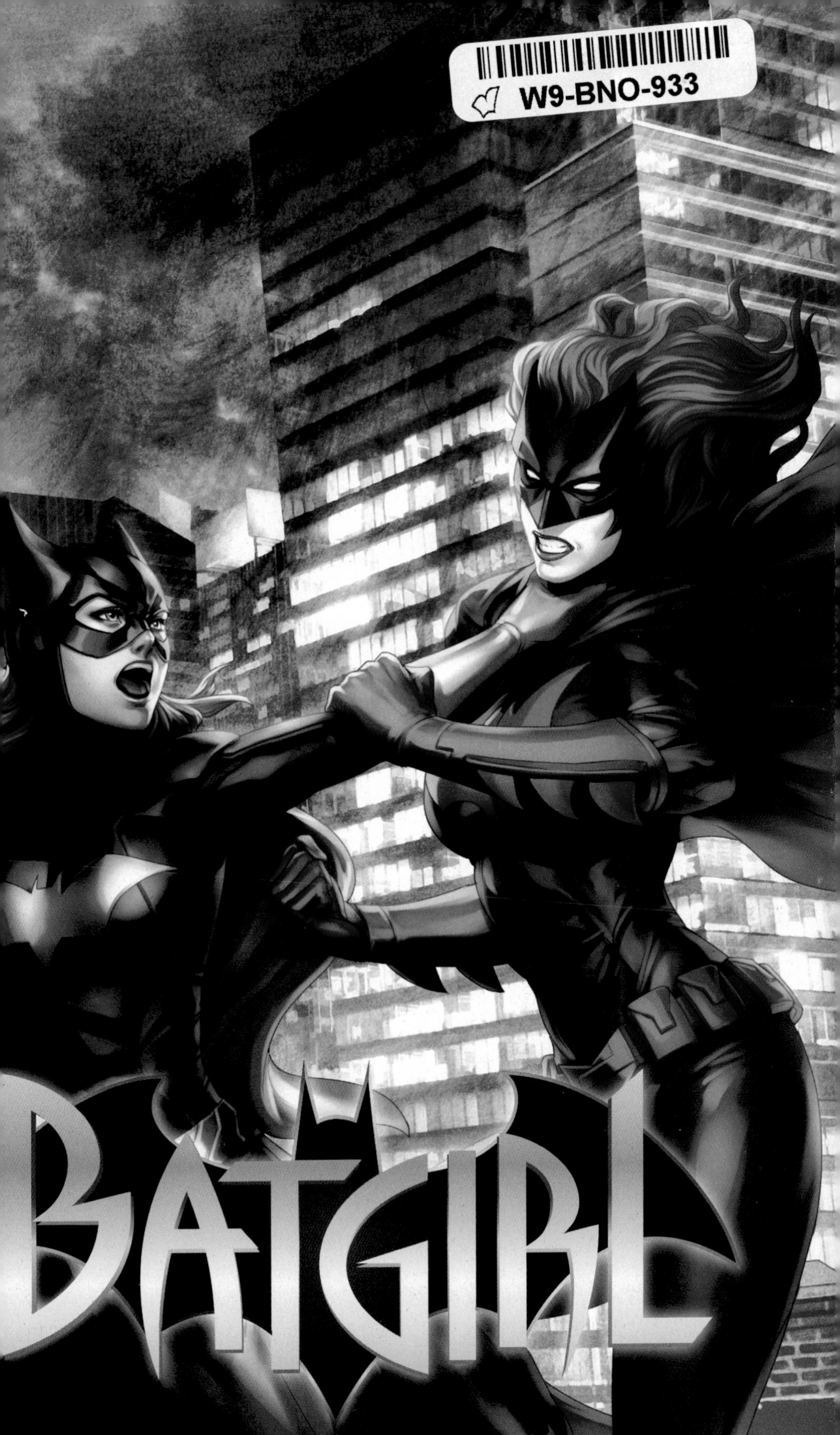

BATGIRL

VOLUME 2 **KNIGHTFALL DESCENDS**

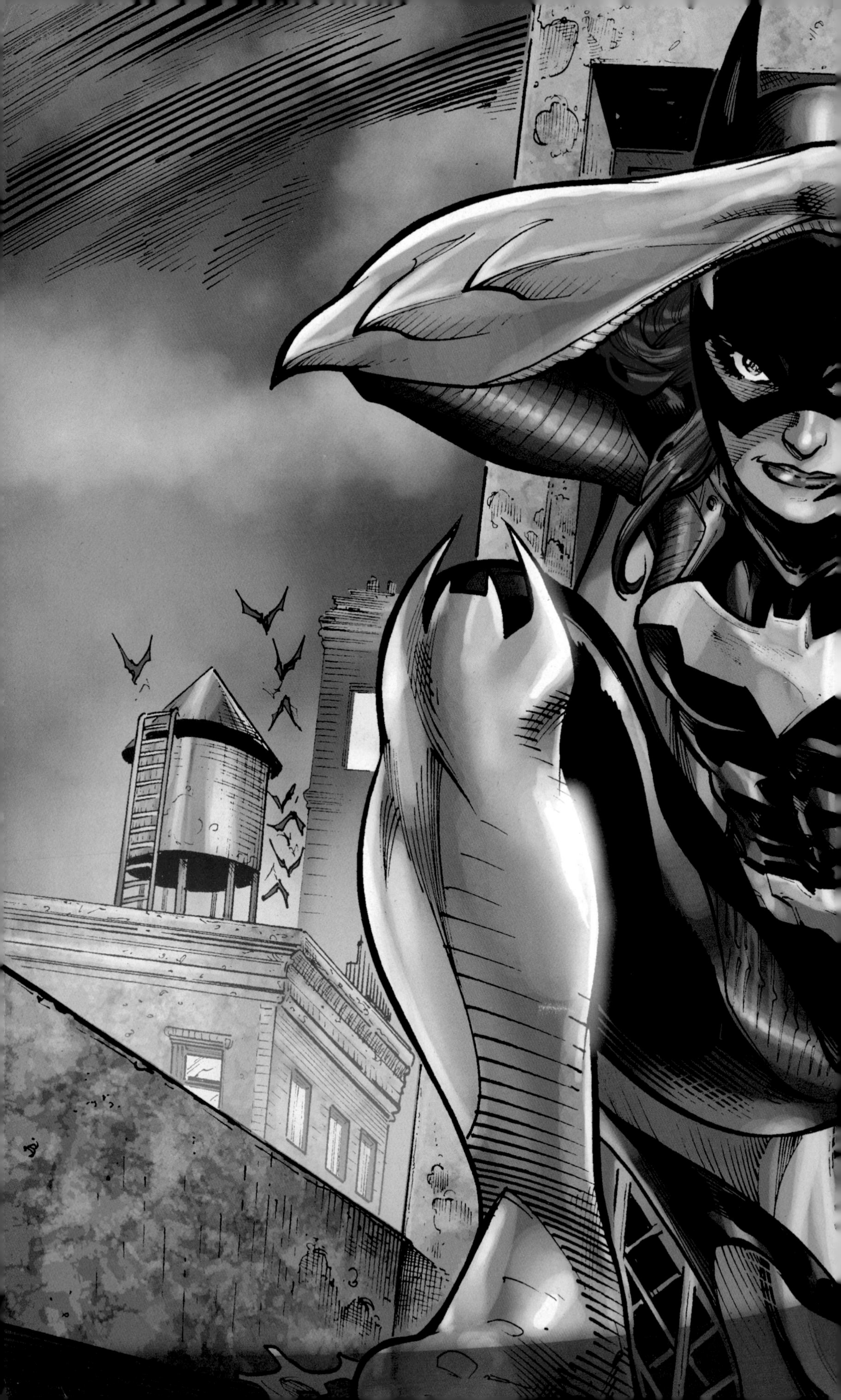

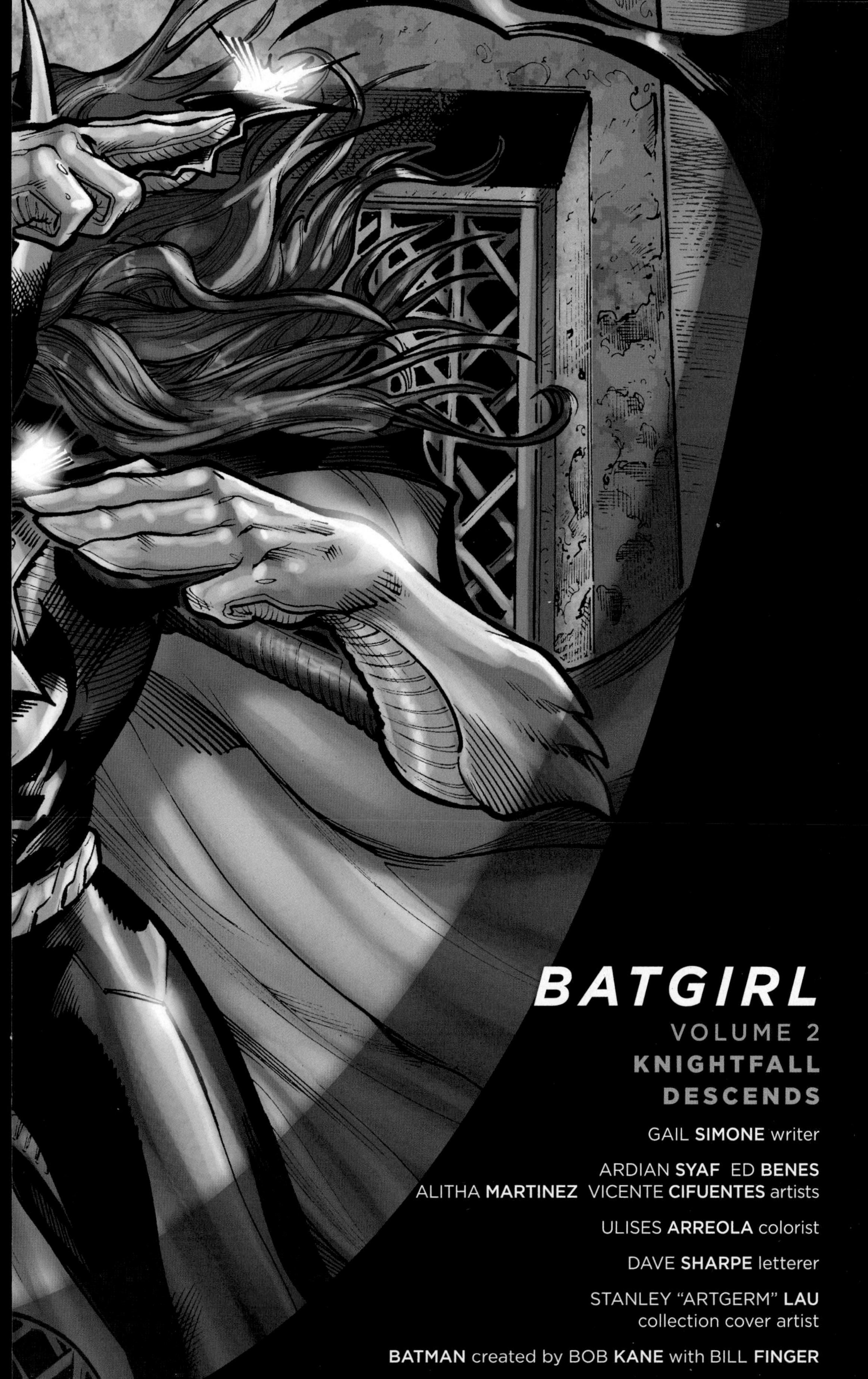

BATGIRL

VOLUME 2
KNIGHTFALL DESCENDS

GAIL **SIMONE** writer

ARDIAN **SYAF** ED **BENES**
ALITHA **MARTINEZ** VICENTE **CIFUENTES** artists

ULISES **ARREOLA** colorist

DAVE **SHARPE** letterer

STANLEY "ARTGERM" **LAU**
collection cover artist

BATMAN created by BOB **KANE** with BILL **FINGER**

BRIAN SMITH BOBBIE CHASE Editors – Original Series KATIE KUBERT Assistant Editor – Original Series
JEB WOODARD Group Editor – Collected Editions ROBIN WILDMAN Editor – Collected Edition
STEVE COOK Design Director – Books ROBBIE BIEDERMAN Publication Design

BOB HARRAS Senior VP – Editor-in-Chief, DC Comics

DIANE NELSON President DAN DIDIO and JIM LEE Co-Publishers
GEOFF JOHNS Chief Creative Officer AMIT DESAI Senior VP – Marketing & Global Franchise Management
NAIRI GARDINER Senior VP – Finance SAM ADES VP – Digital Marketing BOBBIE CHASE VP – Talent Development
MARK CHIARELLO Senior VP – Art, Design & Collected Editions JOHN CUNNINGHAM VP – Content Strategy
ANNE DEPIES VP – Strategy Planning & Reporting DON FALLETTI VP – Manufacturing Operations
LAWRENCE GANEM VP – Editorial Administration & Talent Relations ALISON GILL Senior VP – Manufacturing & Operations
HANK KANALZ Senior VP – Editorial Strategy & Administration JAY KOGAN VP – Legal Affairs
DEREK MADDALENA Senior VP – Sales & Business Development JACK MAHAN VP – Business Affairs
DAN MIRON VP – Sales Planning & Trade Development NICK NAPOLITANO VP – Manufacturing Administration
CAROL ROEDER VP – Marketing EDDIE SCANNELL VP – Mass Account & Digital Sales
COURTNEY SIMMONS Senior VP – Publicity & Communications JIM (SKI) SOKOLOWSKI VP – Comic Book Specialty & Newsstand Sales
SANDY YI Senior VP – Global Franchise Management

BATGIRL VOLUME 2: KNIGHTFALL DESCENDS

DC Comics, 2900 W. Alameda Avenue, Burbank, CA 91505
Printed by Solisco Printers, Scott, QC, Canada. 2/5/16. Third Printing.
ISBN: 978-1-4012-3817-9

Library of Congress Cataloging-in-Publication Data

Simone, Gail.
Batgirl. Volume 2, Knightfall descends / Gail Simone, Ardian Syaf, Ed Benes, Vicente Cifuentes.
p. cm.
"Originally published in single magazine form in Batgirl 7-13, 0."
ISBN 978-1-4012-3817-9
1. Graphic novels. I. Syaf, Ardian. II. Benes, Ed. III. Cifuentes, Vicente. IV. Title. V. Title: Knightfall descends.
PN6728.B358S57 2012
741.5'973—dc23
2012040571

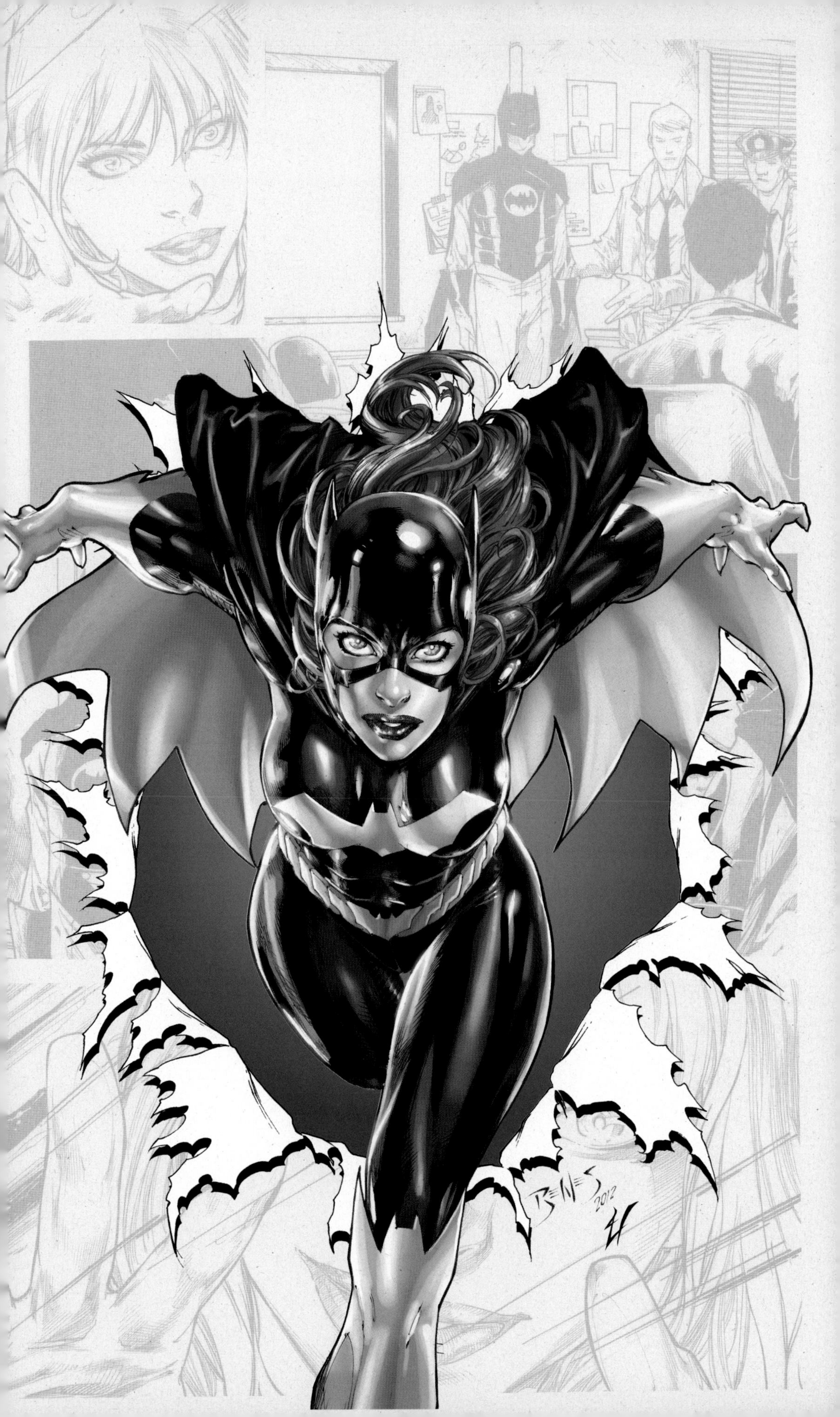
BENES 2012

A FIRE IN THE HEAVENS

GAIL SIMONE writer **ED BENES** artist cover by **ED BENES** and **ULISES ARREOLA**

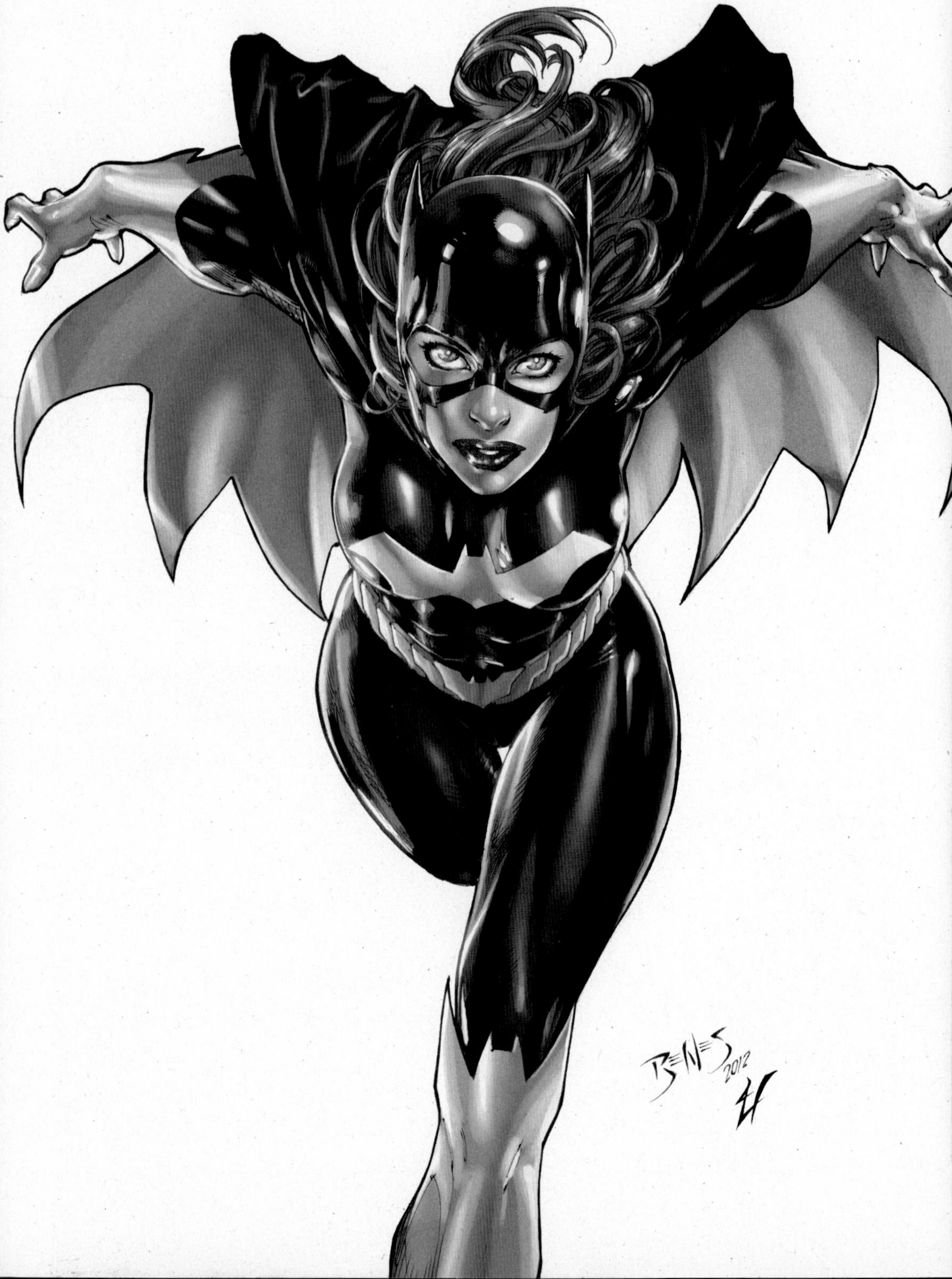

BENES 2012

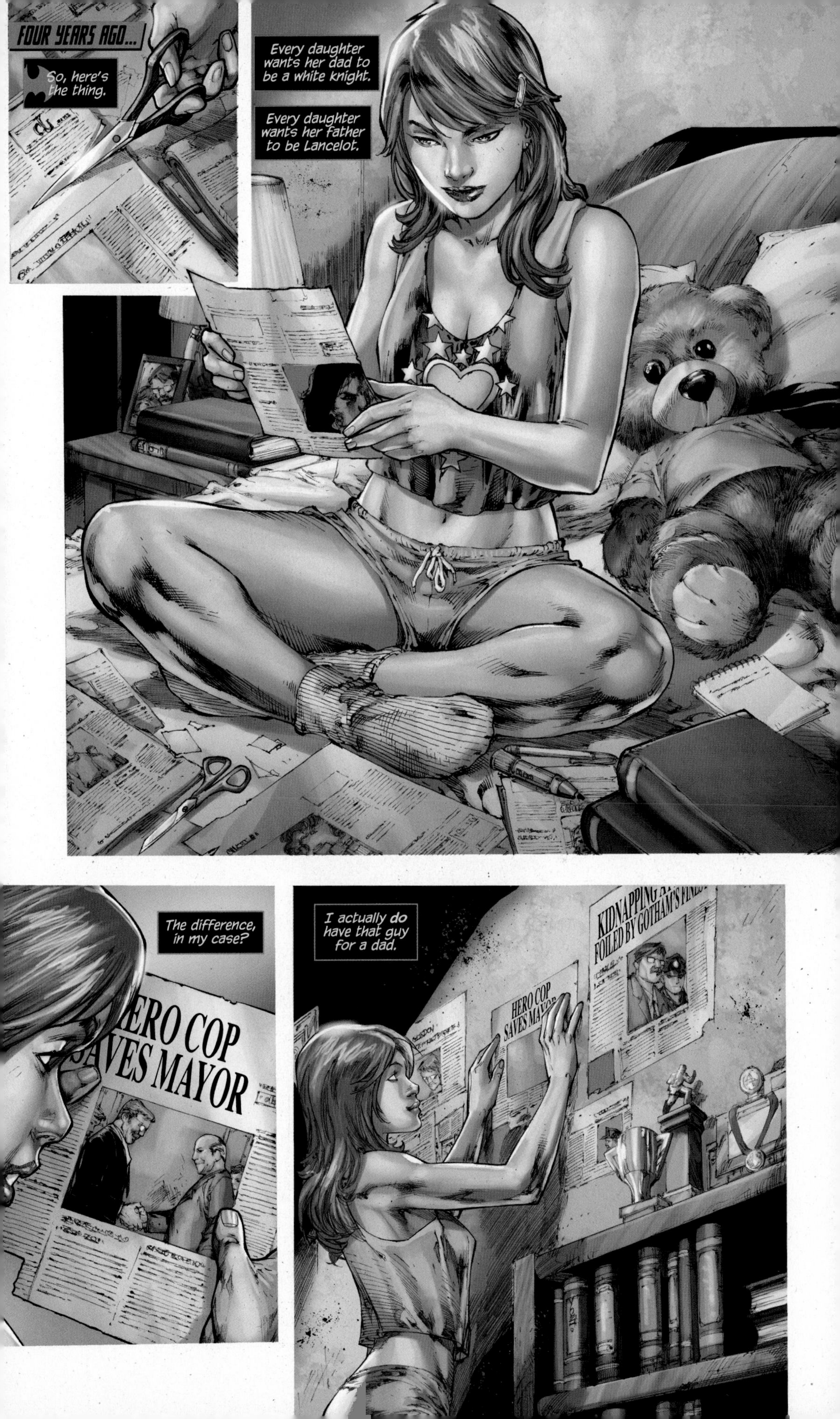
FOUR YEARS AGO...
So, here's the thing.
Every daughter wants her dad to be a white knight.
Every daughter wants her father to be Lancelot.
The difference, in my case?
HERO COP SAVES MAYOR
I actually do have that guy for a dad.
KIDNAPPING A
FOILED BY GOTHAM'S FINEST
HERO COP SAVES MAYOR

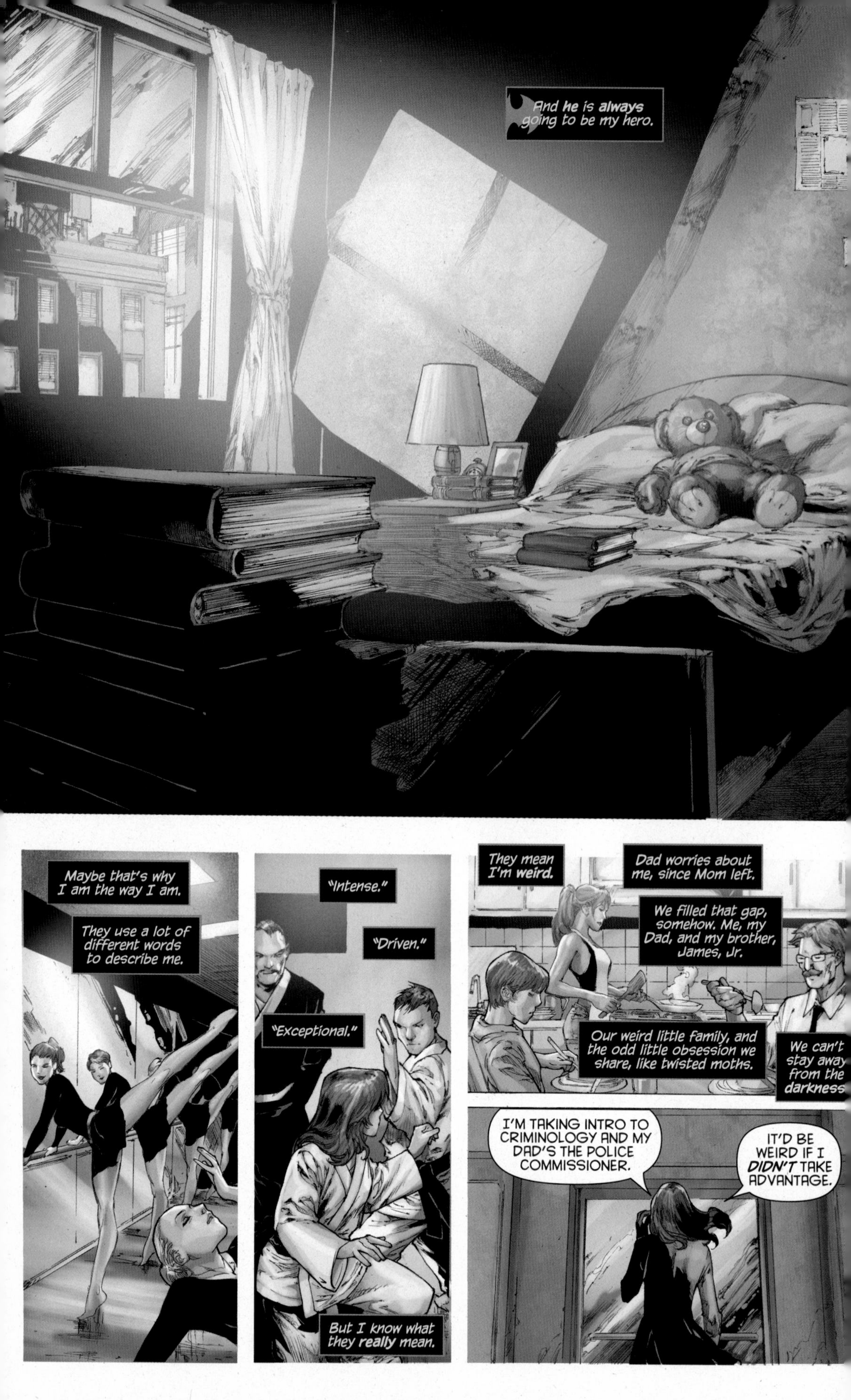
And he is always going to be my hero.
Maybe that's why I am the way I am.
They use a lot of different words to describe me.
"Intense."
"Driven."
"Exceptional."
But I know what they really mean.
They mean I'm weird.
Dad worries about me, since Mom left.
We filled that gap, somehow. Me, my Dad, and my brother, James, Jr.
Our weird little family, and the odd little obsession we share, like twisted moths.
We can't stay away from the darkness
I'M TAKING INTRO TO CRIMINOLOGY AND MY DAD'S THE POLICE COMMISSIONER.
IT'D BE WEIRD IF I DIDN'T TAKE ADVANTAGE.

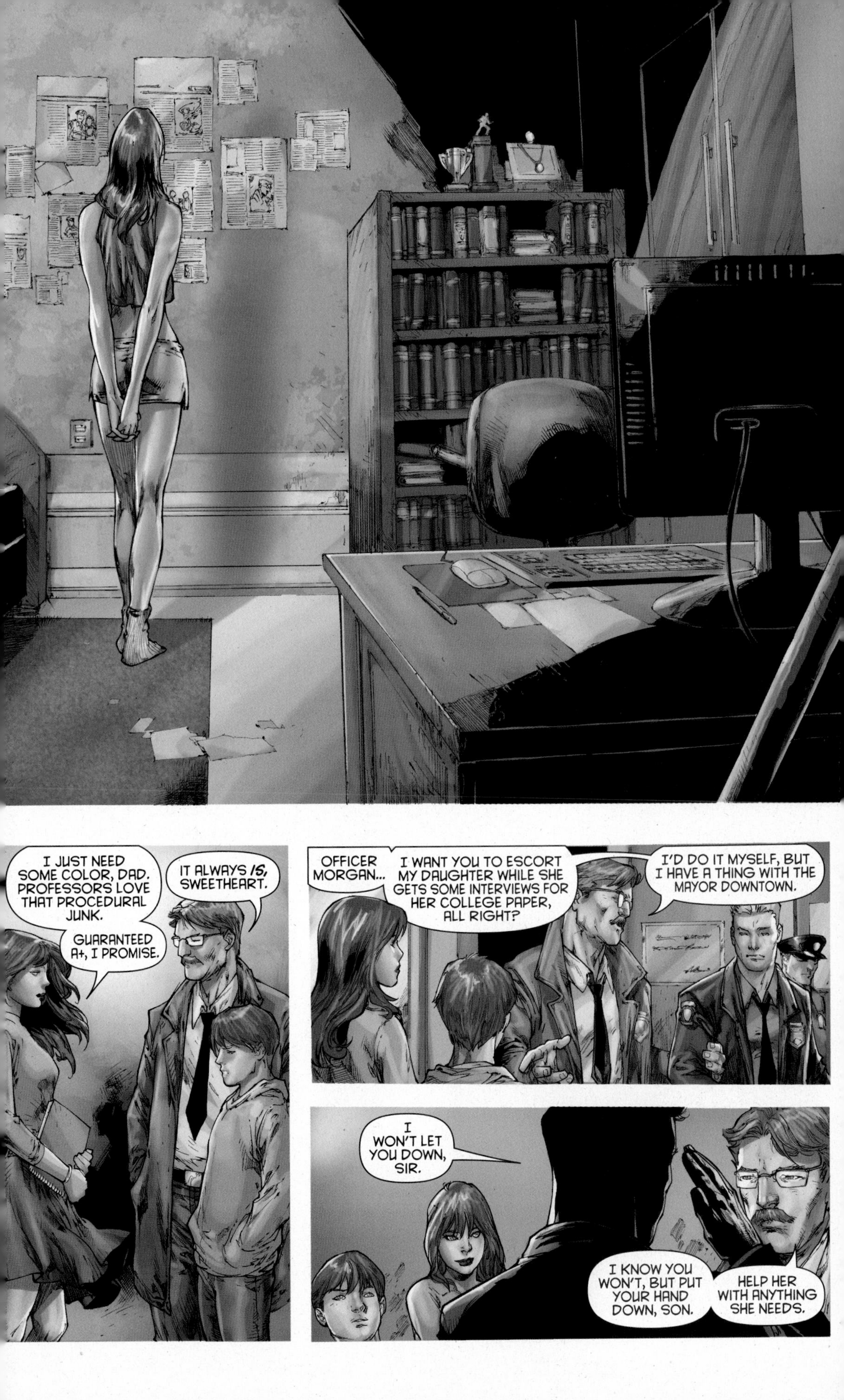
I JUST NEED SOME COLOR, DAD. PROFESSORS LOVE THAT PROCEDURAL JUNK.
GUARANTEED A+, I PROMISE.
IT ALWAYS *IS*, SWEETHEART.
OFFICER MORGAN...
I WANT YOU TO ESCORT MY DAUGHTER WHILE SHE GETS SOME INTERVIEWS FOR HER COLLEGE PAPER, ALL RIGHT?
I'D DO IT MYSELF, BUT I HAVE A THING WITH THE MAYOR DOWNTOWN.
I WON'T LET YOU DOWN, SIR.
I KNOW YOU WON'T, BUT PUT YOUR HAND DOWN, SON.
HELP HER WITH ANYTHING SHE NEEDS.

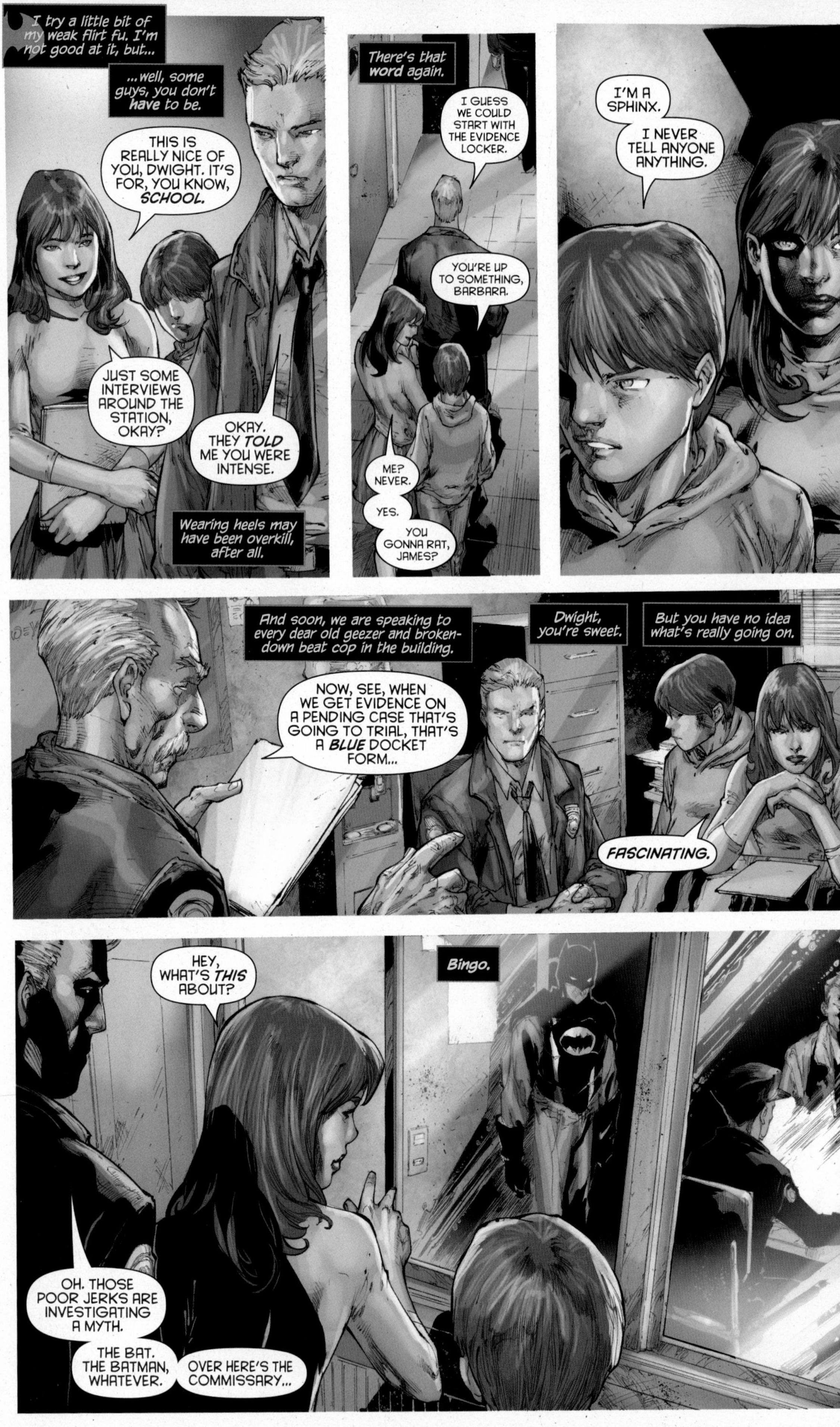

I try a little bit of my weak flirt fu. I'm not good at it, but...
...well, some guys, you don't have to be.
THIS IS REALLY NICE OF YOU, DWIGHT. IT'S FOR, YOU KNOW, SCHOOL.
JUST SOME INTERVIEWS AROUND THE STATION, OKAY?
OKAY. THEY TOLD ME YOU WERE INTENSE.
Wearing heels may have been overkill, after all.
There's that word again.
I GUESS WE COULD START WITH THE EVIDENCE LOCKER.
YOU'RE UP TO SOMETHING, BARBARA.
ME? NEVER.
YES.
YOU GONNA RAT, JAMES?
I'M A SPHINX.
I NEVER TELL ANYONE ANYTHING.
And soon, we are speaking to every dear old geezer and broken-down beat cop in the building.
NOW, SEE, WHEN WE GET EVIDENCE ON A PENDING CASE THAT'S GOING TO TRIAL, THAT'S A BLUE DOCKET FORM...
Dwight, you're sweet.
But you have no idea what's really going on.
FASCINATING.
HEY, WHAT'S THIS ABOUT?
Bingo.
OH. THOSE POOR JERKS ARE INVESTIGATING A MYTH.
THE BAT. THE BATMAN, WHATEVER.
OVER HERE'S THE COMMISSARY...

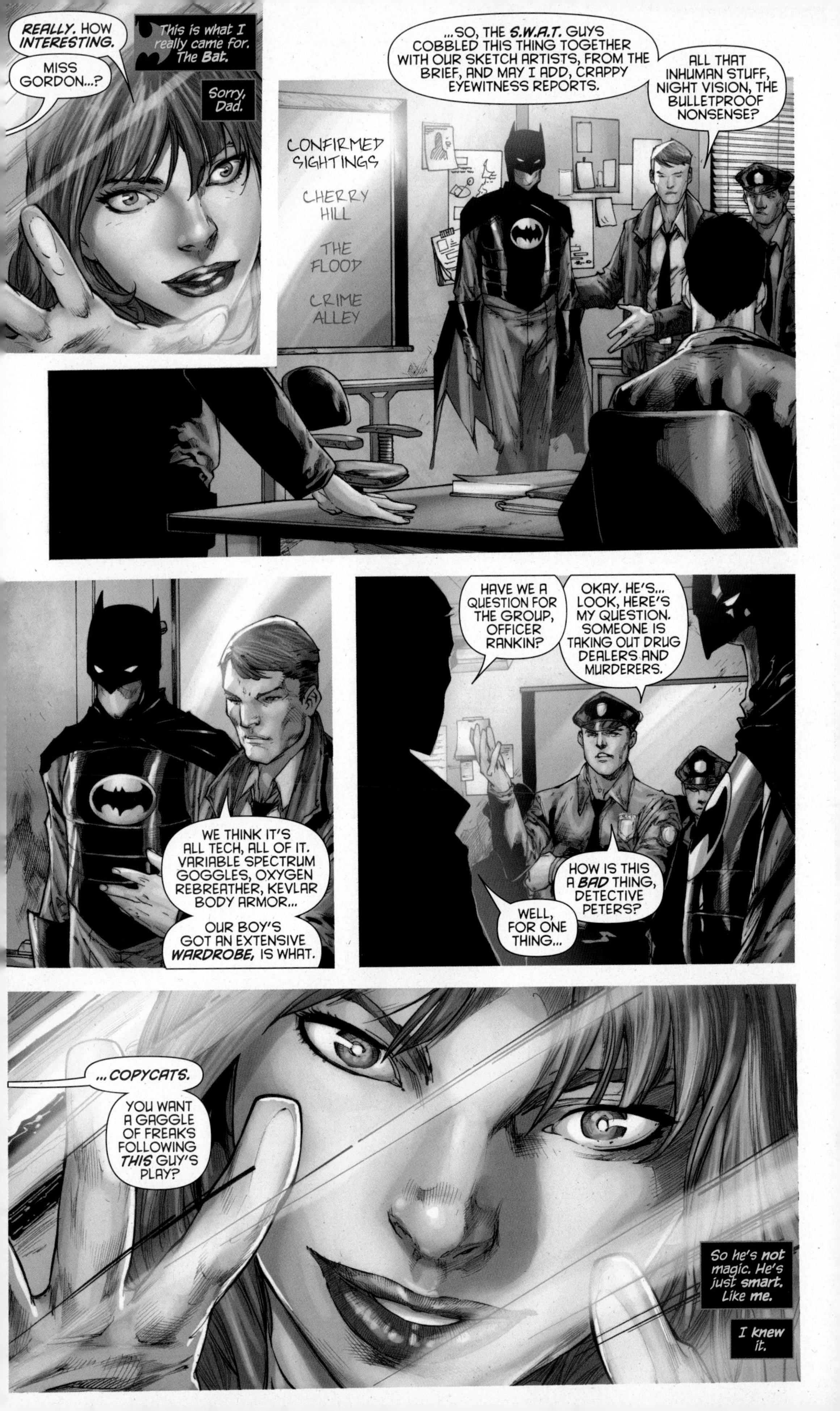
REALLY. HOW INTERESTING.
MISS GORDON...?
This is what I really came for. The Bat.
Sorry, Dad.
...SO, THE S.W.A.T. GUYS COBBLED THIS THING TOGETHER WITH OUR SKETCH ARTISTS, FROM THE BRIEF, AND MAY I ADD, CRAPPY EYEWITNESS REPORTS.
ALL THAT INHUMAN STUFF, NIGHT VISION, THE BULLETPROOF NONSENSE?
CONFIRMED SIGHTINGS
CHERRY HILL
THE FLOOD
CRIME ALLEY
WE THINK IT'S ALL TECH, ALL OF IT. VARIABLE SPECTRUM GOGGLES, OXYGEN REBREATHER, KEVLAR BODY ARMOR...
OUR BOY'S GOT AN EXTENSIVE WARDROBE, IS WHAT.
HAVE WE A QUESTION FOR THE GROUP, OFFICER RANKIN?
OKAY. HE'S... LOOK, HERE'S MY QUESTION. SOMEONE IS TAKING OUT DRUG DEALERS AND MURDERERS.
HOW IS THIS A BAD THING, DETECTIVE PETERS?
WELL, FOR ONE THING...
...COPYCATS.
YOU WANT A GAGGLE OF FREAKS FOLLOWING THIS GUY'S PLAY?
So he's not magic. He's just smart. Like me.
I knew it.

A weird feeling, like a ghost just walked over my grave.

Seems like bad news waiting to happen.

And just then...

...speak of the Devil.

I know this guy.

STAY BACK, MISS GORDON.

This long stick of walking nightmare calls himself *Harry X*, awaiting possible extradition. He's *Canadian*, of all things.

Made his bones in human trafficking...*RCMP* raided his compound while he was vacationing in the States.

Found an abandoned well *full* of missing women from Eastern Europe, all deceased.

All with broken necks... his *signature* move.

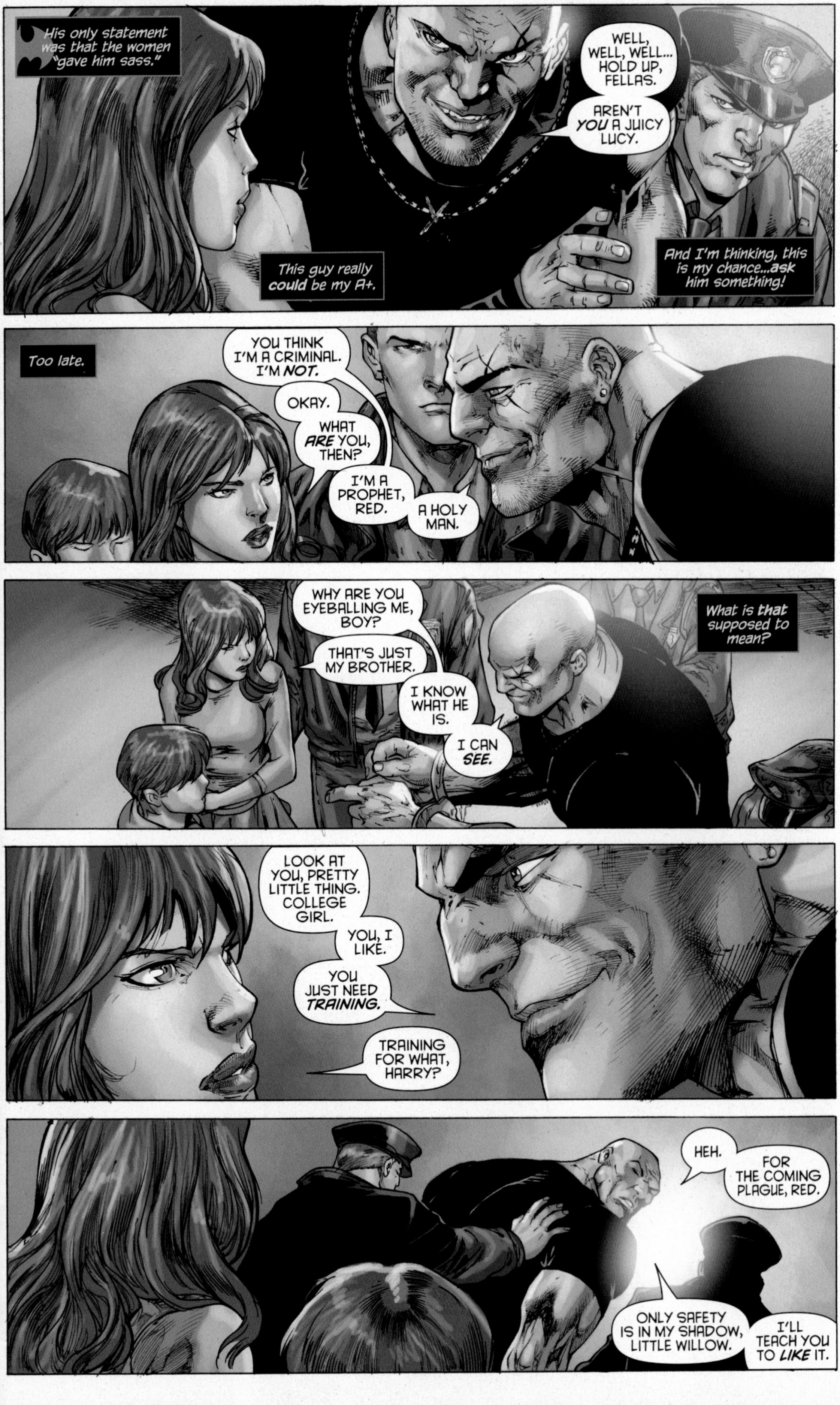
His only statement was that the women "gave him sass."
WELL, WELL, WELL... HOLD UP, FELLAS.
AREN'T YOU A JUICY LUCY.
This guy really could be my A+.
And I'm thinking, this is my chance...ask him something!
Too late.
YOU THINK I'M A CRIMINAL. I'M NOT.
OKAY.
WHAT ARE YOU, THEN?
I'M A PROPHET, RED.
A HOLY MAN.
WHY ARE YOU EYEBALLING ME, BOY?
THAT'S JUST MY BROTHER.
I KNOW WHAT HE IS.
I CAN SEE.
What is that supposed to mean?
LOOK AT YOU, PRETTY LITTLE THING. COLLEGE GIRL.
YOU, I LIKE.
YOU JUST NEED TRAINING.
TRAINING FOR WHAT, HARRY?
HEH.
FOR THE COMING PLAGUE, RED.
ONLY SAFETY IS IN MY SHADOW, LITTLE WILLOW.
I'LL TEACH YOU TO LIKE IT.

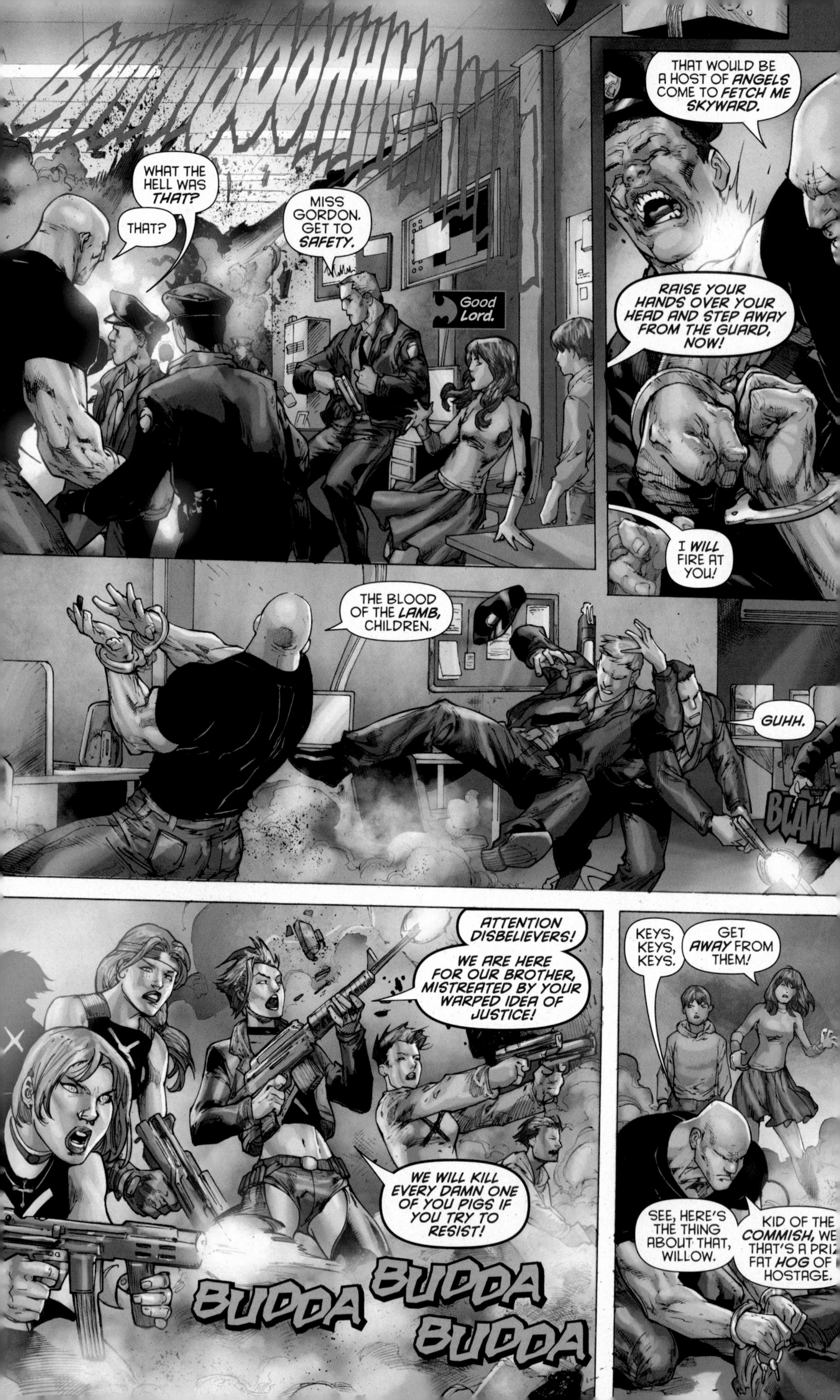

BOOOOOOOMMM
WHAT THE HELL WAS THAT?
THAT?
MISS GORDON. GET TO SAFETY.
Good Lord.
THAT WOULD BE A HOST OF ANGELS COME TO FETCH ME SKYWARD.
RAISE YOUR HANDS OVER YOUR HEAD AND STEP AWAY FROM THE GUARD, NOW!
I WILL FIRE AT YOU!
THE BLOOD OF THE LAMB, CHILDREN.
GUHH.
BLAM
ATTENTION DISBELIEVERS!
WE ARE HERE FOR OUR BROTHER, MISTREATED BY YOUR WARPED IDEA OF JUSTICE!
WE WILL KILL EVERY DAMN ONE OF YOU PIGS IF YOU TRY TO RESIST!
BUDDA BUDDA BUDDA
KEYS, KEYS, KEYS.
GET AWAY FROM THEM!
SEE, HERE'S THE THING ABOUT THAT, WILLOW.
KID OF THE COMMISH, WE THAT'S A PRI FAT HOG OF HOSTAGE.

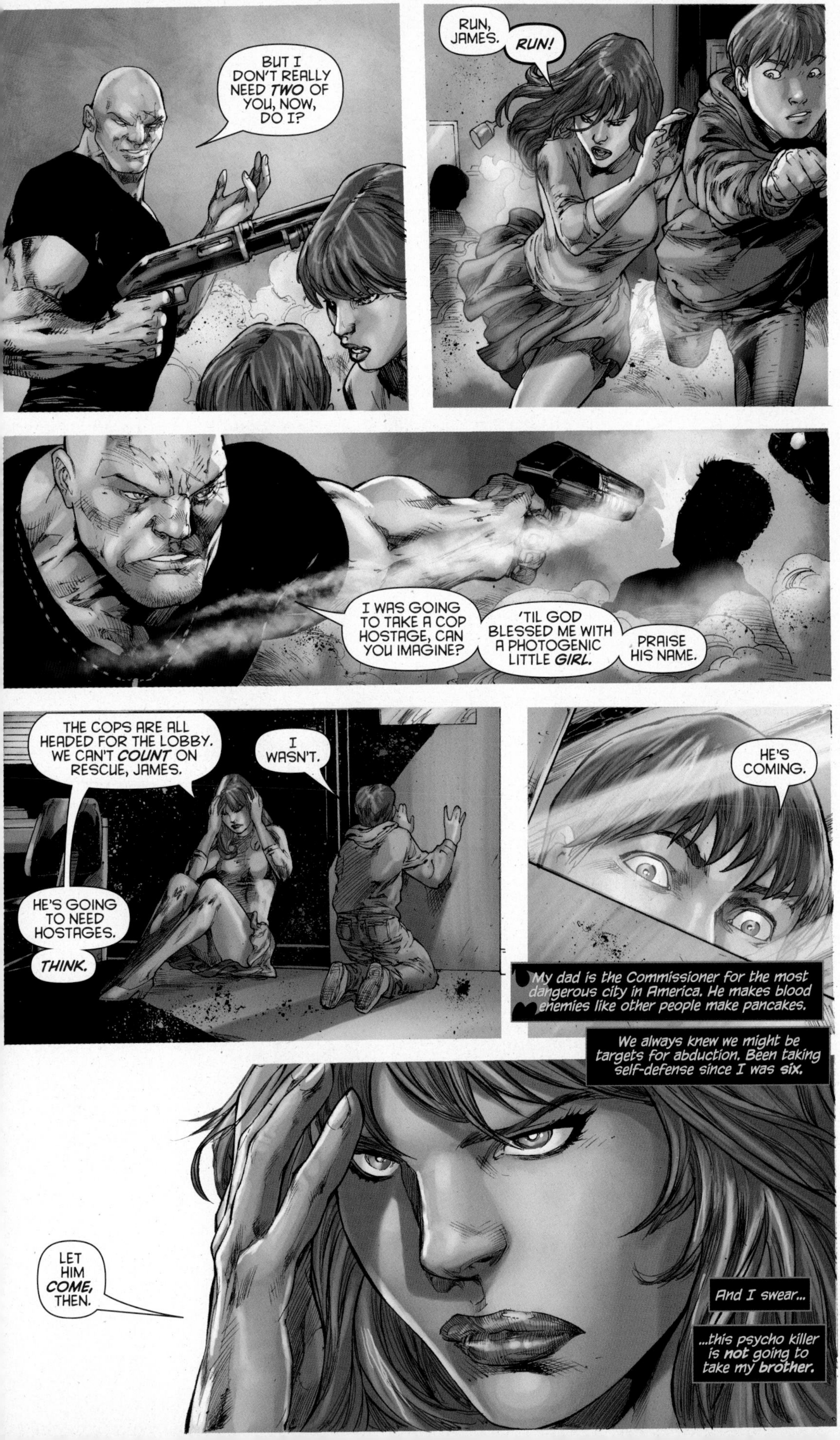

BUT I DON'T REALLY NEED TWO OF YOU, NOW, DO I?
RUN, JAMES.
RUN!
I WAS GOING TO TAKE A COP HOSTAGE, CAN YOU IMAGINE?
'TIL GOD BLESSED ME WITH A PHOTOGENIC LITTLE GIRL.
PRAISE HIS NAME.
THE COPS ARE ALL HEADED FOR THE LOBBY. WE CAN'T COUNT ON RESCUE, JAMES.
I WASN'T.
HE'S GOING TO NEED HOSTAGES.
THINK.
HE'S COMING.
My dad is the Commissioner for the most dangerous city in America. He makes blood enemies like other people make pancakes.
We always knew we might be targets for abduction. Been taking self-defense since I was six.
LET HIM COME, THEN.
And I swear...
...this psycho killer is not going to take my brother.

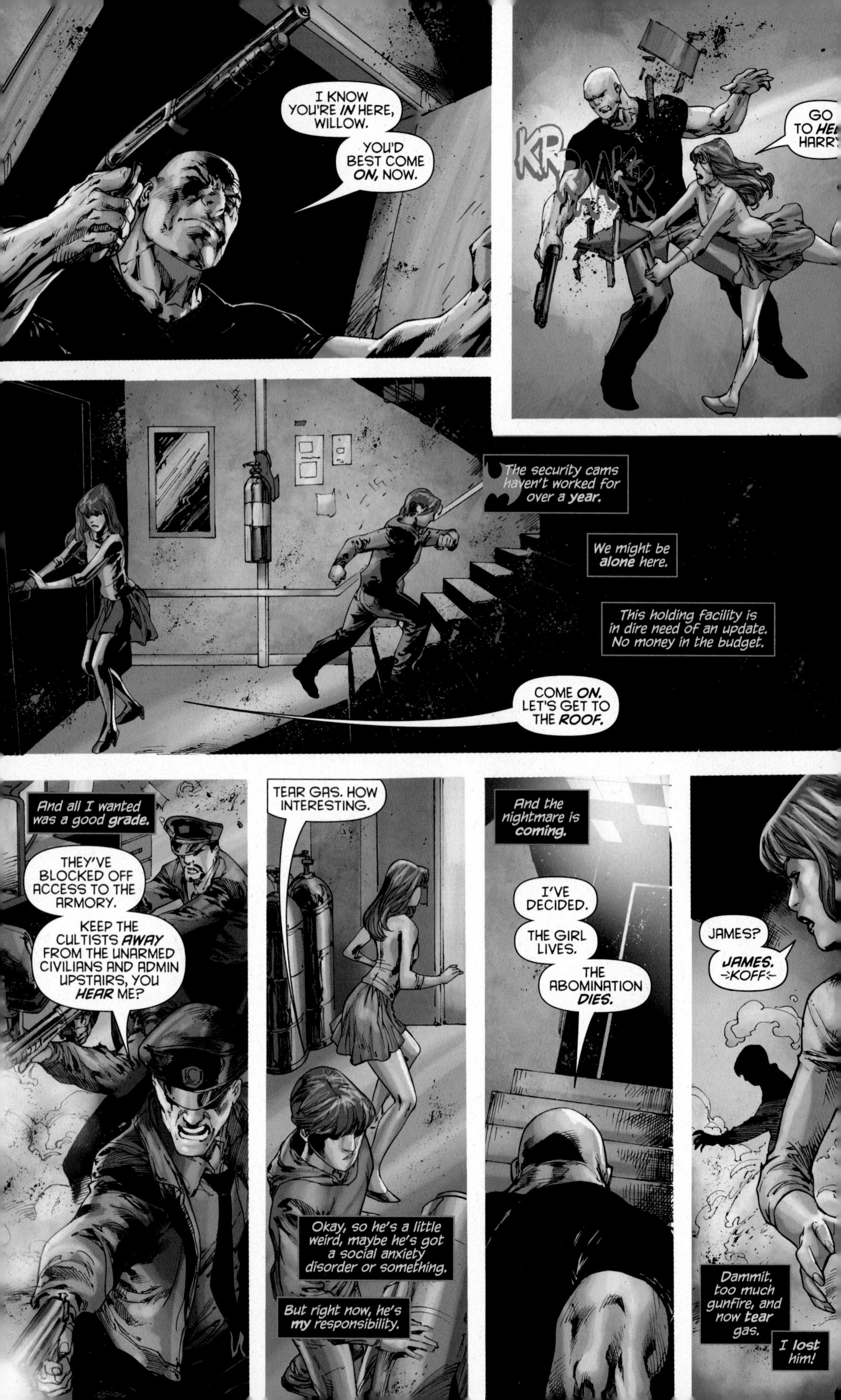

I KNOW YOU'RE *IN* HERE, WILLOW.
YOU'D BEST COME *ON,* NOW.
KRAKK
GO TO *HEL*
HARRY
The security cams haven't worked for over a **year.**
We might be **alone** here.
This holding facility is in dire need of an update. No money in the budget.
COME *ON.* LET'S GET TO THE *ROOF.*
And all I wanted was a good **grade.**
THEY'VE BLOCKED OFF ACCESS TO THE ARMORY.
KEEP THE CULTISTS *AWAY* FROM THE UNARMED CIVILIANS AND ADMIN UPSTAIRS, YOU *HEAR* ME?
TEAR GAS. HOW INTERESTING.
Okay, so he's a little weird, maybe he's got a social anxiety disorder or something.
But right now, he's **my** responsibility.
And the nightmare is **coming.**
I'VE DECIDED.
THE GIRL LIVES.
THE ABOMINATION *DIES.*
JAMES?
JAMES. KOFF
Dammit, too much gunfire, and now **tear** gas.
I lost him!

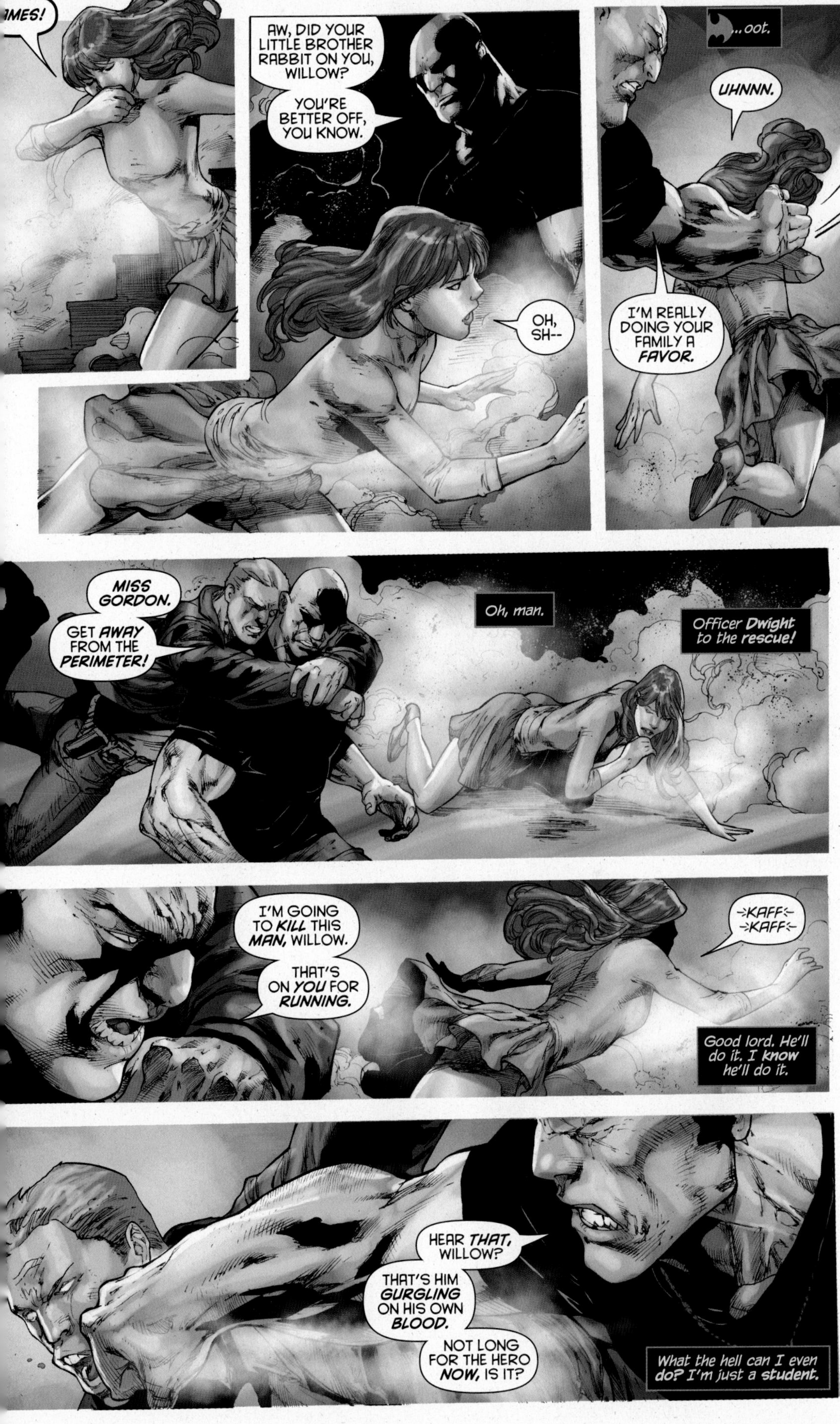
...AMES!
AW, DID YOUR LITTLE BROTHER RABBIT ON YOU, WILLOW?
YOU'RE BETTER OFF, YOU KNOW.
OH, SH--
...oot.
UHNNN.
I'M REALLY DOING YOUR FAMILY A FAVOR.
MISS GORDON.
GET AWAY FROM THE PERIMETER!
Oh, man.
Officer Dwight to the rescue!
I'M GOING TO KILL THIS MAN, WILLOW.
THAT'S ON YOU FOR RUNNING.
-KAFF- -KAFF-
Good lord. He'll do it. I know he'll do it.
HEAR THAT, WILLOW?
THAT'S HIM GURGLING ON HIS OWN BLOOD.
NOT LONG FOR THE HERO NOW, IS IT?
What the hell can I even do? I'm just a student.

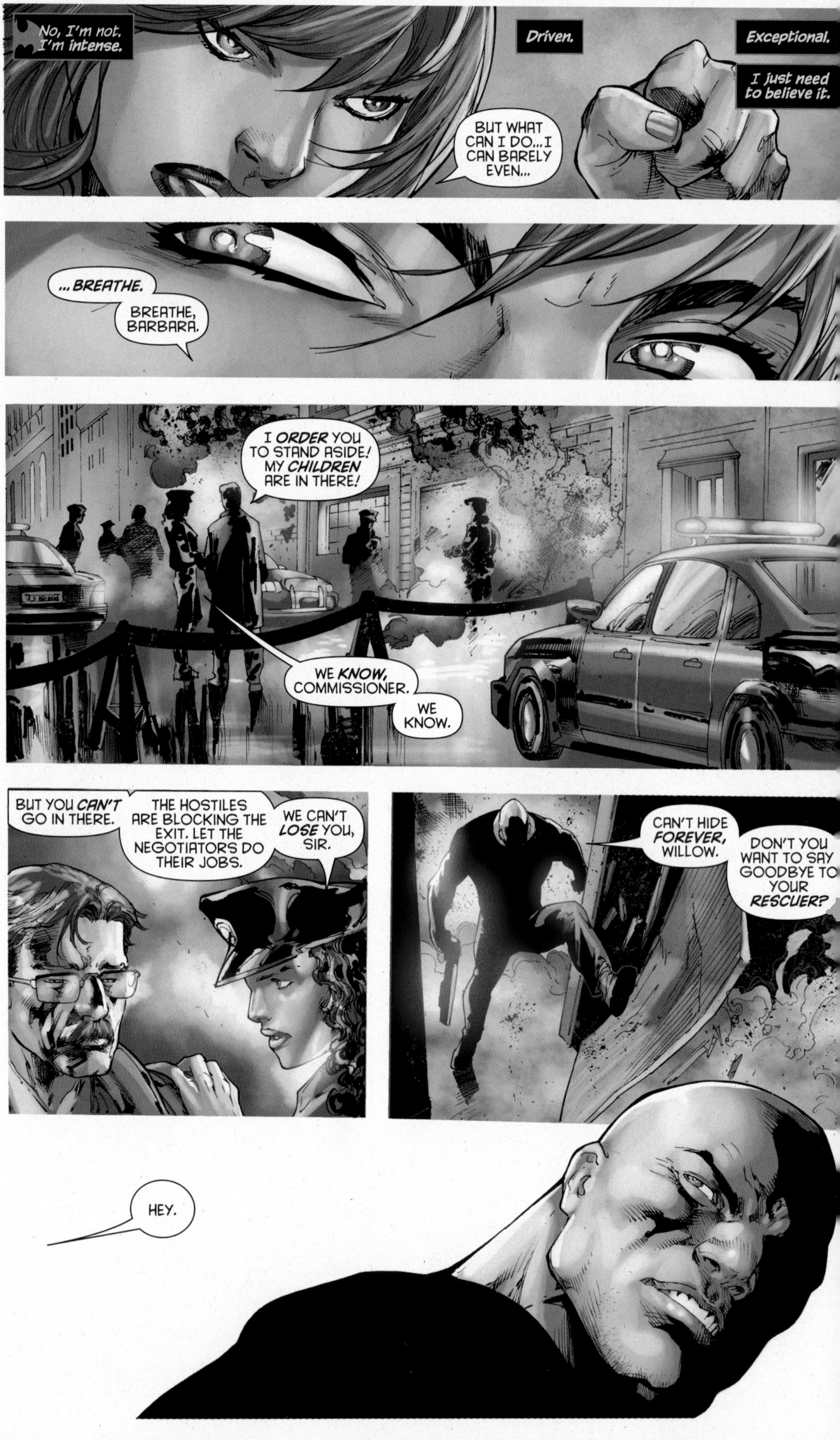
No, I'm not. I'm intense.
Driven.
Exceptional.
I just need to believe it.
BUT WHAT CAN I DO...I CAN BARELY EVEN...
...BREATHE.
BREATHE, BARBARA.
I ORDER YOU TO STAND ASIDE! MY CHILDREN ARE IN THERE!
WE KNOW, COMMISSIONER.
WE KNOW.
BUT YOU CAN'T GO IN THERE.
THE HOSTILES ARE BLOCKING THE EXIT. LET THE NEGOTIATORS DO THEIR JOBS.
WE CAN'T LOSE YOU, SIR.
CAN'T HIDE FOREVER, WILLOW.
DON'T YOU WANT TO SAY GOODBYE TO YOUR RESCUER?
HEY.

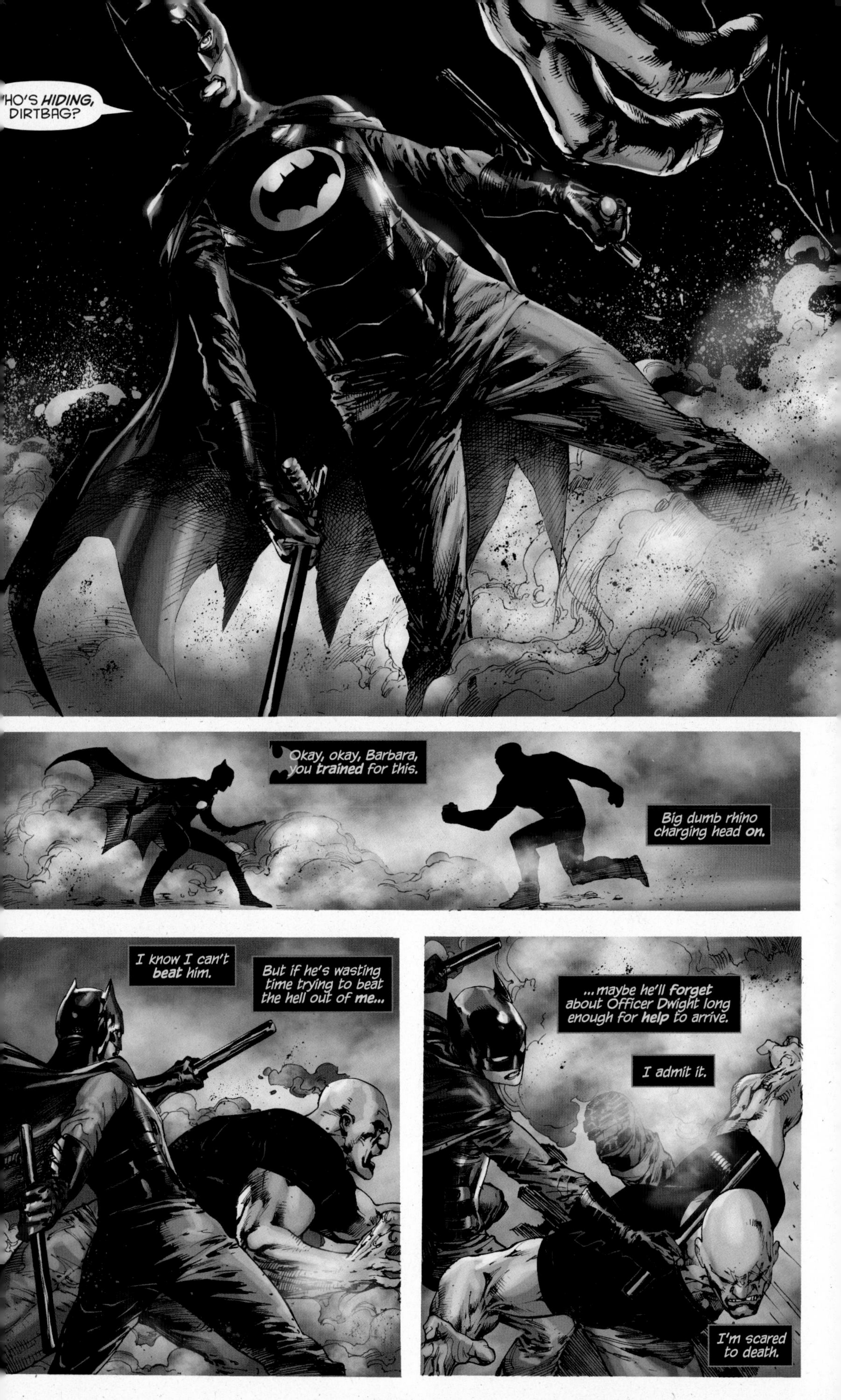

'HO'S HIDING, DIRTBAG?
Okay, okay, Barbara, you trained for this.
Big dumb rhino charging head on.
I know I can't beat him.
But if he's wasting time trying to beat the hell out of me...
...maybe he'll forget about Officer Dwight long enough for help to arrive.
I admit it.
I'm scared to death.

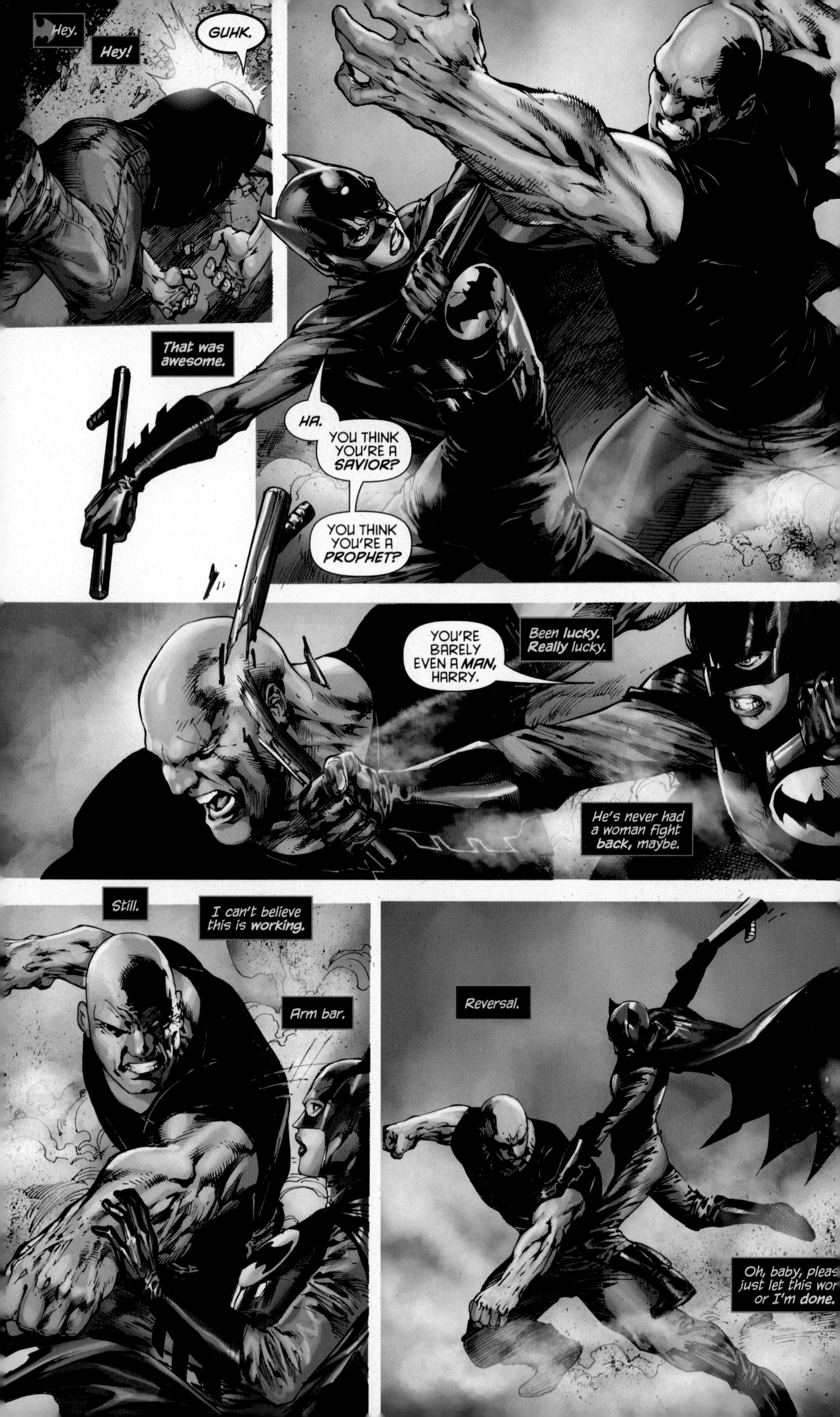
Hey.
Hey!
GUHK.
That was awesome.
HA.
YOU THINK YOU'RE A SAVIOR?
YOU THINK YOU'RE A PROPHET?
YOU'RE BARELY EVEN A MAN, HARRY.
Been lucky. Really lucky.
He's never had a woman fight back, maybe.
Still.
I can't believe this is working.
Arm bar.
Reversal.
Oh, baby, pleas just let this wor or I'm done.

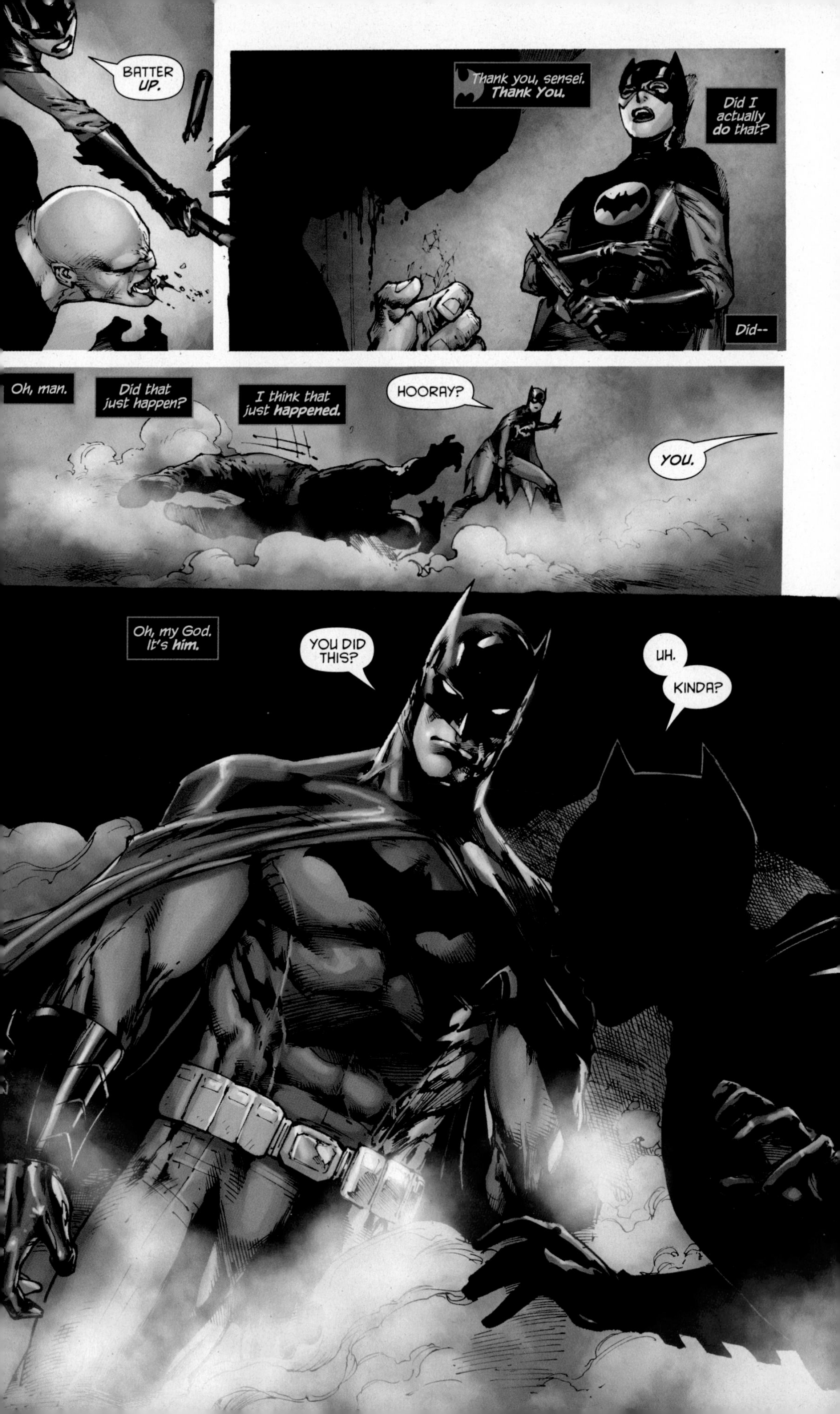

BATTER UP.
Thank you, sensei. Thank You.
Did I actually do that?
Did--
Oh, man.
Did that just happen?
I think that just happened.
HOORAY?
YOU.
Oh, my God. It's him.
YOU DID THIS?
UH.
KINDA?

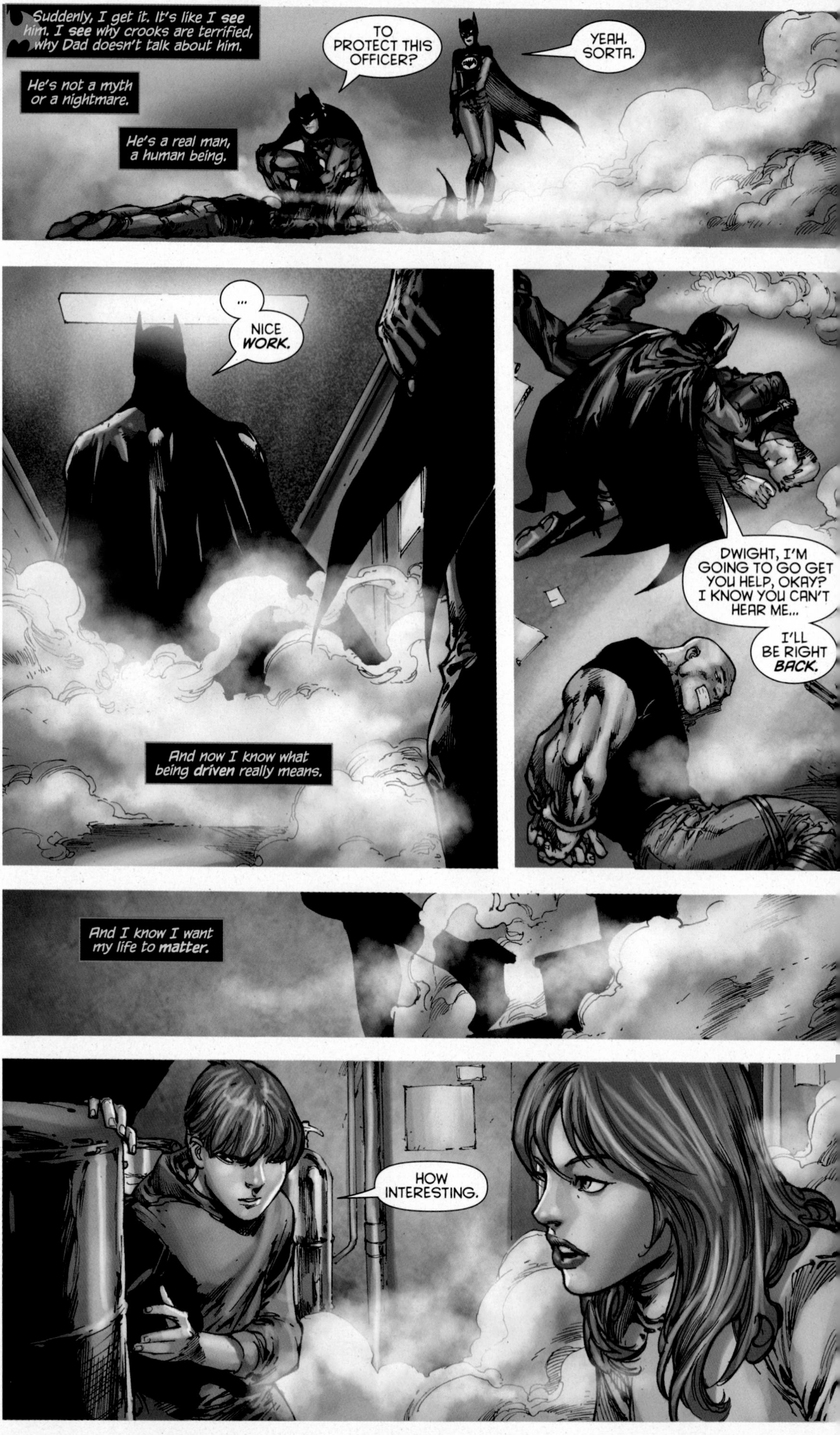
Suddenly, I get it. It's like I see him. I see why crooks are terrified, why Dad doesn't talk about him.
He's not a myth or a nightmare.
He's a real man, a human being.
TO PROTECT THIS OFFICER?
YEAH. SORTA.
... NICE WORK.
And now I know what being driven really means.
DWIGHT, I'M GOING TO GO GET YOU HELP, OKAY? I KNOW YOU CAN'T HEAR ME...
I'LL BE RIGHT BACK.
And I know I want my life to matter.
HOW INTERESTING.

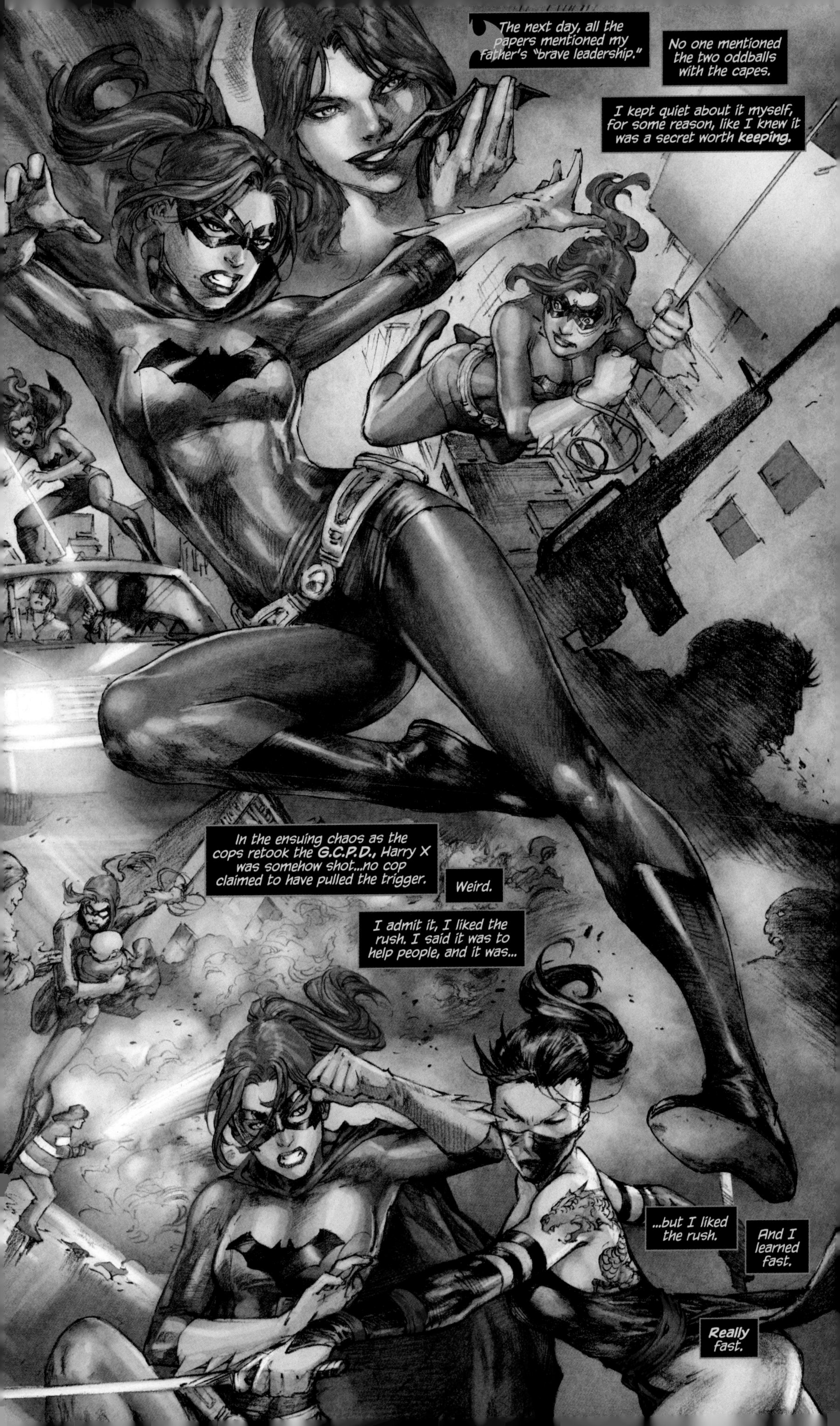
The next day, all the papers mentioned my father's "brave leadership."
No one mentioned the two oddballs with the capes.
I kept quiet about it myself, for some reason, like I knew it was a secret worth **keeping.**
In the ensuing chaos as the cops retook the **G.C.P.D.,** Harry X was somehow shot...no cop claimed to have pulled the trigger.
Weird.
I admit it, I liked the rush. I said it was to help people, and it was...
...but I liked the rush.
And I learned fast.
Really fast.

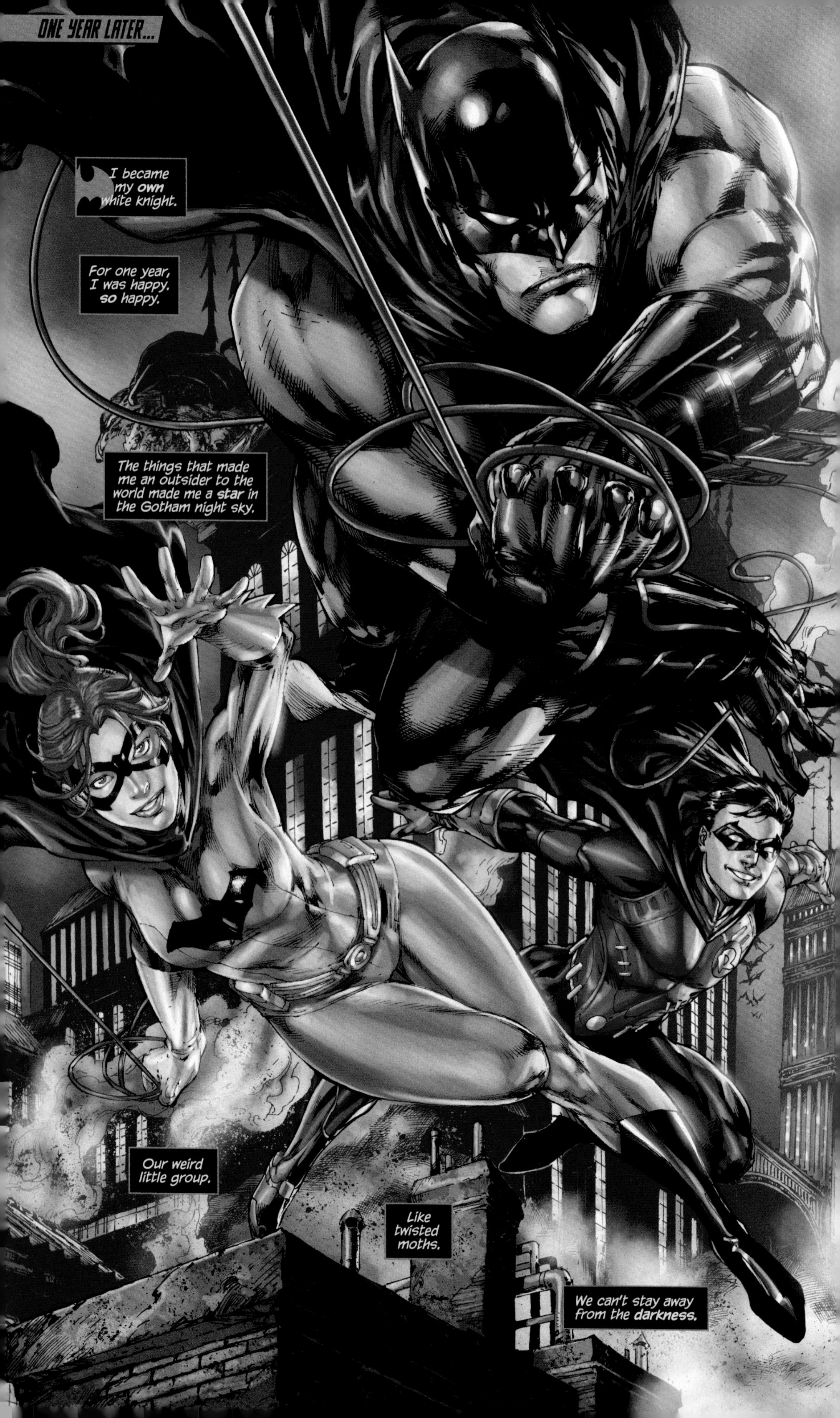
ONE YEAR LATER...
I became my own white knight.
For one year, I was happy. so happy.
The things that made me an outsider to the world made me a star in the Gotham night sky.
Our weird little group.
Like twisted moths.
We can't stay away from the darkness.

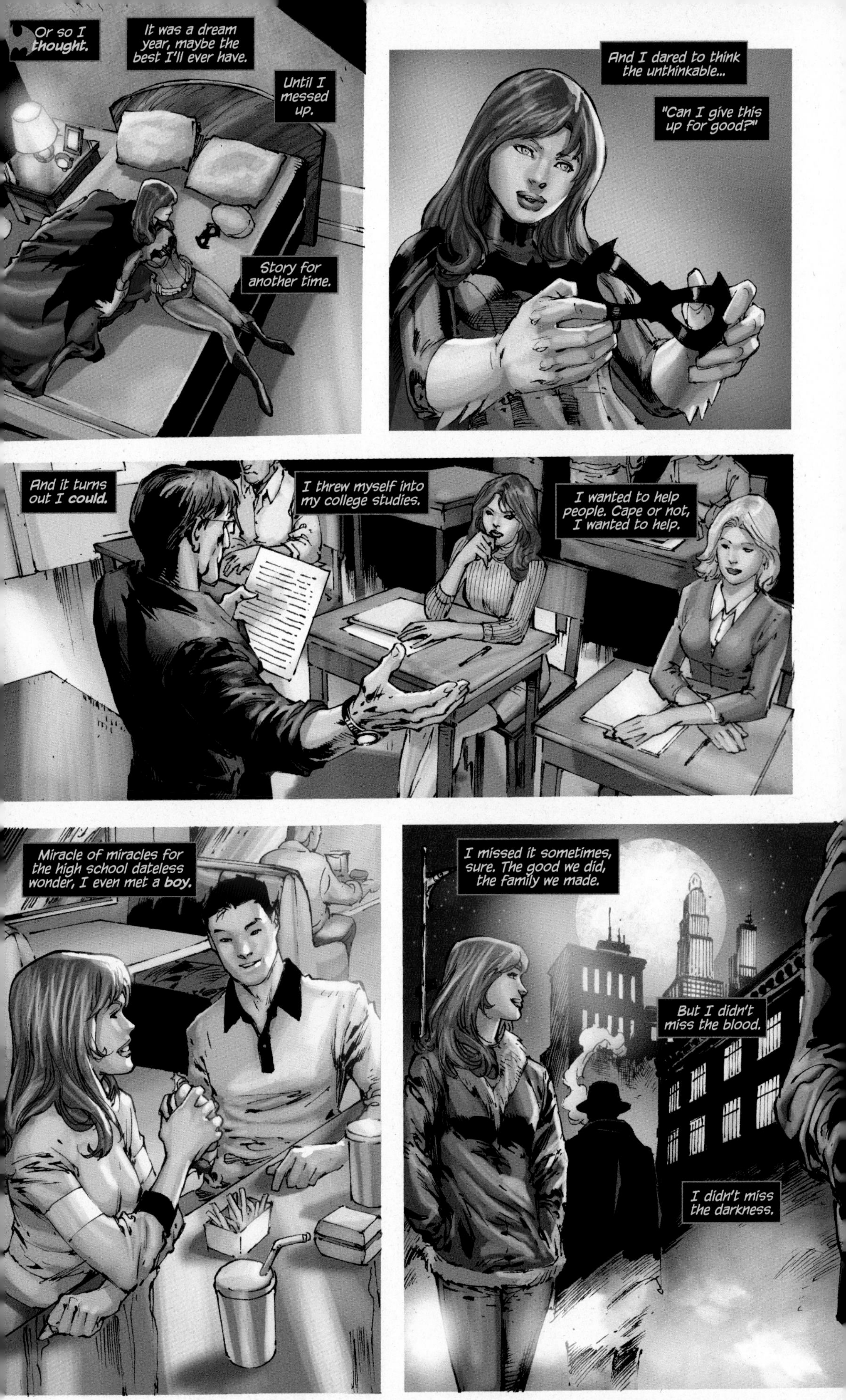
Or so I thought.
It was a dream year, maybe the best I'll ever have.
Until I messed up.
Story for another time.
And I dared to think the unthinkable...
"Can I give this up for good?"
And it turns out I could.
I threw myself into my college studies.
I wanted to help people. Cape or not, I wanted to help.
Miracle of miracles for the high school dateless wonder, I even met a boy.
I missed it sometimes, sure. The good we did, the family we made.
But I didn't miss the blood.
I didn't miss the darkness.

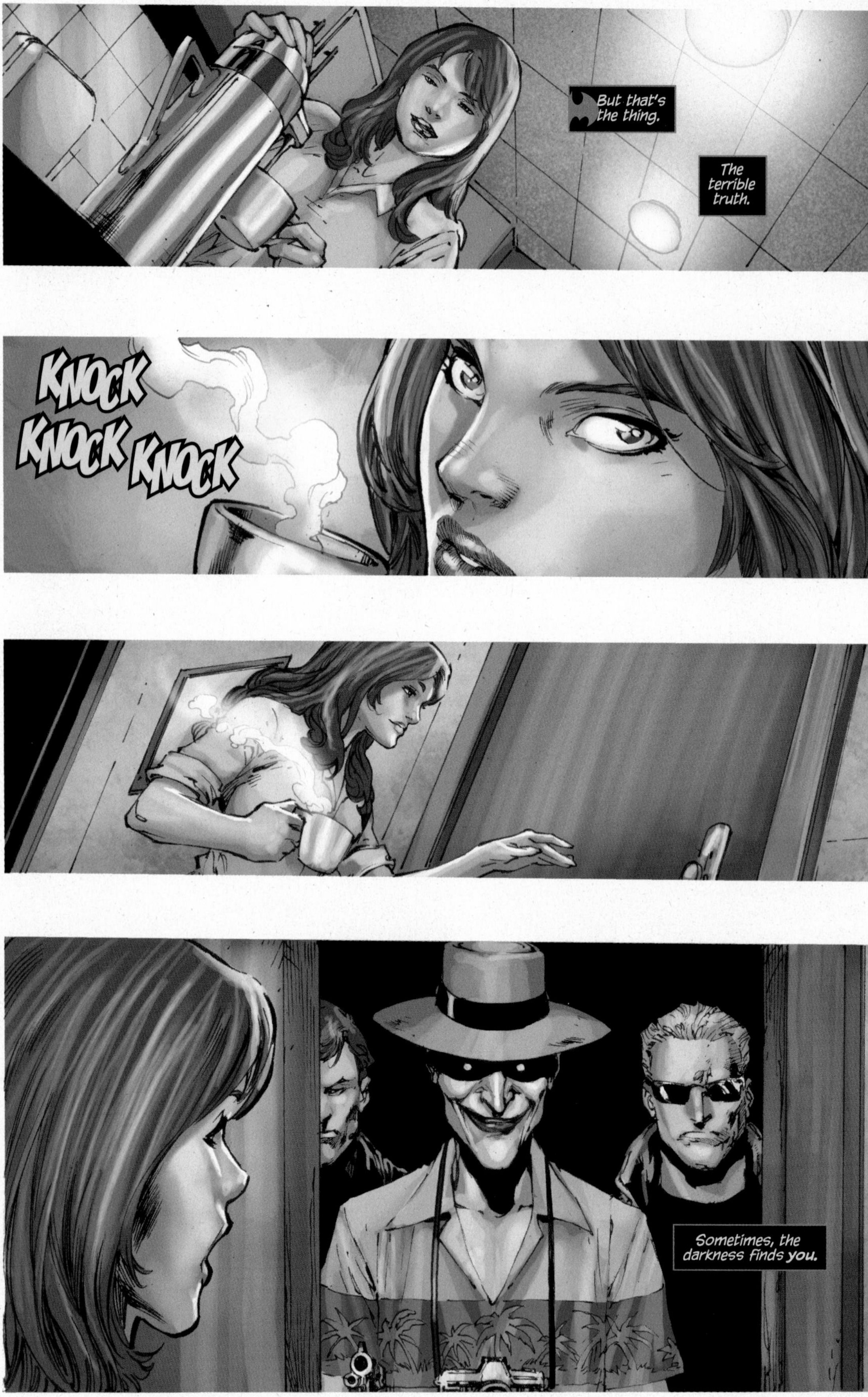
But that's the thing.
The terrible truth.
KNOCK KNOCK KNOCK
Sometimes, the darkness finds **you**.

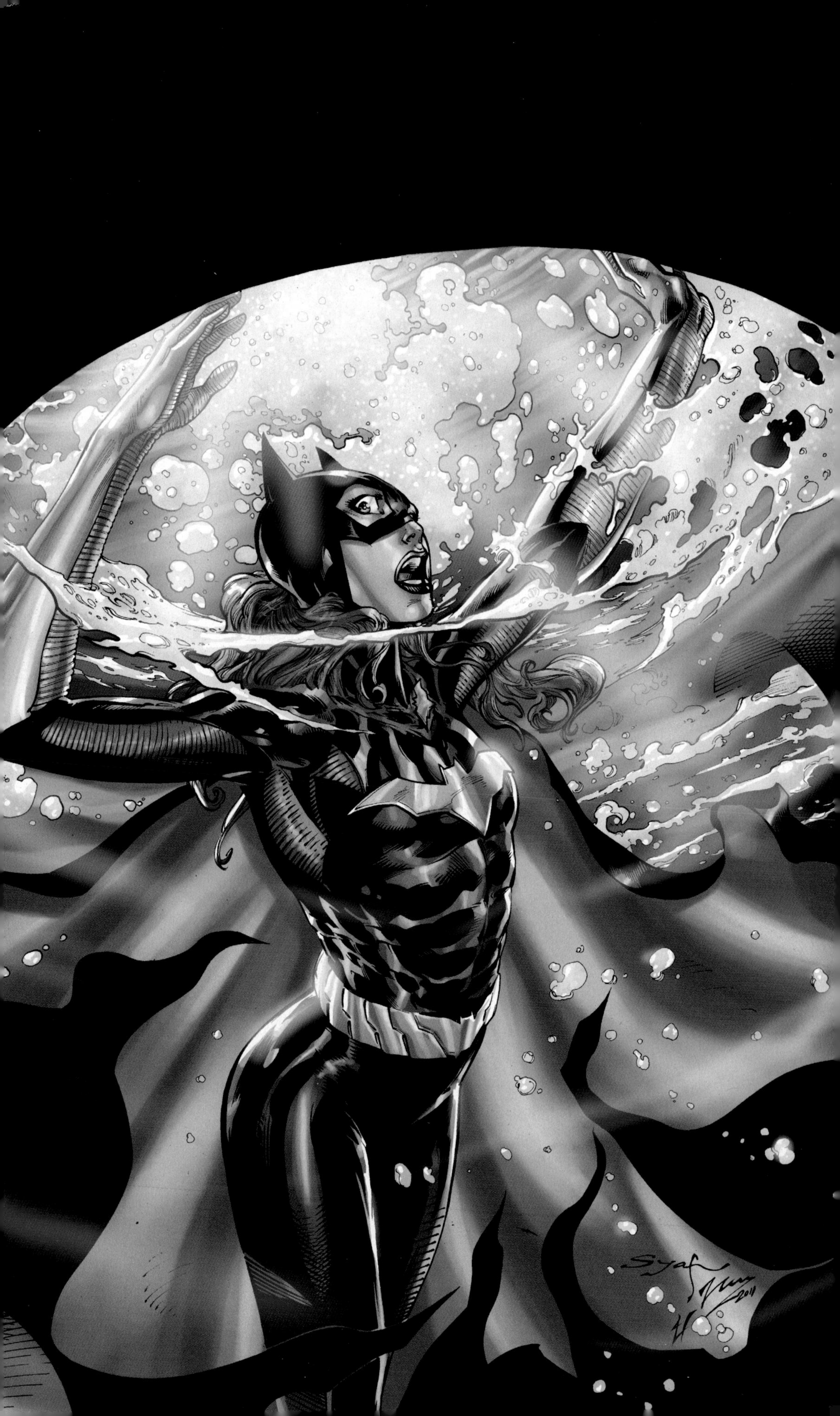

A VIEW FROM BELOW

GAIL SIMONE writer **ARDIAN SYAF & ALITHA MARTINEZ** pencillers **VICENTE CIFUENTES** inker
cover by ARDIAN SYAF, VICENTE CIFUENTES & ULISES ARREOLA

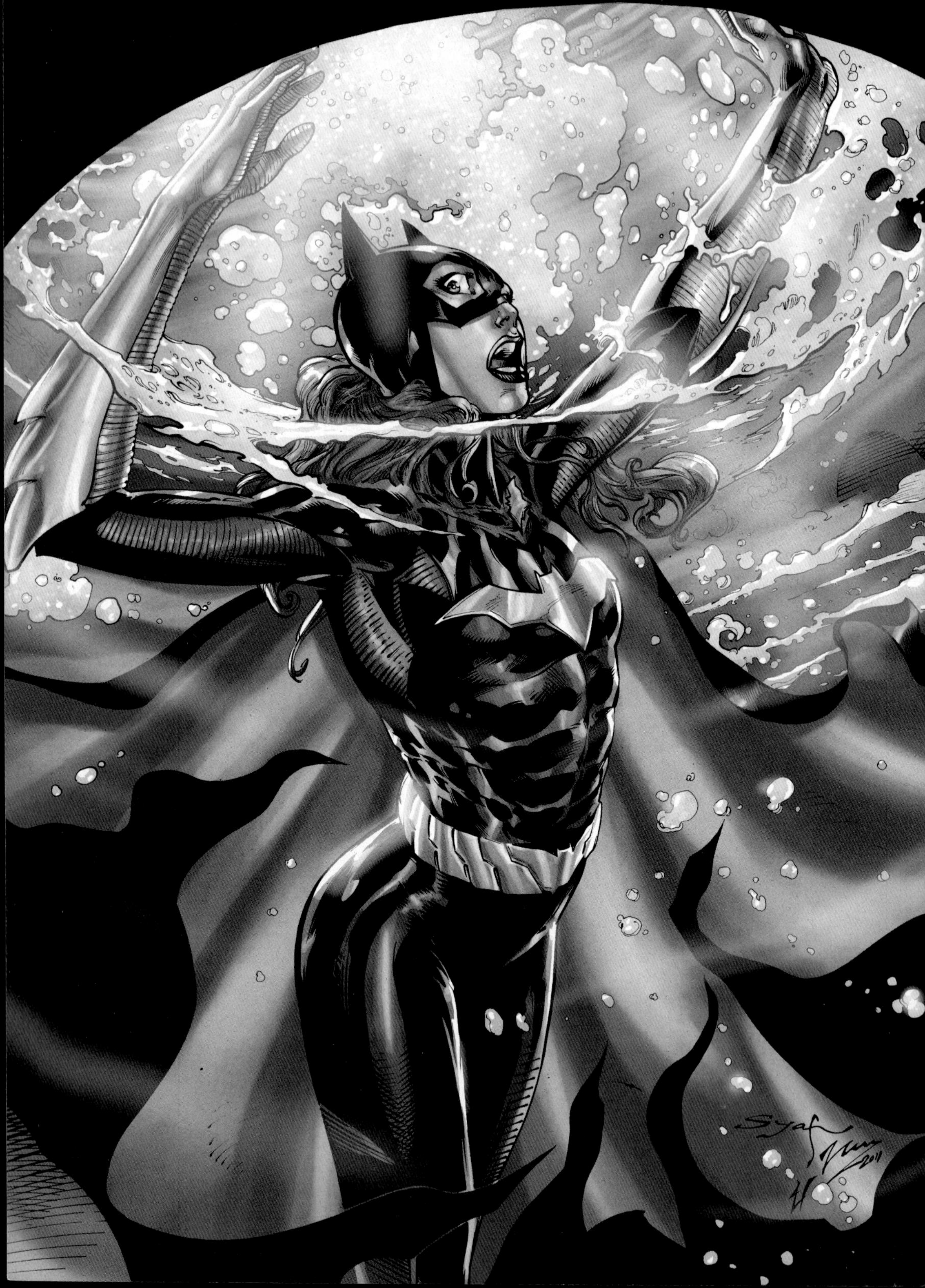

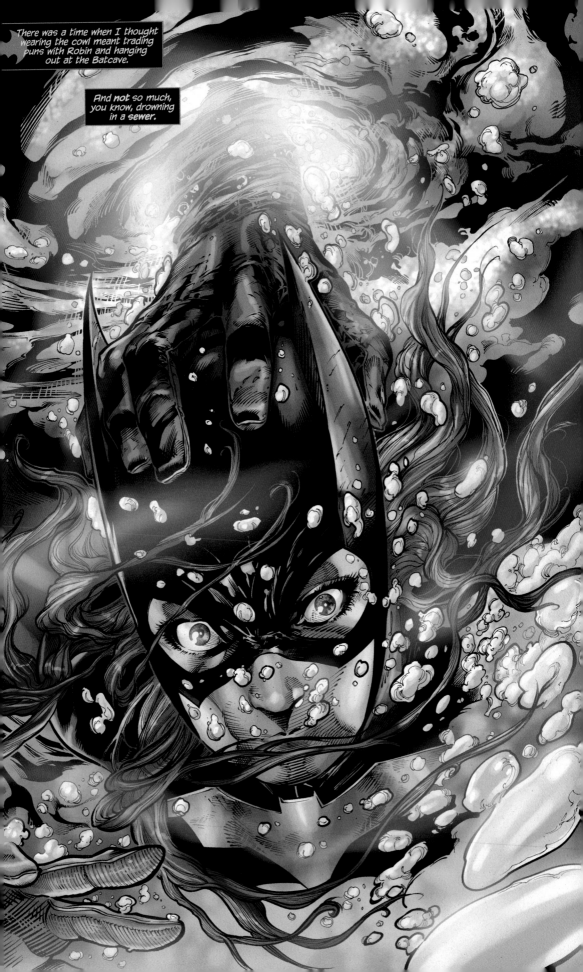

There was a time when I thought wearing the cowl meant trading puns with Robin and hanging out at the Batcave.

And *not* so much, you know, drowning in a sewer.

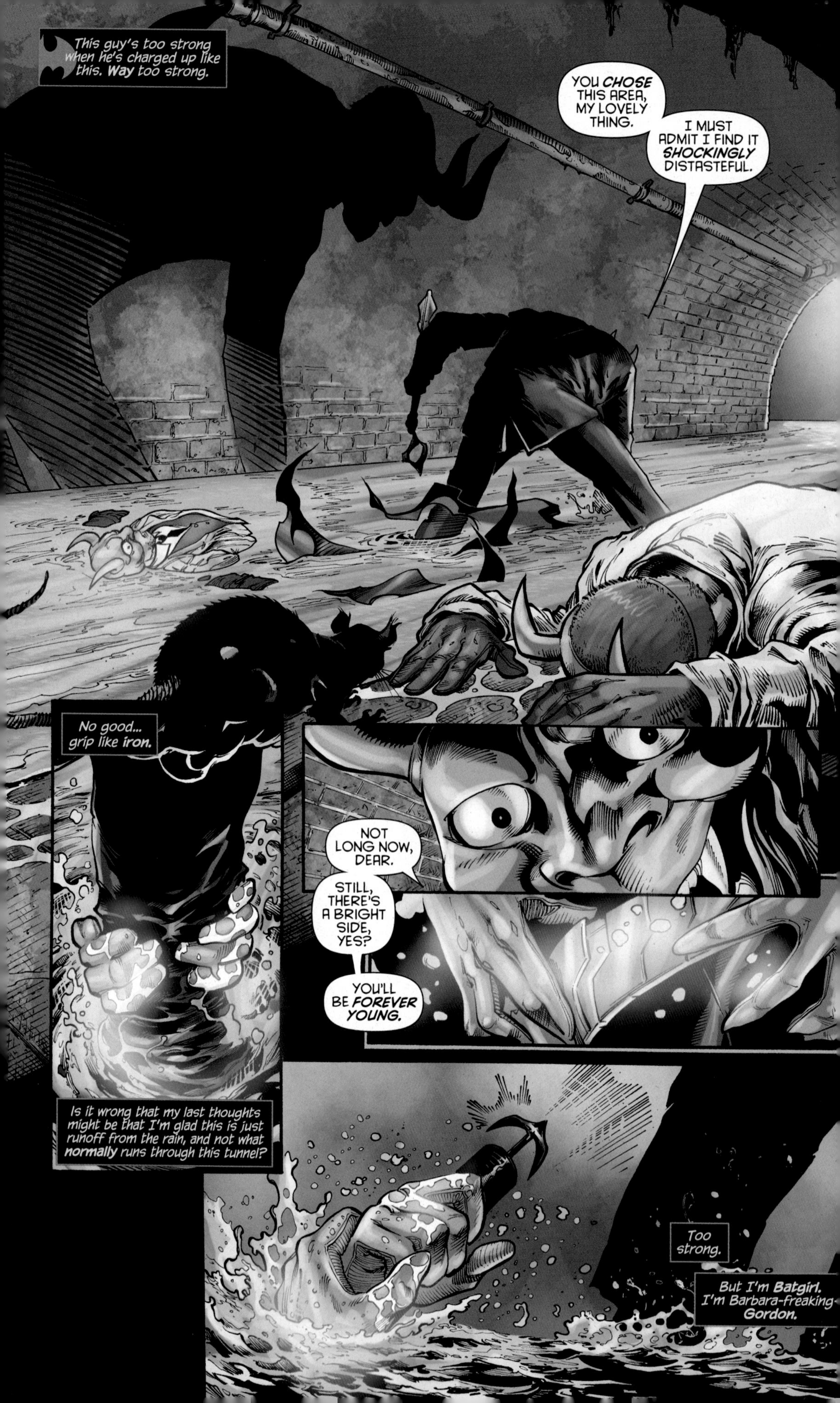

This guy's too strong when he's charged up like this. Way too strong.
YOU CHOSE THIS AREA, MY LOVELY THING.
I MUST ADMIT I FIND IT SHOCKINGLY DISTASTEFUL.
No good... grip like iron.
NOT LONG NOW, DEAR.
STILL, THERE'S A BRIGHT SIDE, YES?
YOU'LL BE FOREVER YOUNG.
Is it wrong that my last thoughts might be that I'm glad this is just runoff from the rain, and not what normally runs through this tunnel?
Too strong.
But I'm Batgirl. I'm Barbara-freaking Gordon.

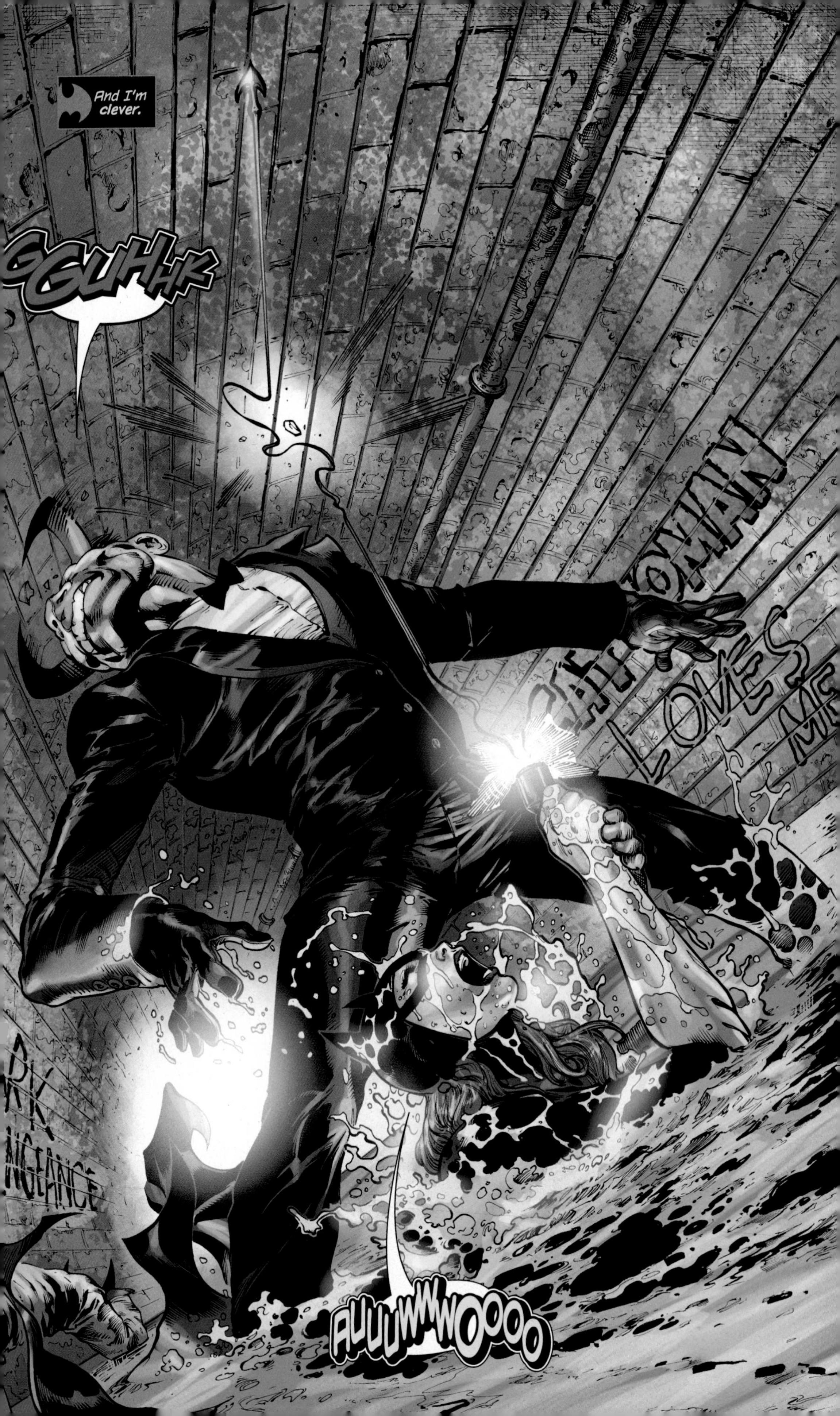
And I'm clever.
GGUHHK
LOVES ME
AUUUWWWOOOO

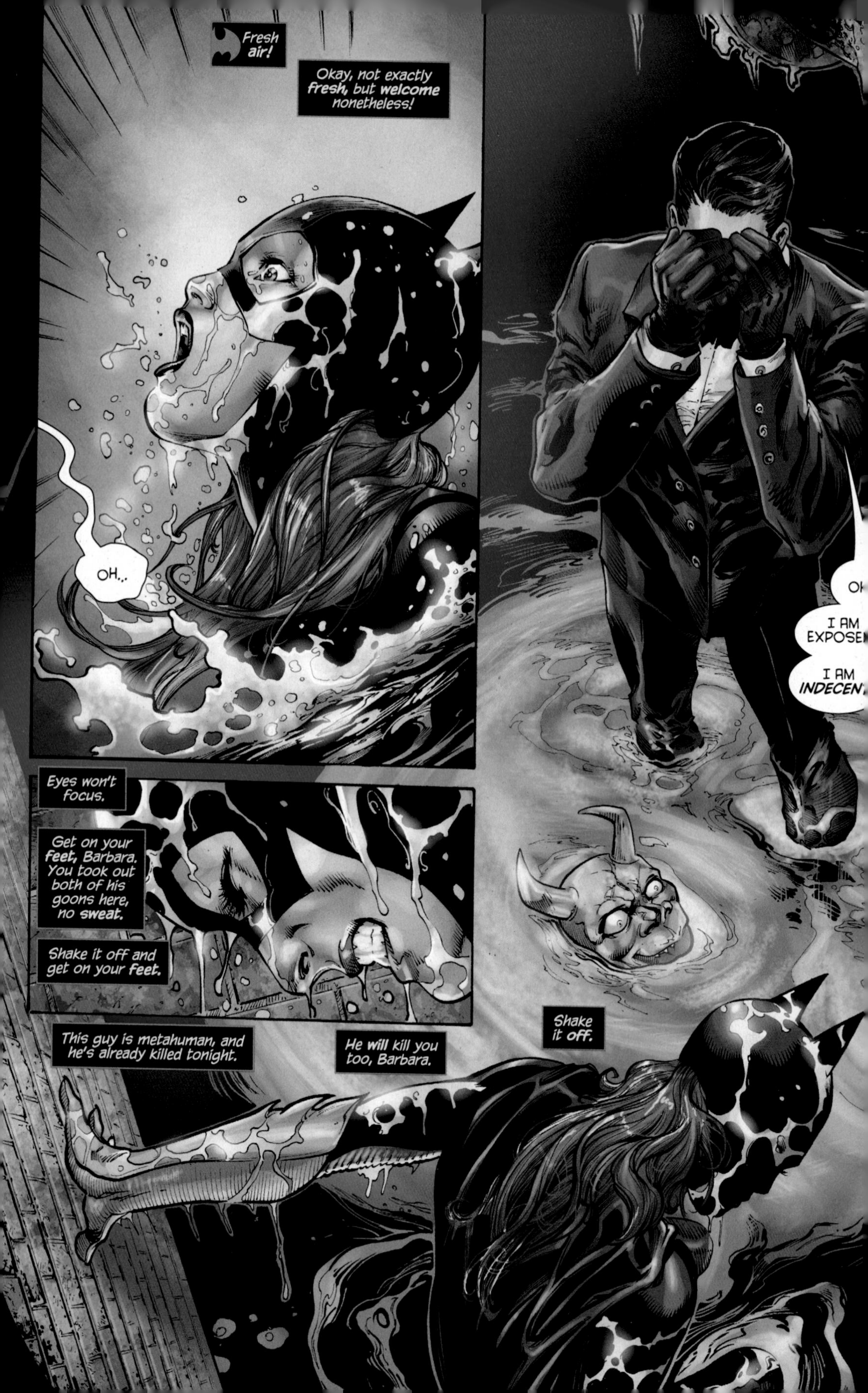
Fresh air!
Okay, not exactly fresh, but welcome nonetheless!
OH...
Eyes won't focus.
Get on your feet, Barbara. You took out both of his goons here, no sweat.
Shake it off and get on your feet.
OH
I AM EXPOSE
I AM INDECEN
This guy is metahuman, and he's already killed tonight.
He will kill you too, Barbara.
Shake it off.

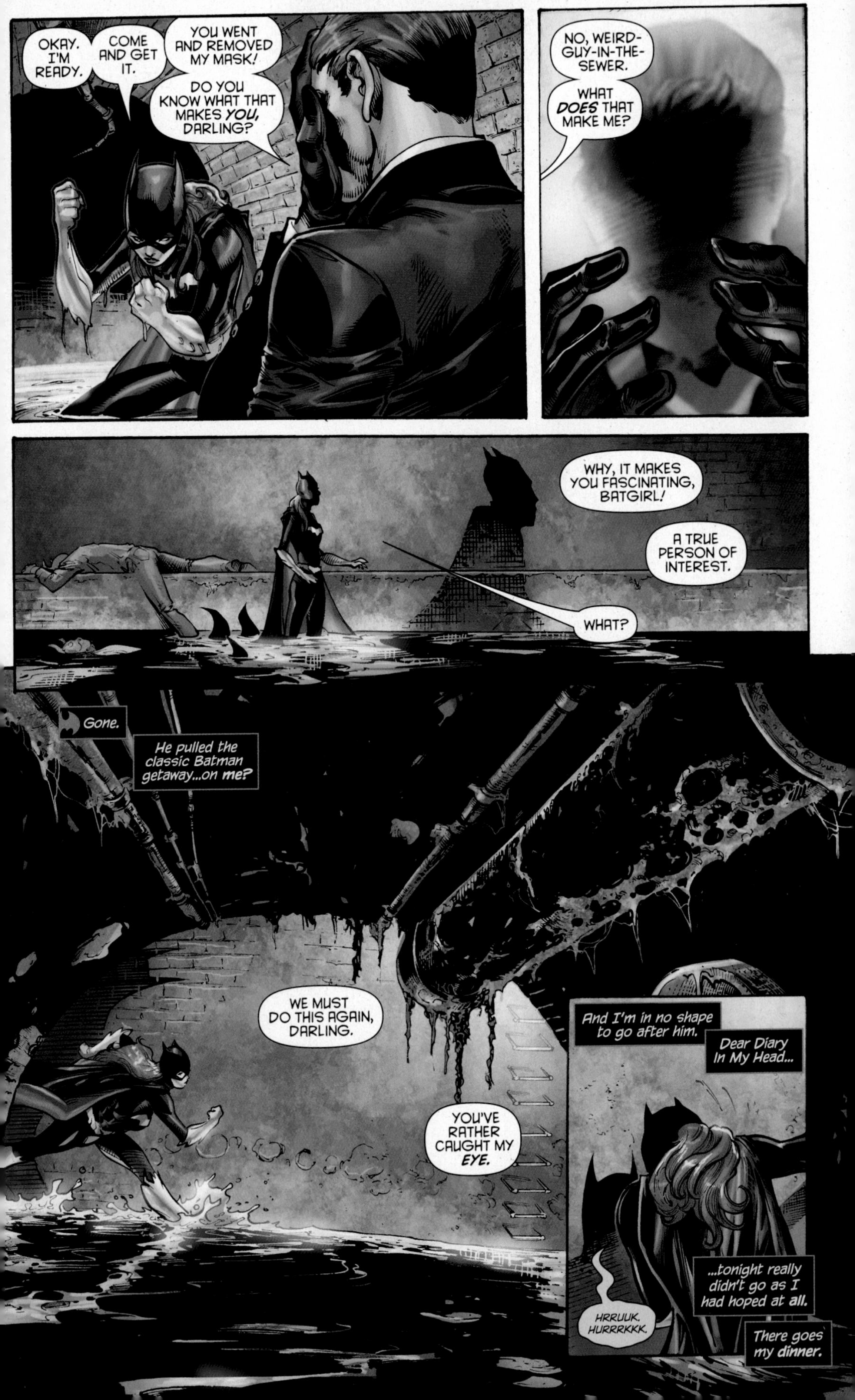
OKAY. I'M READY.
COME AND GET IT.
YOU WENT AND REMOVED MY MASK!
DO YOU KNOW WHAT THAT MAKES YOU, DARLING?
NO, WEIRD-GUY-IN-THE-SEWER.
WHAT DOES THAT MAKE ME?
WHY, IT MAKES YOU FASCINATING, BATGIRL!
A TRUE PERSON OF INTEREST.
WHAT?
Gone.
He pulled the classic Batman getaway...on me?
WE MUST DO THIS AGAIN, DARLING.
YOU'VE RATHER CAUGHT MY EYE.
And I'm in no shape to go after him.
Dear Diary In My Head...
...tonight really didn't go as I had hoped at all.
HRRUUK. HURRRKKK.
There goes my dinner.

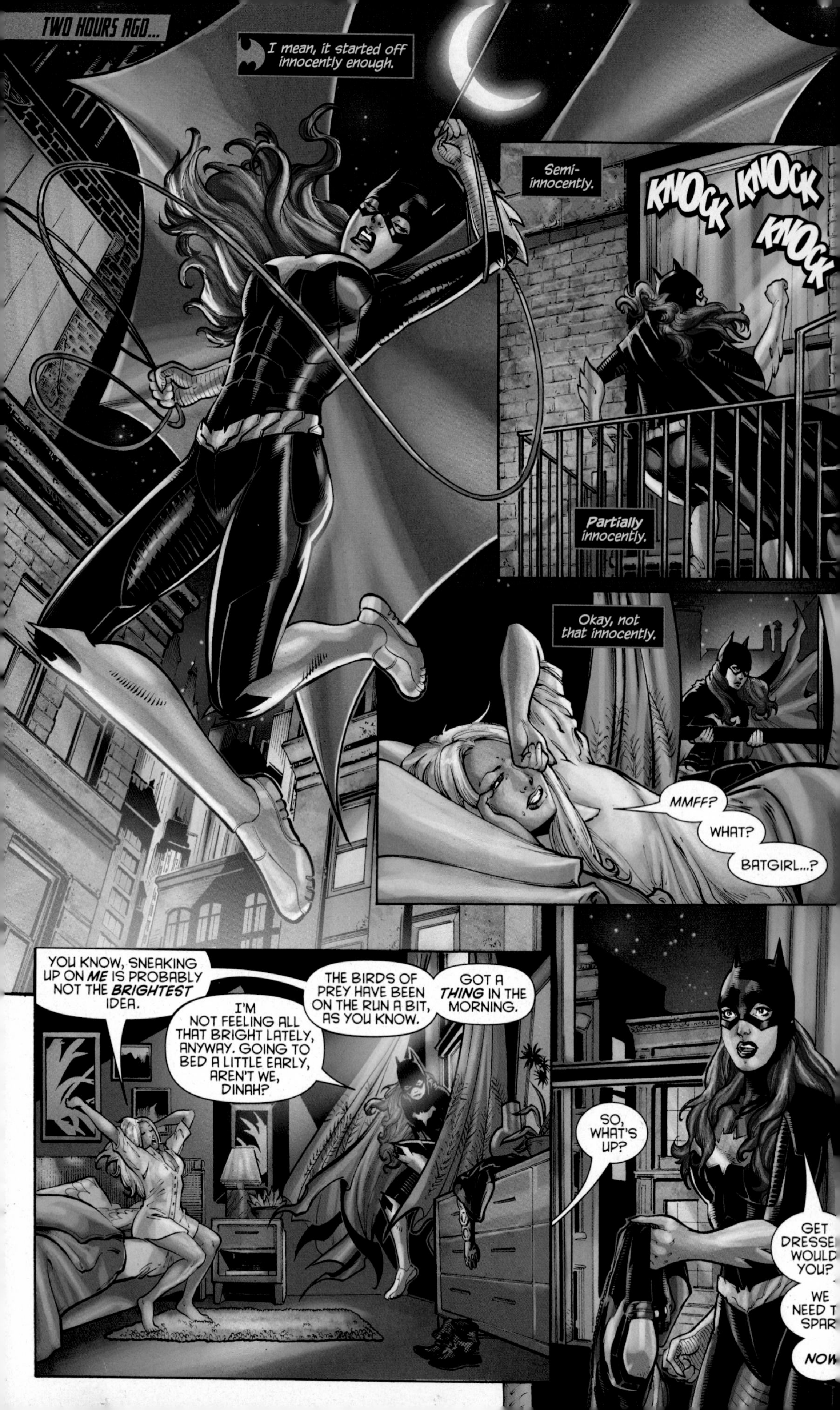

TWO HOURS AGO...
I mean, it started off innocently enough.
Semi-innocently.
KNOCK KNOCK KNOCK
Partially innocently.
Okay, not that innocently.
MMFF?
WHAT?
BATGIRL...?
YOU KNOW, SNEAKING UP ON ME IS PROBABLY NOT THE BRIGHTEST IDEA.
I'M NOT FEELING ALL THAT BRIGHT LATELY, ANYWAY. GOING TO BED A LITTLE EARLY, AREN'T WE, DINAH?
THE BIRDS OF PREY HAVE BEEN ON THE RUN A BIT, AS YOU KNOW.
GOT A THING IN THE MORNING.
SO, WHAT'S UP?

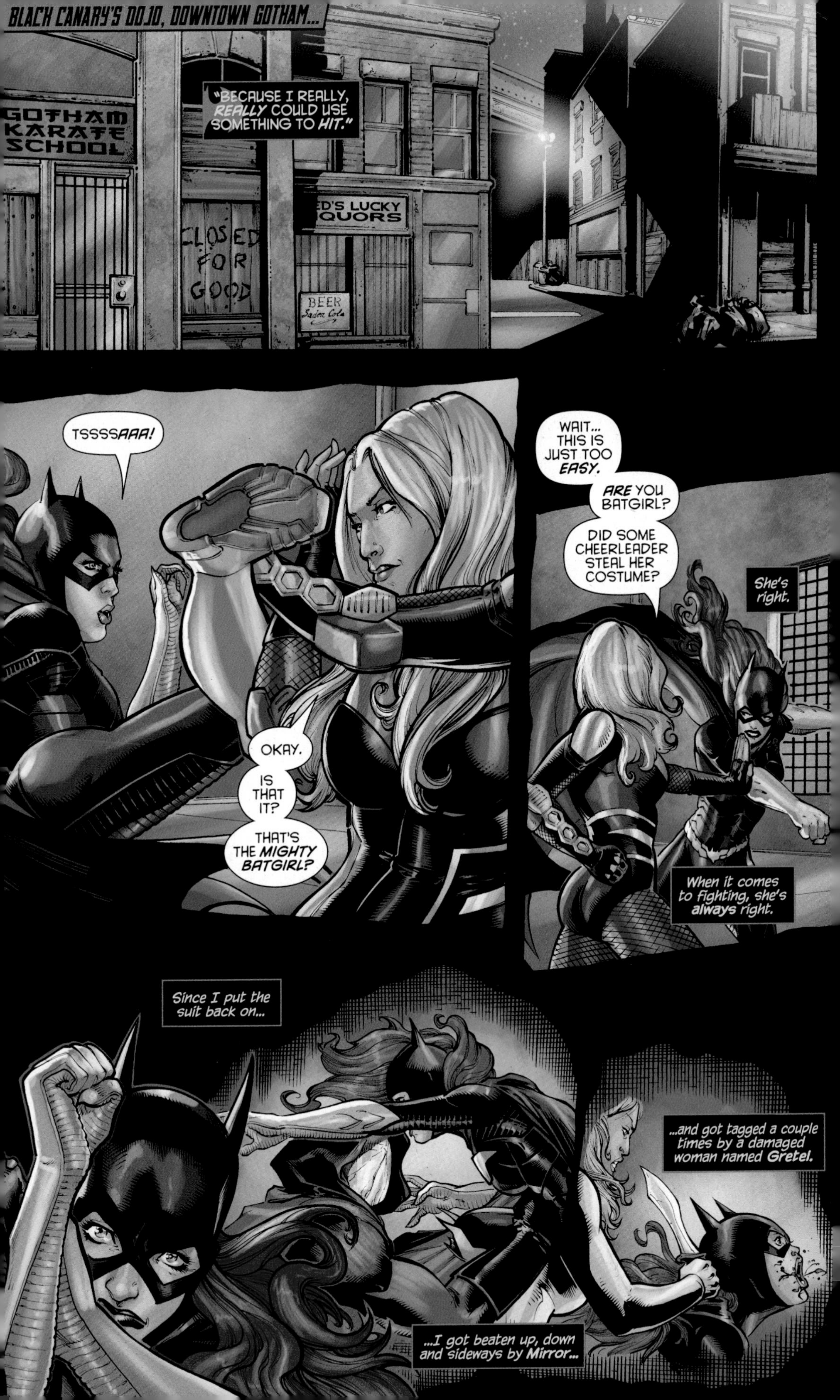
BLACK CANARY'S DOJO, DOWNTOWN GOTHAM...
GOTHAM KARATE SCHOOL
"BECAUSE I REALLY, REALLY COULD USE SOMETHING TO HIT."
CLOSED FOR GOOD
ED'S LUCKY QUORS
BEER
TSSSSAAA!
OKAY.
IS THAT IT?
THAT'S THE MIGHTY BATGIRL?
WAIT... THIS IS JUST TOO EASY.
ARE YOU BATGIRL?
DID SOME CHEERLEADER STEAL HER COSTUME?
She's right.
When it comes to fighting, she's always right.
Since I put the suit back on...
...I got beaten up, down and sideways by Mirror...
...and got tagged a couple times by a damaged woman named Gretel.

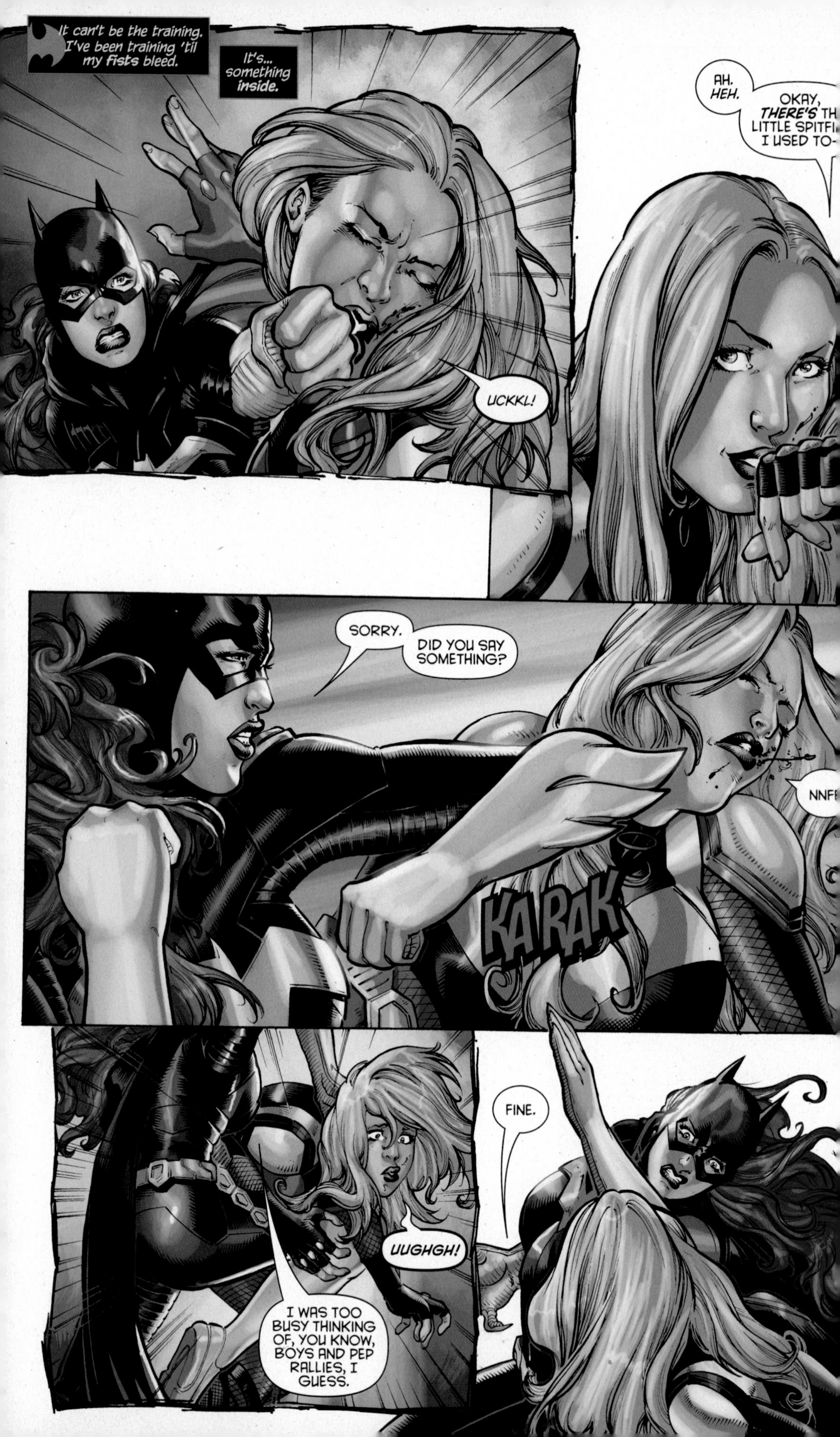
It can't be the training. I've been training 'til my fists bleed.
It's... something inside.
UCKKL!
AH. HEH.
OKAY, THERE'S TH LITTLE SPITFI I USED TO-
SORRY.
DID YOU SAY SOMETHING?
NNFF
KA RAK
UUGHGH!
I WAS TOO BUSY THINKING OF, YOU KNOW, BOYS AND PEP RALLIES, I GUESS.
FINE.

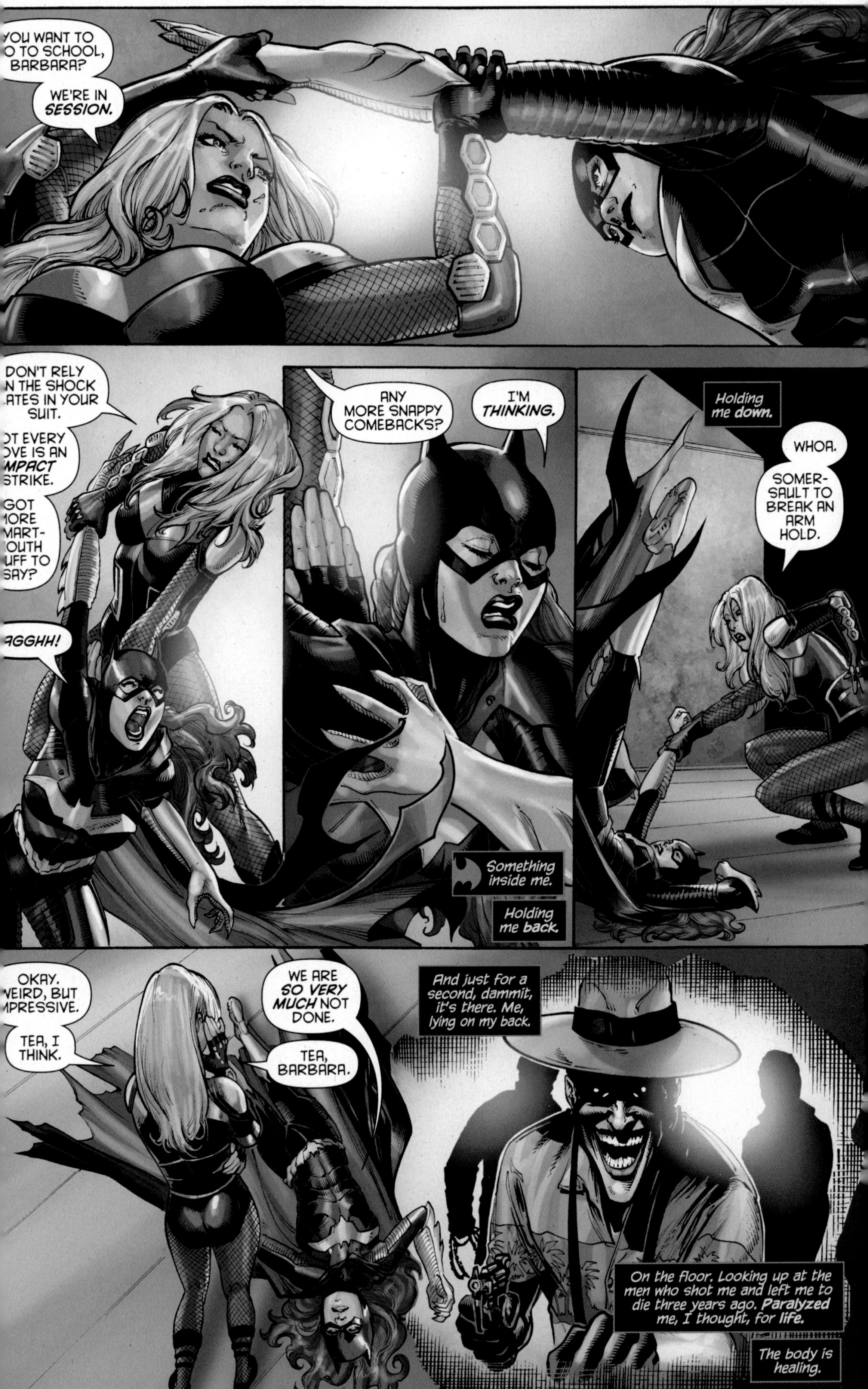

YOU WANT TO
O TO SCHOOL,
BARBARA?
WE'RE IN SESSION.
DON'T RELY
N THE SHOCK
ATES IN YOUR
SUIT.
OT EVERY
OVE IS AN
MPACT
STRIKE.
GOT
MORE
MART-
OUTH
UFF TO
SAY?
AGGHH!
ANY MORE SNAPPY COMEBACKS?
I'M THINKING.
Something inside me.
Holding me back.
Holding me down.
WHOA.
SOMER-SAULT TO BREAK AN ARM HOLD.
OKAY.
VEIRD, BUT
MPRESSIVE.
TEA, I THINK.
WE ARE SO VERY MUCH NOT DONE.
TEA, BARBARA.
And just for a second, dammit, it's there. Me, lying on my back.
On the floor. Looking up at the men who shot me and left me to die three years ago. Paralyzed me, I thought, for life.
The body is healing.

The spirit remains wounded.

GOOD LORD, THE *TECH* IN THIS SUIT, BARBARA. HOW IN THE WORLD DID YOU AFFORD IT?

IT'S *INCREDIBLY* ELEGANT.

THAT'S A BIT OF A STORY, DINAH.

SORRY I GOT A LITTLE HAYWIRE FOR A SECOND.

IT'S OKAY. I MEAN...

...I *AM* THE BLACK CANARY. I CAN HANDLE IT.

She is.

And I love her dearly for it.

SO, WHAT'S WITH ALL THE AGITA?

WHAT'S SO BAD IT MAKES YOU *WANT* TO GET PUMMELED?

WELL, FOR STARTERS, THE MOTHER WHO ABANDONED ME WANTS BACK IN MY LIFE, FROM OUT OF NOWHERE.

WHOA.

DOES YOUR DAD KNOW?

GOTHAM CITY POLICE DEPARTMENT...

"NOT YET, I DON'T THINK.

"HE NEVER STOPPED LOVING HER, NEVER SAID A BAD WORD *ABOUT* HER. I DON'T KNOW *WHAT* HE'LL DO."

COMMISSIONER? YOU HAVE A VISITOR.

McKENNA, I SPECIFICALLY SAID *NO* VISITORS TONIGHT, AND I EXPECT MY *DETECTIVES* TO BE ABLE TO FOLLOW SIMPLE--

UH, ALL DUE RESPECT, COMMISSIONER...

...I'M PRETTY SURE IT'S TIME FOR AN *EXCEPTION.*

GOTHAM CITY POLICE BLOTTER

GOTHAM CITY POLICE BLOTTER GOTHAM CITY POLICE BLOTTER GOTHAM CITY POLICE BLOTTER GOTHAM CITY POLICE BLOTTER GOTHAM CITY POLICE BLOTTER GOTHAM CITY POLICE BLOTTER

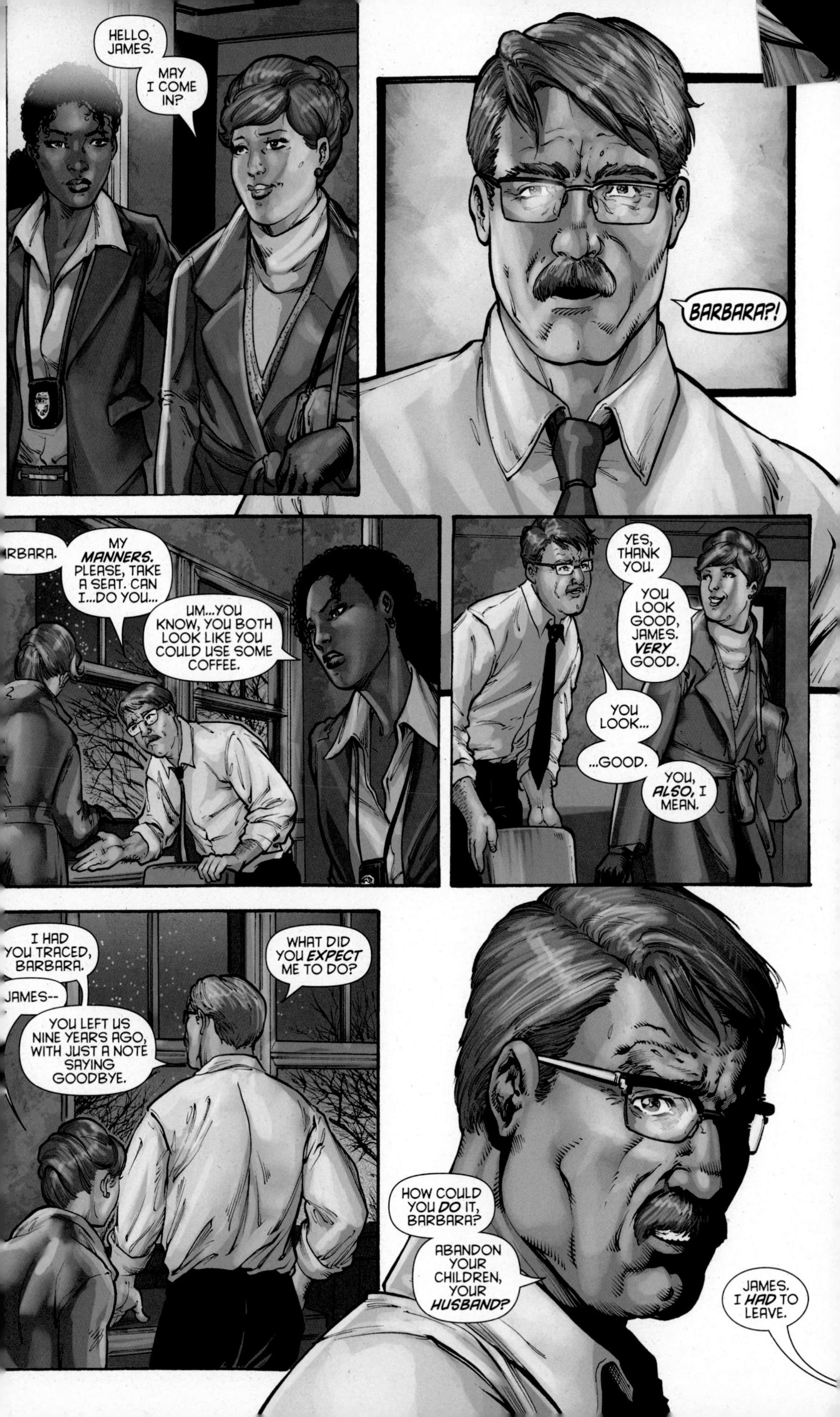
HELLO, JAMES.
MAY I COME IN?
BARBARA?!
RBARA.
MY MANNERS. PLEASE, TAKE A SEAT. CAN I...DO YOU...
UM...YOU KNOW, YOU BOTH LOOK LIKE YOU COULD USE SOME COFFEE.
YES, THANK YOU.
YOU LOOK GOOD, JAMES. VERY GOOD.
YOU LOOK...
...GOOD.
YOU, ALSO, I MEAN.
I HAD YOU TRACED, BARBARA.
JAMES--
YOU LEFT US NINE YEARS AGO, WITH JUST A NOTE SAYING GOODBYE.
WHAT DID YOU EXPECT ME TO DO?
HOW COULD YOU DO IT, BARBARA?
ABANDON YOUR CHILDREN, YOUR HUSBAND?
JAMES. I HAD TO LEAVE.

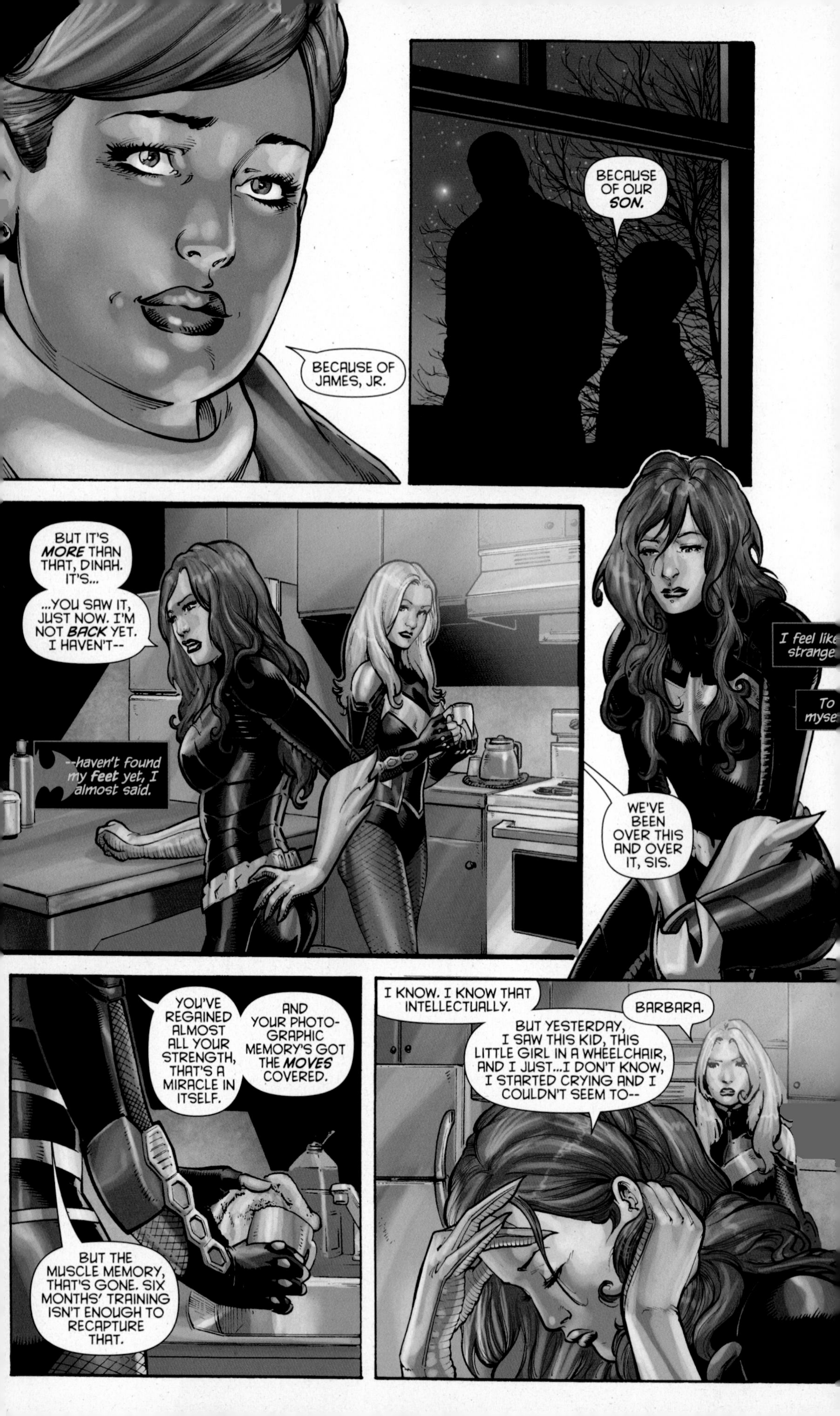
BECAUSE OF JAMES, JR.
BECAUSE OF OUR SON.
BUT IT'S MORE THAN THAT, DINAH. IT'S...
...YOU SAW IT, JUST NOW. I'M NOT BACK YET. I HAVEN'T--
--haven't found my feet yet, I almost said.
WE'VE BEEN OVER THIS AND OVER IT, SIS.
YOU'VE REGAINED ALMOST ALL YOUR STRENGTH, THAT'S A MIRACLE IN ITSELF.
AND YOUR PHOTO-GRAPHIC MEMORY'S GOT THE MOVES COVERED.
BUT THE MUSCLE MEMORY, THAT'S GONE. SIX MONTHS' TRAINING ISN'T ENOUGH TO RECAPTURE THAT.
I KNOW. I KNOW THAT INTELLECTUALLY.
BARBARA.
BUT YESTERDAY, I SAW THIS KID, THIS LITTLE GIRL IN A WHEELCHAIR, AND I JUST...I DON'T KNOW, I STARTED CRYING AND I COULDN'T SEEM TO--

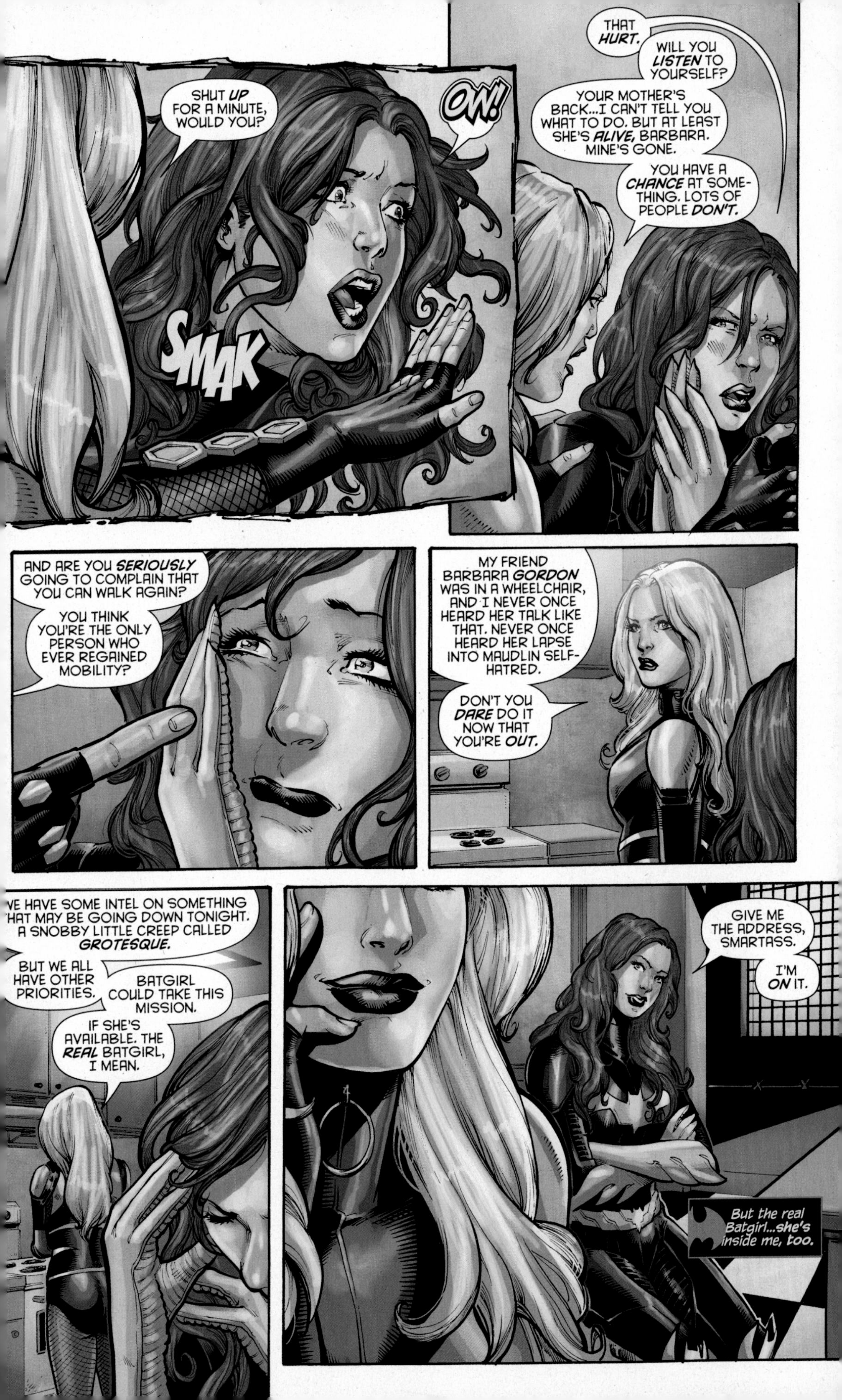
SHUT UP FOR A MINUTE, WOULD YOU?
SMAK
OW!
THAT HURT.
WILL YOU LISTEN TO YOURSELF?
YOUR MOTHER'S BACK...I CAN'T TELL YOU WHAT TO DO. BUT AT LEAST SHE'S ALIVE, BARBARA. MINE'S GONE.
YOU HAVE A CHANCE AT SOMETHING. LOTS OF PEOPLE DON'T.
AND ARE YOU SERIOUSLY GOING TO COMPLAIN THAT YOU CAN WALK AGAIN?
YOU THINK YOU'RE THE ONLY PERSON WHO EVER REGAINED MOBILITY?
MY FRIEND BARBARA GORDON WAS IN A WHEELCHAIR, AND I NEVER ONCE HEARD HER TALK LIKE THAT. NEVER ONCE HEARD HER LAPSE INTO MAUDLIN SELF-HATRED.
DON'T YOU DARE DO IT NOW THAT YOU'RE OUT.
WE HAVE SOME INTEL ON SOMETHING THAT MAY BE GOING DOWN TONIGHT. A SNOBBY LITTLE CREEP CALLED GROTESQUE.
BUT WE ALL HAVE OTHER PRIORITIES.
BATGIRL COULD TAKE THIS MISSION.
IF SHE'S AVAILABLE. THE REAL BATGIRL, I MEAN.
GIVE ME THE ADDRESS, SMARTASS.
I'M ON IT.
But the real Batgirl...she's inside me, too.

CARTIER'S ONE CLUB...

It just took my blonde friend to remind me.

Now let's see how good her intel is.

The most expensive, exclusive private club in town--second only to the Iceberg Casino. Extra security.

Media mogul Theodore Aiklin's birthday. A level of wealth only people like Bruce Wayne can really understand.

Those guards could be legit.

Let's check the roof then, shall we?

Okay, UZIs?

That's not right.

Something definitely w

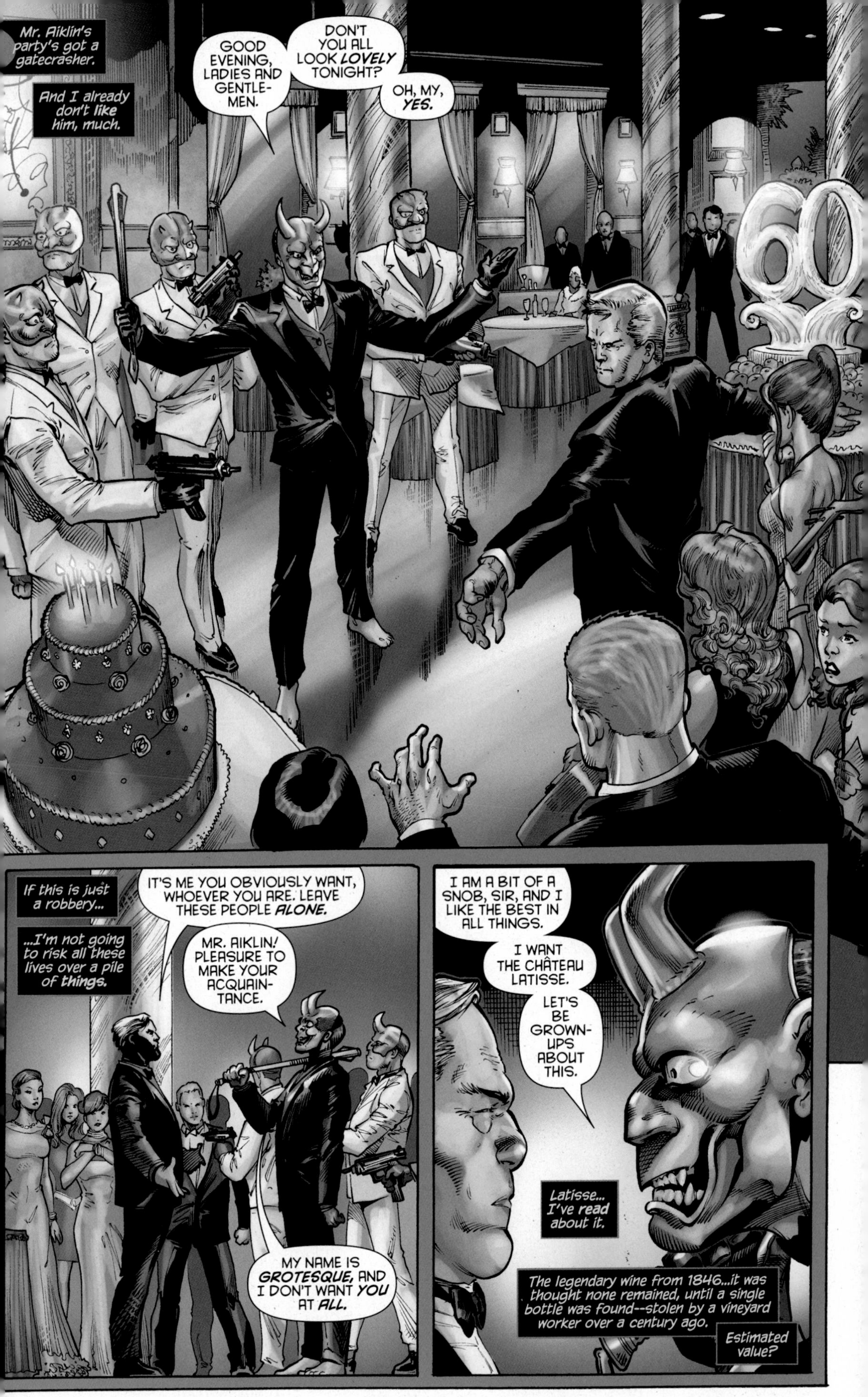

Mr. Aiklin's party's got a gatecrasher.
And I already don't like him, much.
GOOD EVENING, LADIES AND GENTLE-MEN.
DON'T YOU ALL LOOK LOVELY TONIGHT?
OH, MY, YES.
If this is just a robbery...
...I'm not going to risk all these lives over a pile of things.
IT'S ME YOU OBVIOUSLY WANT, WHOEVER YOU ARE. LEAVE THESE PEOPLE ALONE.
MR. AIKLIN! PLEASURE TO MAKE YOUR ACQUAINTANCE.
MY NAME IS GROTESQUE, AND I DON'T WANT YOU AT ALL.
I AM A BIT OF A SNOB, SIR, AND I LIKE THE BEST IN ALL THINGS.
I WANT THE CHÂTEAU LATISSE.
LET'S BE GROWN-UPS ABOUT THIS.
Latisse... I've read about it.
The legendary wine from 1846...it was thought none remained, until a single bottle was found--stolen by a vineyard worker over a century ago.
Estimated value?

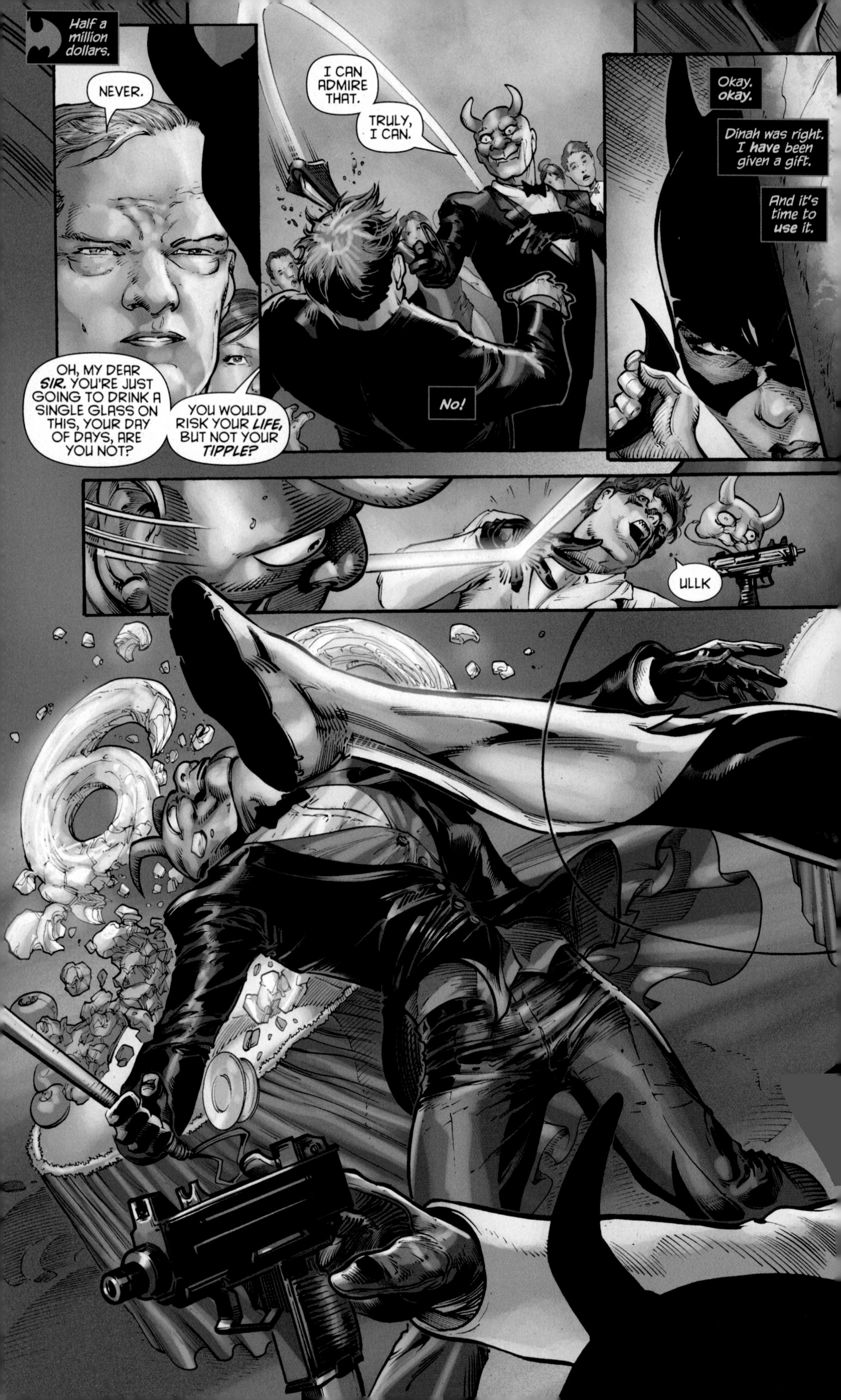
Half a million dollars.
NEVER.
OH, MY DEAR SIR. YOU'RE JUST GOING TO DRINK A SINGLE GLASS ON THIS, YOUR DAY OF DAYS, ARE YOU NOT?
YOU WOULD RISK YOUR LIFE, BUT NOT YOUR TIPPLE?
I CAN ADMIRE THAT.
TRULY, I CAN.
No!
Okay. okay.
Dinah was right. I have been given a gift.
And it's time to use it.
ULLK

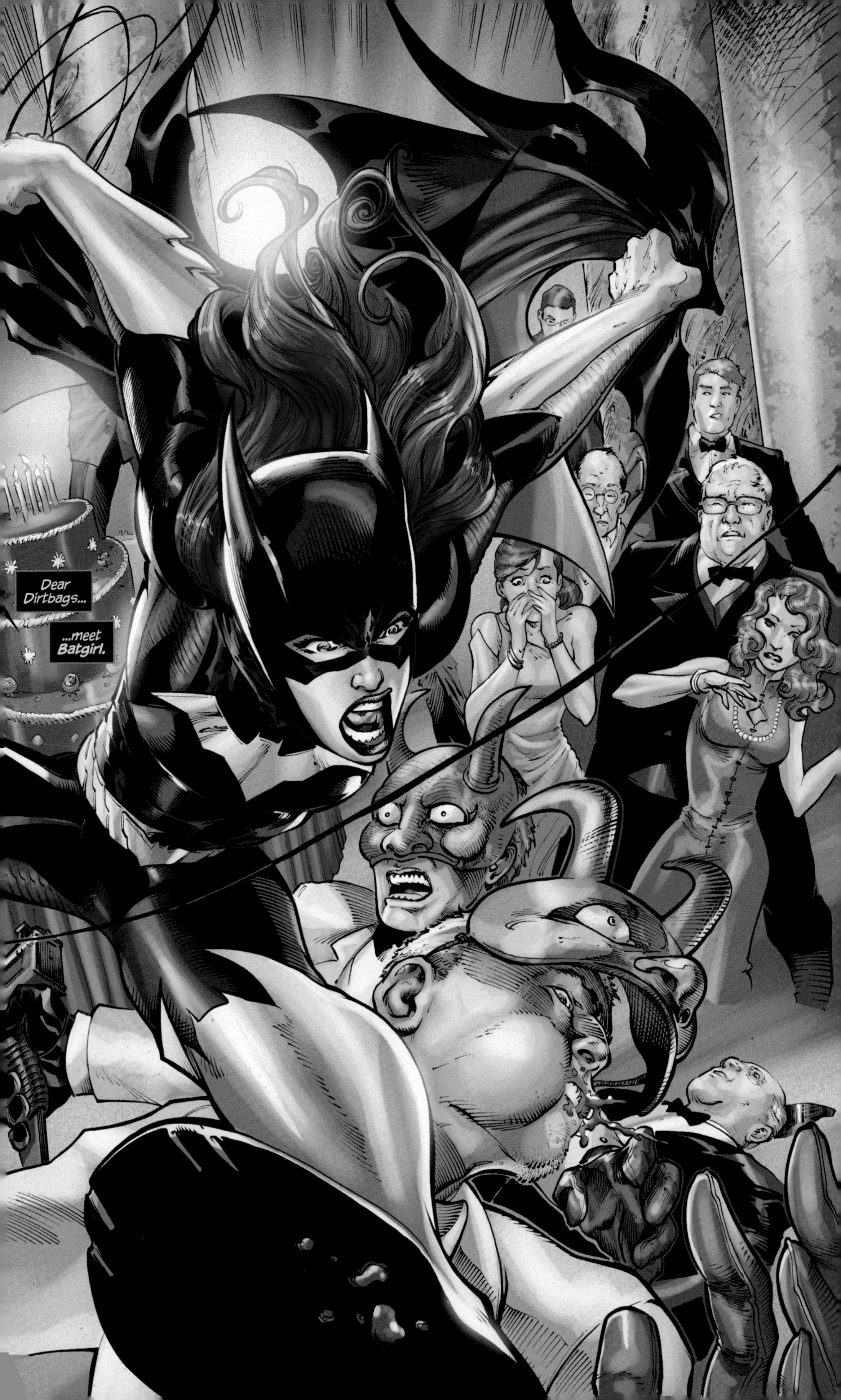
Dear Dirtbags...
...meet Batgirl.

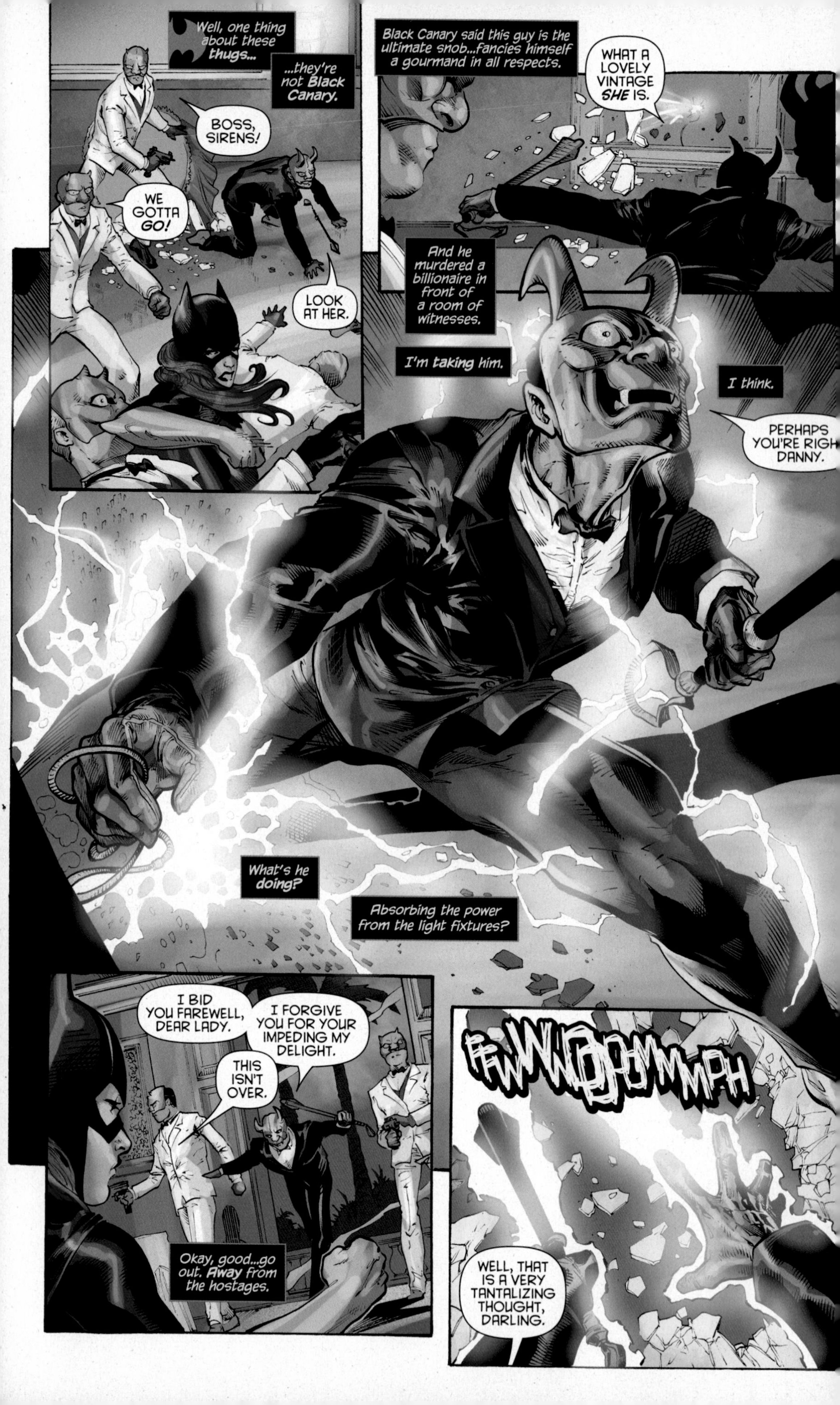
Well, one thing about these thugs...
...they're not Black Canary.
BOSS, SIRENS!
WE GOTTA GO!
LOOK AT HER.
Black Canary said this guy is the ultimate snob...fancies himself a gourmand in all respects.
WHAT A LOVELY VINTAGE SHE IS.
And he murdered a billionaire in front of a room of witnesses.
I'm taking him.
I think.
PERHAPS YOU'RE RIGH DANNY.
What's he doing?
Absorbing the power from the light fixtures?
I BID YOU FAREWELL, DEAR LADY.
I FORGIVE YOU FOR YOUR IMPEDING MY DELIGHT.
THIS ISN'T OVER.
Okay, good...go out. Away from the hostages.
FWWOOOMMMPH
WELL, THAT IS A VERY TANTALIZING THOUGHT, DARLING.

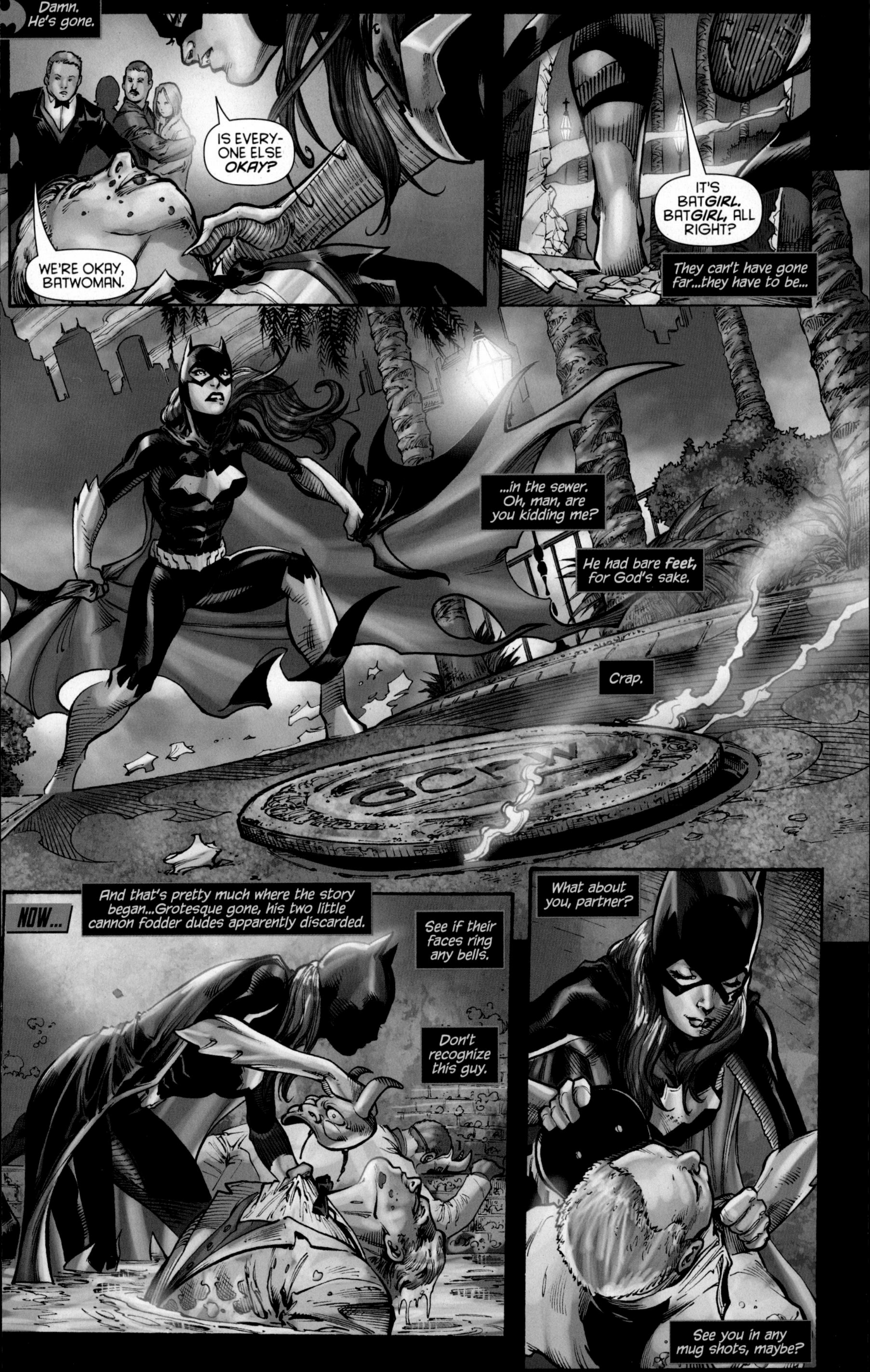
Damn. He's gone.
IS EVERY-ONE ELSE OKAY?
WE'RE OKAY, BATWOMAN.
IT'S BATGIRL. BATGIRL, ALL RIGHT?
They can't have gone far...they have to be...
...in the sewer. Oh, man, are you kidding me?
He had bare feet, for God's sake.
Crap.
NOW...
And that's pretty much where the story began...Grotesque gone, his two little cannon fodder dudes apparently discarded.
See if their faces ring any bells.
Don't recognize this guy.
What about you, partner?
See you in any mug shots, maybe?

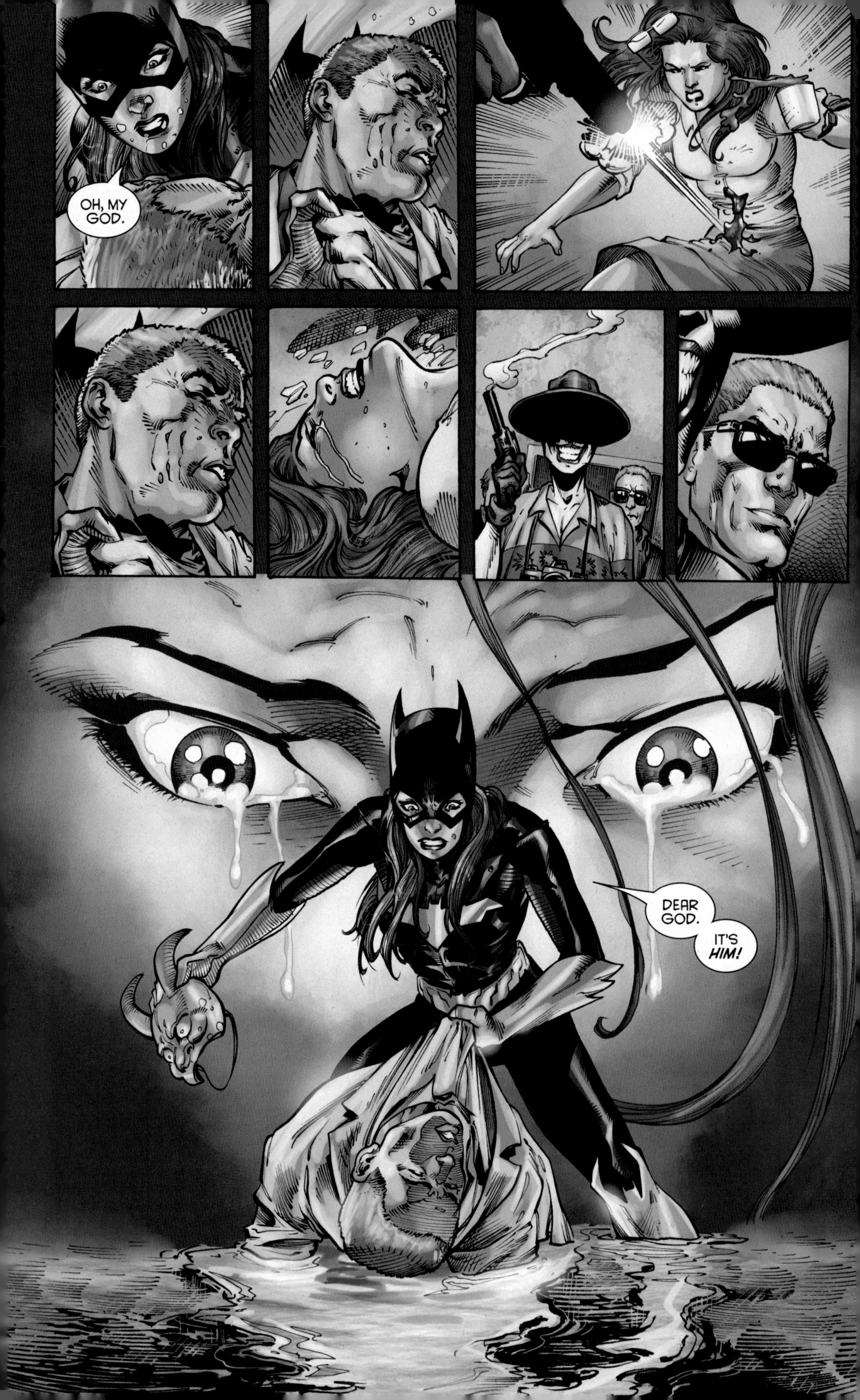
OH, MY GOD.
DEAR GOD.
IT'S *HIM!*

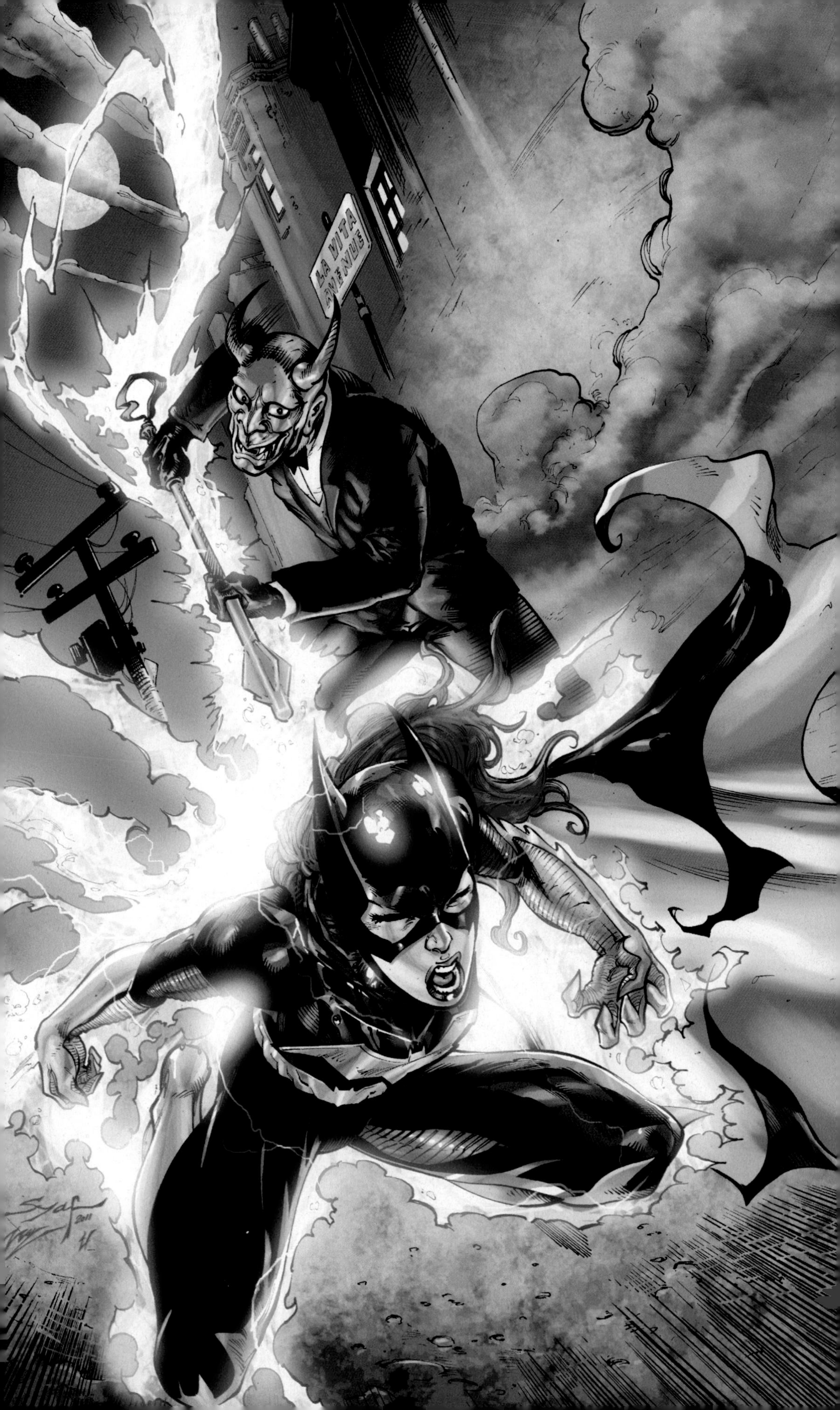
LA VITA AVENUE

cover ARDIAN SYAF, VICENTE CIFUENTES & ULISES ARREOLA

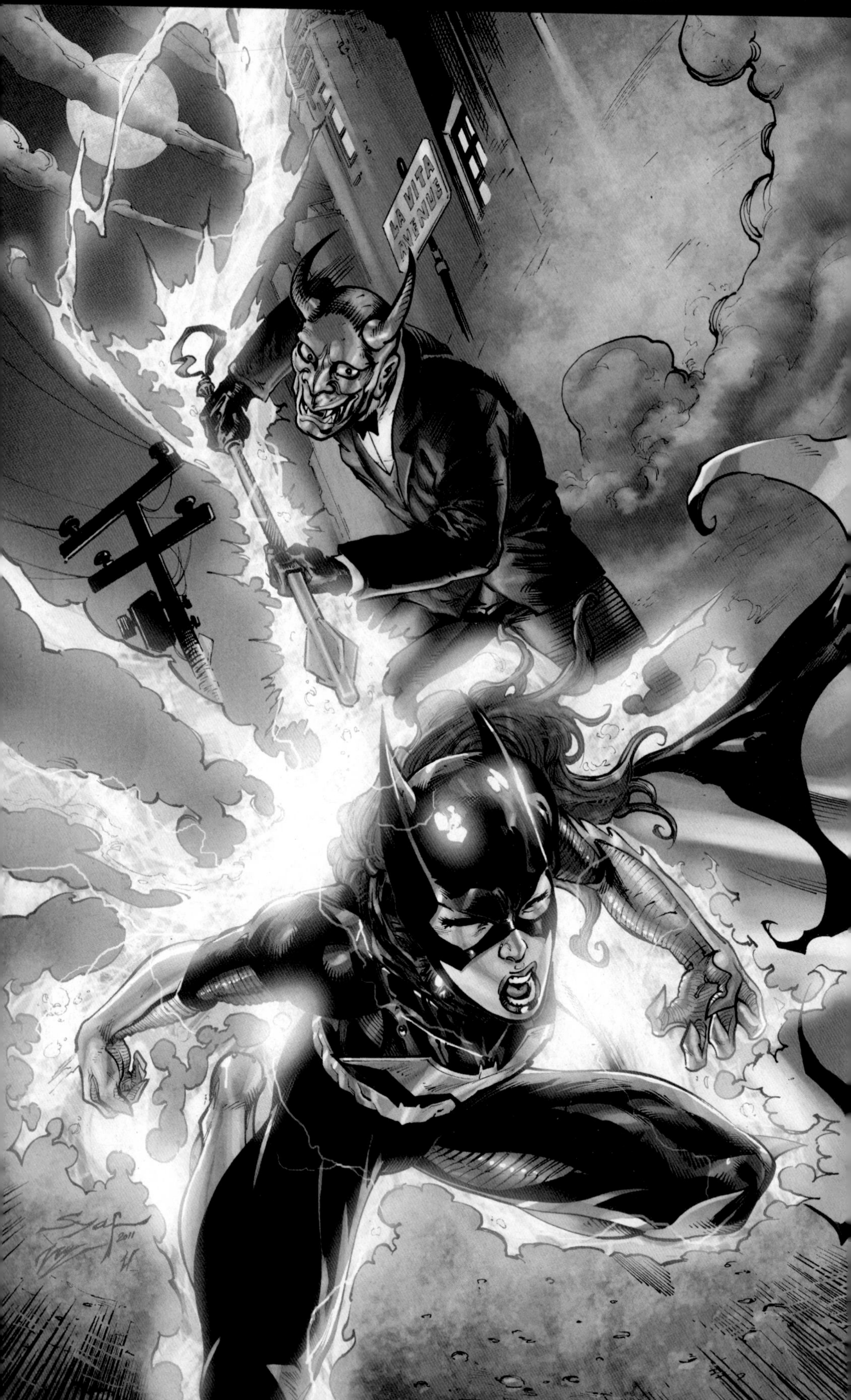
LA VITA AVENUE
Syaf 2011

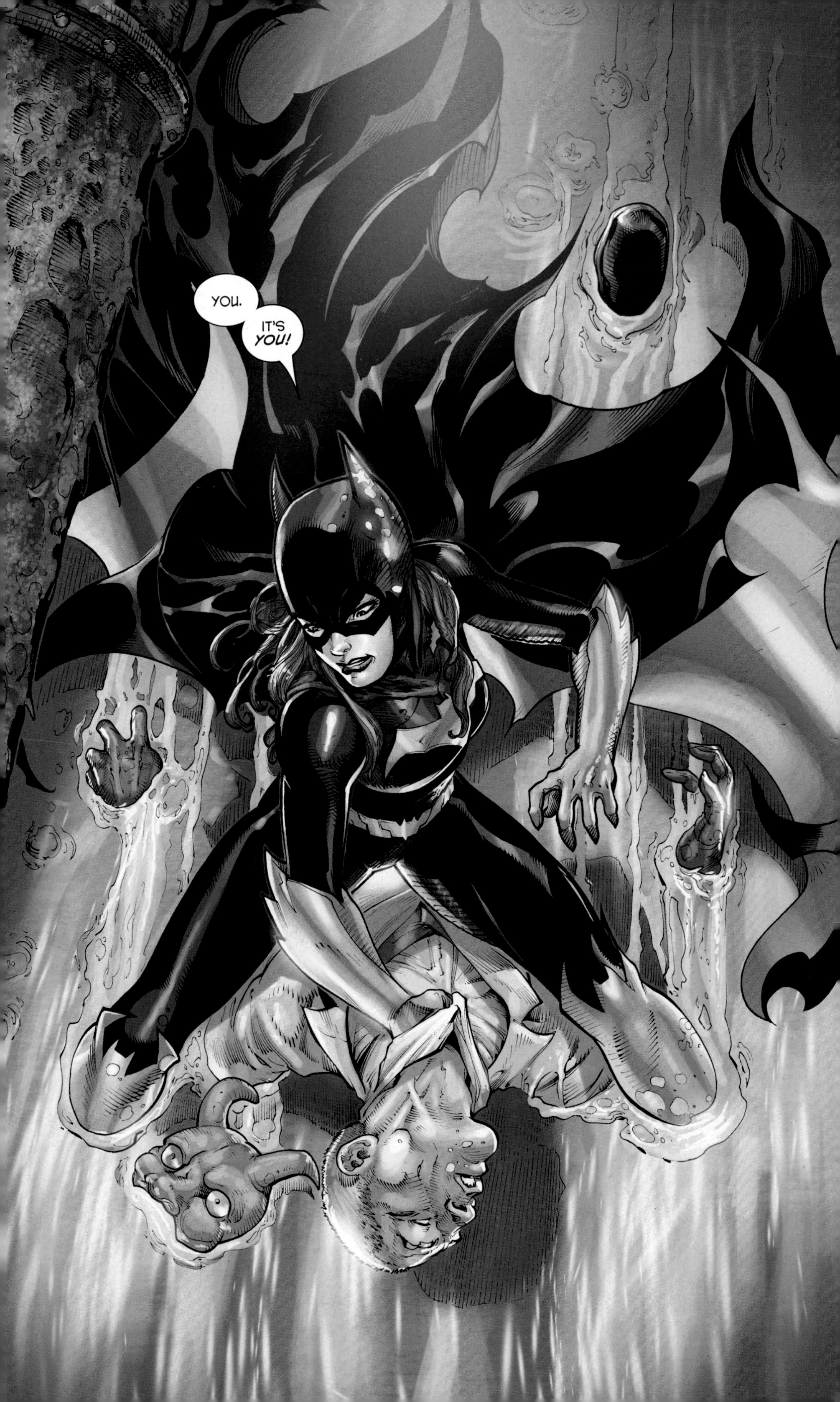
YOU.
IT'S *YOU!*

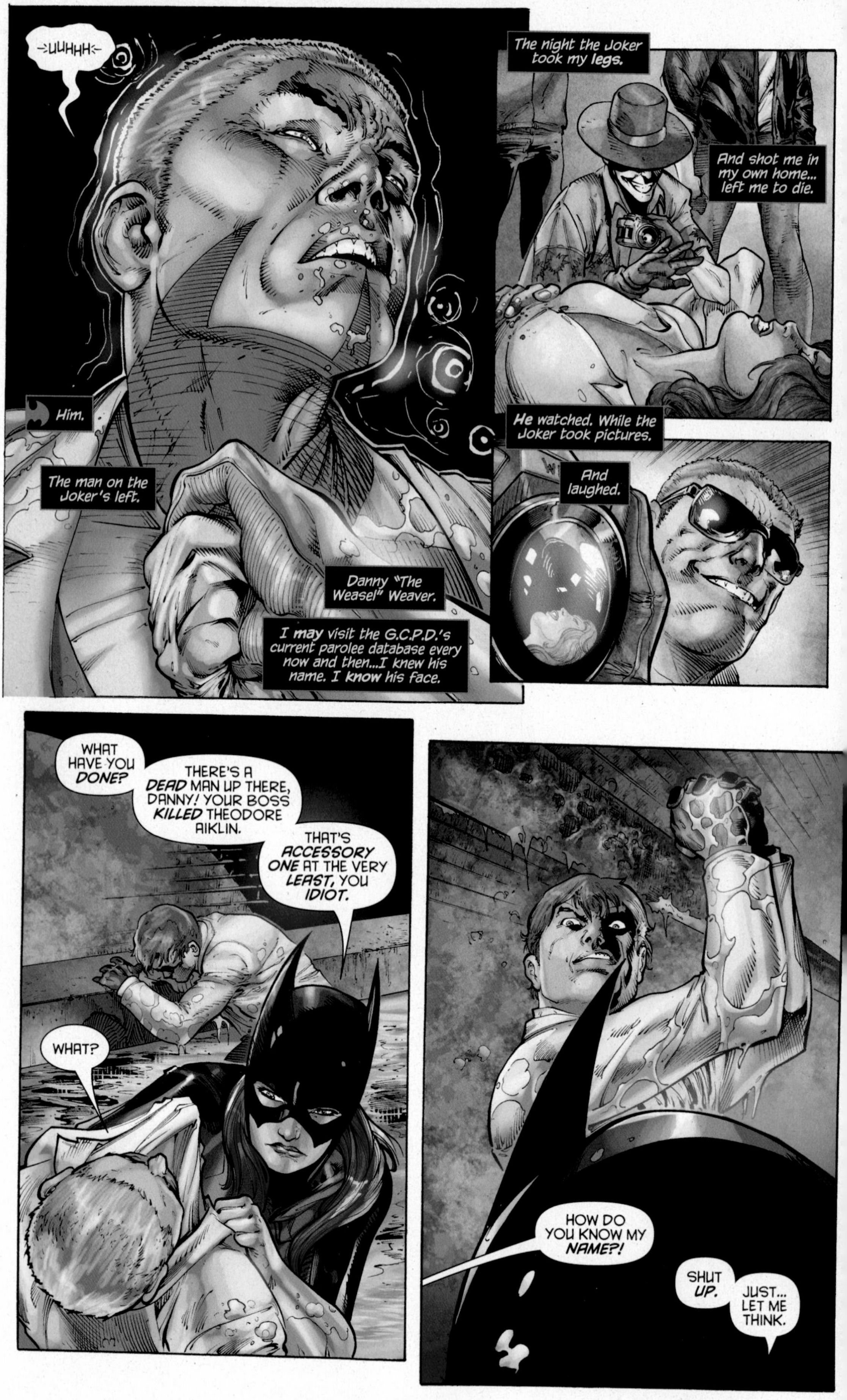

UUHHH
The night the Joker took my legs.
And shot me in my own home... left me to die.
Him.
The man on the Joker's left.
He watched. While the Joker took pictures.
And laughed.
Danny "The Weasel" Weaver.
I may visit the G.C.P.D.'s current parolee database every now and then...I knew his name. I know his face.
WHAT HAVE YOU DONE?
THERE'S A DEAD MAN UP THERE, DANNY! YOUR BOSS KILLED THEODORE AIKLIN.
THAT'S ACCESSORY ONE AT THE VERY LEAST, YOU IDIOT.
WHAT?
HOW DO YOU KNOW MY NAME?!
SHUT UP.
JUST... LET ME THINK.

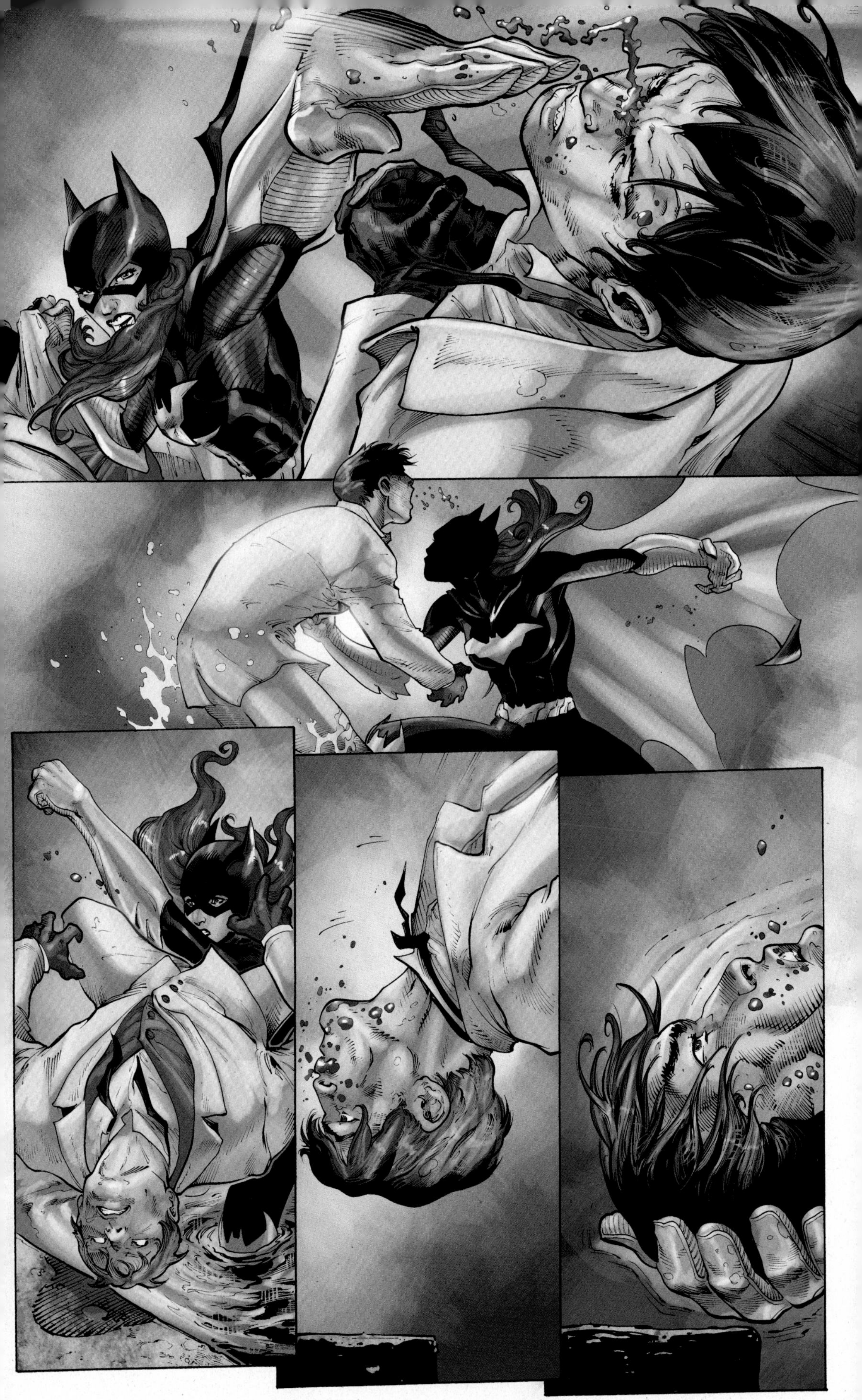

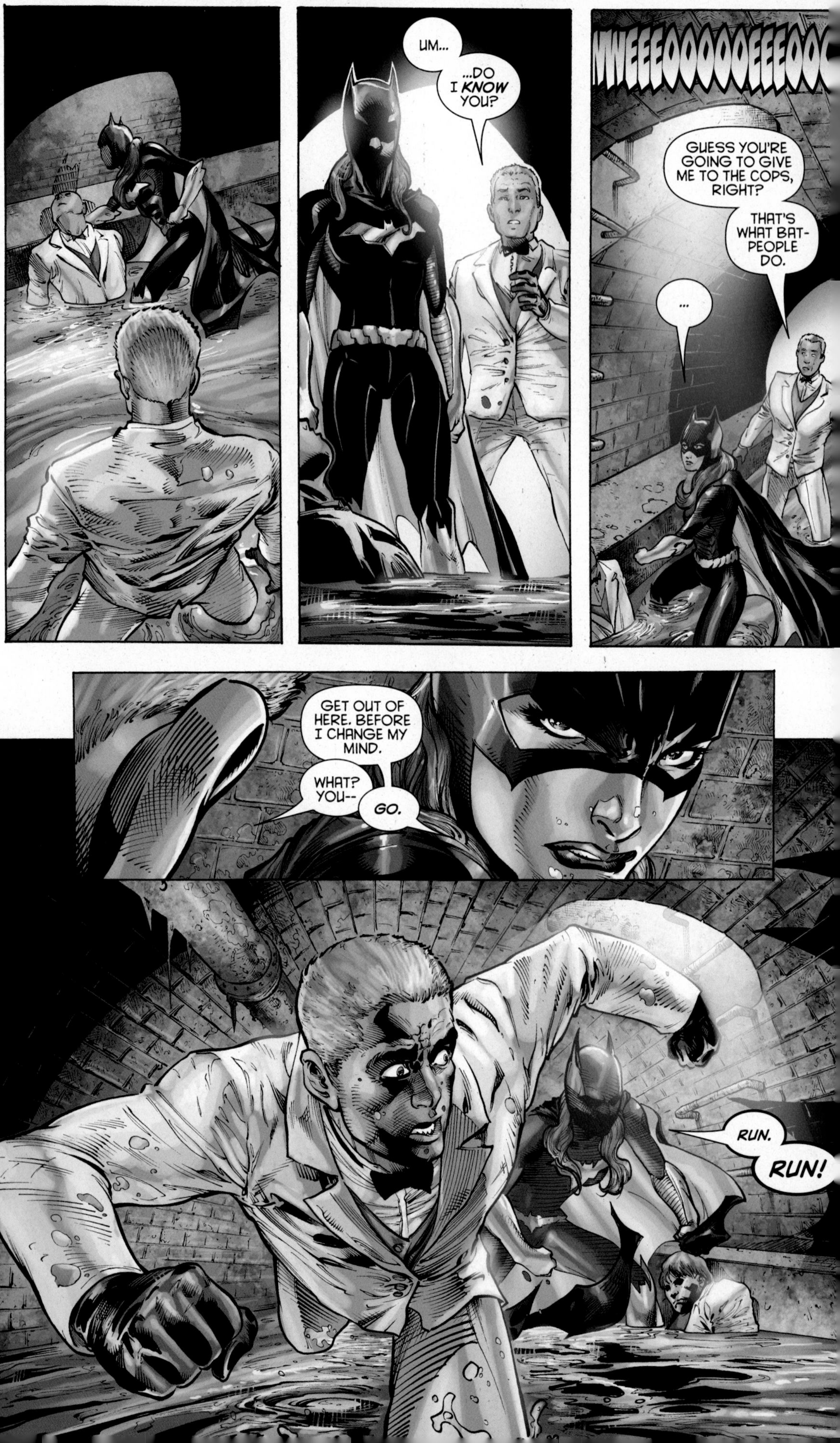

UM...
...DO I KNOW YOU?
MWEEEOOOOOEEEOOO
GUESS YOU'RE GOING TO GIVE ME TO THE COPS, RIGHT?
THAT'S WHAT BAT-PEOPLE DO.
...
GET OUT OF HERE. BEFORE I CHANGE MY MIND.
WHAT? YOU--
GO.
RUN.
RUN!

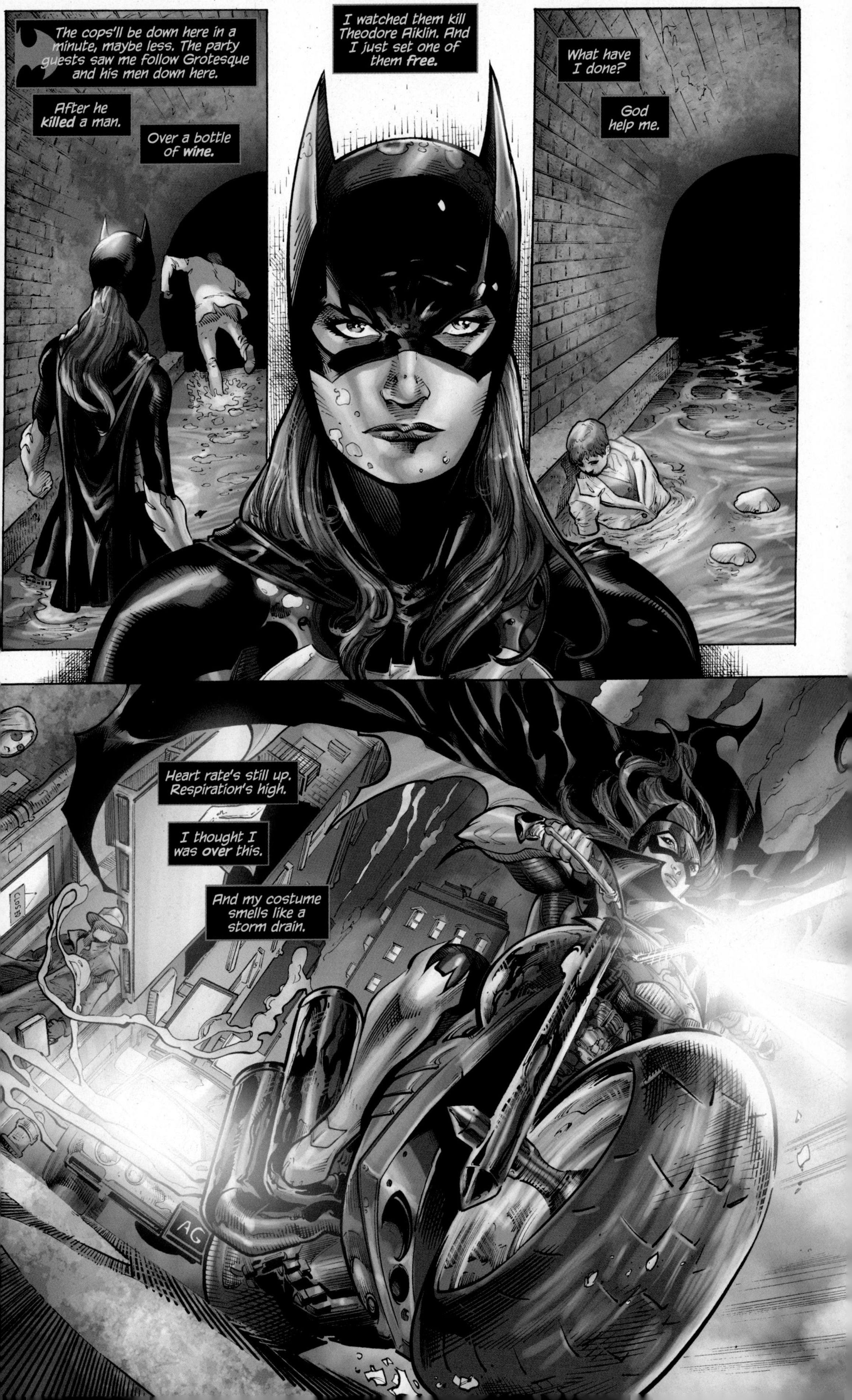
The cops'll be down here in a minute, maybe less. The party guests saw me follow Grotesque and his men down here.
After he killed a man.
Over a bottle of wine.
I watched them kill Theodore Aiklin. And I just set one of them free.
What have I done?
God help me.
Heart rate's still up. Respiration's high.
I thought I was over this.
And my costume smells like a storm drain.
AG

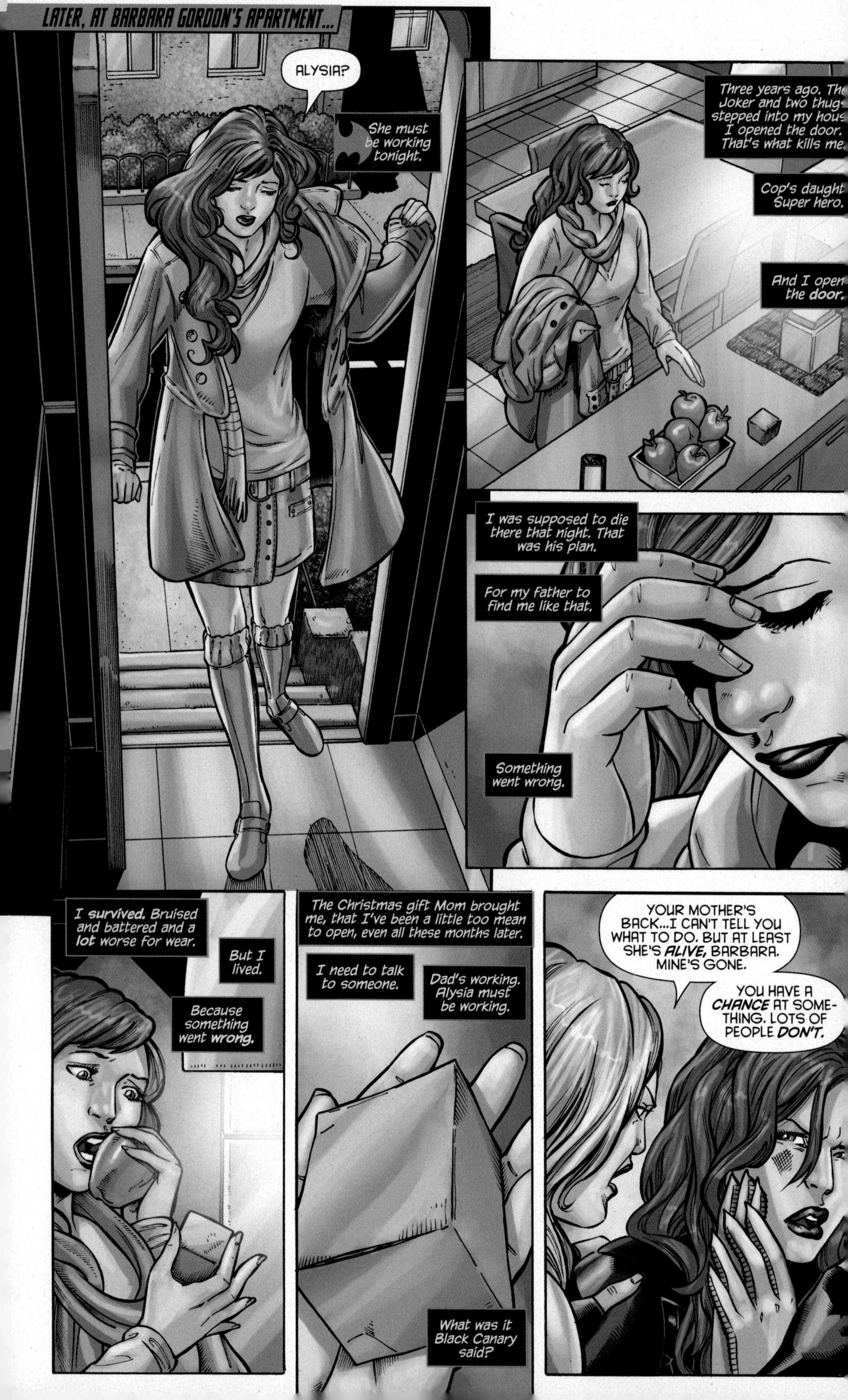

LATER, AT BARBARA GORDON'S APARTMENT...
ALYSIA?
She must be working tonight.
Three years ago. The Joker and two thugs stepped into my house. I opened the door. That's what kills me.
Cop's daught Super hero.
And I open the door.
I was supposed to die there that night. That was his plan.
For my father to find me like that.
Something went wrong.
I survived. Bruised and battered and a lot worse for wear.
But I lived.
Because something went wrong.
The Christmas gift Mom brought me, that I've been a little too mean to open, even all these months later.
I need to talk to someone.
Dad's working. Alysia must be working.
What was it Black Canary said?
YOUR MOTHER'S BACK...I CAN'T TELL YOU WHAT TO DO. BUT AT LEAST SHE'S ALIVE, BARBARA. MINE'S GONE.
YOU HAVE A CHANCE AT SOMETHING. LOTS OF PEOPLE DON'T.

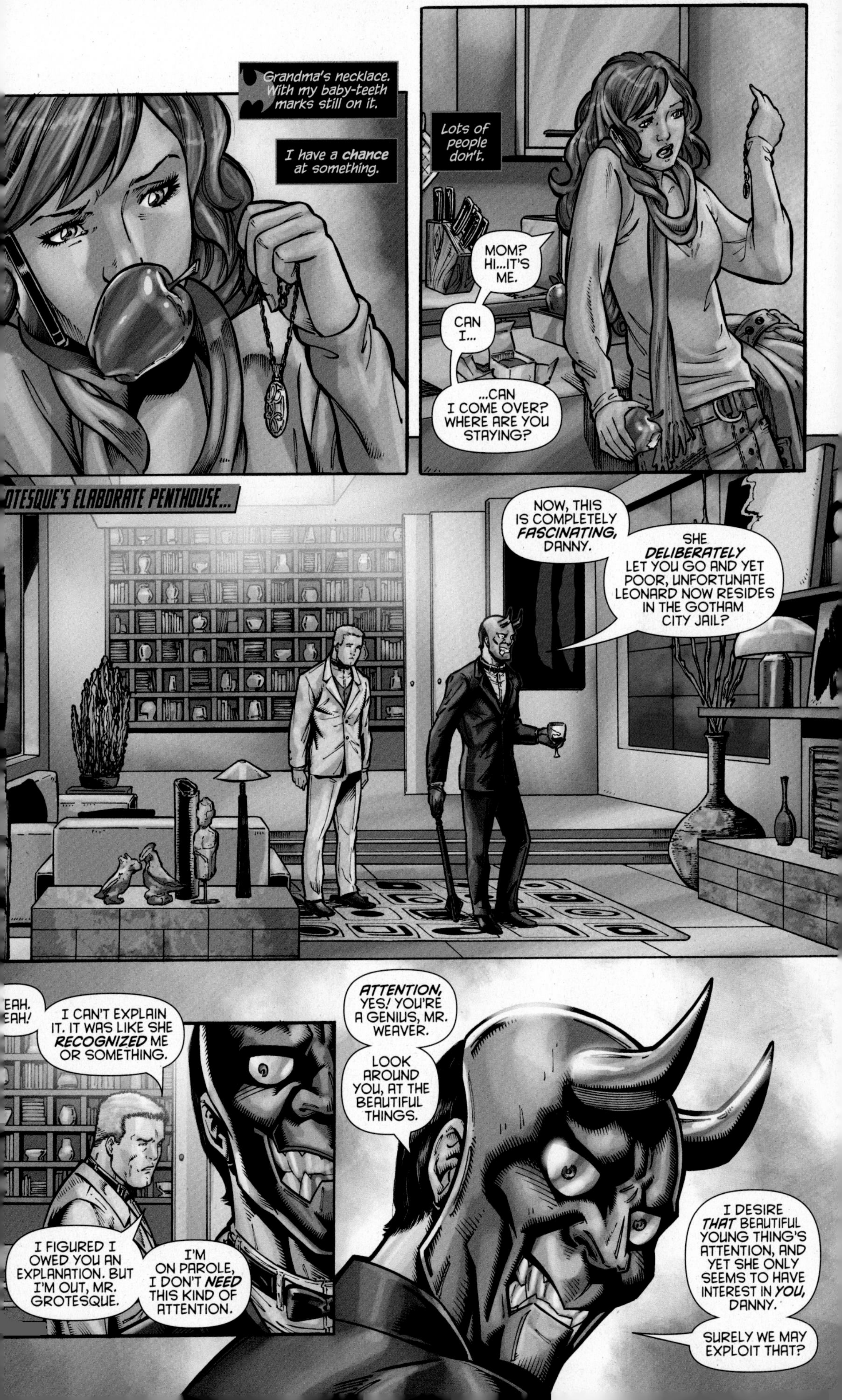

Grandma's necklace. With my baby-teeth marks still on it.
I have a chance at something.
Lots of people don't.
MOM? HI...IT'S ME.
CAN I...
...CAN I COME OVER? WHERE ARE YOU STAYING?
OTESQUE'S ELABORATE PENTHOUSE...
NOW, THIS IS COMPLETELY FASCINATING, DANNY.
SHE DELIBERATELY LET YOU GO AND YET POOR, UNFORTUNATE LEONARD NOW RESIDES IN THE GOTHAM CITY JAIL?
EAH. EAH!
I CAN'T EXPLAIN IT. IT WAS LIKE SHE RECOGNIZED ME OR SOMETHING.
I FIGURED I OWED YOU AN EXPLANATION. BUT I'M OUT, MR. GROTESQUE.
I'M ON PAROLE, I DON'T NEED THIS KIND OF ATTENTION.
ATTENTION, YES! YOU'RE A GENIUS, MR. WEAVER.
LOOK AROUND YOU, AT THE BEAUTIFUL THINGS.
I DESIRE THAT BEAUTIFUL YOUNG THING'S ATTENTION, AND YET SHE ONLY SEEMS TO HAVE INTEREST IN YOU, DANNY.
SURELY WE MAY EXPLOIT THAT?

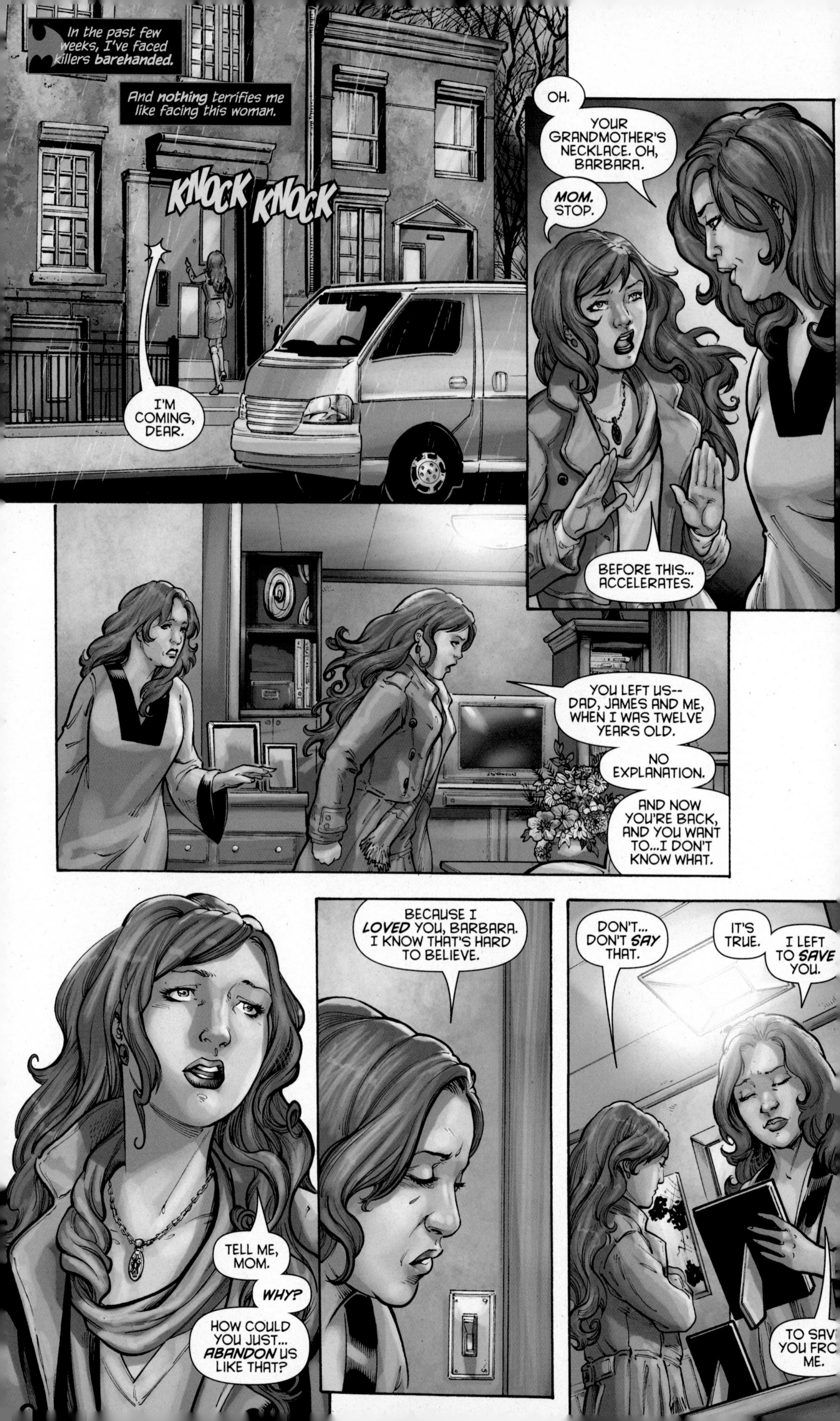
In the past few weeks, I've faced killers barehanded.
And nothing terrifies me like facing this woman.
KNOCK KNOCK
I'M COMING, DEAR.
OH.
YOUR GRANDMOTHER'S NECKLACE. OH, BARBARA.
MOM. STOP.
BEFORE THIS... ACCELERATES.
YOU LEFT US-- DAD, JAMES AND ME, WHEN I WAS TWELVE YEARS OLD.
NO EXPLANATION.
AND NOW YOU'RE BACK, AND YOU WANT TO...I DON'T KNOW WHAT.
TELL ME, MOM.
WHY?
HOW COULD YOU JUST... ABANDON US LIKE THAT?
BECAUSE I LOVED YOU, BARBARA. I KNOW THAT'S HARD TO BELIEVE.
DON'T... DON'T SAY THAT.
IT'S TRUE.
I LEFT TO SAVE YOU.
TO SAV YOU FRO ME.

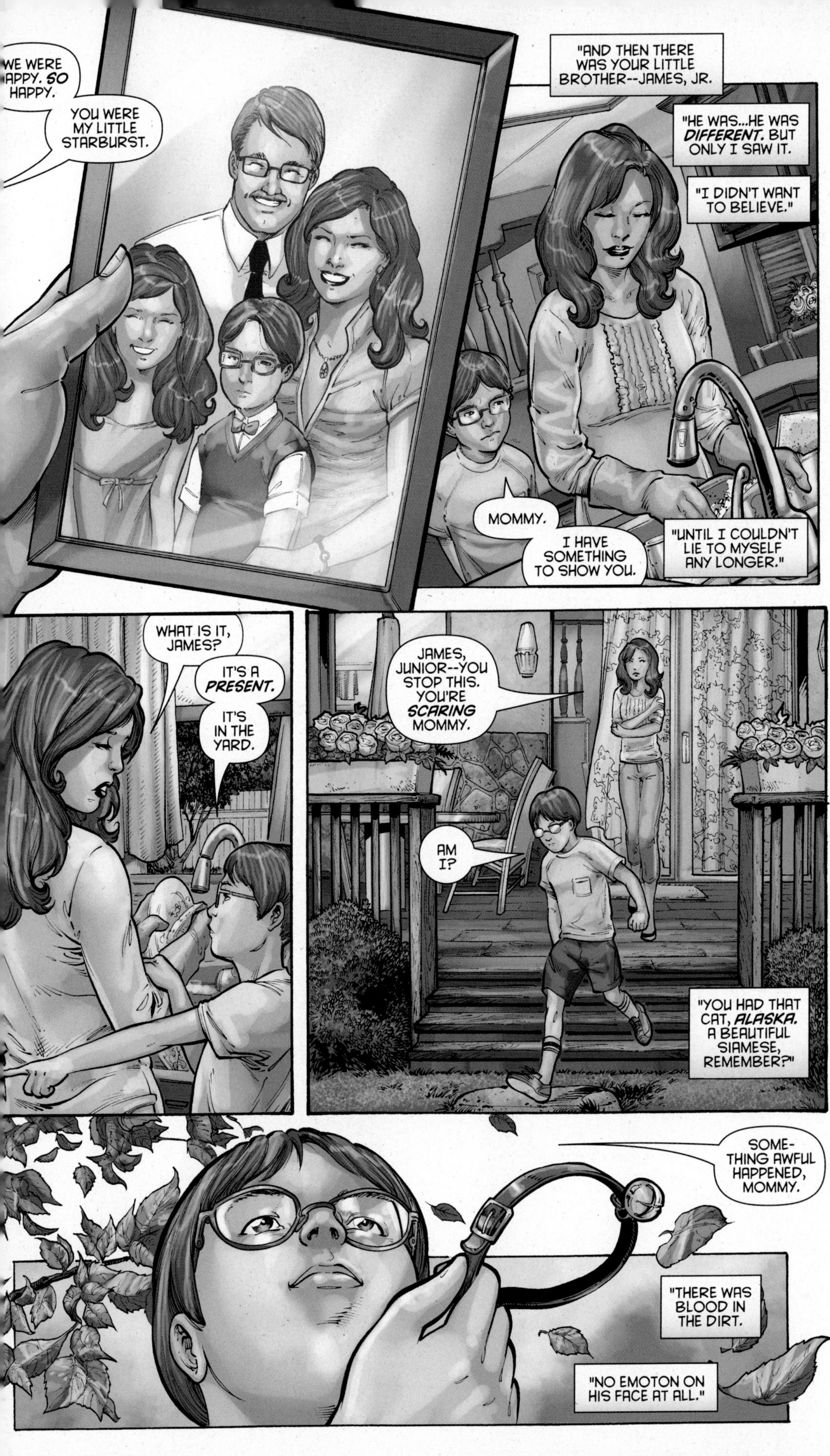
WE WERE HAPPY. SO HAPPY.
YOU WERE MY LITTLE STARBURST.
"AND THEN THERE WAS YOUR LITTLE BROTHER--JAMES, JR.
"HE WAS...HE WAS DIFFERENT. BUT ONLY I SAW IT.
"I DIDN'T WANT TO BELIEVE."
MOMMY.
I HAVE SOMETHING TO SHOW YOU.
"UNTIL I COULDN'T LIE TO MYSELF ANY LONGER."
WHAT IS IT, JAMES?
IT'S A PRESENT.
IT'S IN THE YARD.
JAMES, JUNIOR--YOU STOP THIS. YOU'RE SCARING MOMMY.
AM I?
"YOU HAD THAT CAT, ALASKA. A BEAUTIFUL SIAMESE, REMEMBER?"
SOME-THING AWFUL HAPPENED, MOMMY.
"THERE WAS BLOOD IN THE DIRT.
"NO EMOTON ON HIS FACE AT ALL."

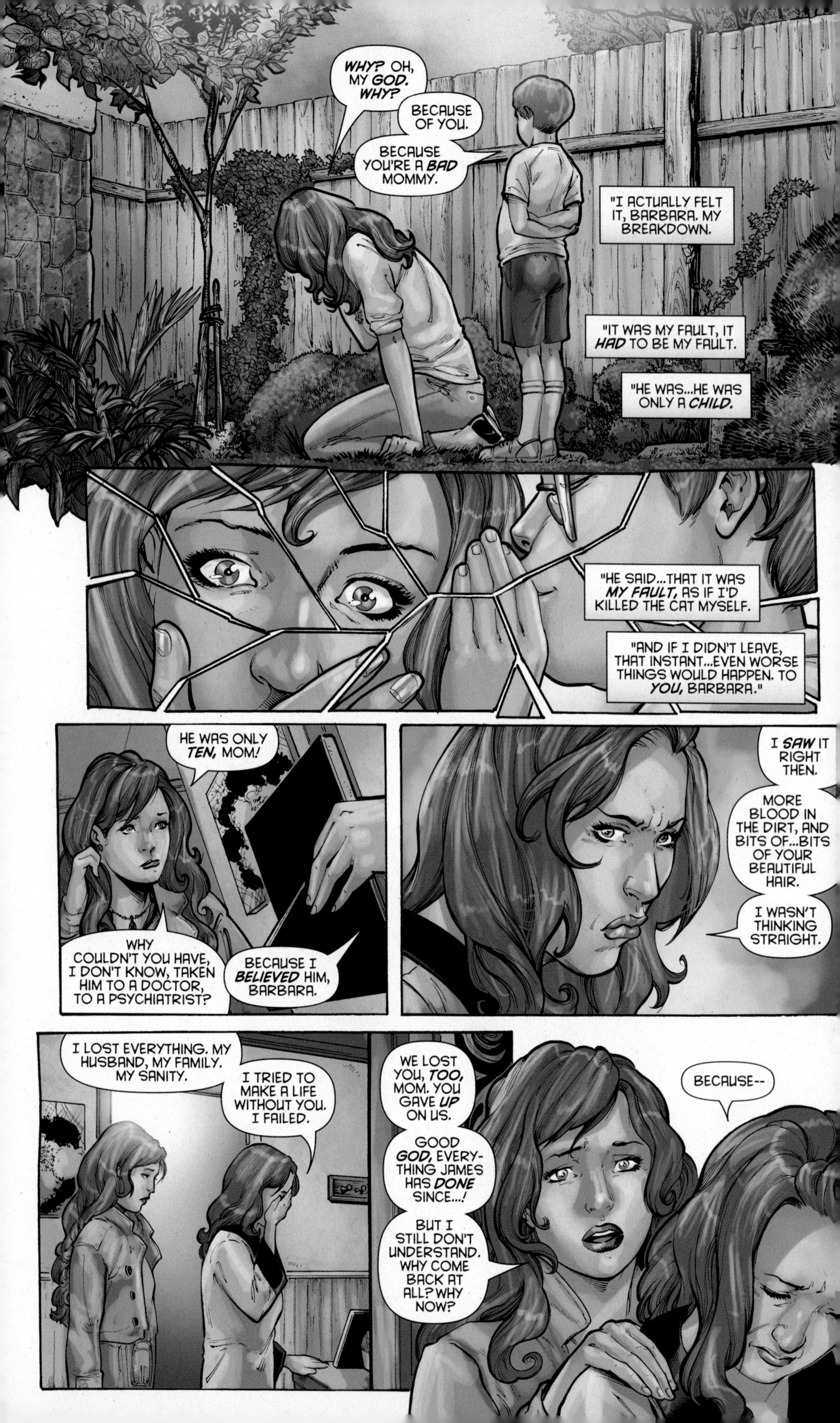
WHY? OH, MY GOD. WHY?
BECAUSE OF YOU.
BECAUSE YOU'RE A BAD MOMMY.
"I ACTUALLY FELT IT, BARBARA. MY BREAKDOWN.
"IT WAS MY FAULT, IT HAD TO BE MY FAULT.
"HE WAS...HE WAS ONLY A CHILD.
"HE SAID...THAT IT WAS MY FAULT, AS IF I'D KILLED THE CAT MYSELF.
"AND IF I DIDN'T LEAVE, THAT INSTANT...EVEN WORSE THINGS WOULD HAPPEN. TO YOU, BARBARA."
HE WAS ONLY TEN, MOM!
WHY COULDN'T YOU HAVE, I DON'T KNOW, TAKEN HIM TO A DOCTOR, TO A PSYCHIATRIST?
BECAUSE I BELIEVED HIM, BARBARA.
I SAW IT RIGHT THEN.
MORE BLOOD IN THE DIRT, AND BITS OF...BITS OF YOUR BEAUTIFUL HAIR.
I WASN'T THINKING STRAIGHT.
I LOST EVERYTHING. MY HUSBAND, MY FAMILY. MY SANITY.
I TRIED TO MAKE A LIFE WITHOUT YOU. I FAILED.
WE LOST YOU, TOO, MOM. YOU GAVE UP ON US.
GOOD GOD, EVERYTHING JAMES HAS DONE SINCE...!
BUT I STILL DON'T UNDERSTAND. WHY COME BACK AT ALL? WHY NOW?
BECAUSE--

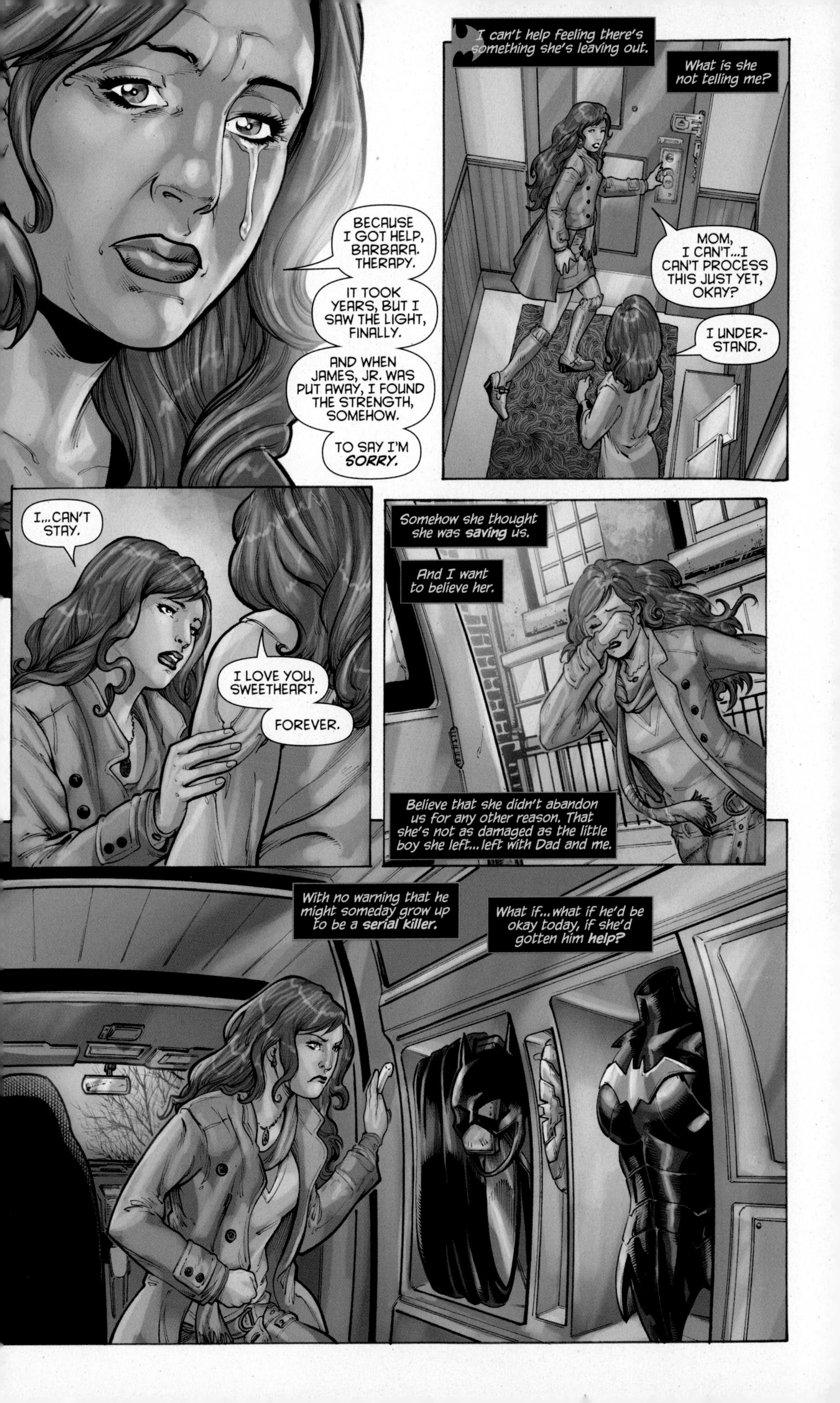
BECAUSE I GOT HELP, BARBARA. THERAPY.
IT TOOK YEARS, BUT I SAW THE LIGHT, FINALLY.
AND WHEN JAMES, JR. WAS PUT AWAY, I FOUND THE STRENGTH, SOMEHOW.
TO SAY I'M SORRY.
I can't help feeling there's something she's leaving out.
What is she not telling me?
MOM, I CAN'T...I CAN'T PROCESS THIS JUST YET, OKAY?
I UNDERSTAND.
I...CAN'T STAY.
I LOVE YOU, SWEETHEART.
FOREVER.
Somehow she thought she was saving us.
And I want to believe her.
Believe that she didn't abandon us for any other reason. That she's not as damaged as the little boy she left...left with Dad and me.
With no warning that he might someday grow up to be a serial killer.
What if...what if he'd be okay today, if she'd gotten him help?

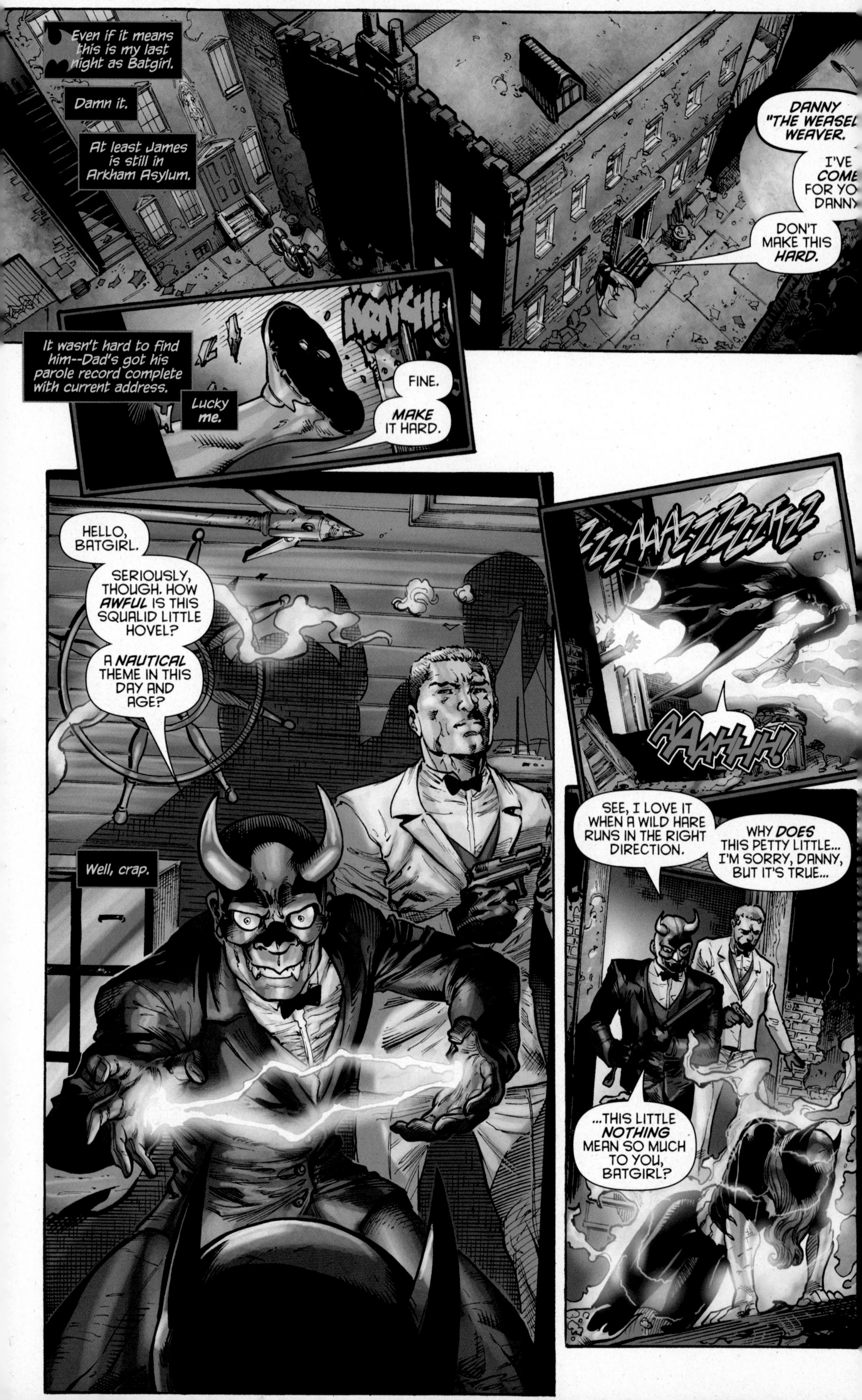
Even if it means this is my last night as Batgirl.
Damn it.
At least James is still in Arkham Asylum.
DANNY "THE WEASEL" WEAVER.
I'VE COME FOR YOU, DANNY.
DON'T MAKE THIS HARD.
KRNCH!
It wasn't hard to find him--Dad's got his parole record complete with current address.
Lucky me.
FINE.
MAKE IT HARD.
HELLO, BATGIRL.
SERIOUSLY, THOUGH. HOW AWFUL IS THIS SQUALID LITTLE HOVEL?
A NAUTICAL THEME IN THIS DAY AND AGE?
Well, crap.
ZZZAAAZZZZZZZZ
AAAHHH!
SEE, I LOVE IT WHEN A WILD HARE RUNS IN THE RIGHT DIRECTION.
WHY DOES THIS PETTY LITTLE... I'M SORRY, DANNY, BUT IT'S TRUE...
...THIS LITTLE NOTHING MEAN SO MUCH TO YOU, BATGIRL?

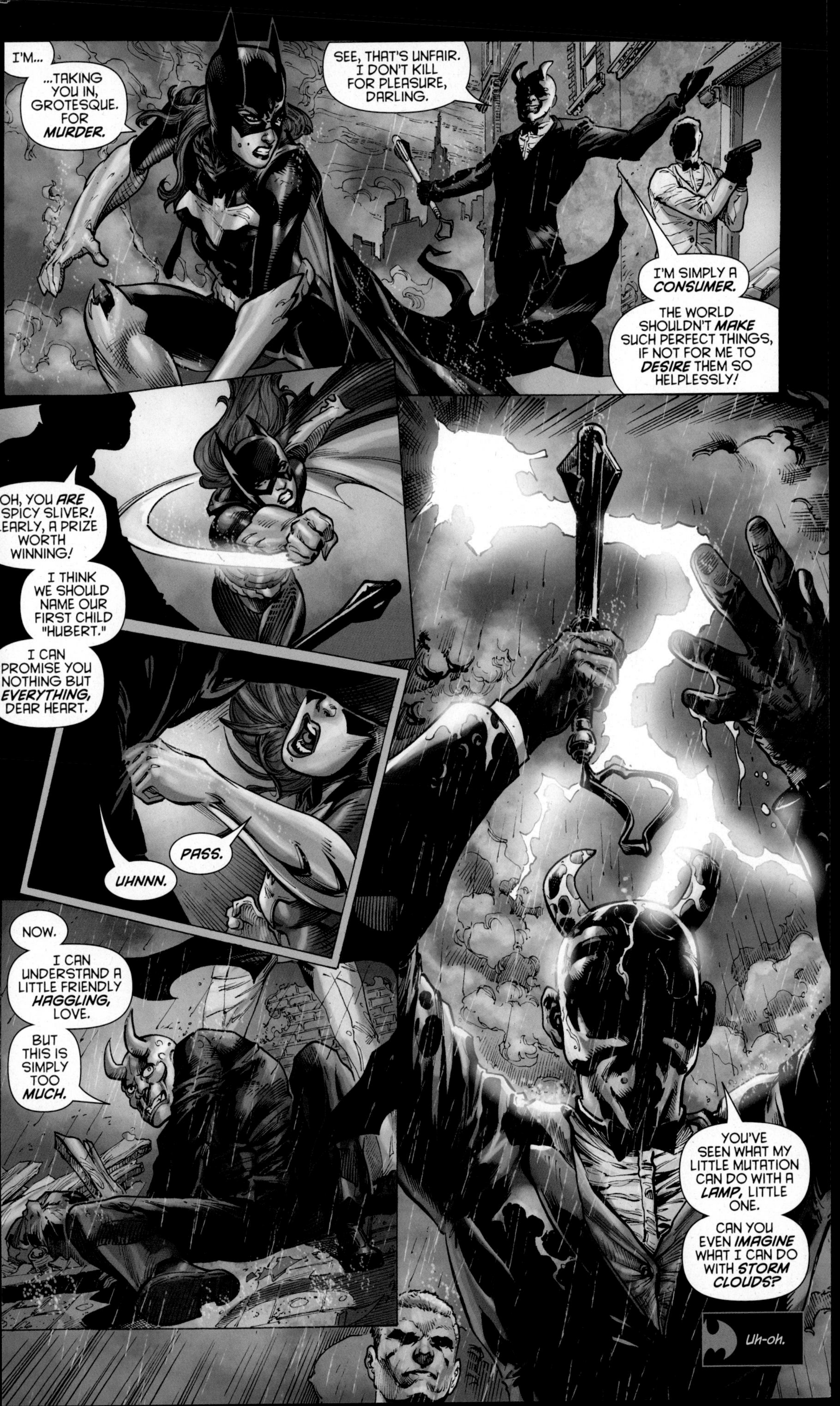
I'M...
...TAKING YOU IN, GROTESQUE. FOR MURDER.
SEE, THAT'S UNFAIR. I DON'T KILL FOR PLEASURE, DARLING.
I'M SIMPLY A CONSUMER.
THE WORLD SHOULDN'T MAKE SUCH PERFECT THINGS, IF NOT FOR ME TO DESIRE THEM SO HELPLESSLY!
OH, YOU ARE SPICY SLIVER! EARLY, A PRIZE WORTH WINNING!
I THINK WE SHOULD NAME OUR FIRST CHILD "HUBERT."
I CAN PROMISE YOU NOTHING BUT EVERYTHING, DEAR HEART.
PASS.
UHNNN.
NOW.
I CAN UNDERSTAND A LITTLE FRIENDLY HAGGLING, LOVE.
BUT THIS IS SIMPLY TOO MUCH.
YOU'VE SEEN WHAT MY LITTLE MUTATION CAN DO WITH A LAMP, LITTLE ONE.
CAN YOU EVEN IMAGINE WHAT I CAN DO WITH STORM CLOUDS?
Uh-oh.

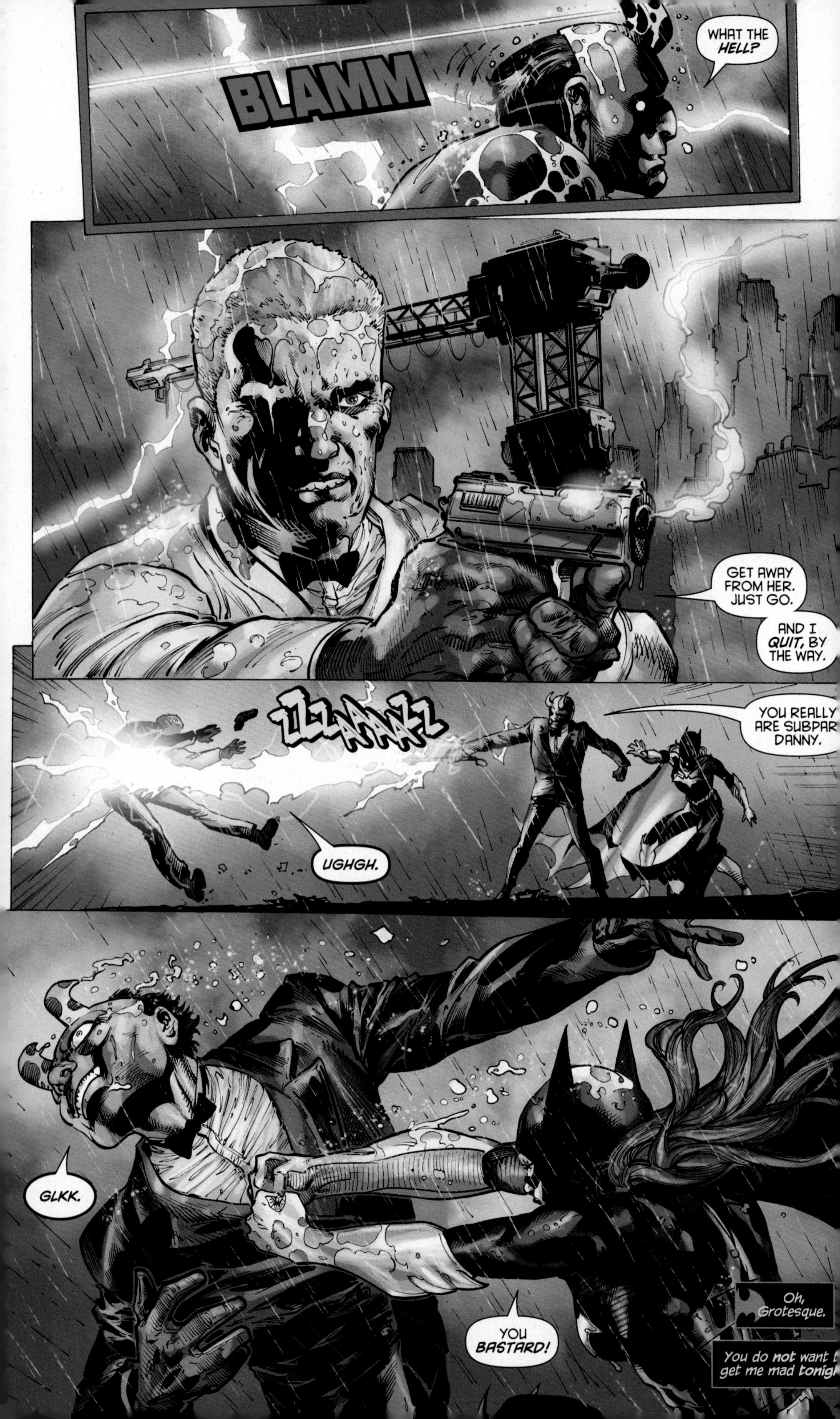
BLAMM
WHAT THE HELL?
GET AWAY FROM HER. JUST GO.
AND I QUIT, BY THE WAY.
ZZZAAAZZ
YOU REALLY ARE SUBPAR DANNY.
UGHGH.
GLKK.
YOU BASTARD!
Oh, Grotesque.
You do not want t get me mad tonig

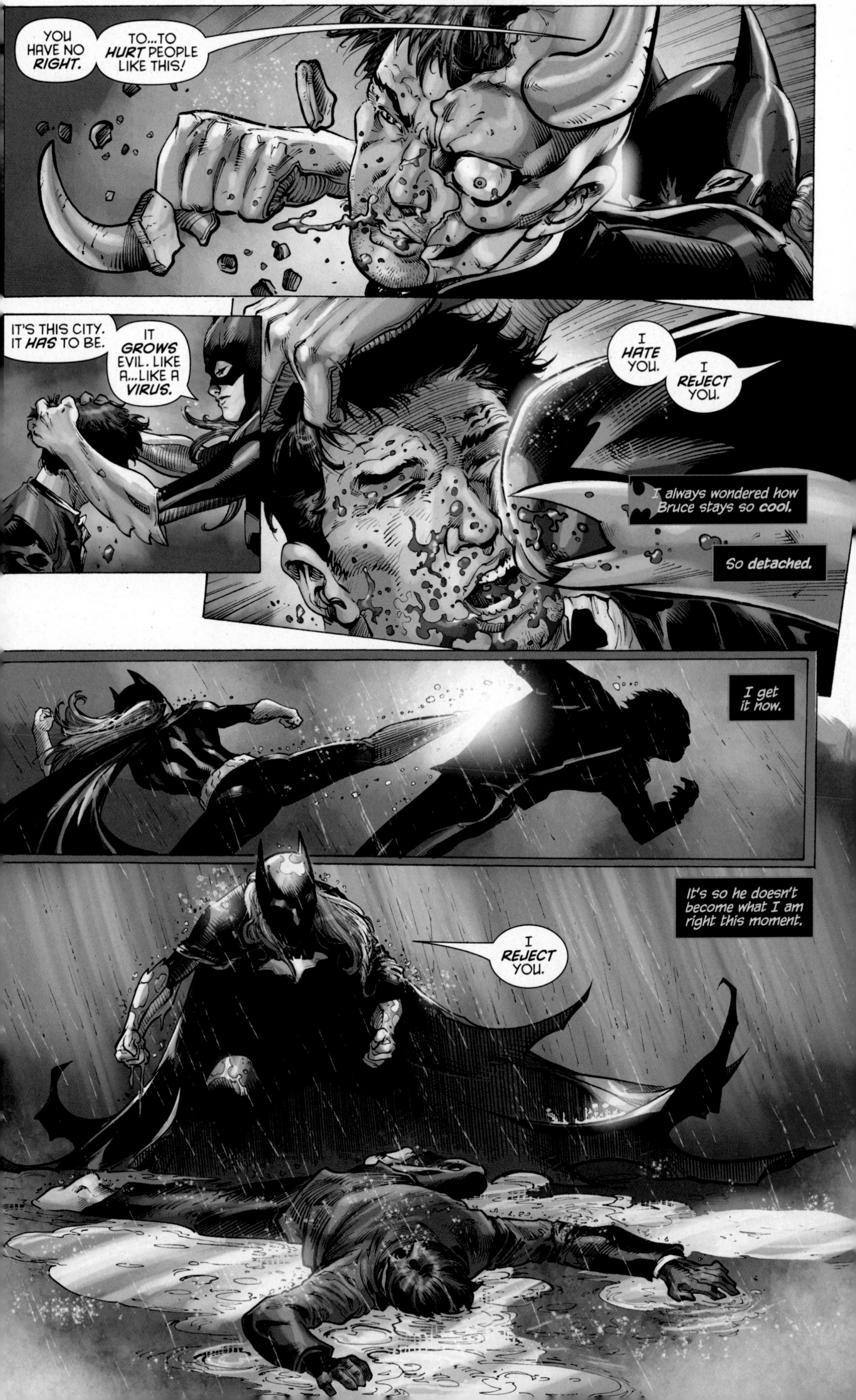
YOU HAVE NO RIGHT.
TO...TO HURT PEOPLE LIKE THIS!
IT'S THIS CITY. IT HAS TO BE.
IT GROWS EVIL. LIKE A...LIKE A VIRUS.
I HATE YOU.
I REJECT YOU.
I always wondered how Bruce stays so cool.
So detached.
I get it now.
It's so he doesn't become what I am right this moment.
I REJECT YOU.

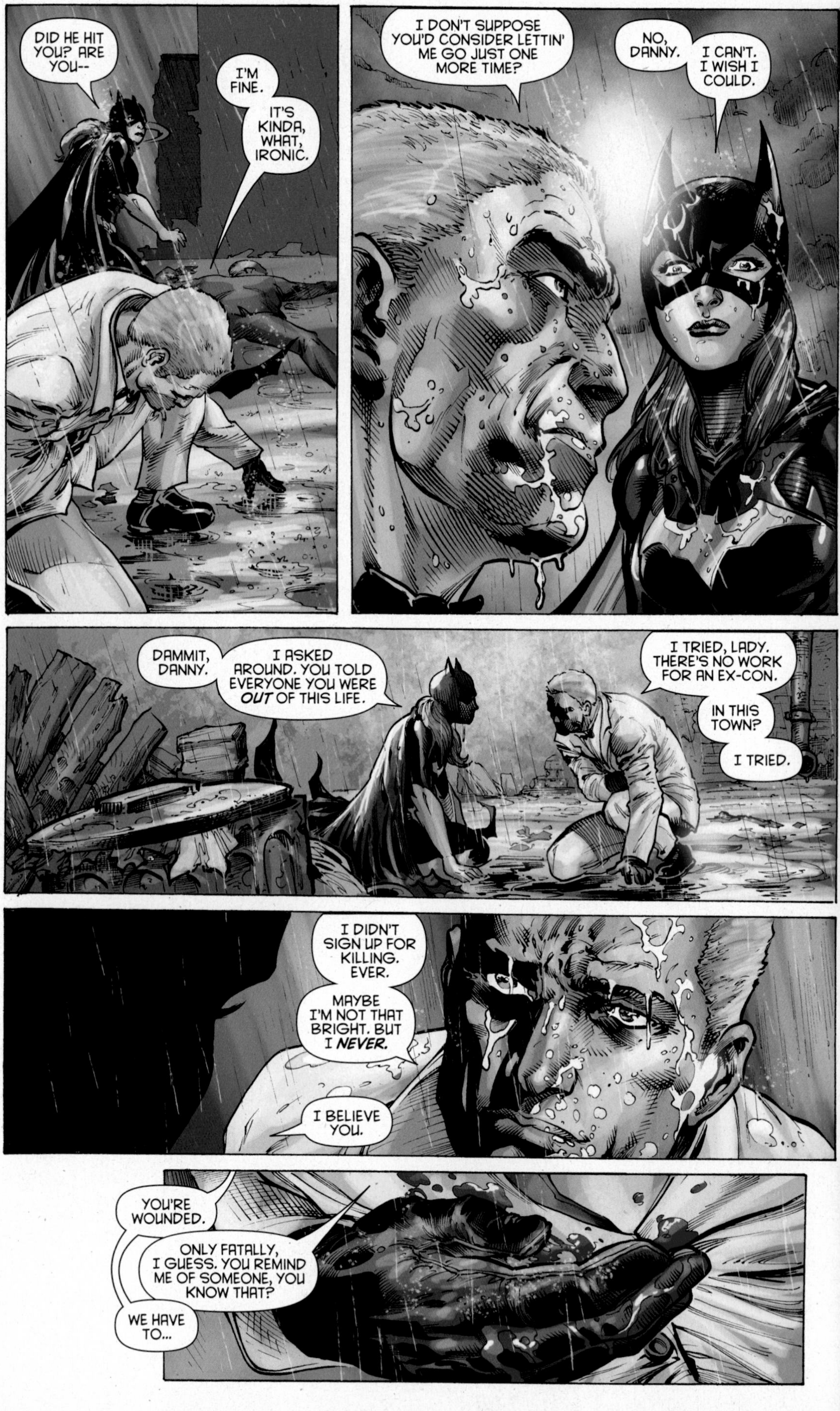

DID HE HIT YOU? ARE YOU--
I'M FINE.
IT'S KINDA, WHAT, IRONIC.
I DON'T SUPPOSE YOU'D CONSIDER LETTIN' ME GO JUST ONE MORE TIME?
NO, DANNY.
I CAN'T. I WISH I COULD.
DAMMIT, DANNY.
I ASKED AROUND. YOU TOLD EVERYONE YOU WERE *OUT* OF THIS LIFE.
I TRIED, LADY. THERE'S NO WORK FOR AN EX-CON.
IN THIS TOWN?
I TRIED.
I DIDN'T SIGN UP FOR KILLING. EVER.
MAYBE I'M NOT THAT BRIGHT. BUT I ***NEVER.***
I BELIEVE YOU.
YOU'RE WOUNDED.
ONLY FATALLY, I GUESS. YOU REMIND ME OF SOMEONE, YOU KNOW THAT?
WE HAVE TO...

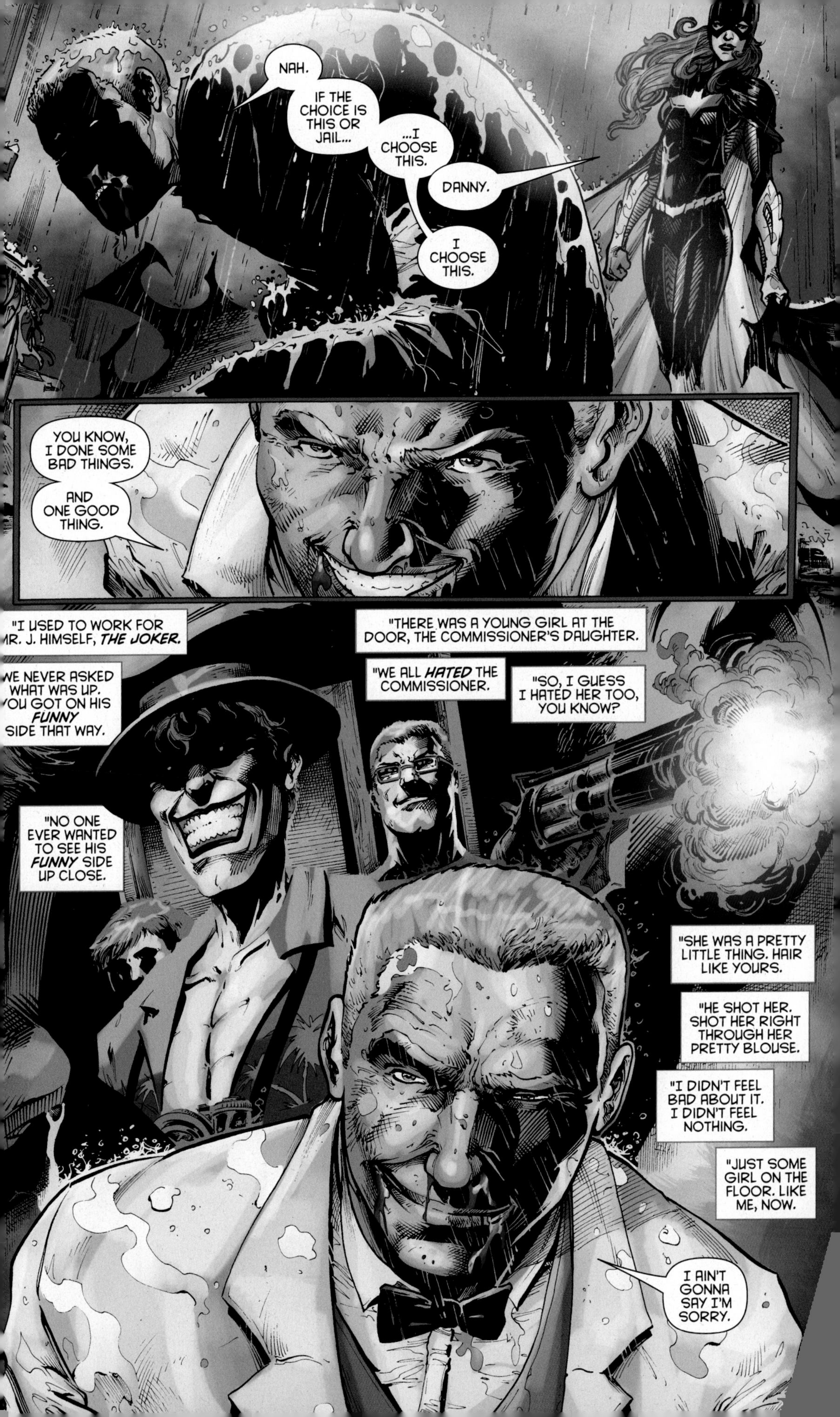
NAH.
IF THE CHOICE IS THIS OR JAIL...
...I CHOOSE THIS.
DANNY.
I CHOOSE THIS.
YOU KNOW, I DONE SOME BAD THINGS.
AND ONE GOOD THING.
"I USED TO WORK FOR MR. J. HIMSELF, *THE JOKER.*
WE NEVER ASKED WHAT WAS UP. YOU GOT ON HIS *FUNNY* SIDE THAT WAY.
"NO ONE EVER WANTED TO SEE HIS *FUNNY* SIDE UP CLOSE.
"THERE WAS A YOUNG GIRL AT THE DOOR, THE COMMISSIONER'S DAUGHTER.
"WE ALL *HATED* THE COMMISSIONER.
"SO, I GUESS I HATED HER TOO, YOU KNOW?
"SHE WAS A PRETTY LITTLE THING. HAIR LIKE YOURS.
"HE SHOT HER. SHOT HER RIGHT THROUGH HER PRETTY BLOUSE.
"I DIDN'T FEEL BAD ABOUT IT. I DIDN'T FEEL NOTHING.
"JUST SOME GIRL ON THE FLOOR. LIKE ME, NOW.
I AIN'T GONNA SAY I'M SORRY.

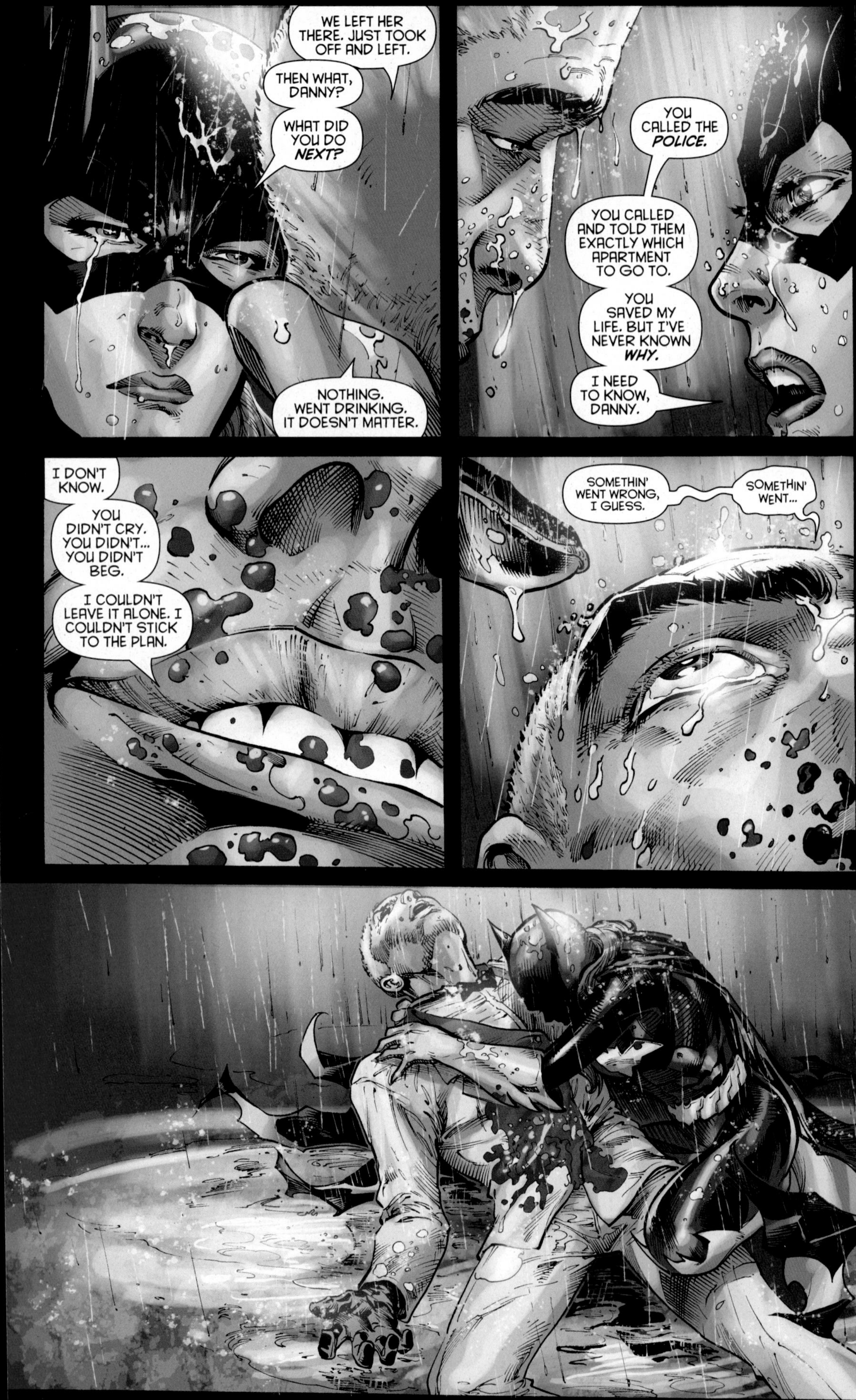
WE LEFT HER THERE. JUST TOOK OFF AND LEFT.
THEN WHAT, DANNY?
WHAT DID YOU DO *NEXT?*
NOTHING. WENT DRINKING. IT DOESN'T MATTER.
YOU CALLED THE *POLICE.*
YOU CALLED AND TOLD THEM EXACTLY WHICH APARTMENT TO GO TO.
YOU SAVED MY LIFE. BUT I'VE NEVER KNOWN *WHY.*
I NEED TO KNOW, DANNY.
I DON'T KNOW.
YOU DIDN'T CRY. YOU DIDN'T... YOU DIDN'T BEG.
I COULDN'T LEAVE IT ALONE. I COULDN'T STICK TO THE PLAN.
SOMETHIN' WENT WRONG, I GUESS.
SOMETHIN' WENT...

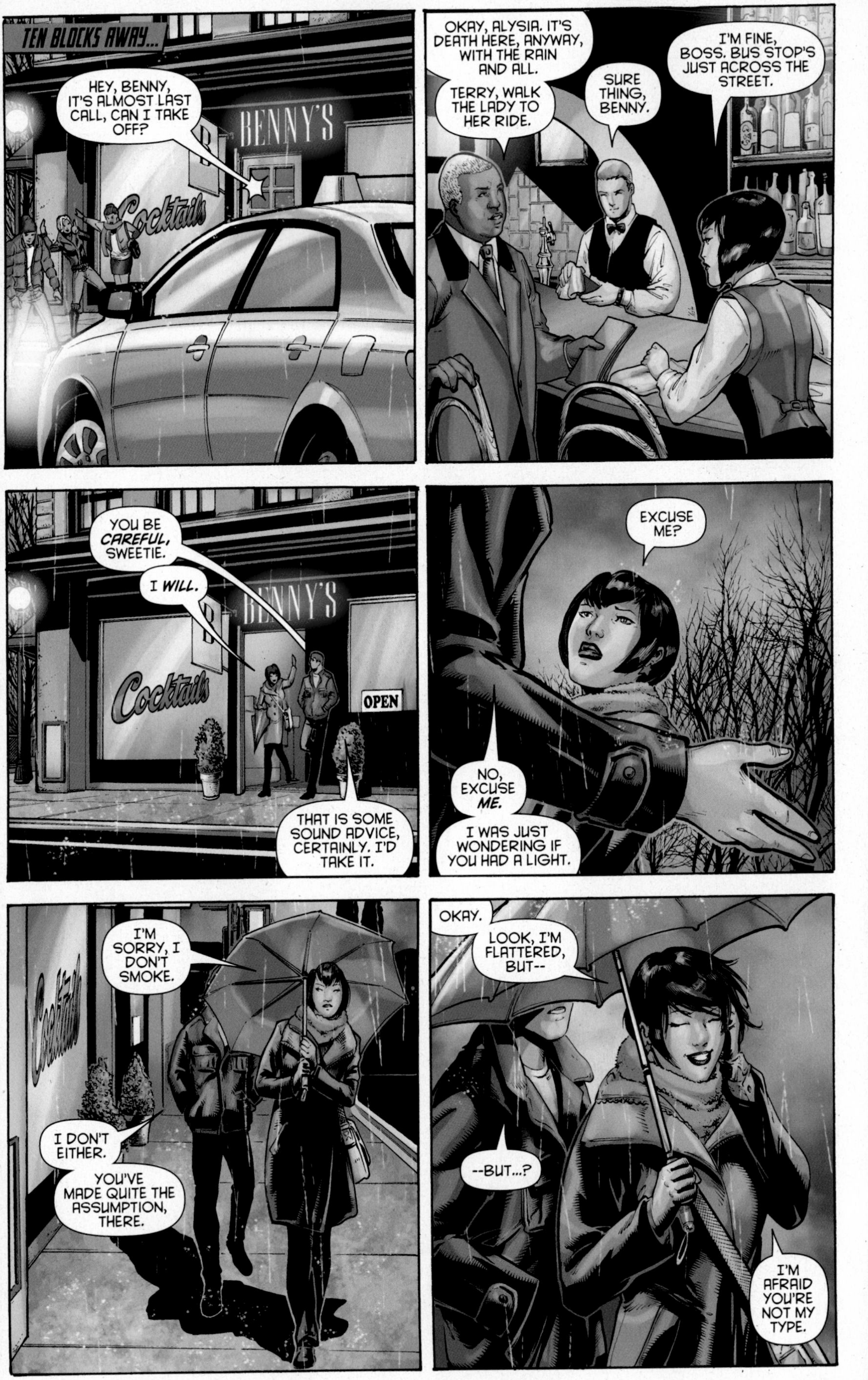
TEN BLOCKS AWAY...
HEY, BENNY, IT'S ALMOST LAST CALL, CAN I TAKE OFF?
BENNY'S
Cocktails
OKAY, ALYSIA. IT'S DEATH HERE, ANYWAY, WITH THE RAIN AND ALL.
TERRY, WALK THE LADY TO HER RIDE.
SURE THING, BENNY.
I'M FINE, BOSS. BUS STOP'S JUST ACROSS THE STREET.
YOU BE CAREFUL, SWEETIE.
I WILL.
BENNY'S
Cocktails
OPEN
THAT IS SOME SOUND ADVICE, CERTAINLY. I'D TAKE IT.
EXCUSE ME?
NO, EXCUSE ME.
I WAS JUST WONDERING IF YOU HAD A LIGHT.
I'M SORRY, I DON'T SMOKE.
I DON'T EITHER.
YOU'VE MADE QUITE THE ASSUMPTION, THERE.
OKAY.
LOOK, I'M FLATTERED, BUT--
--BUT...?
I'M AFRAID YOU'RE NOT MY TYPE.

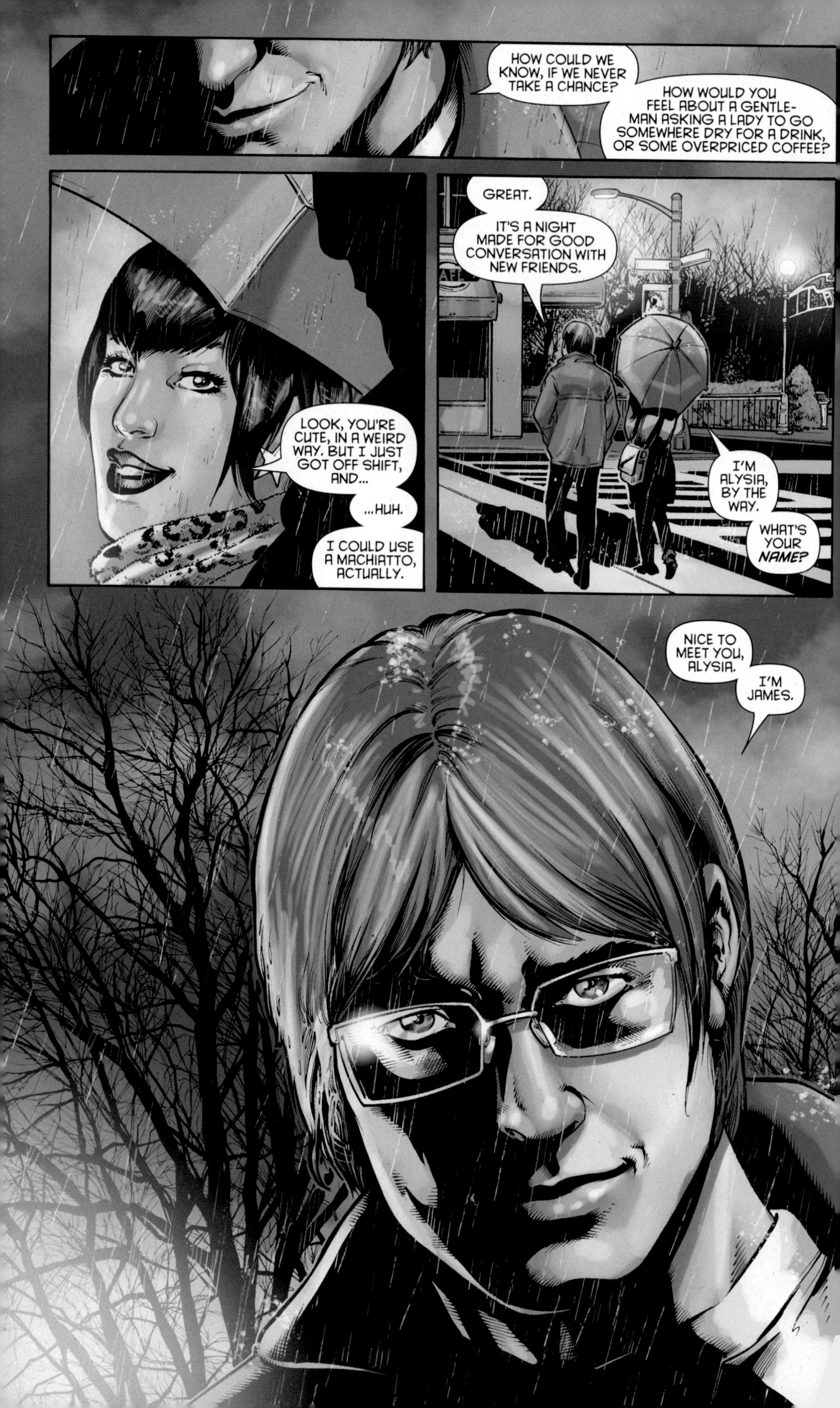
HOW COULD WE KNOW, IF WE NEVER TAKE A CHANCE?
HOW WOULD YOU FEEL ABOUT A GENTLE-MAN ASKING A LADY TO GO SOMEWHERE DRY FOR A DRINK, OR SOME OVERPRICED COFFEE?
LOOK, YOU'RE CUTE, IN A WEIRD WAY. BUT I JUST GOT OFF SHIFT, AND...
...HUH.
I COULD USE A MACHIATTO, ACTUALLY.
GREAT.
IT'S A NIGHT MADE FOR GOOD CONVERSATION WITH NEW FRIENDS.
I'M ALYSIA, BY THE WAY.
WHAT'S YOUR *NAME?*
NICE TO MEET YOU, ALYSIA.
I'M JAMES.

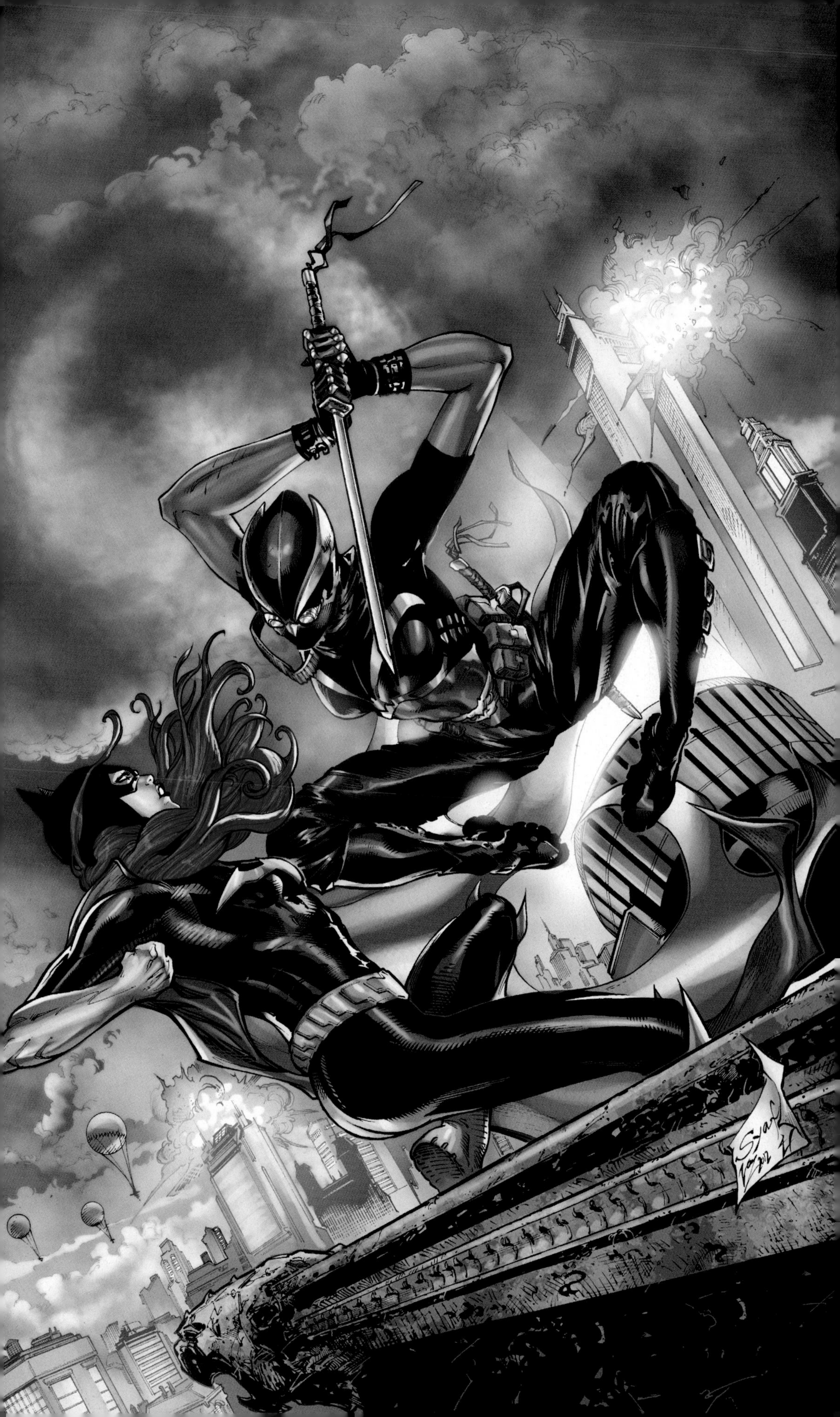

IN THE LINE OF FIRE

GAIL SIMONE writer **ARDIAN SYAF** penciller **VICENTE CIFUENTES** inker cover by ARDIAN SYAF, VICENTE CIFUENTES & ULISES ARREOLA

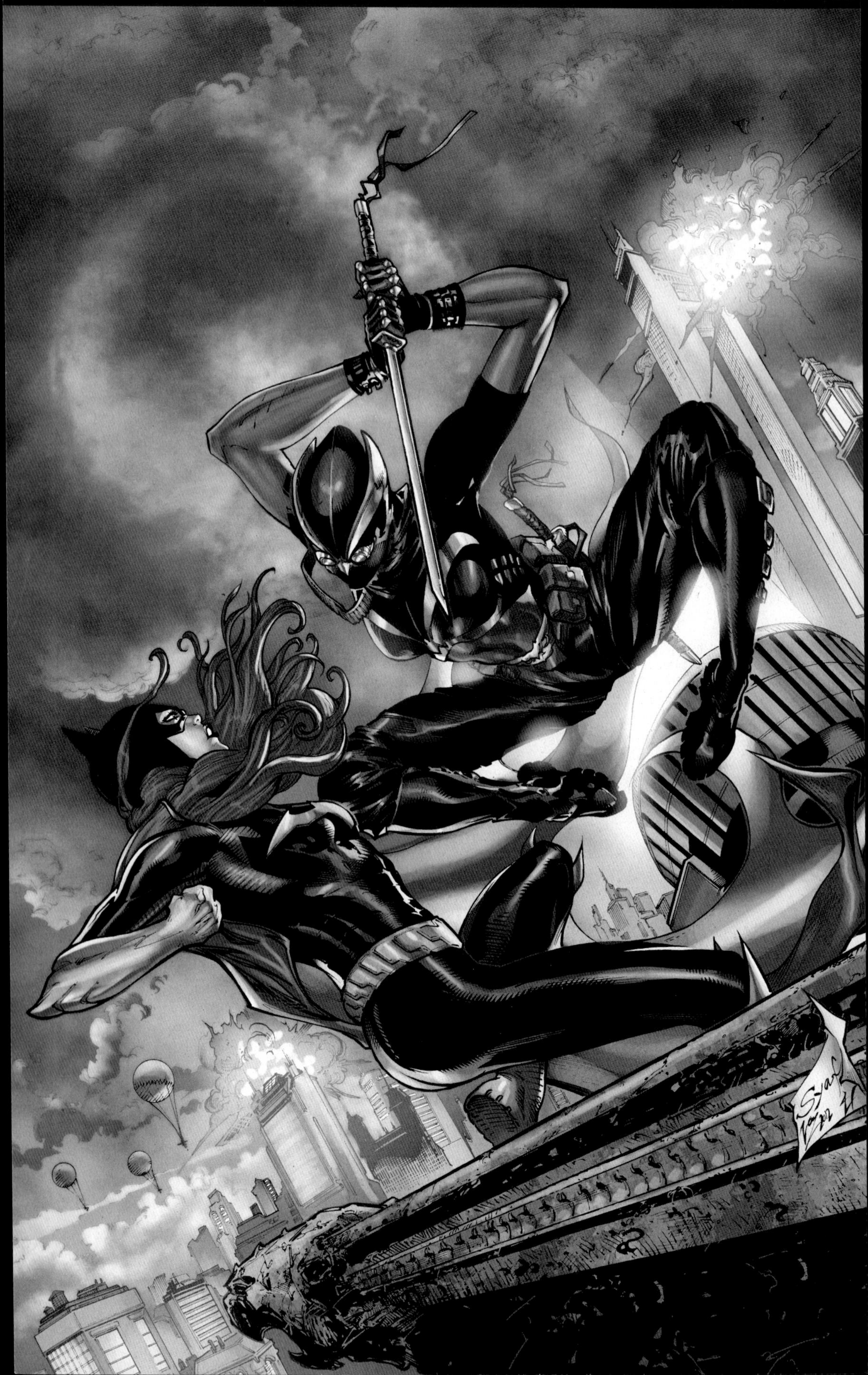

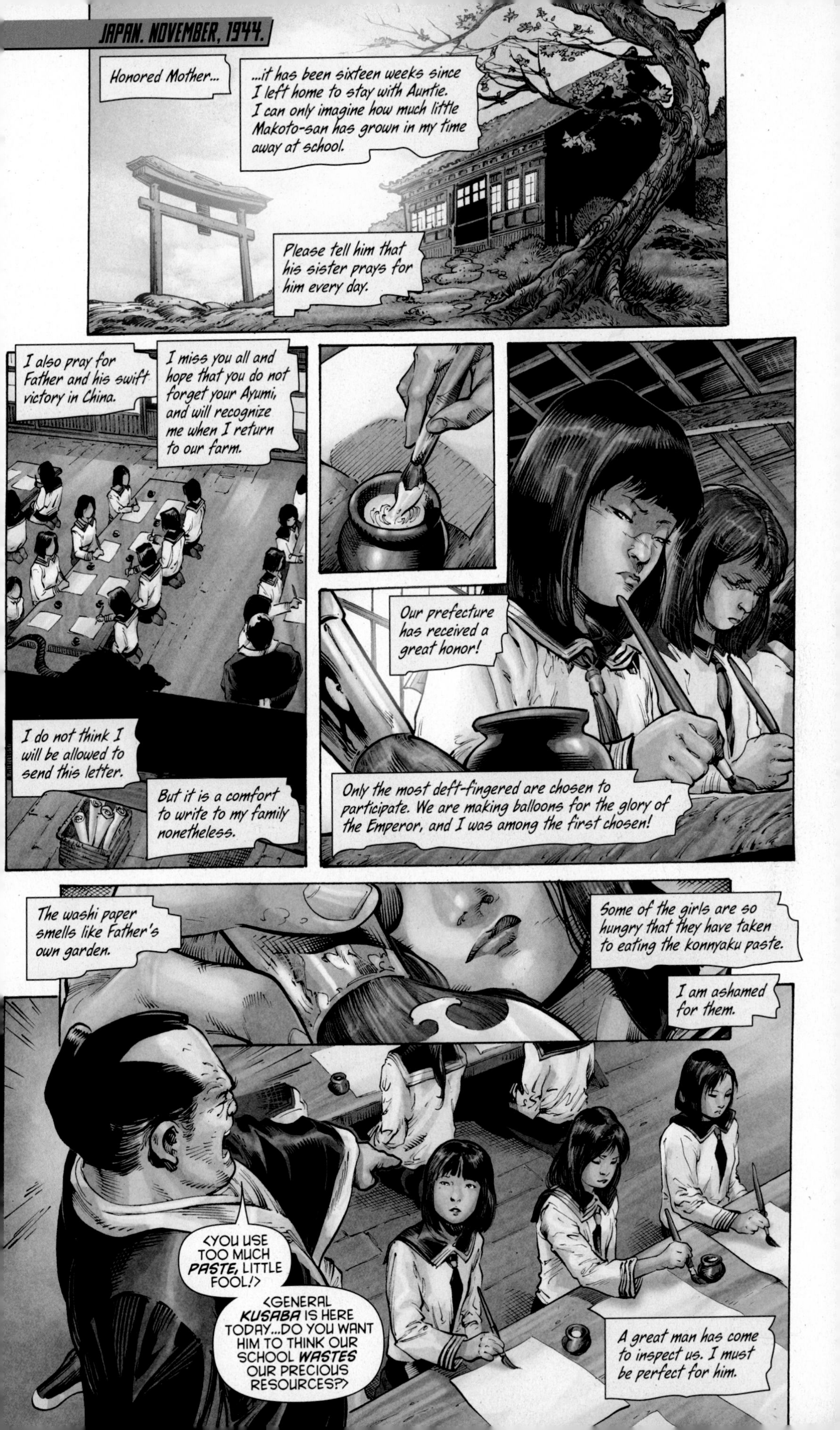

JAPAN. NOVEMBER, 1944.
Honored Mother...
...it has been sixteen weeks since I left home to stay with Auntie. I can only imagine how much little Makoto-san has grown in my time away at school.
Please tell him that his sister prays for him every day.
I also pray for Father and his swift victory in China.
I miss you all and hope that you do not forget your Ayumi, and will recognize me when I return to our farm.
I do not think I will be allowed to send this letter.
But it is a comfort to write to my family nonetheless.
Our prefecture has received a great honor!
Only the most deft-fingered are chosen to participate. We are making balloons for the glory of the Emperor, and I was among the first chosen!
The washi paper smells like Father's own garden.
Some of the girls are so hungry that they have taken to eating the konnyaku paste.
I am ashamed for them.
<YOU USE TOO MUCH PASTE, LITTLE FOOL!>
<GENERAL KUSABA IS HERE TODAY...DO YOU WANT HIM TO THINK OUR SCHOOL WASTES OUR PRECIOUS RESOURCES?>
A great man has come to inspect us. I must be perfect for him.

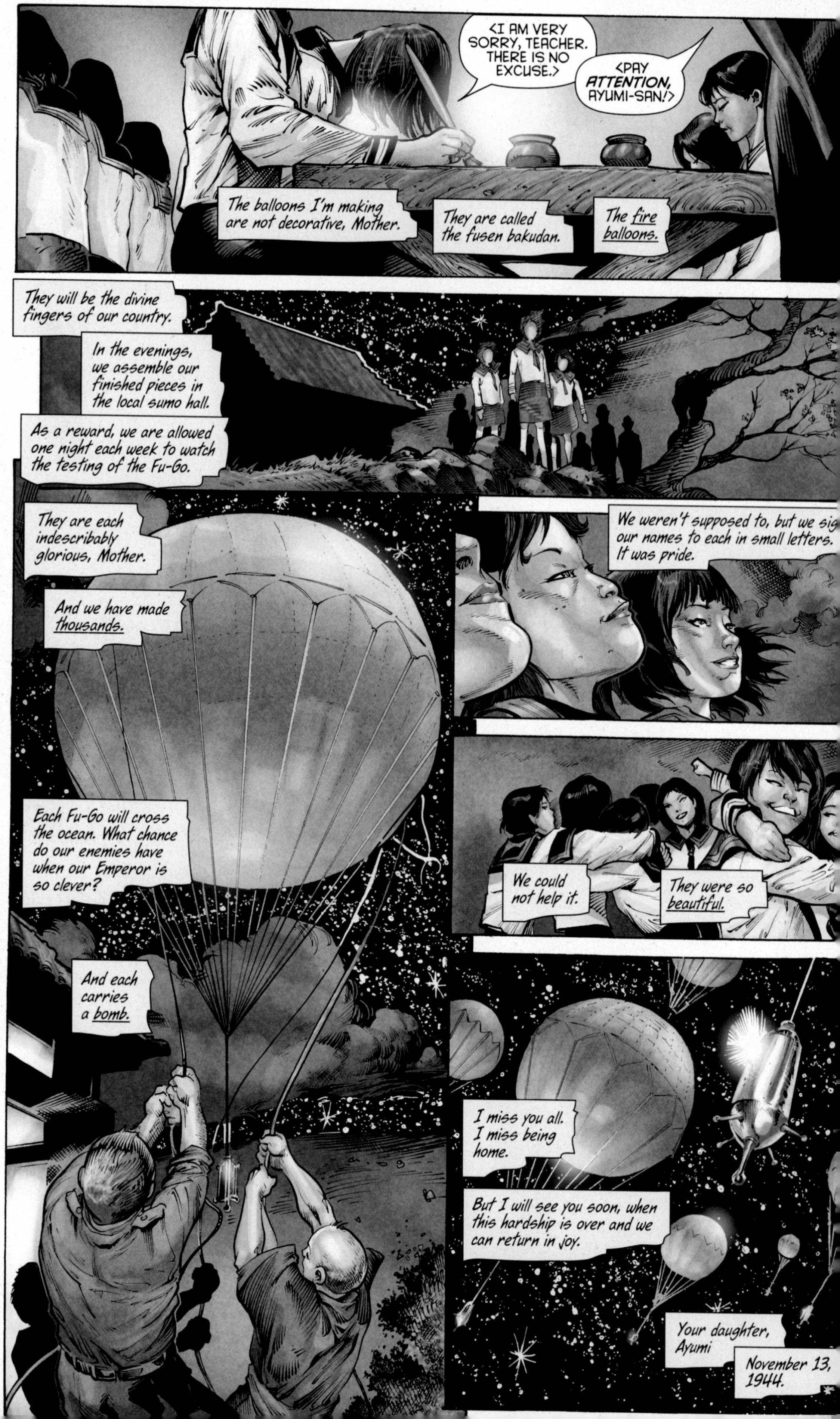
<I AM VERY SORRY, TEACHER. THERE IS NO EXCUSE.>
<PAY ATTENTION, AYUMI-SAN!>
The balloons I'm making are not decorative, Mother.
They are called the fusen bakudan.
The fire balloons.
They will be the divine fingers of our country.
In the evenings, we assemble our finished pieces in the local sumo hall.
As a reward, we are allowed one night each week to watch the testing of the Fu-Go.
They are each indescribably glorious, Mother.
And we have made thousands.
Each Fu-Go will cross the ocean. What chance do our enemies have when our Emperor is so clever?
And each carries a bomb.
We weren't supposed to, but we sig our names to each in small letters. It was pride.
We could not help it.
They were so beautiful.
I miss you all. I miss being home.
But I will see you soon, when this hardship is over and we can return in joy.
Your daughter, Ayumi
November 13, 1944.

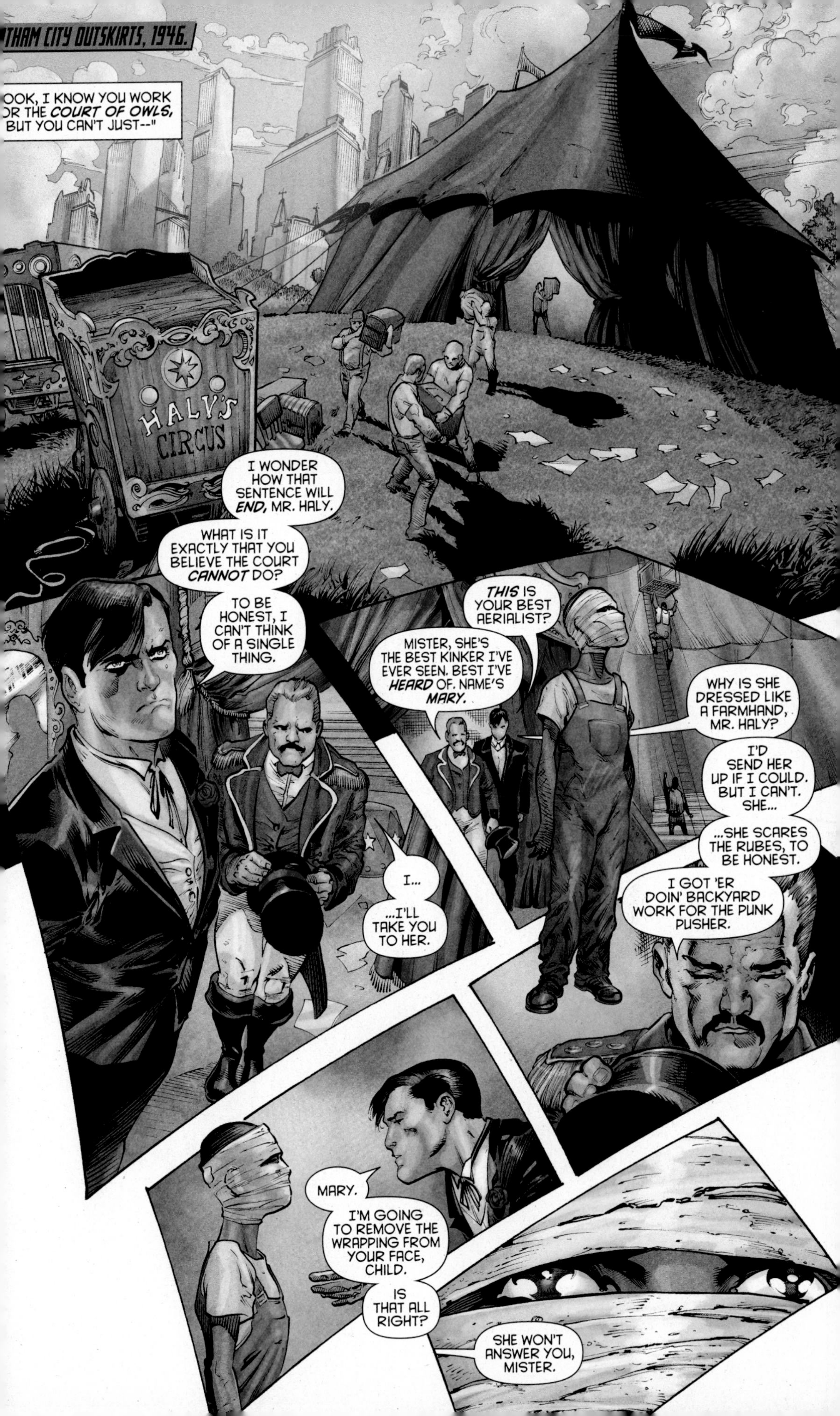
THAM CITY OUTSKIRTS, 1946.
OOK, I KNOW YOU WORK OR THE COURT OF OWLS, BUT YOU CAN'T JUST--"
I WONDER HOW THAT SENTENCE WILL END, MR. HALY.
WHAT IS IT EXACTLY THAT YOU BELIEVE THE COURT CANNOT DO?
TO BE HONEST, I CAN'T THINK OF A SINGLE THING.
I...
...I'LL TAKE YOU TO HER.
THIS IS YOUR BEST AERIALIST?
MISTER, SHE'S THE BEST KINKER I'VE EVER SEEN. BEST I'VE HEARD OF. NAME'S MARY.
WHY IS SHE DRESSED LIKE A FARMHAND, MR. HALY?
I'D SEND HER UP IF I COULD. BUT I CAN'T. SHE...
...SHE SCARES THE RUBES, TO BE HONEST.
I GOT 'ER DOIN' BACKYARD WORK FOR THE PUNK PUSHER.
HALY'S CIRCUS
MARY.
I'M GOING TO REMOVE THE WRAPPING FROM YOUR FACE, CHILD.
IS THAT ALL RIGHT?
SHE WON'T ANSWER YOU, MISTER.

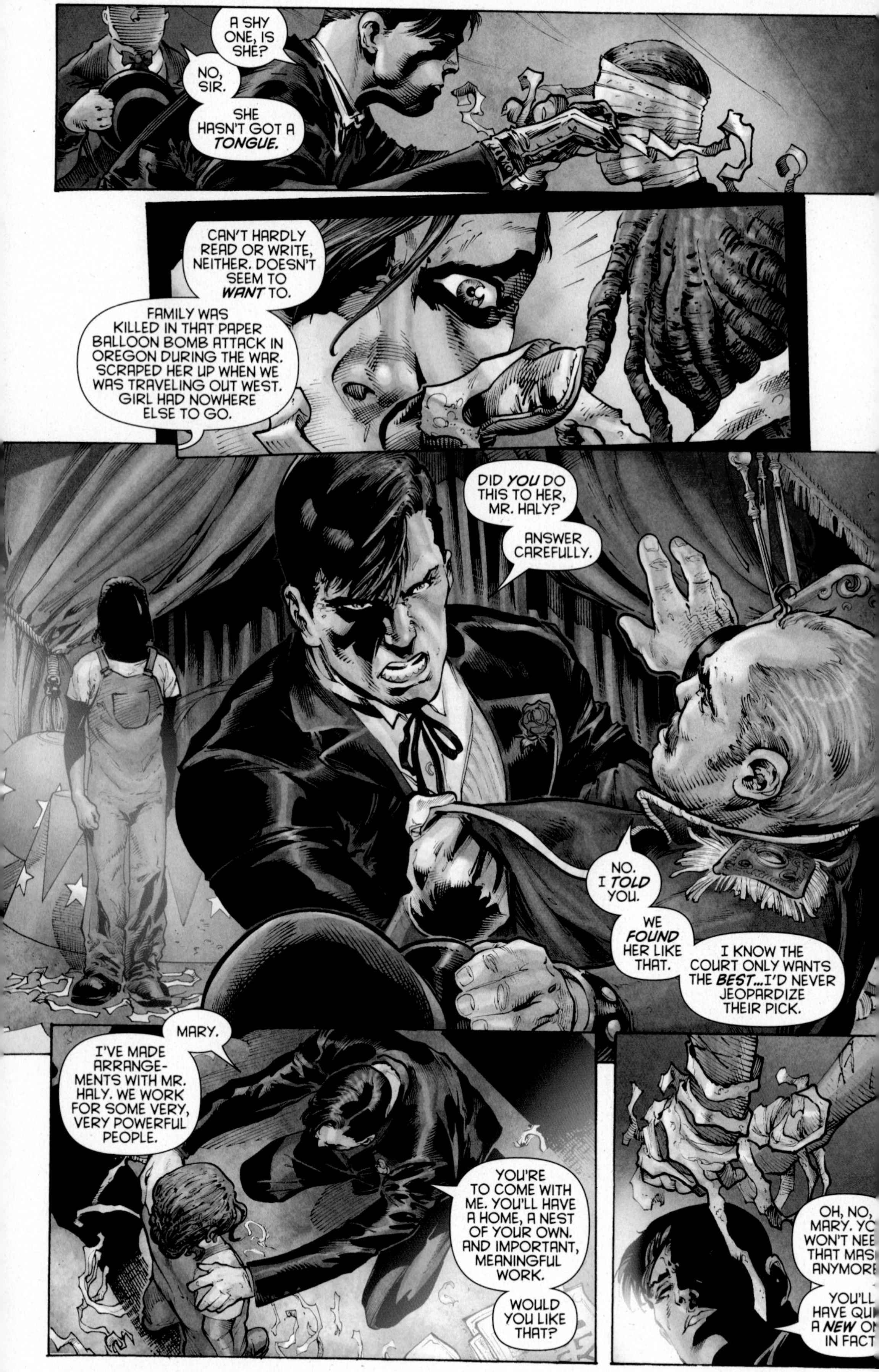
A SHY ONE, IS SHE?
NO, SIR.
SHE HASN'T GOT A *TONGUE.*
CAN'T HARDLY READ OR WRITE, NEITHER. DOESN'T SEEM TO *WANT* TO.
FAMILY WAS KILLED IN THAT PAPER BALLOON BOMB ATTACK IN OREGON DURING THE WAR. SCRAPED HER UP WHEN WE WAS TRAVELING OUT WEST. GIRL HAD NOWHERE ELSE TO GO.
DID *YOU* DO THIS TO HER, MR. HALY?
ANSWER CAREFULLY.
NO. I *TOLD* YOU.
WE *FOUND* HER LIKE THAT.
I KNOW THE COURT ONLY WANTS THE *BEST*...I'D NEVER JEOPARDIZE THEIR PICK.
MARY.
I'VE MADE ARRANGE-MENTS WITH MR. HALY. WE WORK FOR SOME VERY, VERY POWERFUL PEOPLE.
YOU'RE TO COME WITH ME. YOU'LL HAVE A HOME, A NEST OF YOUR OWN. AND IMPORTANT, MEANINGFUL WORK.
WOULD YOU LIKE THAT?

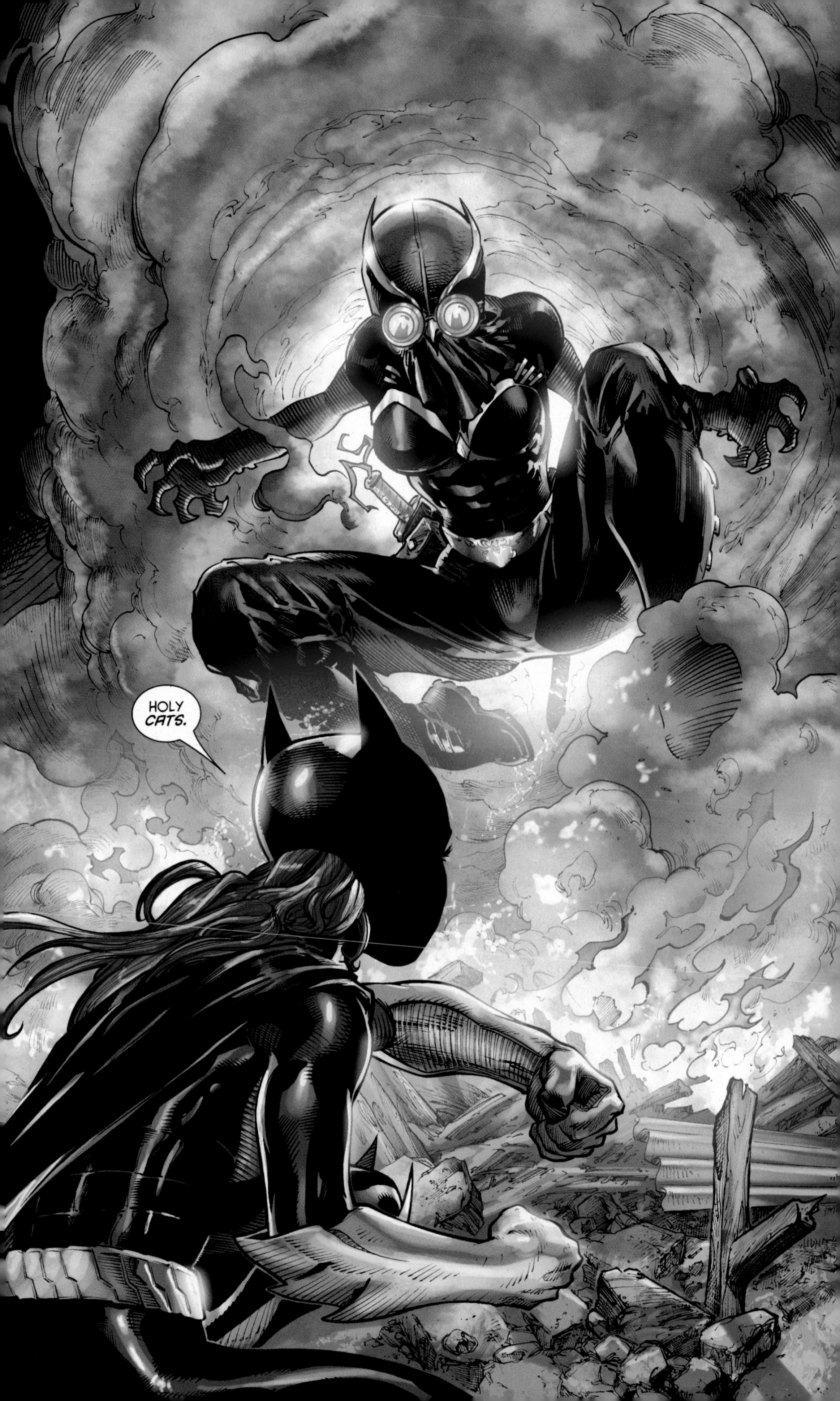
HOLY CATS.

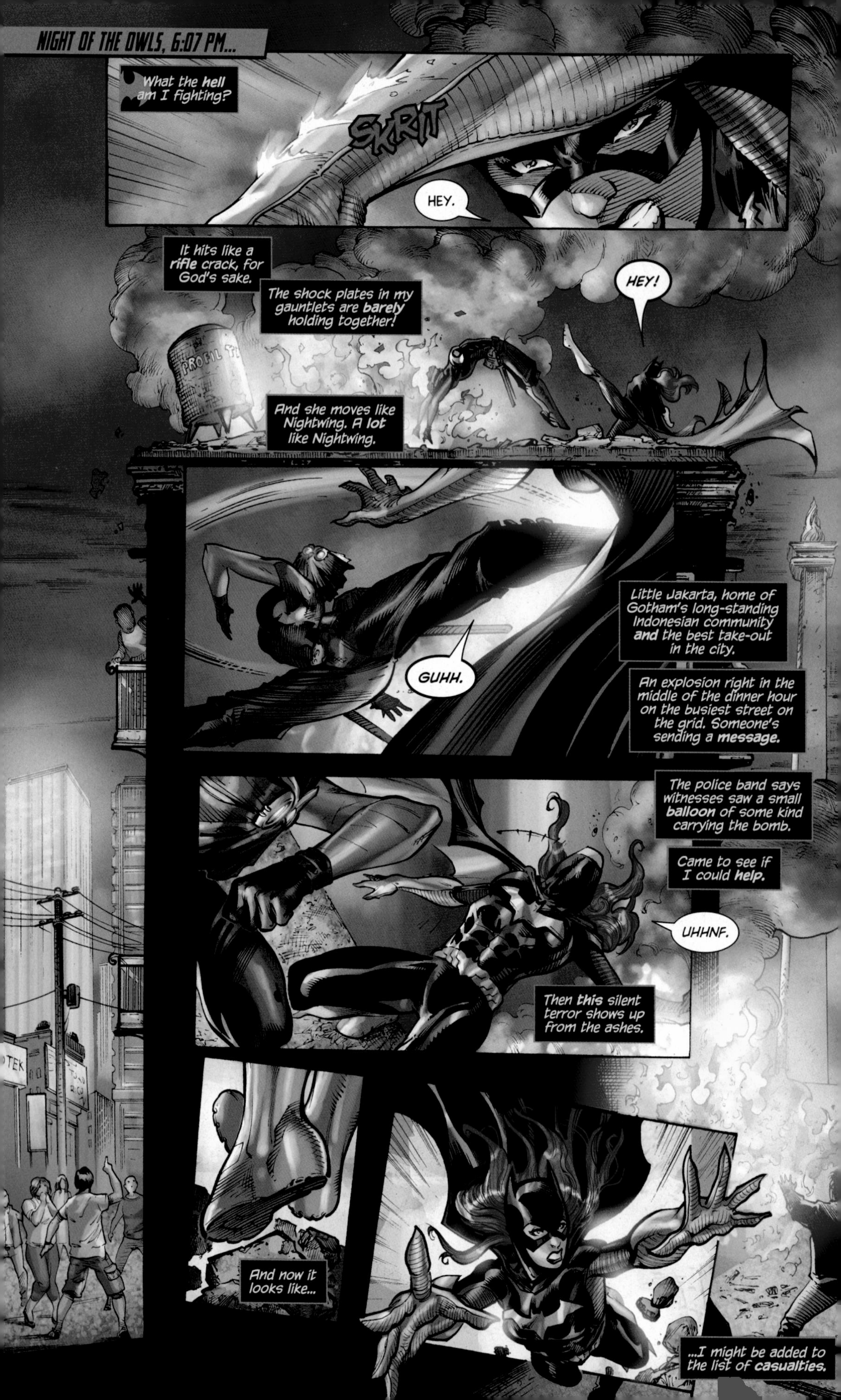

NIGHT OF THE OWLS, 6:07 PM...
What the hell am I fighting?
SKRIT
HEY.
It hits like a rifle crack, for God's sake.
The shock plates in my gauntlets are barely holding together!
HEY!
And she moves like Nightwing. A lot like Nightwing.
PROFIL TE
Little Jakarta, home of Gotham's long-standing Indonesian community and the best take-out in the city.
GUHH.
An explosion right in the middle of the dinner hour on the busiest street on the grid. Someone's sending a message.
The police band says witnesses saw a small balloon of some kind carrying the bomb.
Came to see if I could help.
UHHNF.
Then this silent terror shows up from the ashes.
TEK
And now it looks like...
...I might be added to the list of casualties.

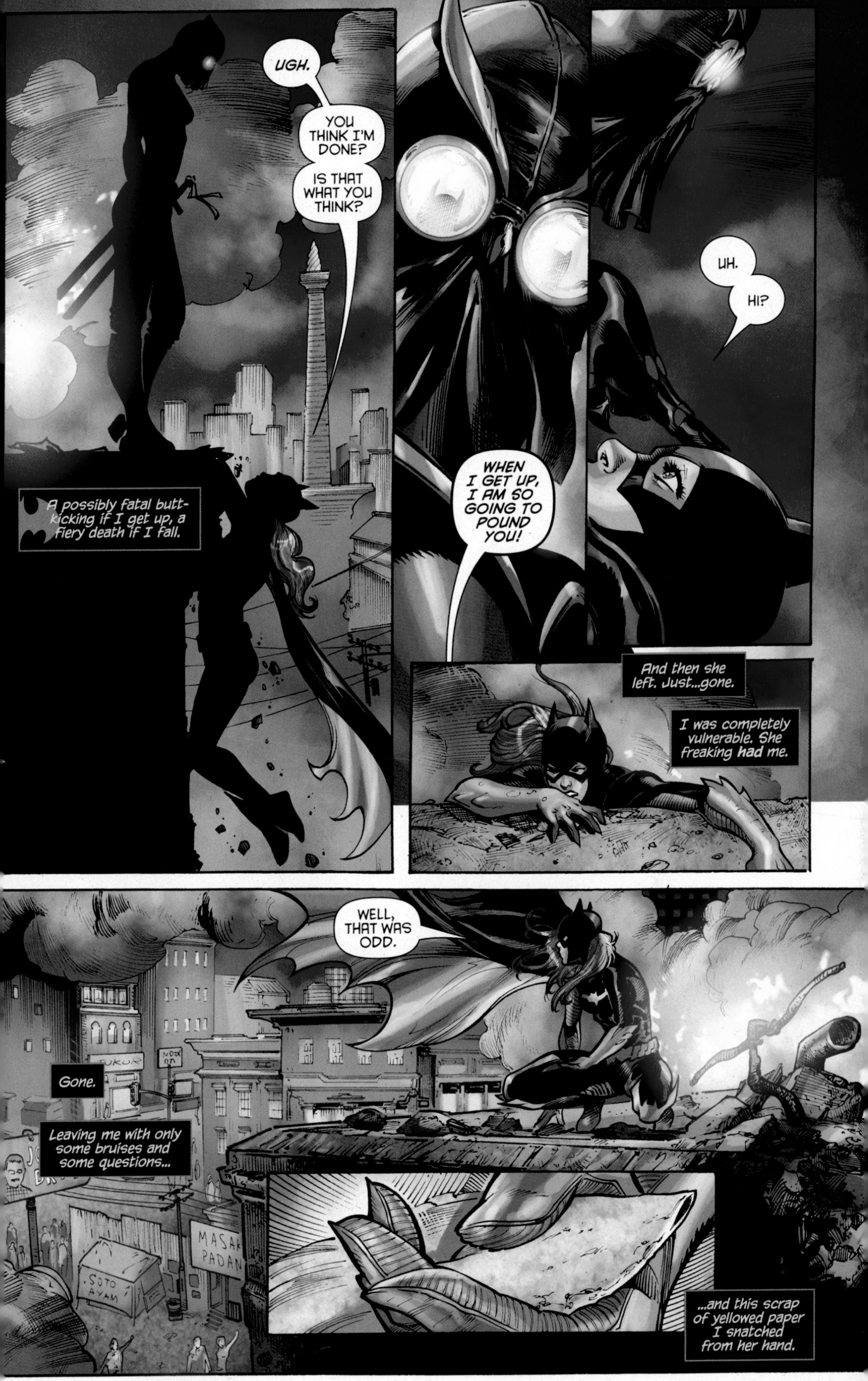

UGH.
YOU THINK I'M DONE?
IS THAT WHAT YOU THINK?
A possibly fatal butt-kicking if I get up, a fiery death if I fall.
WHEN I GET UP, I AM SO GOING TO POUND YOU!
UH.
HI?
And then she left. Just...gone.
I was completely vulnerable. She freaking had me.
WELL, THAT WAS ODD.
Gone.
Leaving me with only some bruises and some questions...
MASAK PADAN
SOTO AYAM
...and this scrap of yellowed paper I snatched from her hand.

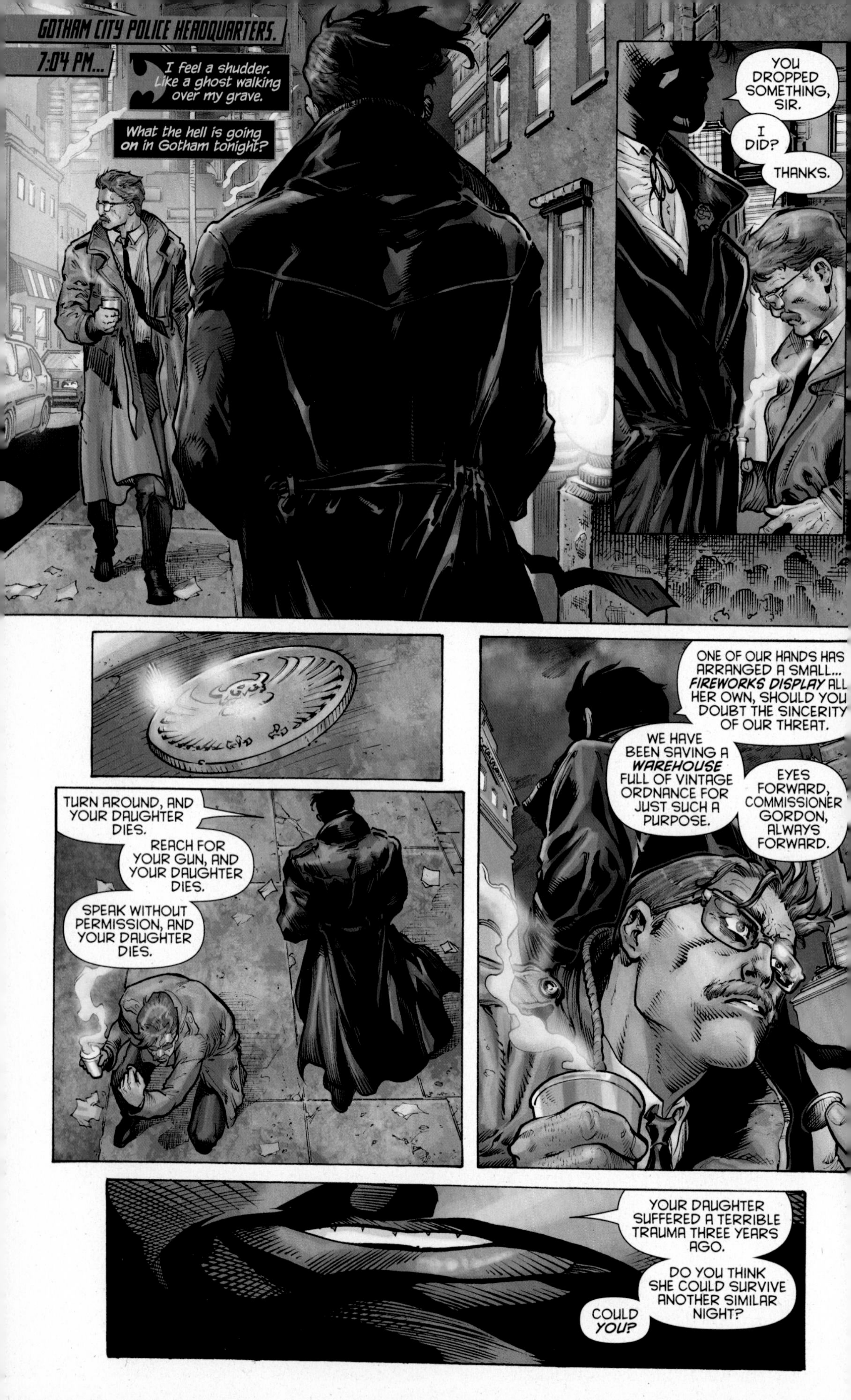

GOTHAM CITY POLICE HEADQUARTERS.
7:04 PM...
I feel a shudder. Like a ghost walking over my grave.
What the hell is going on in Gotham tonight?
YOU DROPPED SOMETHING, SIR.
I DID?
THANKS.
TURN AROUND, AND YOUR DAUGHTER DIES.
REACH FOR YOUR GUN, AND YOUR DAUGHTER DIES.
SPEAK WITHOUT PERMISSION, AND YOUR DAUGHTER DIES.
ONE OF OUR HANDS HAS ARRANGED A SMALL... FIREWORKS DISPLAY ALL HER OWN, SHOULD YOU DOUBT THE SINCERITY OF OUR THREAT.
WE HAVE BEEN SAVING A WAREHOUSE FULL OF VINTAGE ORDNANCE FOR JUST SUCH A PURPOSE.
EYES FORWARD, COMMISSIONER GORDON, ALWAYS FORWARD.
YOUR DAUGHTER SUFFERED A TERRIBLE TRAUMA THREE YEARS AGO.
DO YOU THINK SHE COULD SURVIVE ANOTHER SIMILAR NIGHT?
COULD YOU?

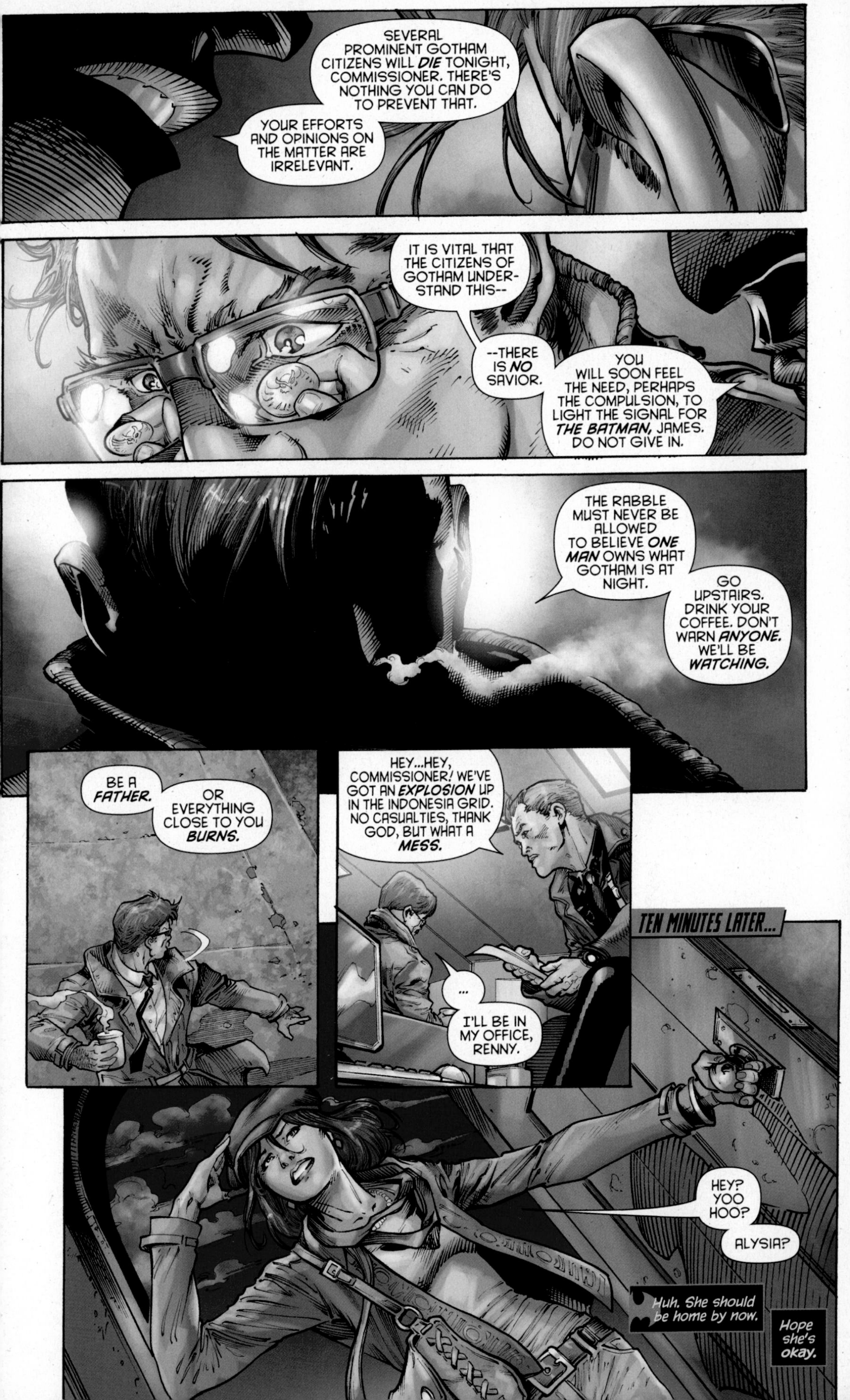
SEVERAL PROMINENT GOTHAM CITIZENS WILL DIE TONIGHT, COMMISSIONER. THERE'S NOTHING YOU CAN DO TO PREVENT THAT.
YOUR EFFORTS AND OPINIONS ON THE MATTER ARE IRRELEVANT.
IT IS VITAL THAT THE CITIZENS OF GOTHAM UNDER-STAND THIS--
--THERE IS NO SAVIOR.
YOU WILL SOON FEEL THE NEED, PERHAPS THE COMPULSION, TO LIGHT THE SIGNAL FOR THE BATMAN, JAMES. DO NOT GIVE IN.
THE RABBLE MUST NEVER BE ALLOWED TO BELIEVE ONE MAN OWNS WHAT GOTHAM IS AT NIGHT.
GO UPSTAIRS. DRINK YOUR COFFEE. DON'T WARN ANYONE. WE'LL BE WATCHING.
BE A FATHER.
OR EVERYTHING CLOSE TO YOU BURNS.
HEY...HEY, COMMISSIONER! WE'VE GOT AN EXPLOSION UP IN THE INDONESIA GRID. NO CASUALTIES, THANK GOD, BUT WHAT A MESS.
...
I'LL BE IN MY OFFICE, RENNY.
TEN MINUTES LATER...
HEY? YOO HOO?
ALYSIA?
Huh. She should be home by now.
Hope she's okay.

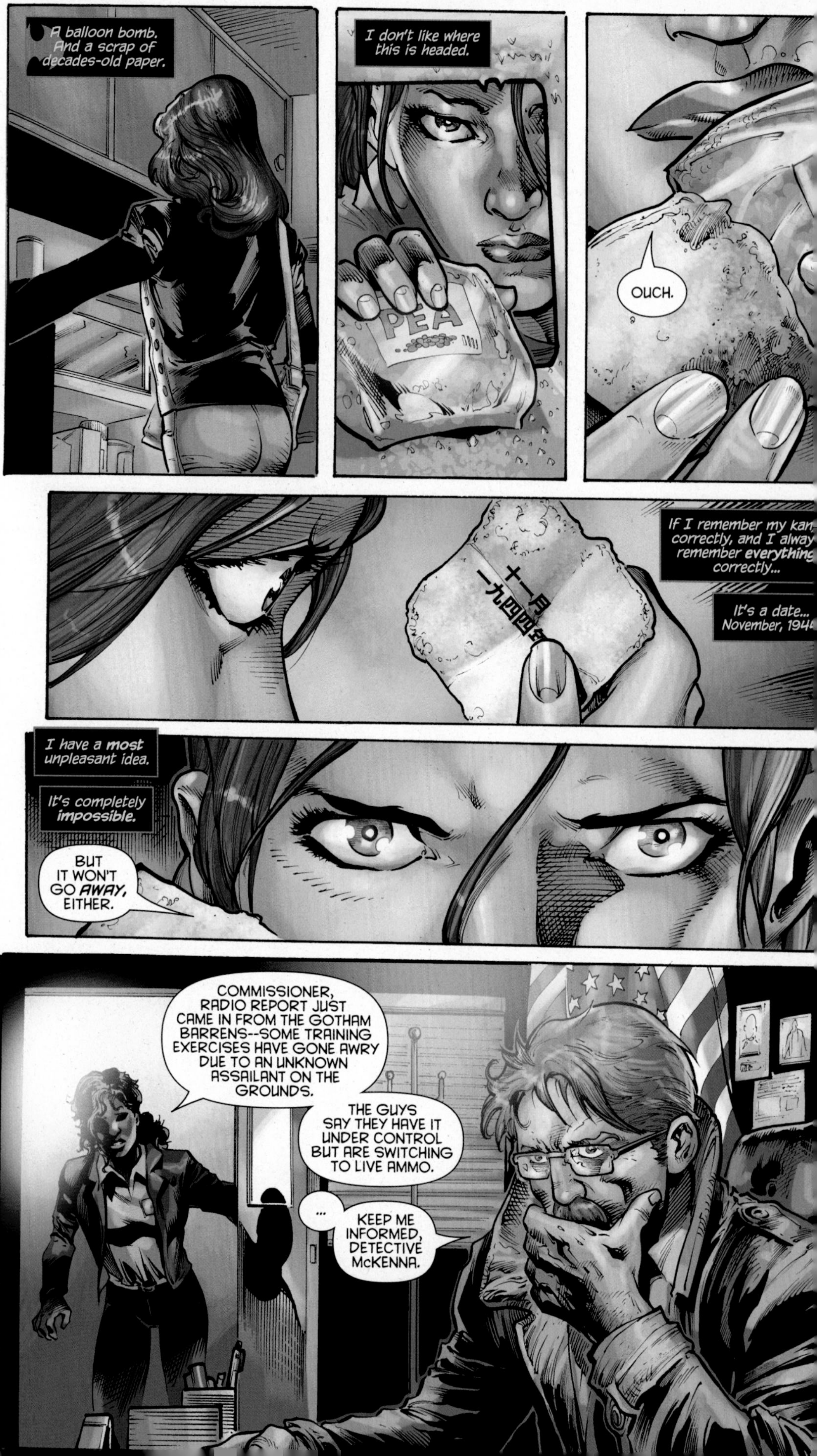

A balloon bomb. And a scrap of decades-old paper.
I don't like where this is headed.
PEA
OUCH.
十一月
一九四四年
If I remember my kan correctly, and I alway remember everything correctly...
It's a date... November, 194
I have a most unpleasant idea.
It's completely impossible.
BUT IT WON'T GO AWAY, EITHER.
COMMISSIONER, RADIO REPORT JUST CAME IN FROM THE GOTHAM BARRENS--SOME TRAINING EXERCISES HAVE GONE AWRY DUE TO AN UNKNOWN ASSAILANT ON THE GROUNDS.
THE GUYS SAY THEY HAVE IT UNDER CONTROL BUT ARE SWITCHING TO LIVE AMMO.
...
KEEP ME INFORMED, DETECTIVE McKENNA.

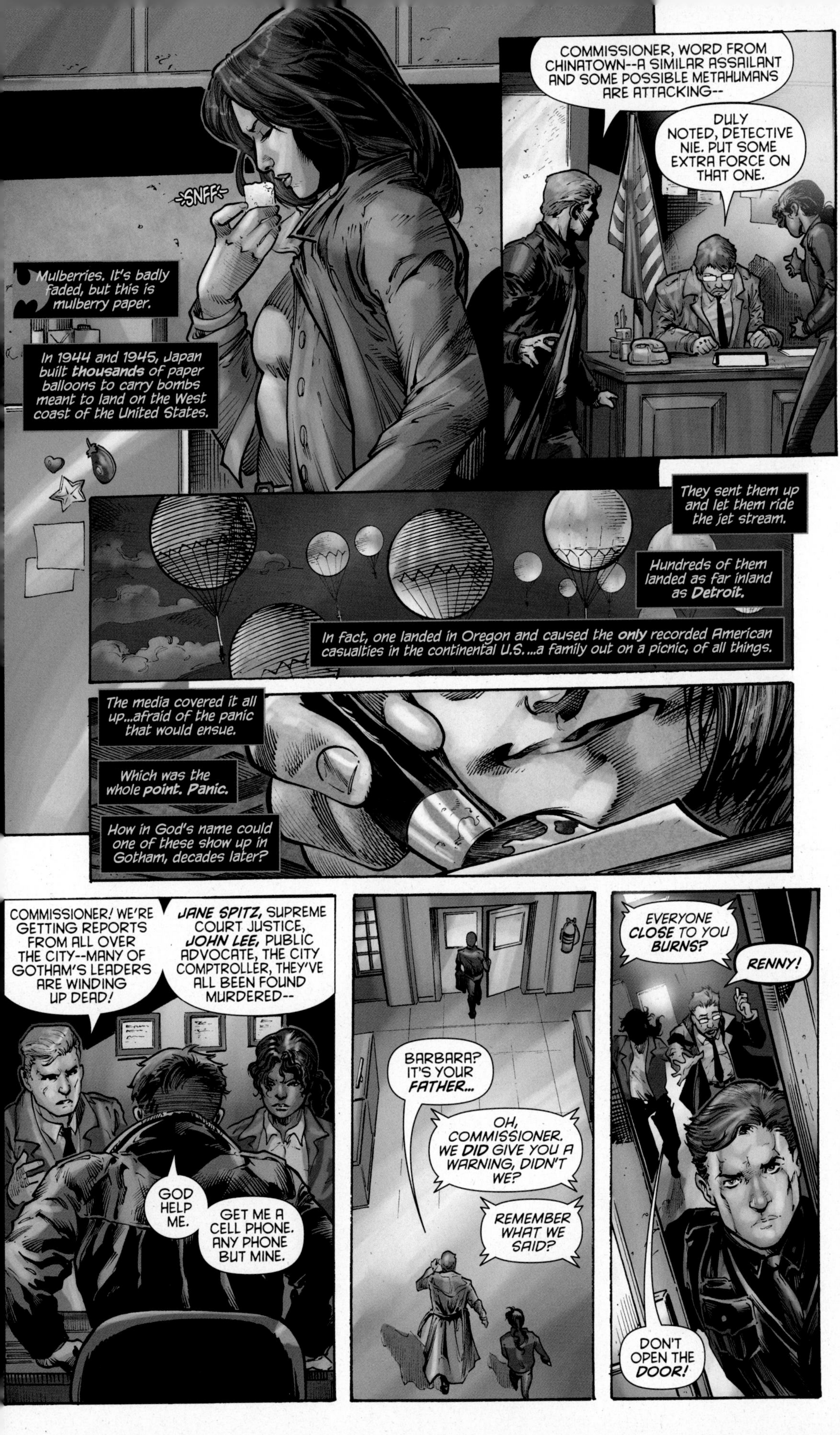

-SNFF-
Mulberries. It's badly faded, but this is mulberry paper.
In 1944 and 1945, Japan built **thousands** of paper balloons to carry bombs meant to land on the West coast of the United States.
COMMISSIONER, WORD FROM CHINATOWN--A SIMILAR ASSAILANT AND SOME POSSIBLE METAHUMANS ARE ATTACKING--
DULY NOTED, DETECTIVE NIE. PUT SOME EXTRA FORCE ON THAT ONE.
They sent them up and let them ride the jet stream.
Hundreds of them landed as far inland as **Detroit.**
In fact, one landed in Oregon and caused the **only** recorded American casualties in the continental U.S....a family out on a picnic, of all things.
The media covered it all up...afraid of the panic that would ensue.
Which was the whole **point. Panic.**
How in God's name could one of these show up in Gotham, decades later?
COMMISSIONER! WE'RE GETTING REPORTS FROM ALL OVER THE CITY--MANY OF GOTHAM'S LEADERS ARE WINDING UP DEAD!
JANE SPITZ, SUPREME COURT JUSTICE, **JOHN LEE,** PUBLIC ADVOCATE, THE CITY COMPTROLLER, THEY'VE ALL BEEN FOUND MURDERED--
GOD HELP ME.
GET ME A CELL PHONE. ANY PHONE BUT MINE.
BARBARA? IT'S YOUR **FATHER...**
OH, COMMISSIONER. WE **DID** GIVE YOU A WARNING, DIDN'T WE?
REMEMBER WHAT WE SAID?
EVERYONE **CLOSE** TO YOU **BURNS?**
RENNY!
DON'T OPEN THE **DOOR!**

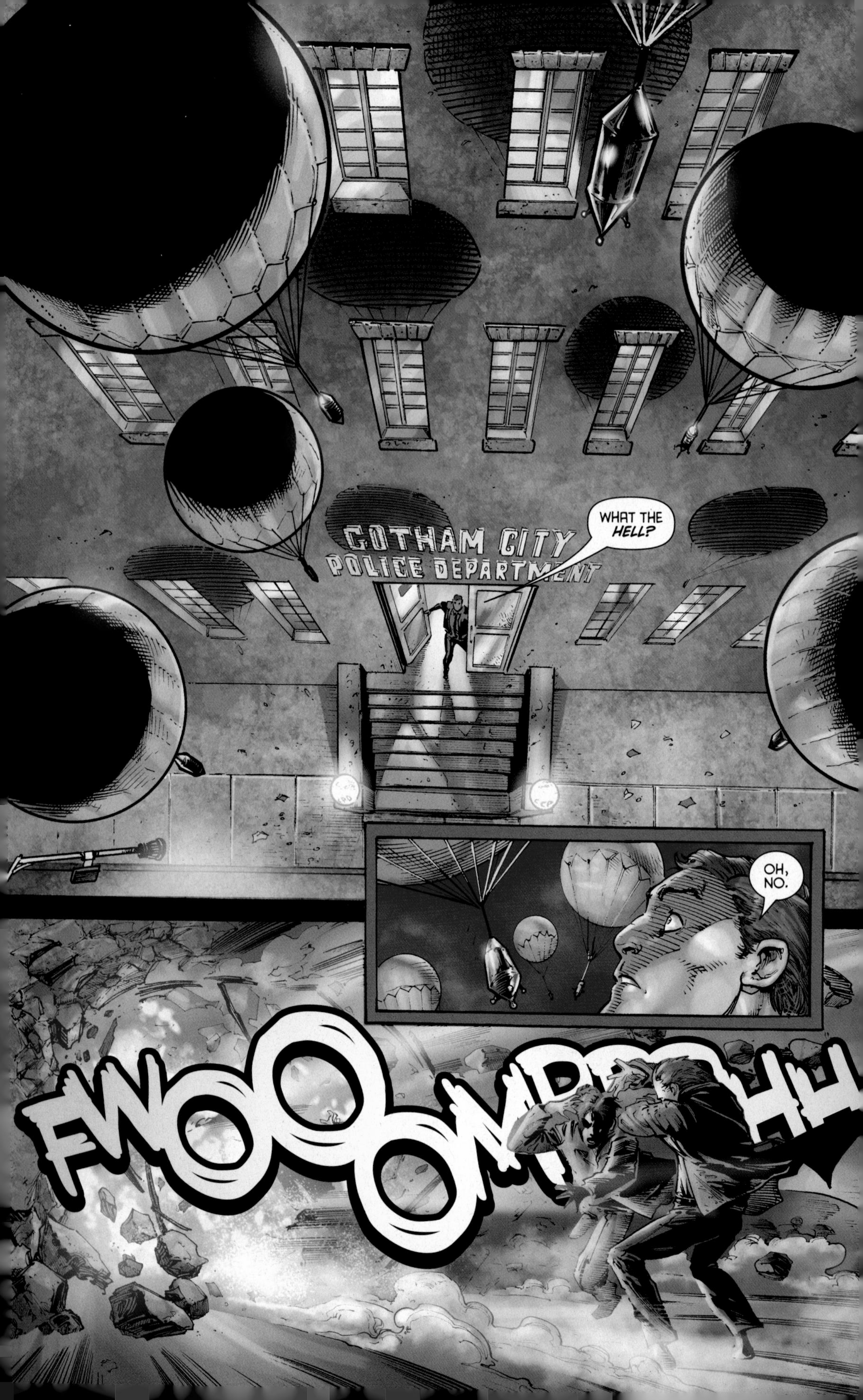
GOTHAM CITY
POLICE DEPARTMENT
WHAT THE HELL?
OH, NO.

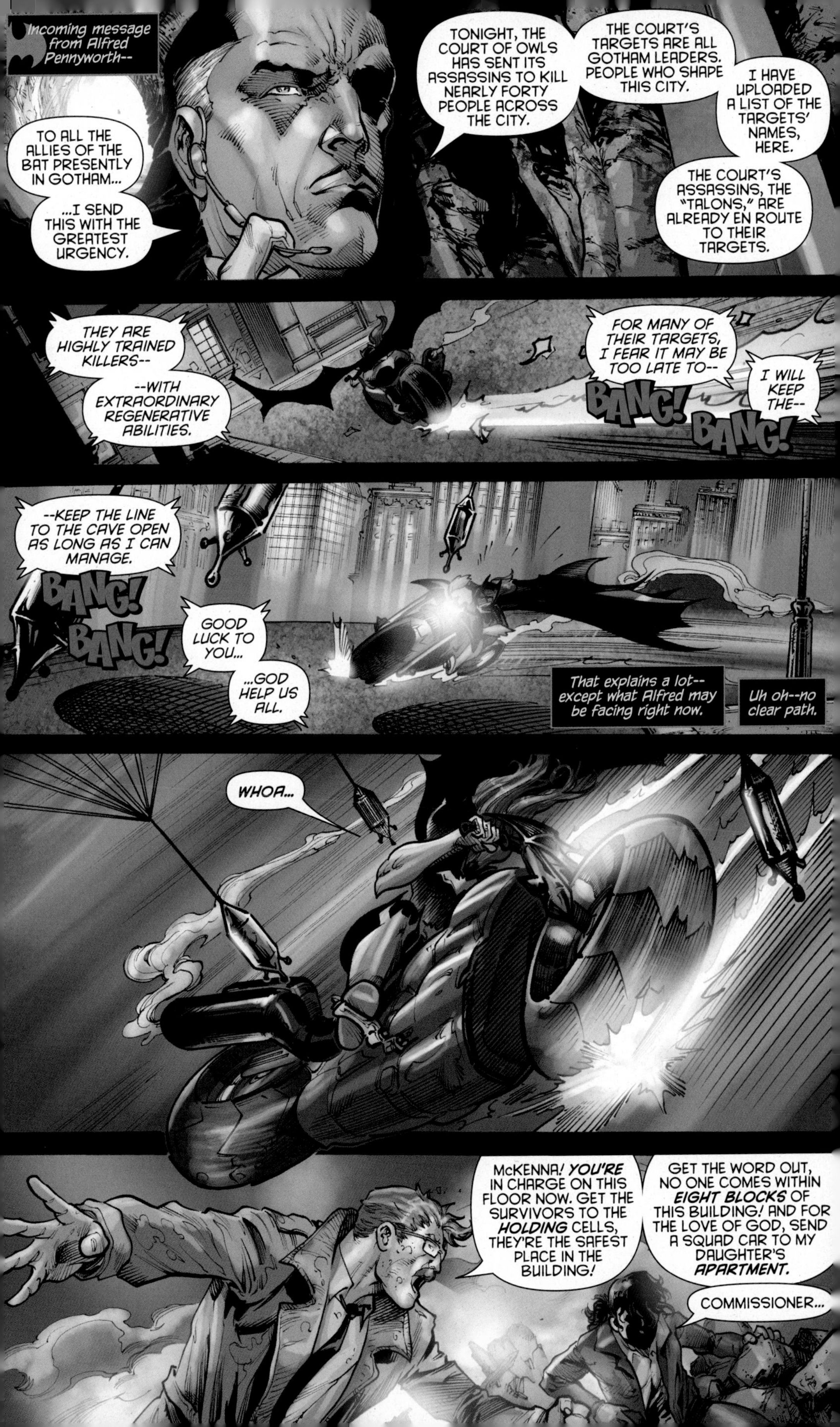
Incoming message from Alfred Pennyworth--
TO ALL THE ALLIES OF THE BAT PRESENTLY IN GOTHAM...
...I SEND THIS WITH THE GREATEST URGENCY.
TONIGHT, THE COURT OF OWLS HAS SENT ITS ASSASSINS TO KILL NEARLY FORTY PEOPLE ACROSS THE CITY.
THE COURT'S TARGETS ARE ALL GOTHAM LEADERS. PEOPLE WHO SHAPE THIS CITY.
I HAVE UPLOADED A LIST OF THE TARGETS' NAMES, HERE.
THE COURT'S ASSASSINS, THE "TALONS," ARE ALREADY EN ROUTE TO THEIR TARGETS.
THEY ARE HIGHLY TRAINED KILLERS--
--WITH EXTRAORDINARY REGENERATIVE ABILITIES.
FOR MANY OF THEIR TARGETS, I FEAR IT MAY BE TOO LATE TO--
BANG!
I WILL KEEP THE--
BANG!
--KEEP THE LINE TO THE CAVE OPEN AS LONG AS I CAN MANAGE.
BANG!
BANG!
GOOD LUCK TO YOU...
...GOD HELP US ALL.
That explains a lot--except what Alfred may be facing right now.
Uh oh--no clear path.
WHOA...
McKENNA! YOU'RE IN CHARGE ON THIS FLOOR NOW. GET THE SURVIVORS TO THE HOLDING CELLS, THEY'RE THE SAFEST PLACE IN THE BUILDING!
GET THE WORD OUT, NO ONE COMES WITHIN EIGHT BLOCKS OF THIS BUILDING! AND FOR THE LOVE OF GOD, SEND A SQUAD CAR TO MY DAUGHTER'S APARTMENT.
COMMISSIONER...

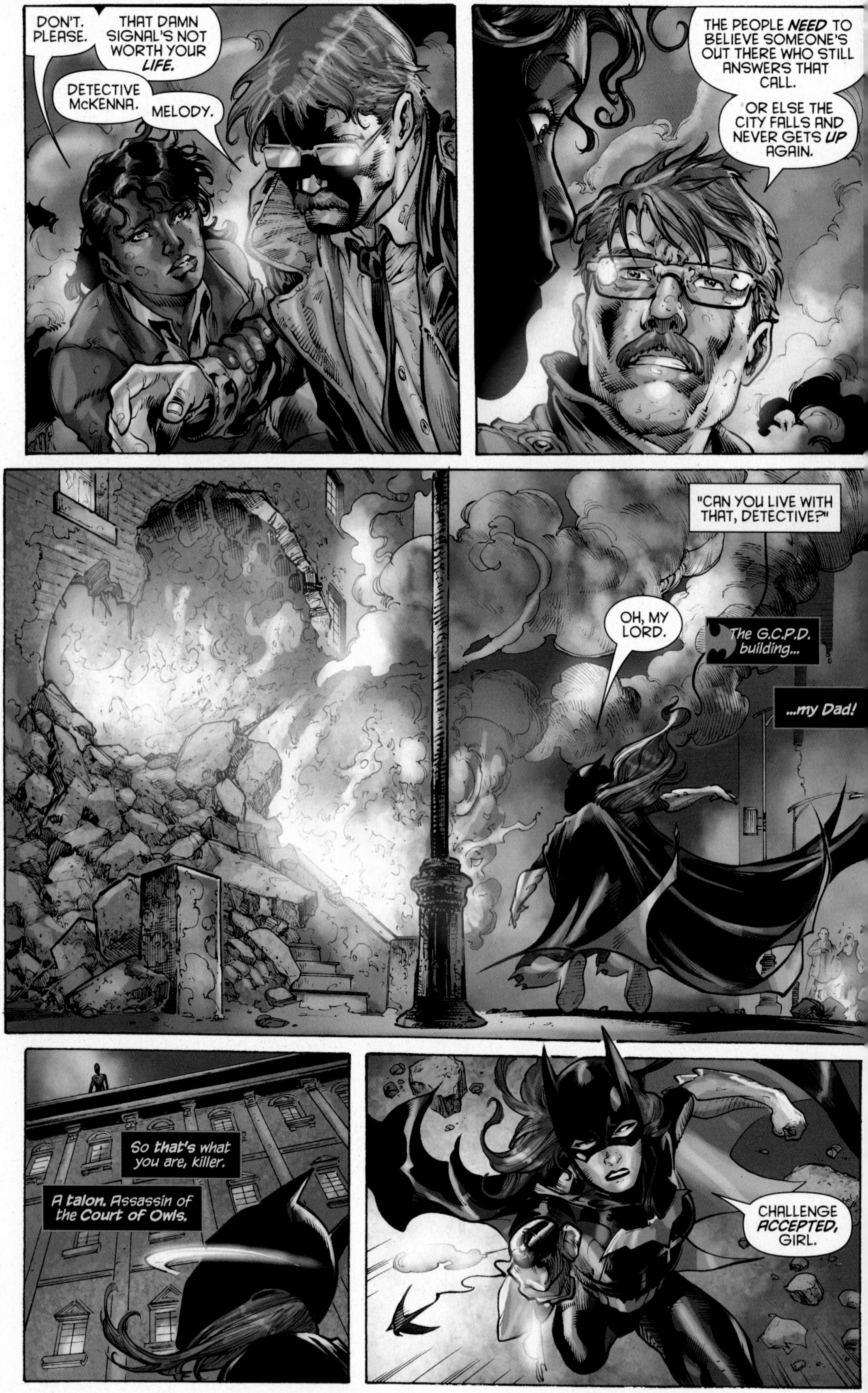

DON'T. PLEASE.
THAT DAMN SIGNAL'S NOT WORTH YOUR *LIFE.*
DETECTIVE McKENNA.
MELODY.
THE PEOPLE *NEED* TO BELIEVE SOMEONE'S OUT THERE WHO STILL ANSWERS THAT CALL.
OR ELSE THE CITY FALLS AND NEVER GETS *UP* AGAIN.
"CAN YOU LIVE WITH THAT, DETECTIVE?"
OH, MY LORD.
The G.C.P.D. building...
...my Dad!
So *that's* what you are, killer.
A *talon.* Assassin of the *Court of Owls.*
CHALLENGE *ACCEPTED,* GIRL.

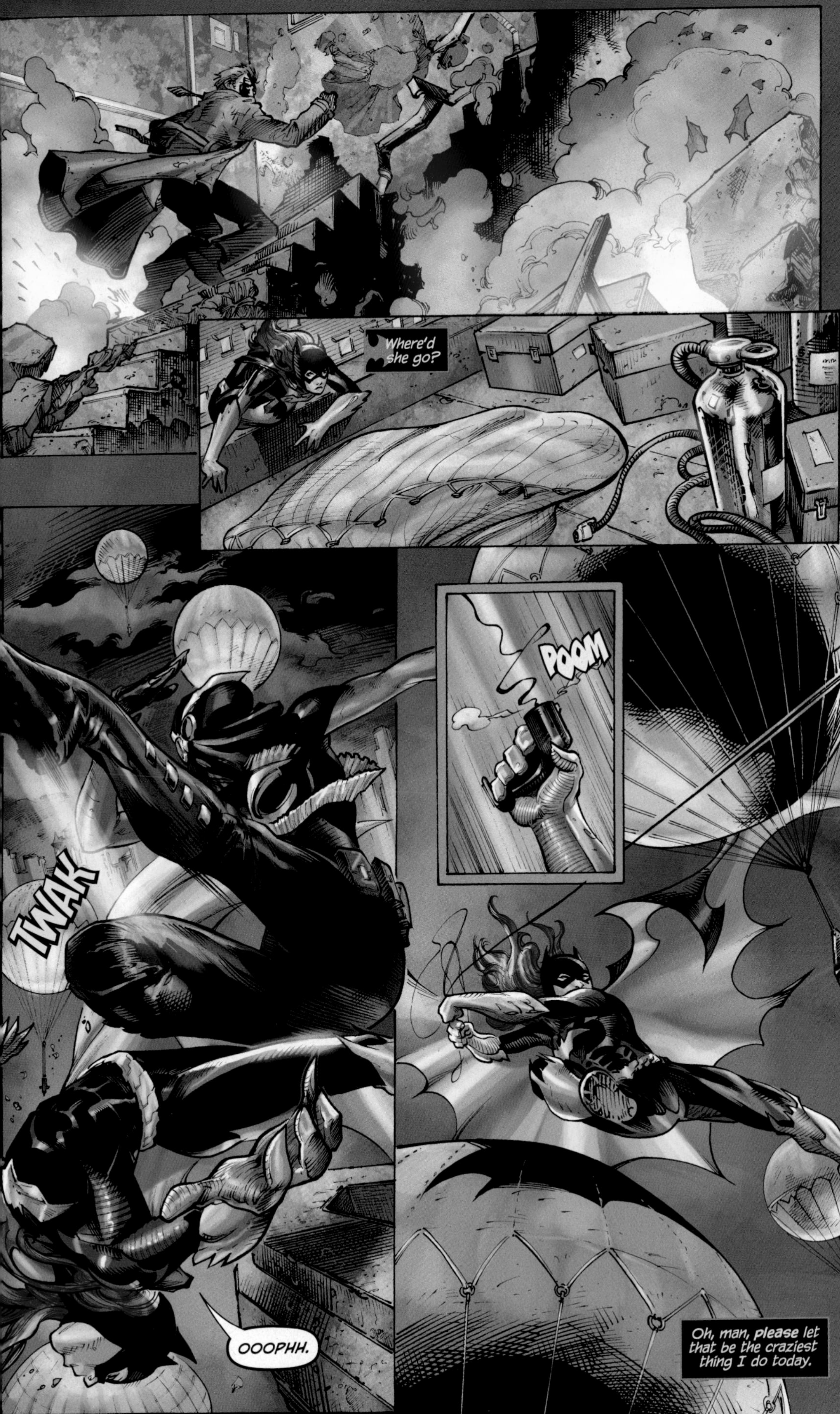
Where'd she go?
POOM
TWAK
OOOPHH.
Oh, man, please let that be the craziest thing I do today.

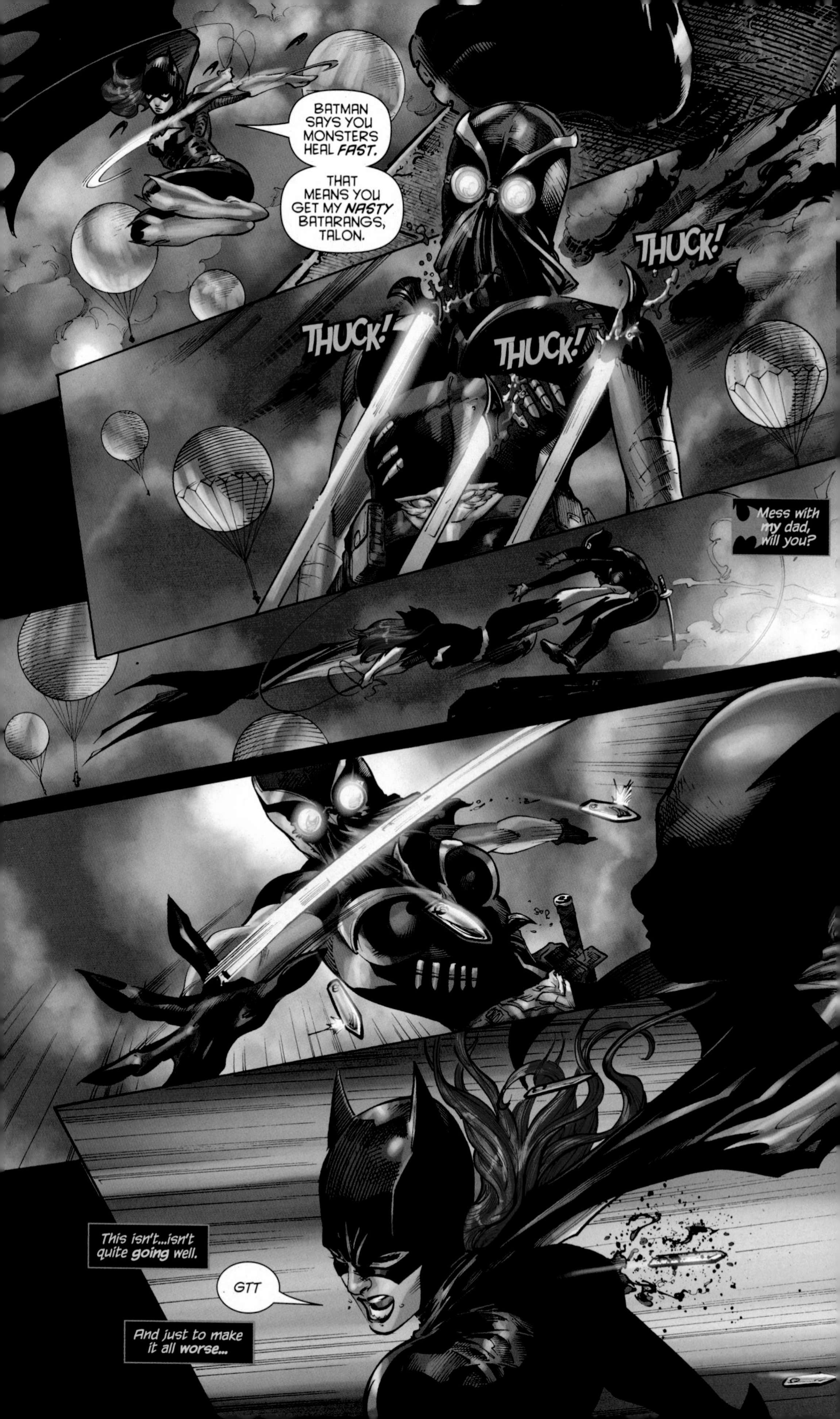
BATMAN SAYS YOU MONSTERS HEAL *FAST.*
THAT MEANS YOU GET MY *NASTY* BATARANGS, TALON.
THUCK!
THUCK!
THUCK!
Mess with my dad, will you?
This isn't...isn't quite going well.
GTT
And just to make it all worse...

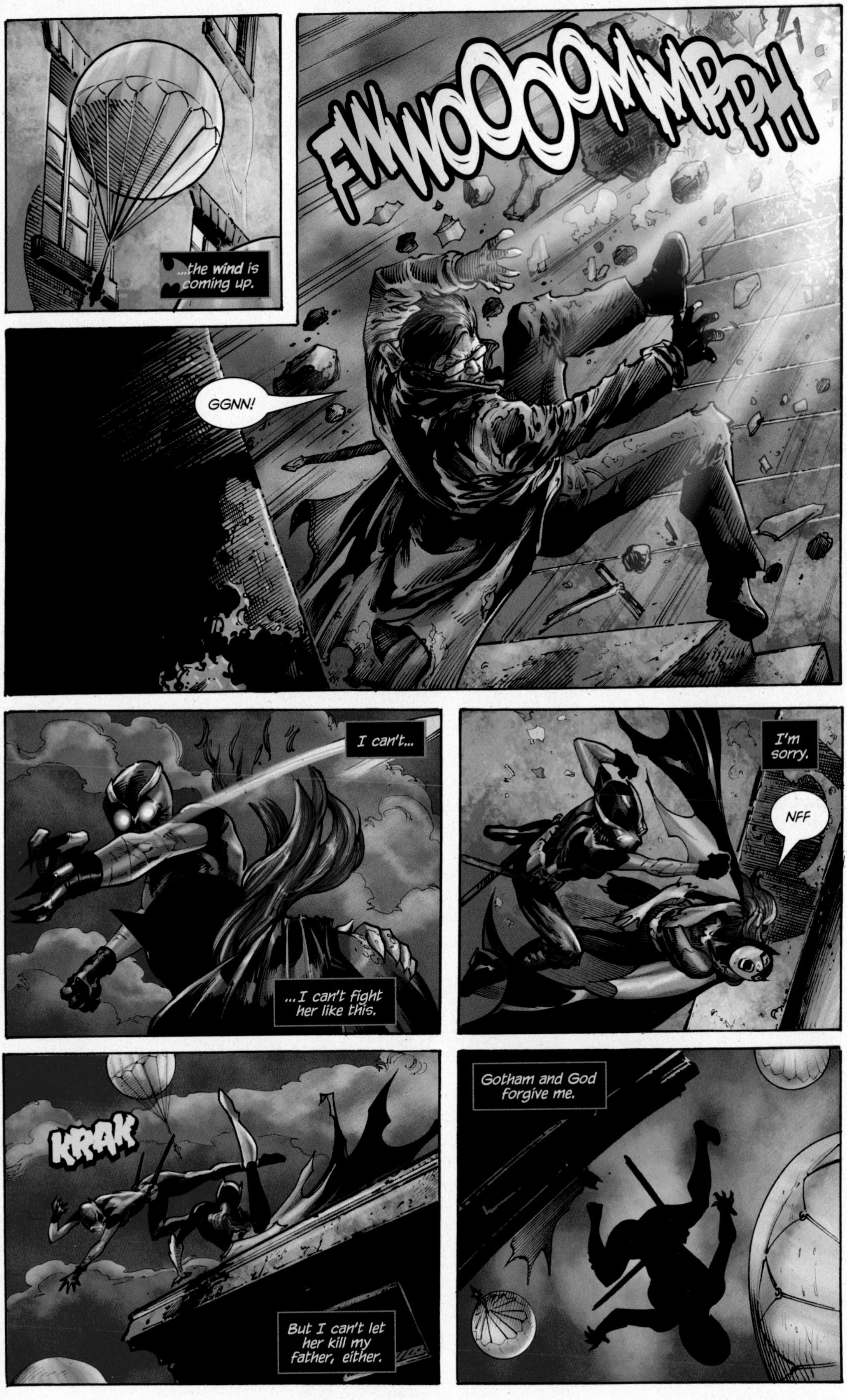
...the wind is coming up.
FWWOOOOMMPPH
GGNN!
I can't...
...I can't fight her like this.
I'm sorry.
NFF
KRAK
But I can't let her kill my father, either.
Gotham and God forgive me.

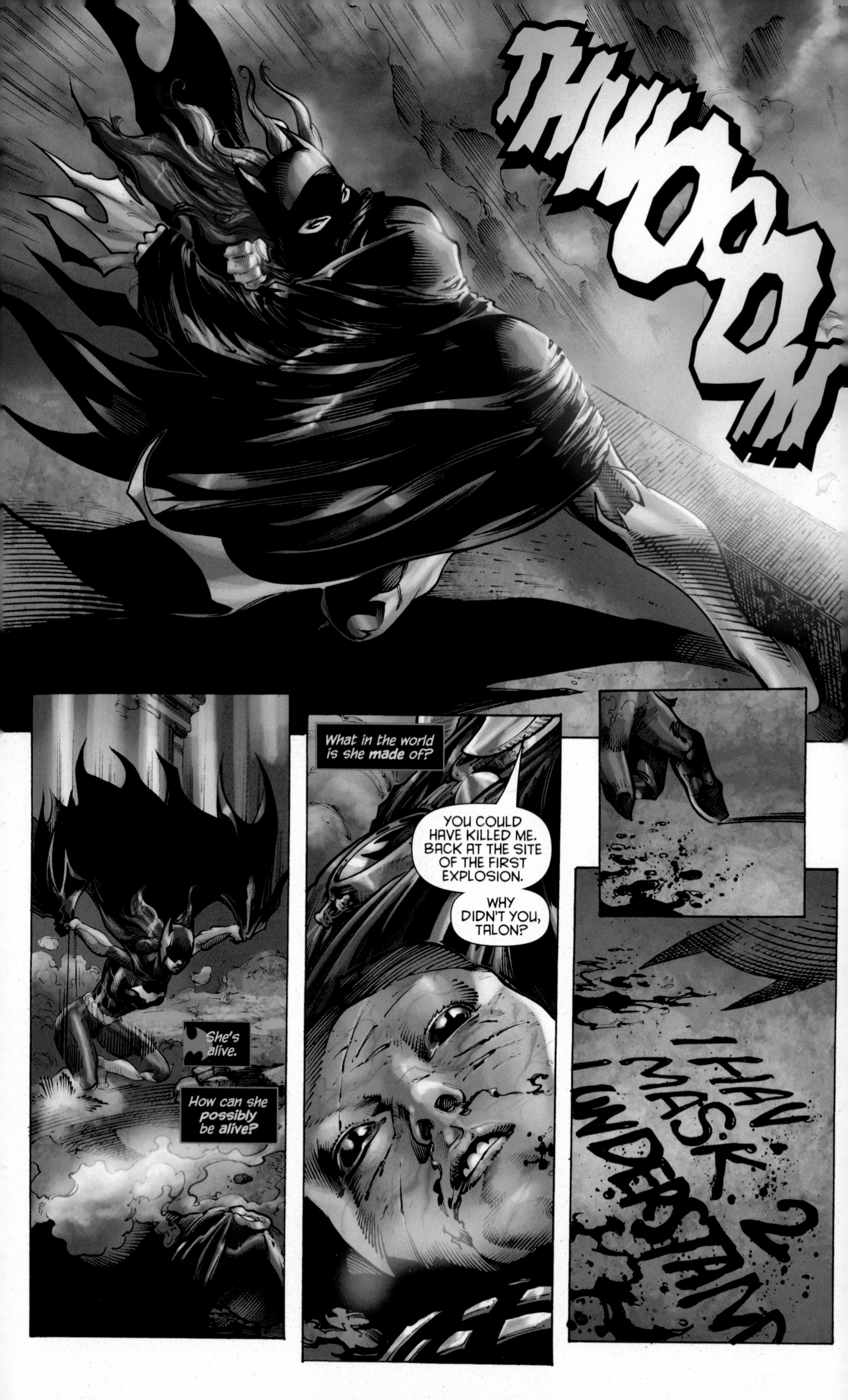
THWOOOM
She's alive.
How can she possibly be alive?
What in the world is she made of?
YOU COULD HAVE KILLED ME. BACK AT THE SITE OF THE FIRST EXPLOSION.
WHY DIDN'T YOU, TALON?
I HAV
MASK.
UNDERSTAN?

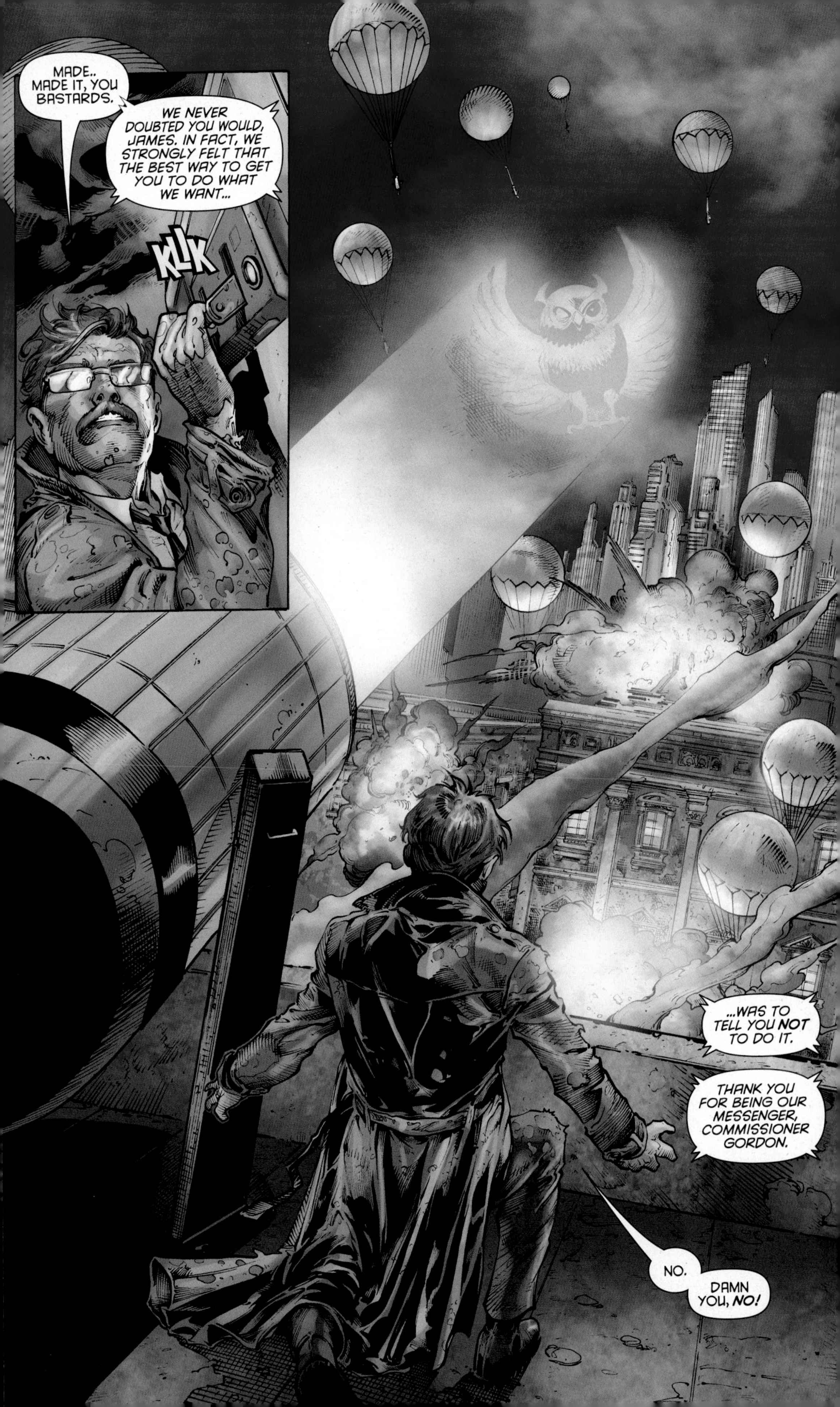

MADE.. MADE IT, YOU BASTARDS.
WE NEVER DOUBTED YOU WOULD, JAMES. IN FACT, WE STRONGLY FELT THAT THE BEST WAY TO GET YOU TO DO WHAT WE WANT...
KLIK
...WAS TO TELL YOU NOT TO DO IT.
THANK YOU FOR BEING OUR MESSENGER, COMMISSIONER GORDON.
NO.
DAMN YOU, NO!

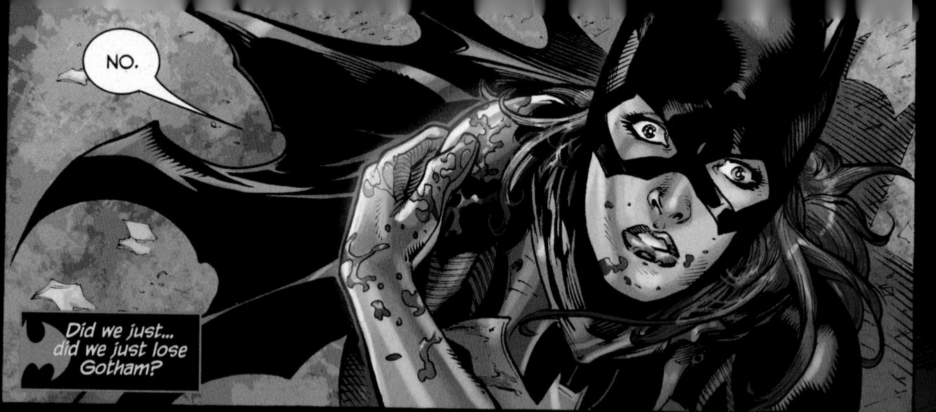
NO.
Did we just... did we just lose Gotham?

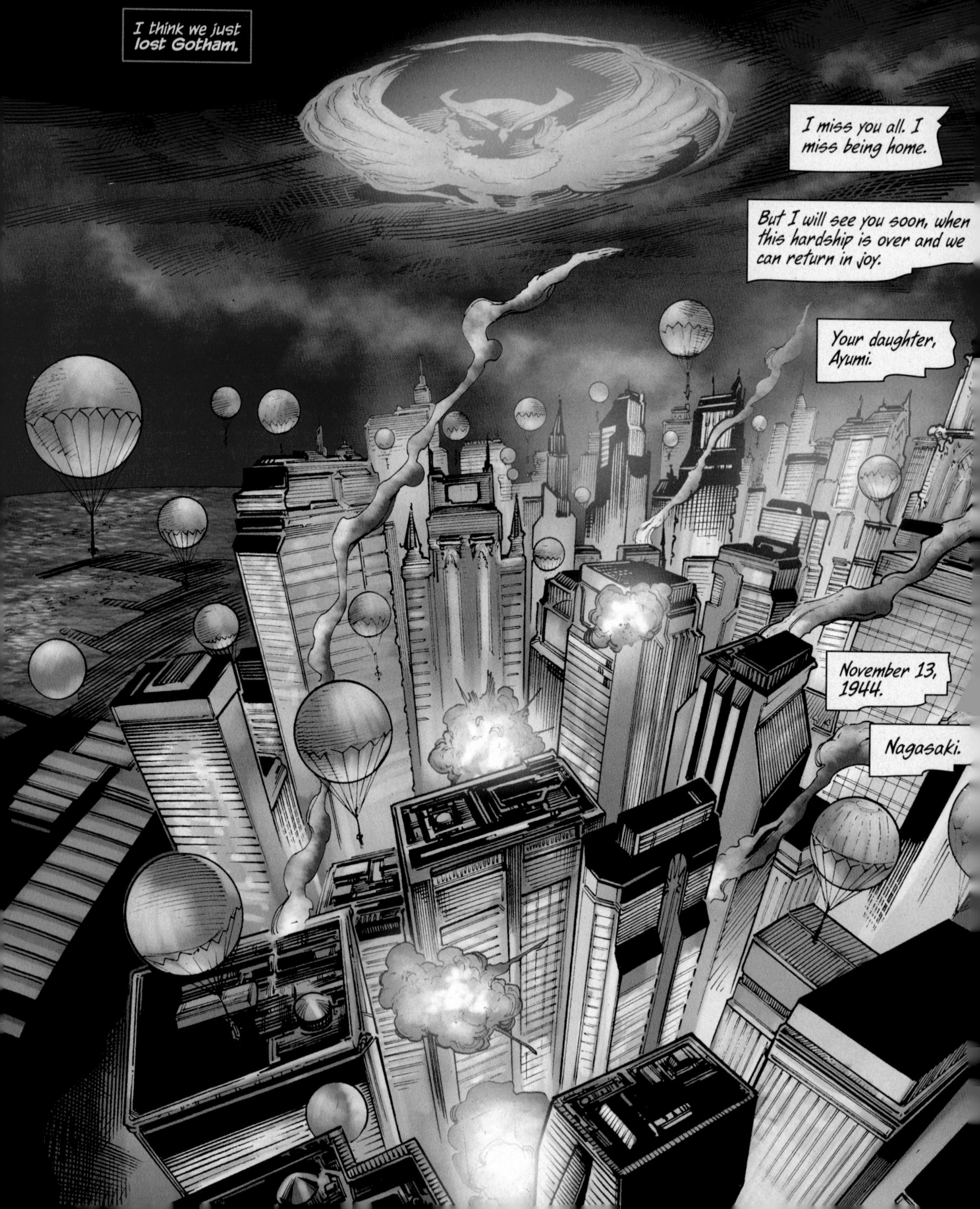
I think we just lost Gotham.
I miss you all. I miss being home.
But I will see you soon, when this hardship is over and we can return in joy.
Your daughter, Ayumi.
November 13, 1944.
Nagasaki.

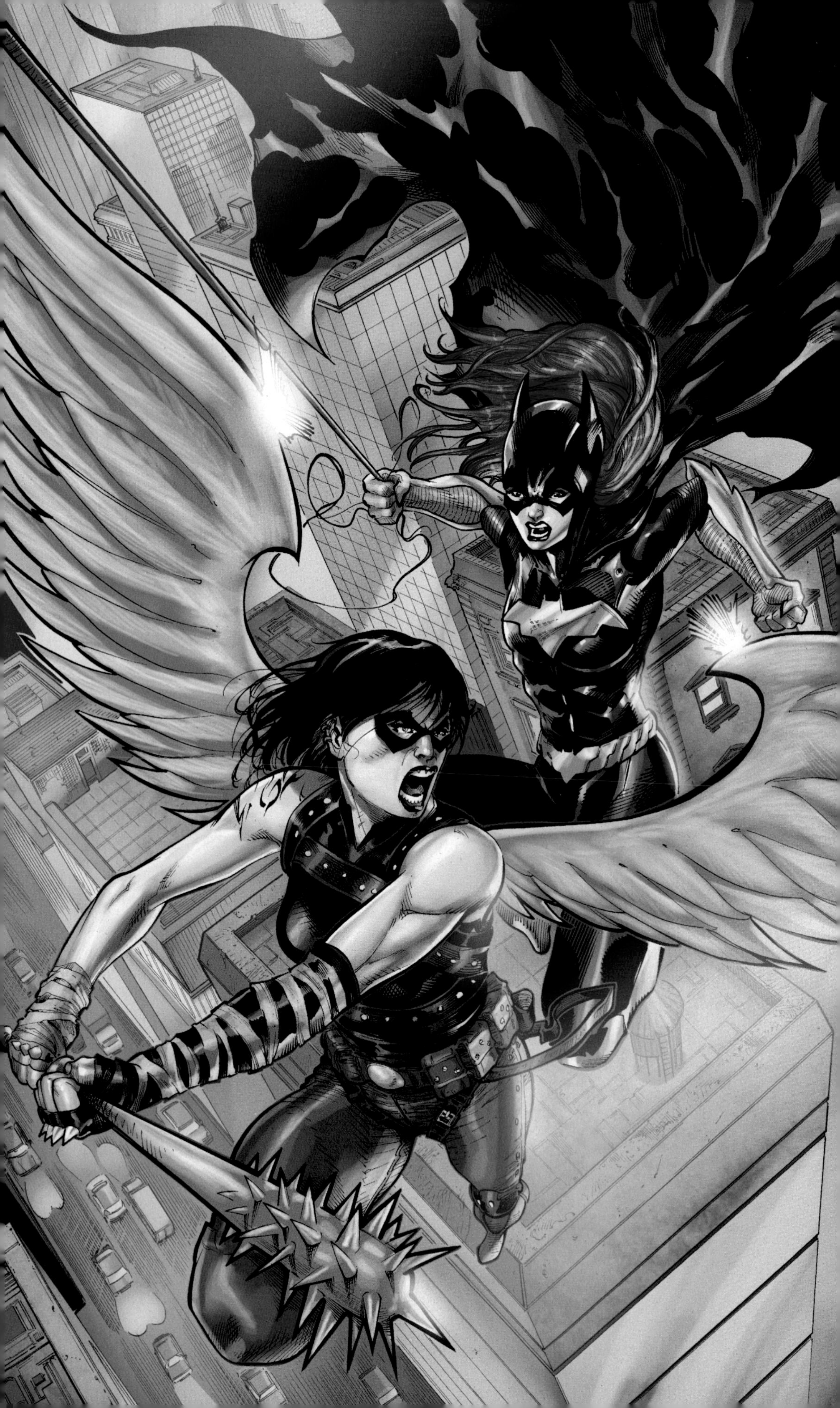

GAIL SIMONE writer ALITHA MARTINEZ penciller VICENTE CIFUENTES inker cover by ARDIAN SYAF, VICENTE CIFUENTES & ULISES ARREOLA

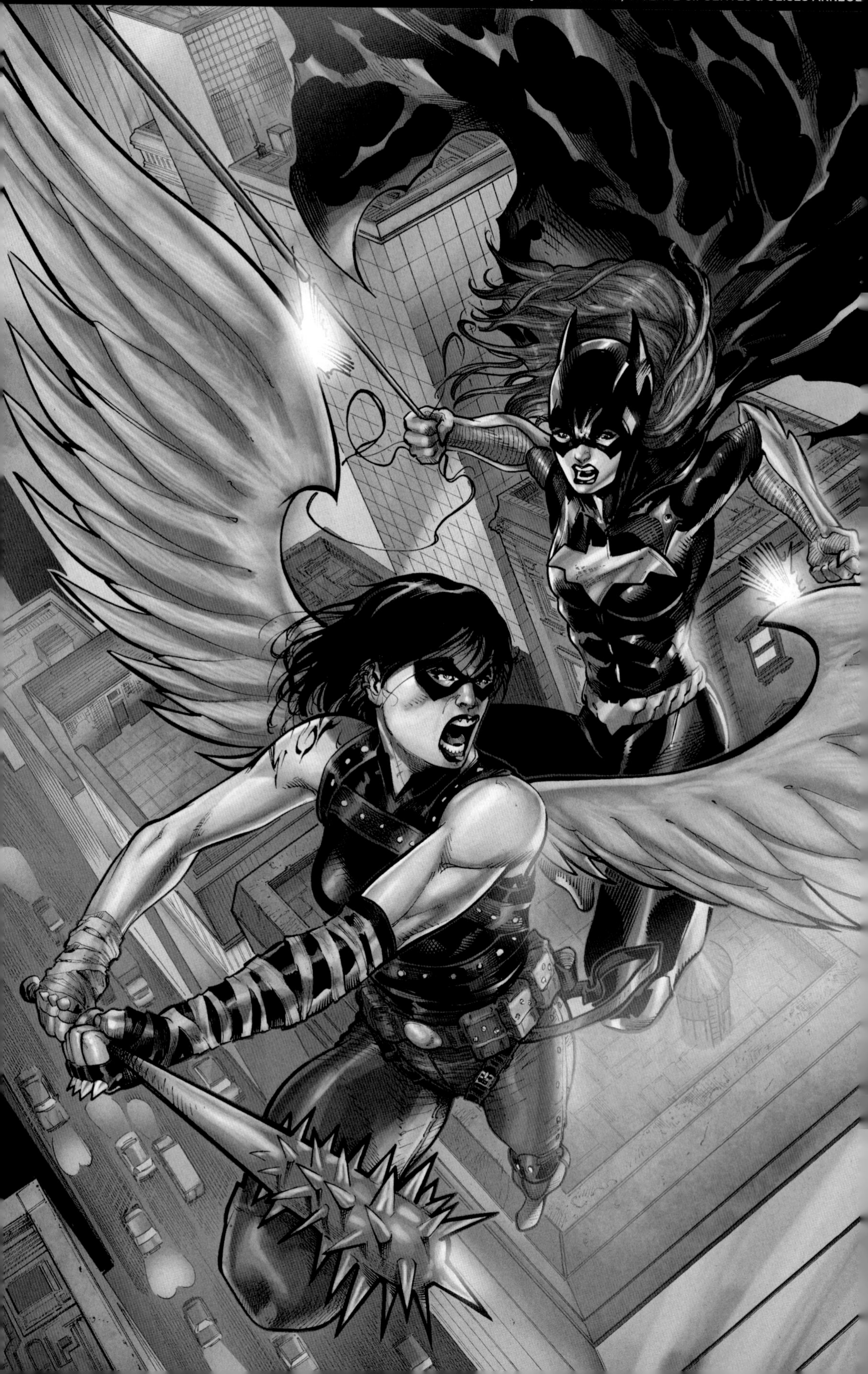

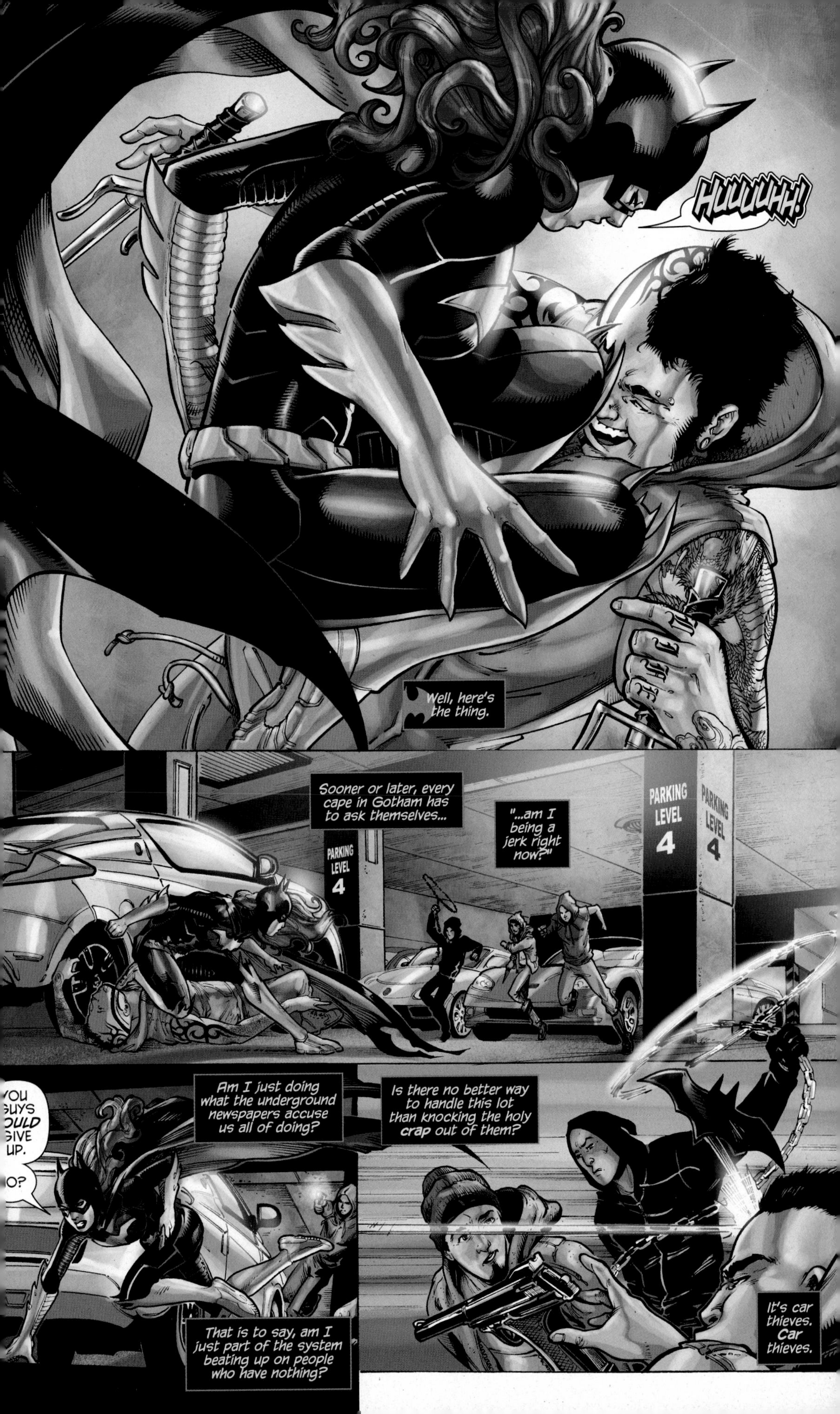

HUUUUHH!
Well, here's the thing.
Sooner or later, every cape in Gotham has to ask themselves...
"...am I being a jerk right now?"
PARKING LEVEL 4
PARKING LEVEL 4
PARKING LEVEL 4
YOU GUYS OULD GIVE UP.
O?
Am I just doing what the underground newspapers accuse us all of doing?
Is there no better way to handle this lot than knocking the holy **crap** out of them?
That is to say, am I just part of the system beating up on people who have nothing?
It's car thieves. **Car** thieves.

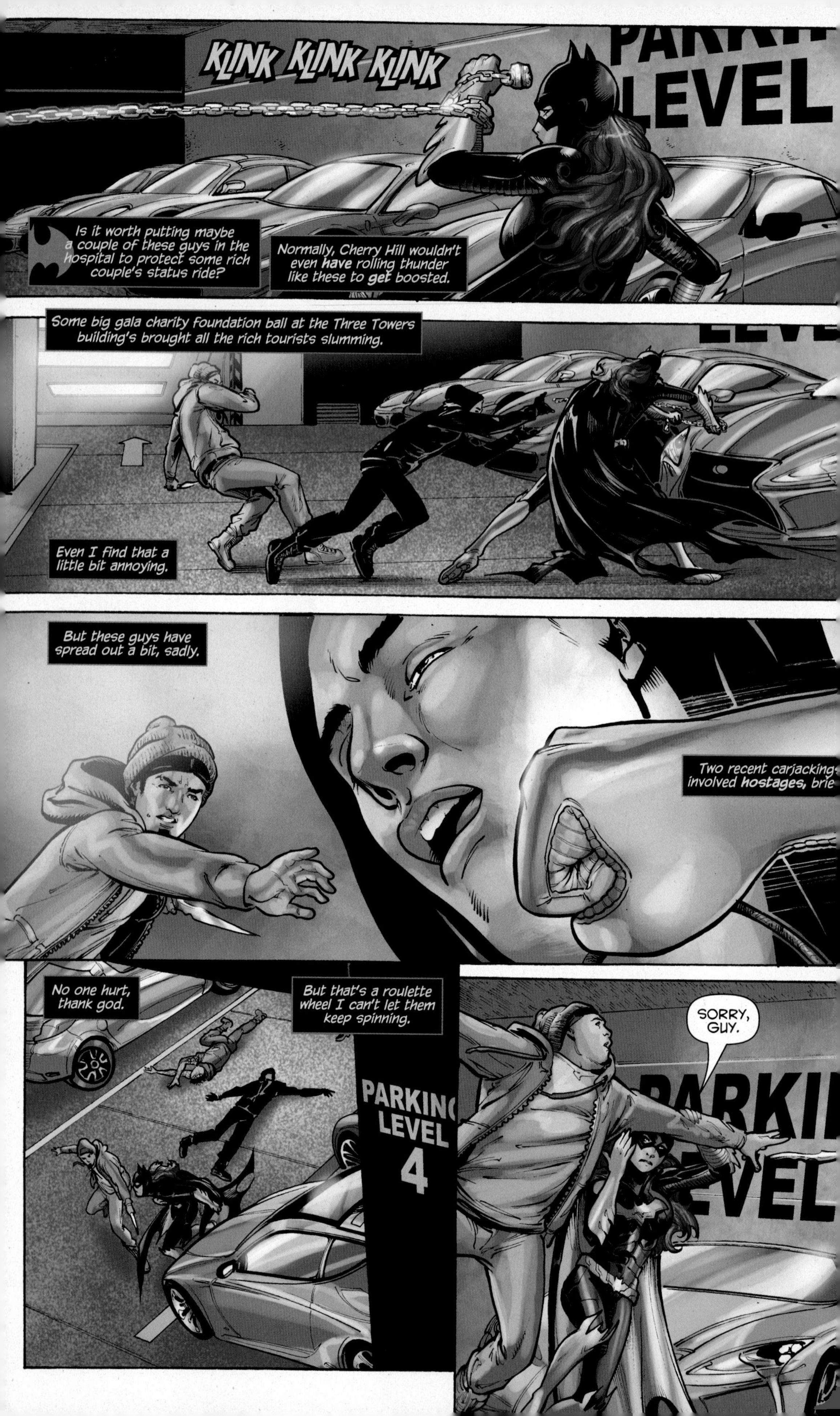
KLINK KLINK KLINK
PARKI
LEVEL
Is it worth putting maybe a couple of these guys in the hospital to protect some rich couple's status ride?
Normally, Cherry Hill wouldn't even **have** rolling thunder like these to **get** boosted.
Some big gala charity foundation ball at the Three Towers building's brought all the rich tourists slumming.
Even I find that a little bit annoying.
But these guys have spread out a bit, sadly.
Two recent carjacking involved **hostages,** brie
No one hurt, thank god.
But that's a roulette wheel I can't let them keep spinning.
PARKING LEVEL 4
SORRY, GUY.

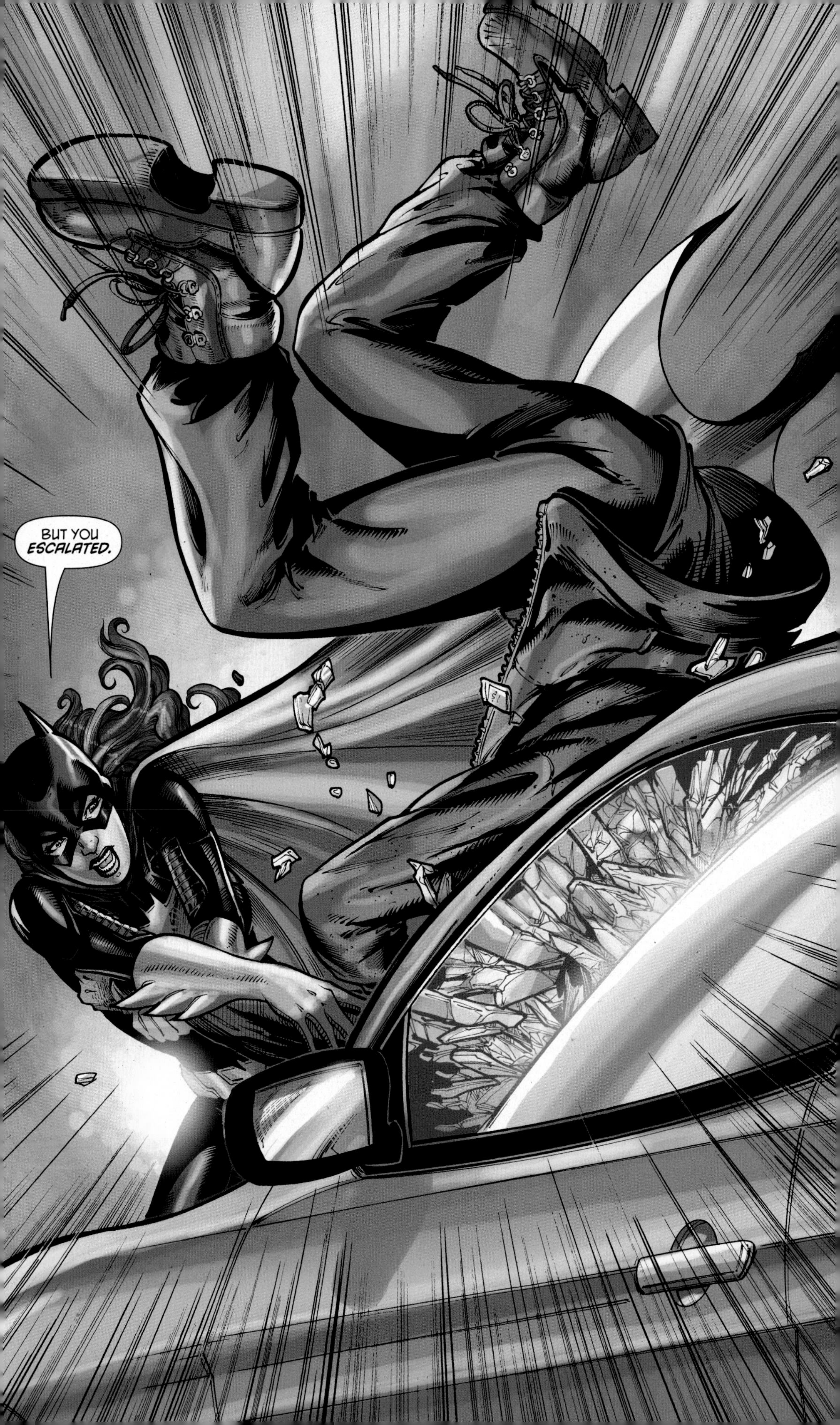
BUT YOU *ESCALATED.*

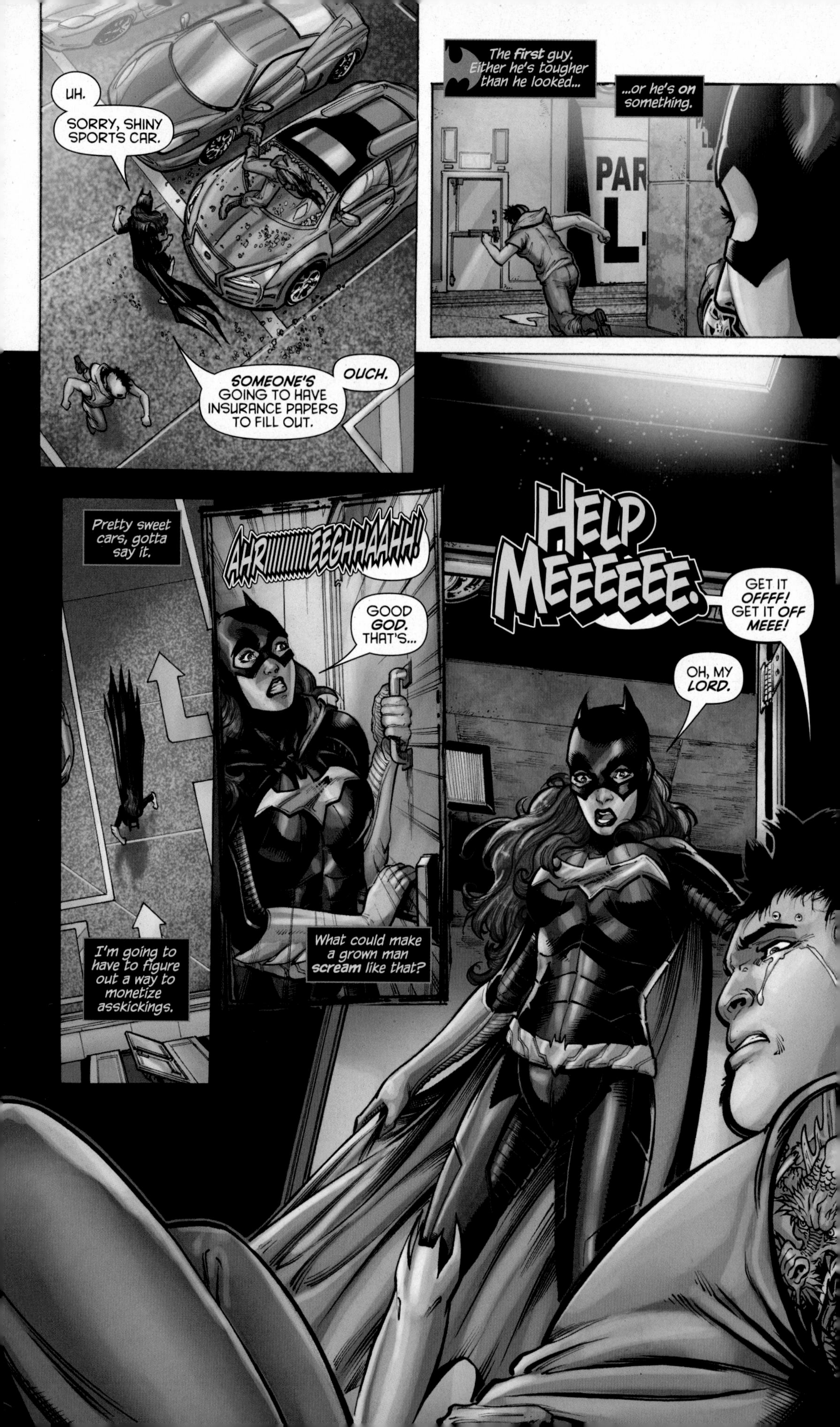

UH.
SORRY, SHINY SPORTS CAR.
SOMEONE'S GOING TO HAVE INSURANCE PAPERS TO FILL OUT.
OUCH.
The first guy. Either he's tougher than he looked...
...or he's on something.
PAR
L.
Pretty sweet cars, gotta say it.
I'm going to have to figure out a way to monetize asskickings.
AHR!!!!!!!EEGHHAAAHH!
GOOD GOD. THAT'S...
What could make a grown man scream like that?
HELP MEEEEEE.
GET IT OFFFF! GET IT OFF MEEE!
OH, MY LORD.

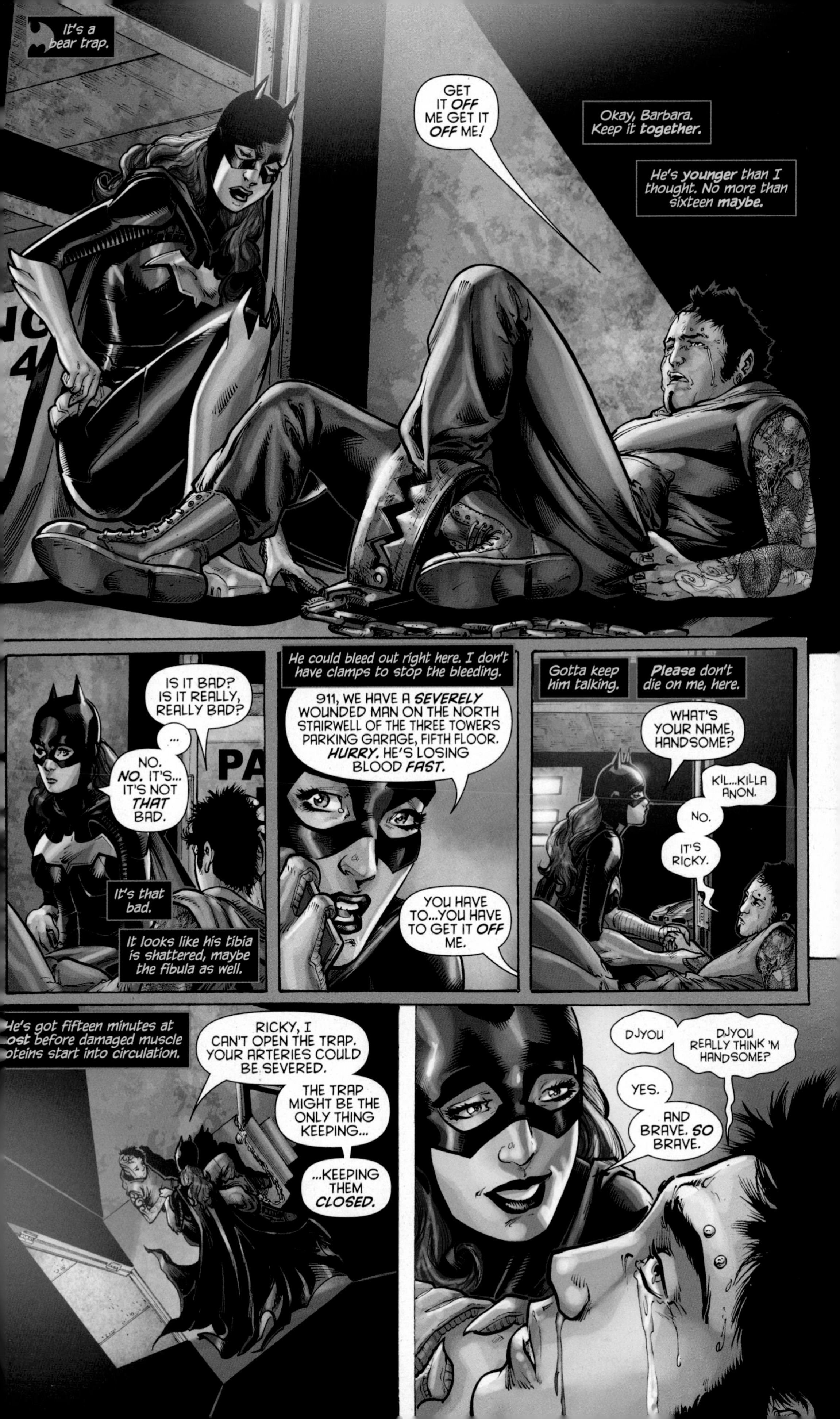
It's a bear trap.
GET IT OFF ME GET IT OFF ME!
Okay, Barbara. Keep it together.
He's younger than I thought. No more than sixteen maybe.
IS IT BAD? IS IT REALLY, REALLY BAD?
...
NO. NO. IT'S... IT'S NOT THAT BAD.
It's that bad.
It looks like his tibia is shattered, maybe the fibula as well.
He could bleed out right here. I don't have clamps to stop the bleeding.
911, WE HAVE A SEVERELY WOUNDED MAN ON THE NORTH STAIRWELL OF THE THREE TOWERS PARKING GARAGE, FIFTH FLOOR. HURRY. HE'S LOSING BLOOD FAST.
YOU HAVE TO...YOU HAVE TO GET IT OFF ME.
Gotta keep him talking.
Please don't die on me, here.
WHAT'S YOUR NAME, HANDSOME?
KIL...KILLA ANON.
NO.
IT'S RICKY.
He's got fifteen minutes at
ost before damaged muscle
oteins start into circulation.
RICKY, I CAN'T OPEN THE TRAP. YOUR ARTERIES COULD BE SEVERED.
THE TRAP MIGHT BE THE ONLY THING KEEPING...
...KEEPING THEM CLOSED.
DJYOU
DJYOU REALLY THINK 'M HANDSOME?
YES.
AND BRAVE. SO BRAVE.

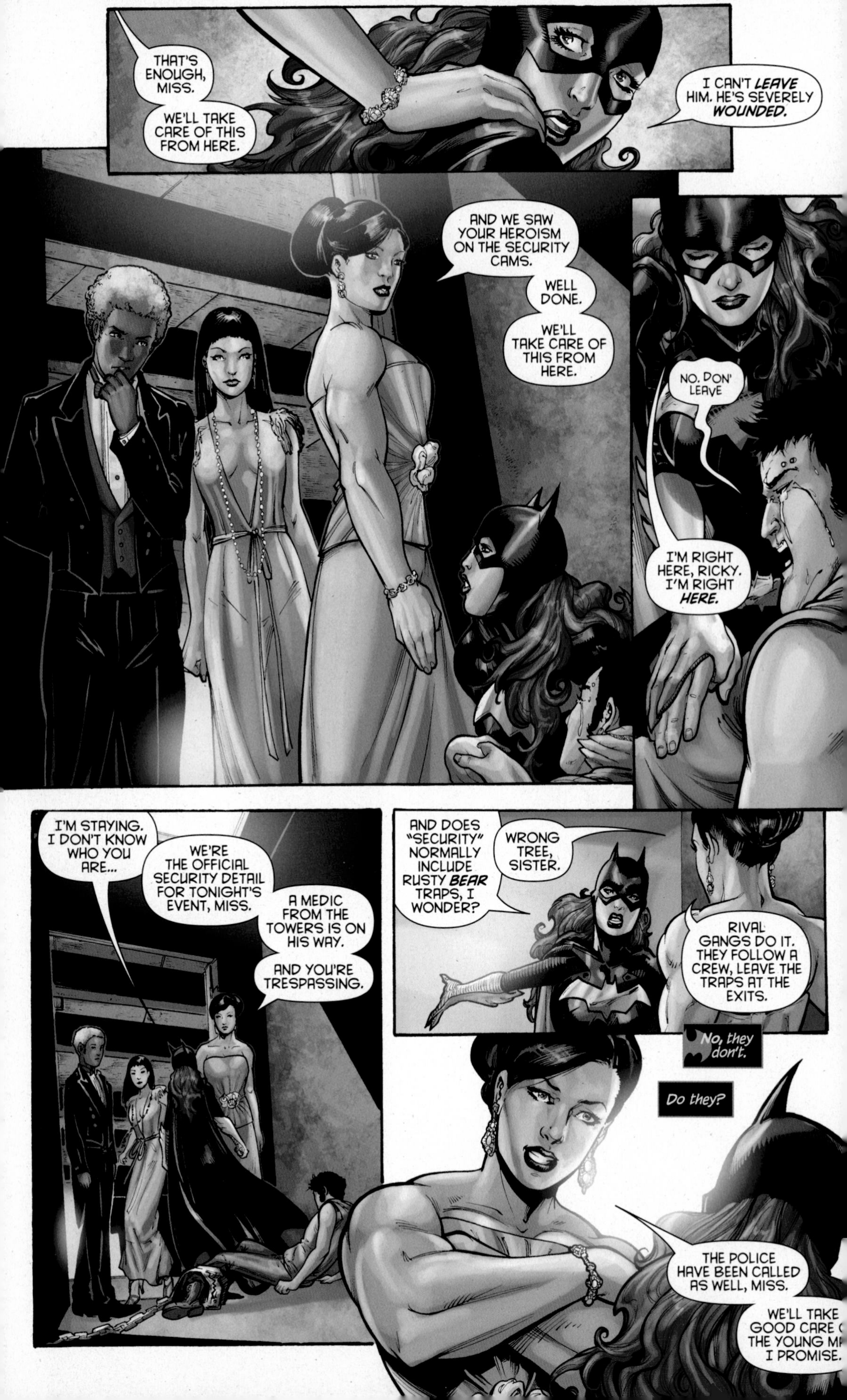
THAT'S ENOUGH, MISS.
WE'LL TAKE CARE OF THIS FROM HERE.
I CAN'T LEAVE HIM. HE'S SEVERELY WOUNDED.
AND WE SAW YOUR HEROISM ON THE SECURITY CAMS.
WELL DONE.
WE'LL TAKE CARE OF THIS FROM HERE.
NO. DON' LEAVE
I'M RIGHT HERE, RICKY. I'M RIGHT HERE.
I'M STAYING. I DON'T KNOW WHO YOU ARE...
WE'RE THE OFFICIAL SECURITY DETAIL FOR TONIGHT'S EVENT, MISS.
A MEDIC FROM THE TOWERS IS ON HIS WAY.
AND YOU'RE TRESPASSING.
AND DOES "SECURITY" NORMALLY INCLUDE RUSTY BEAR TRAPS, I WONDER?
WRONG TREE, SISTER.
RIVAL GANGS DO IT. THEY FOLLOW A CREW, LEAVE THE TRAPS AT THE EXITS.
No, they don't.
Do they?
THE POLICE HAVE BEEN CALLED AS WELL, MISS.
WE'LL TAKE GOOD CARE THE YOUNG I PROMISE.

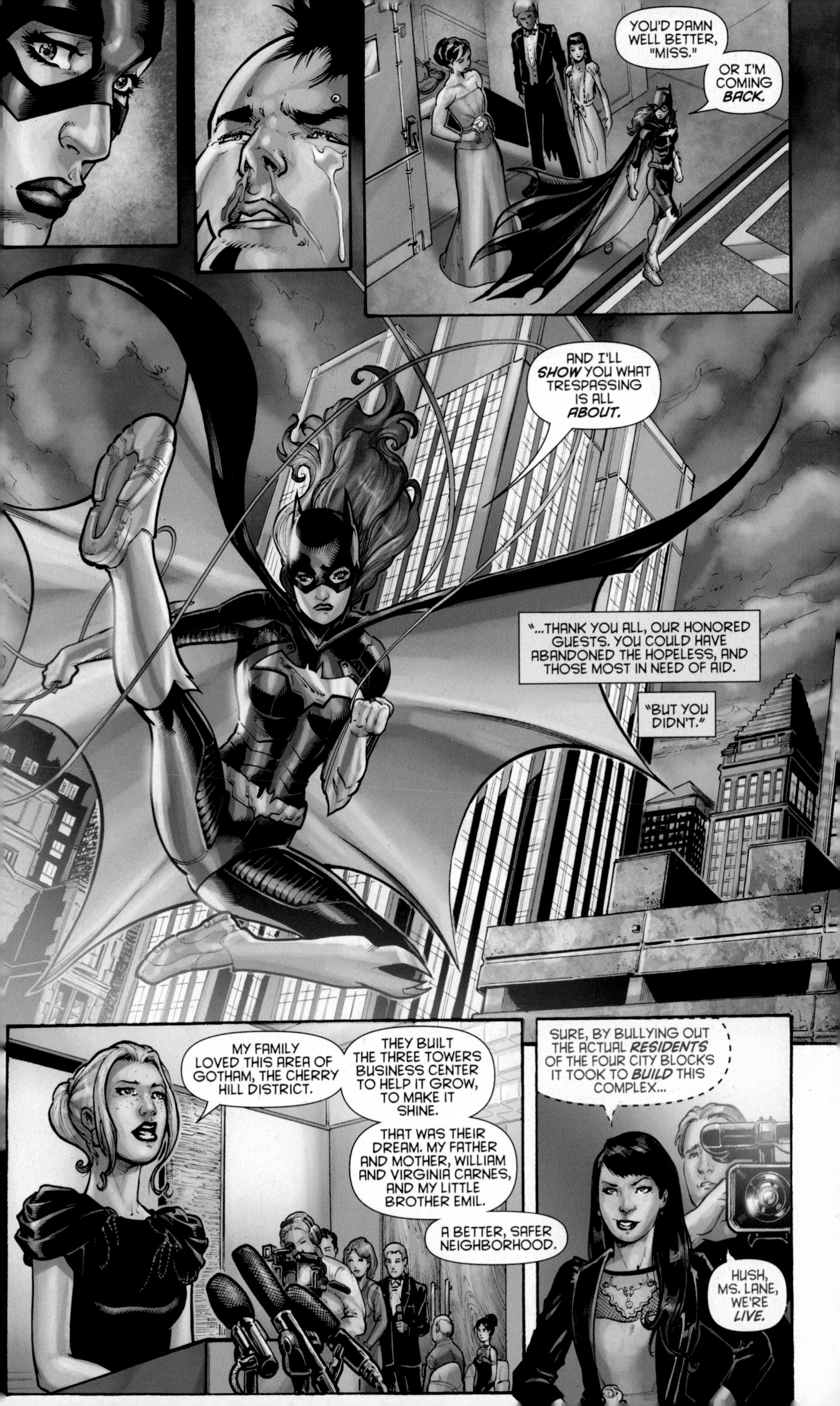
YOU'D DAMN WELL BETTER, "MISS."
OR I'M COMING BACK.
AND I'LL SHOW YOU WHAT TRESPASSING IS ALL ABOUT.
"...THANK YOU ALL, OUR HONORED GUESTS. YOU COULD HAVE ABANDONED THE HOPELESS, AND THOSE MOST IN NEED OF AID.
"BUT YOU DIDN'T."
MY FAMILY LOVED THIS AREA OF GOTHAM, THE CHERRY HILL DISTRICT.
THEY BUILT THE THREE TOWERS BUSINESS CENTER TO HELP IT GROW, TO MAKE IT SHINE.
THAT WAS THEIR DREAM. MY FATHER AND MOTHER, WILLIAM AND VIRGINIA CARNES, AND MY LITTLE BROTHER EMIL.
A BETTER, SAFER NEIGHBORHOOD.
SURE, BY BULLYING OUT THE ACTUAL RESIDENTS OF THE FOUR CITY BLOCKS IT TOOK TO BUILD THIS COMPLEX...
HUSH, MS. LANE, WE'RE LIVE.

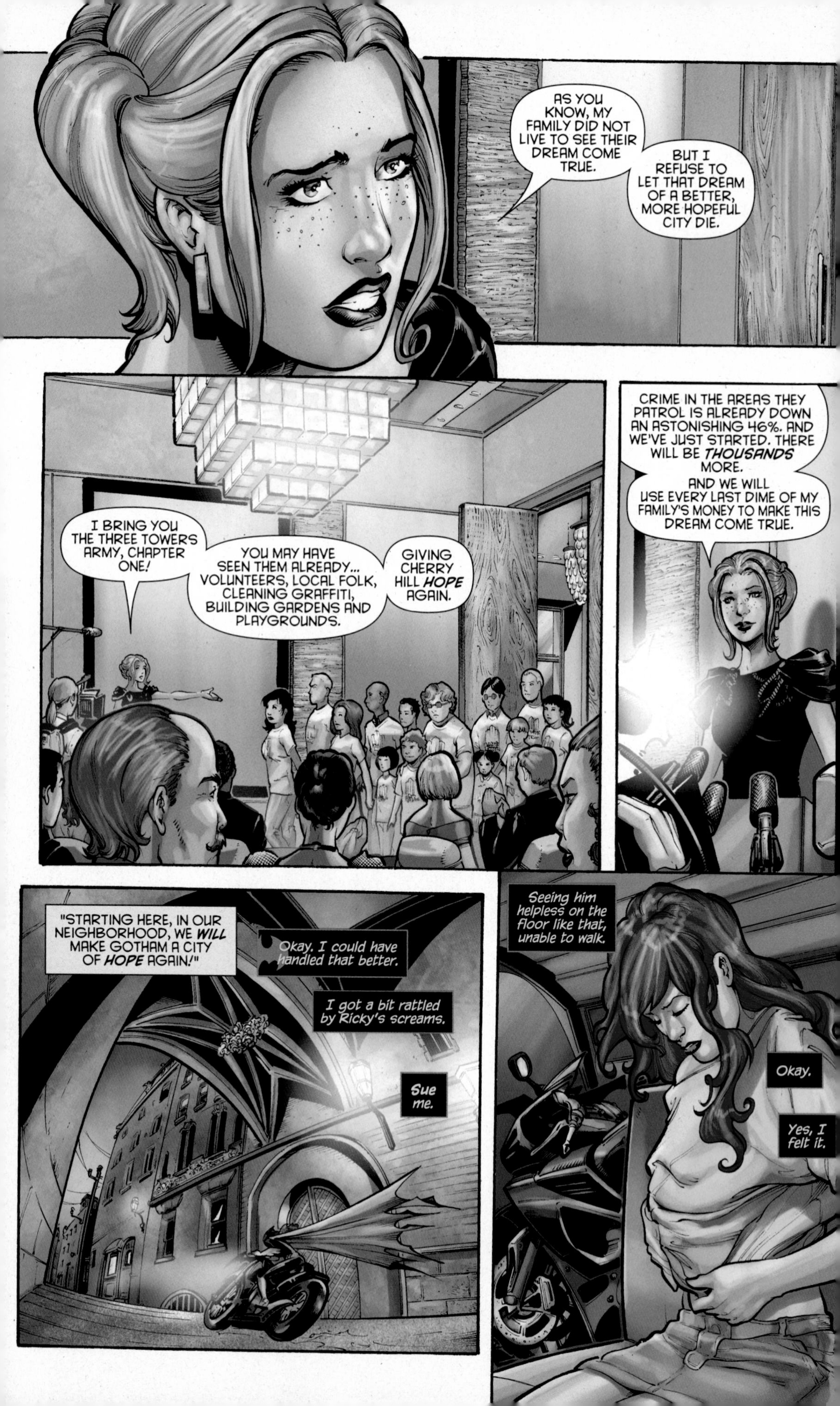
AS YOU KNOW, MY FAMILY DID NOT LIVE TO SEE THEIR DREAM COME TRUE.
BUT I REFUSE TO LET THAT DREAM OF A BETTER, MORE HOPEFUL CITY DIE.
I BRING YOU THE THREE TOWERS ARMY, CHAPTER ONE!
YOU MAY HAVE SEEN THEM ALREADY... VOLUNTEERS, LOCAL FOLK, CLEANING GRAFFITI, BUILDING GARDENS AND PLAYGROUNDS.
GIVING CHERRY HILL HOPE AGAIN.
CRIME IN THE AREAS THEY PATROL IS ALREADY DOWN AN ASTONISHING 46%. AND WE'VE JUST STARTED. THERE WILL BE THOUSANDS MORE.
AND WE WILL USE EVERY LAST DIME OF MY FAMILY'S MONEY TO MAKE THIS DREAM COME TRUE.
"STARTING HERE, IN OUR NEIGHBORHOOD, WE WILL MAKE GOTHAM A CITY OF HOPE AGAIN!"
Okay. I could have handled that better.
I got a bit rattled by Ricky's screams.
Sue me.
Seeing him helpless on the floor like that, unable to walk.
Okay.
Yes, I felt it.

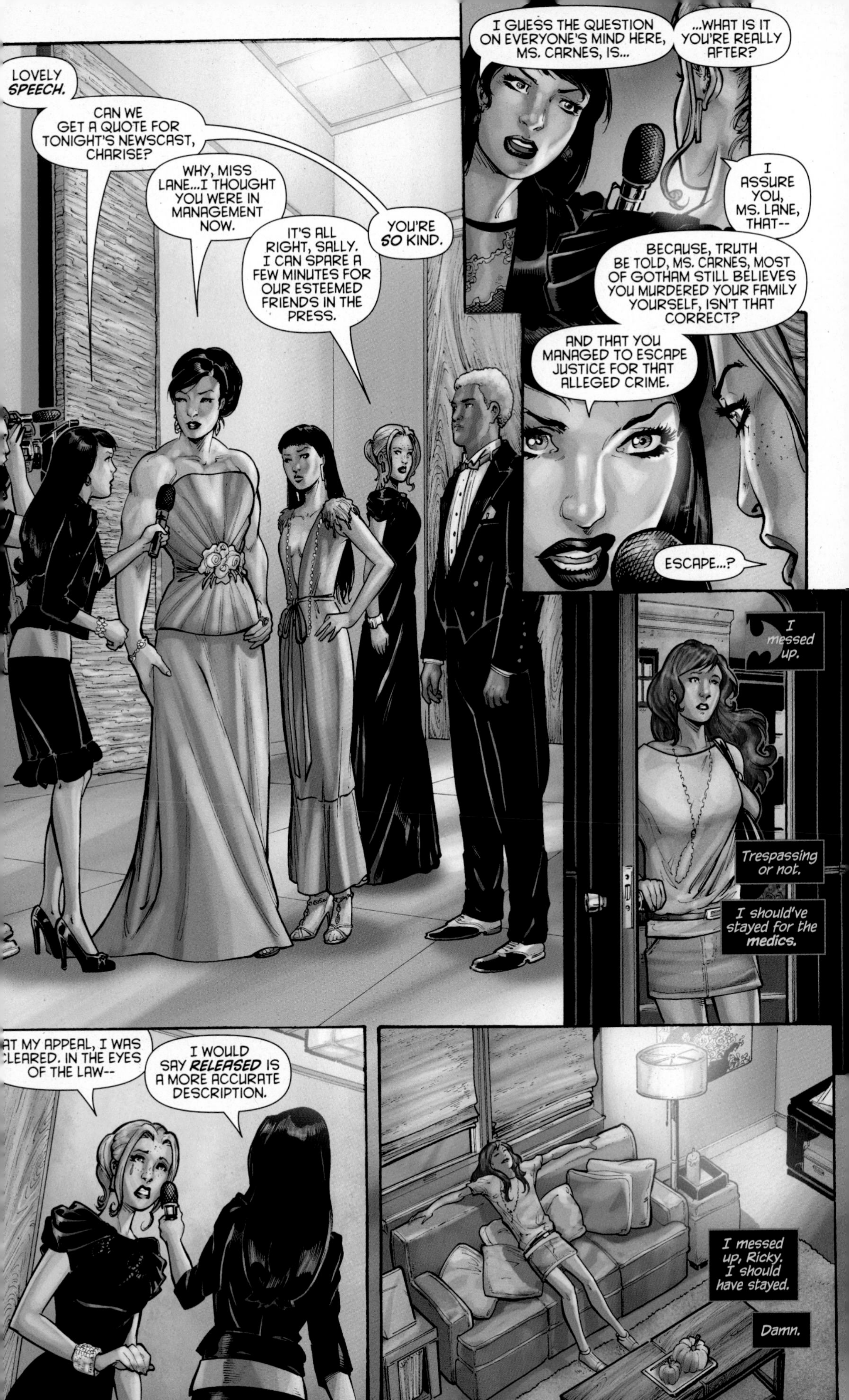
LOVELY SPEECH.
CAN WE GET A QUOTE FOR TONIGHT'S NEWSCAST, CHARISE?
WHY, MISS LANE...I THOUGHT YOU WERE IN MANAGEMENT NOW.
IT'S ALL RIGHT, SALLY. I CAN SPARE A FEW MINUTES FOR OUR ESTEEMED FRIENDS IN THE PRESS.
YOU'RE SO KIND.
I GUESS THE QUESTION ON EVERYONE'S MIND HERE, MS. CARNES, IS...
...WHAT IS IT YOU'RE REALLY AFTER?
I ASSURE YOU, MS. LANE, THAT--
BECAUSE, TRUTH BE TOLD, MS. CARNES, MOST OF GOTHAM STILL BELIEVES YOU MURDERED YOUR FAMILY YOURSELF, ISN'T THAT CORRECT?
AND THAT YOU MANAGED TO ESCAPE JUSTICE FOR THAT ALLEGED CRIME.
ESCAPE...?
I messed up.
Trespassing or not.
I should've stayed for the medics.
AT MY APPEAL, I WAS CLEARED. IN THE EYES OF THE LAW--
I WOULD SAY RELEASED IS A MORE ACCURATE DESCRIPTION.
I messed up, Ricky. I should have stayed.
Damn.

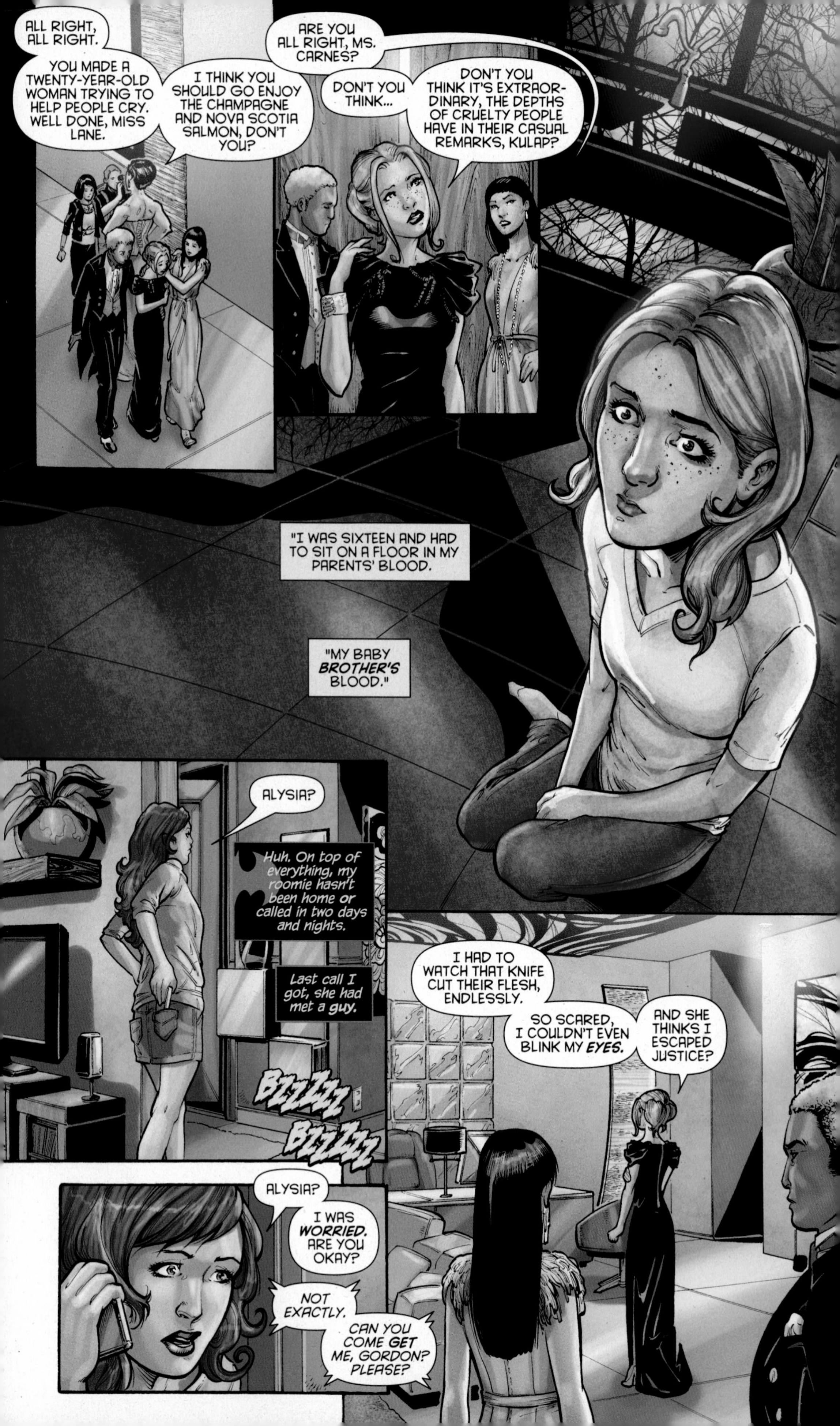
ALL RIGHT, ALL RIGHT.
YOU MADE A TWENTY-YEAR-OLD WOMAN TRYING TO HELP PEOPLE CRY. WELL DONE, MISS LANE.
I THINK YOU SHOULD GO ENJOY THE CHAMPAGNE AND NOVA SCOTIA SALMON, DON'T YOU?
ARE YOU ALL RIGHT, MS. CARNES?
DON'T YOU THINK...
DON'T YOU THINK IT'S EXTRAORDINARY, THE DEPTHS OF CRUELTY PEOPLE HAVE IN THEIR CASUAL REMARKS, KULAP?
"I WAS SIXTEEN AND HAD TO SIT ON A FLOOR IN MY PARENTS' BLOOD.
"MY BABY ***BROTHER'S*** BLOOD."
ALYSIA?
*Huh. On top of everything, my roomie hasn't been home **or** called in two days and nights.*
*Last call I got, she had met a **guy**.*
BZZZZZ
BZZZZZ
I HAD TO WATCH THAT KNIFE CUT THEIR FLESH, ENDLESSLY.
SO SCARED, I COULDN'T EVEN BLINK MY ***EYES.***
AND SHE THINKS I ESCAPED JUSTICE?
ALYSIA?
I WAS ***WORRIED.*** ARE YOU OKAY?
NOT EXACTLY.
*CAN YOU COME **GET** ME, GORDON? PLEASE?*

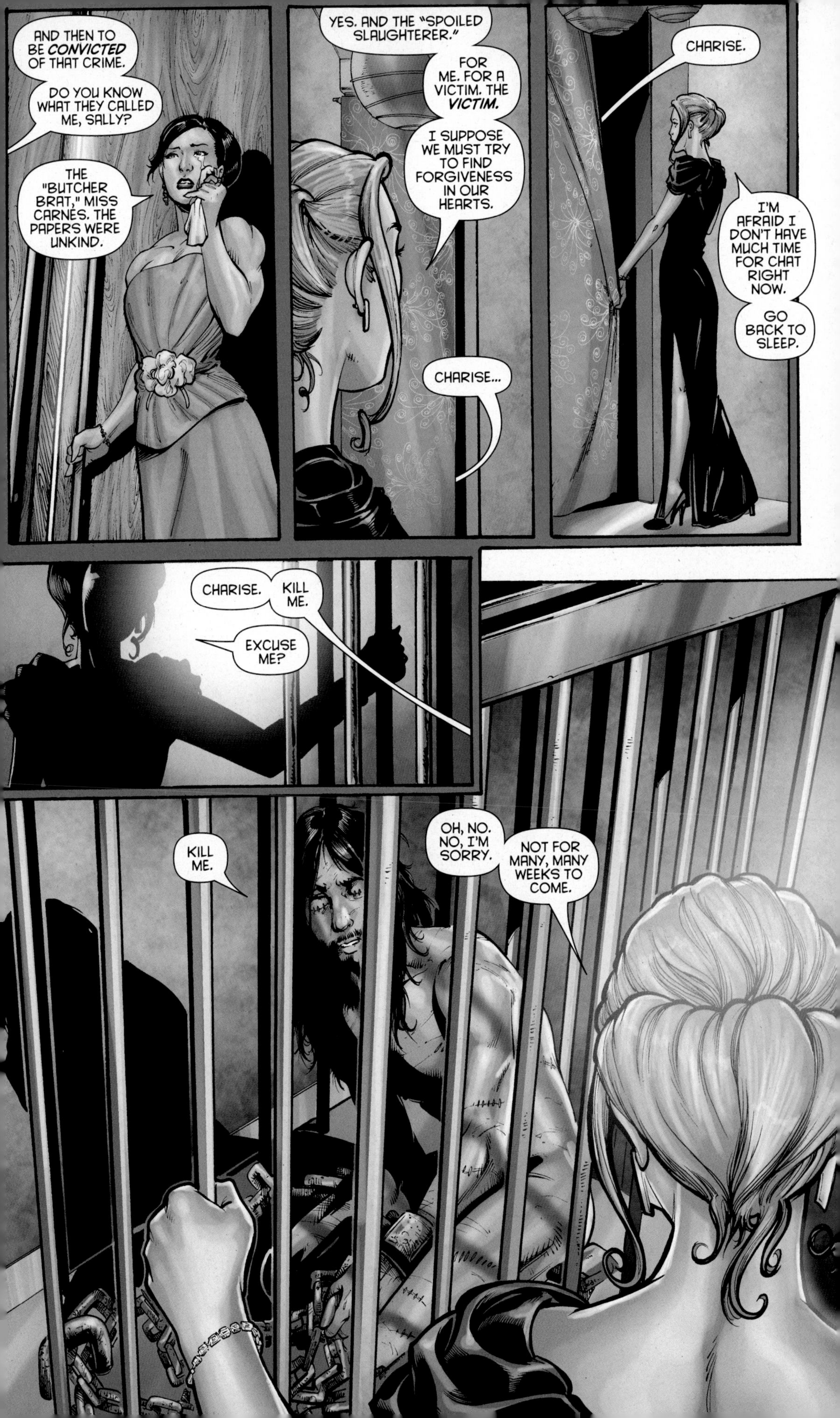
AND THEN TO BE *CONVICTED* OF THAT CRIME.
DO YOU KNOW WHAT THEY CALLED ME, SALLY?
THE "BUTCHER BRAT," MISS CARNES. THE PAPERS WERE UNKIND.
YES. AND THE "SPOILED SLAUGHTERER."
FOR ME. FOR A VICTIM. THE *VICTIM.*
I SUPPOSE WE MUST TRY TO FIND FORGIVENESS IN OUR HEARTS.
CHARISE...
CHARISE.
I'M AFRAID I DON'T HAVE MUCH TIME FOR CHAT RIGHT NOW.
GO BACK TO SLEEP.
CHARISE.
KILL ME.
EXCUSE ME?
KILL ME.
OH, NO. NO, I'M SORRY.
NOT FOR MANY, MANY WEEKS TO COME.

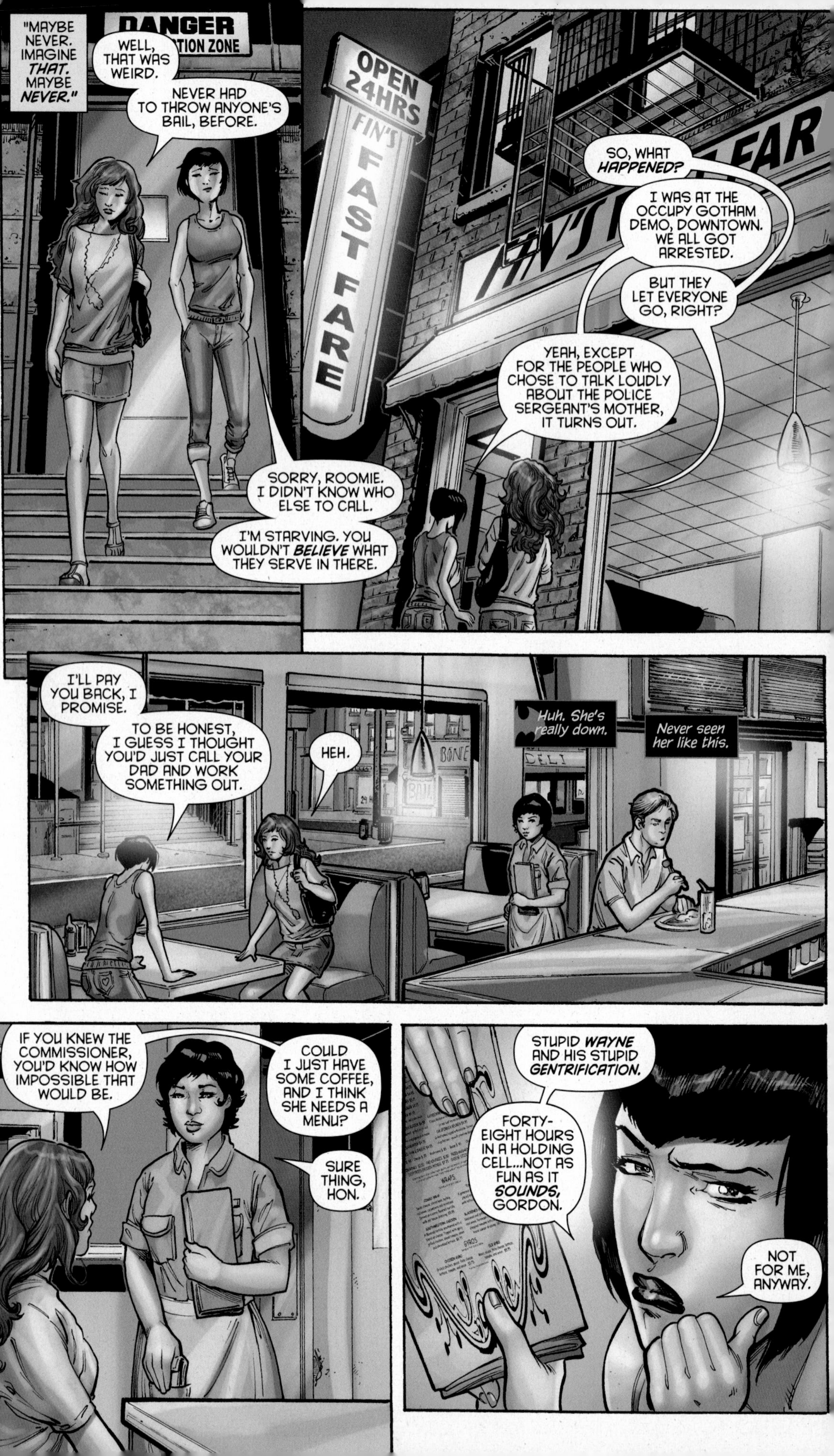

"MAYBE NEVER. IMAGINE *THAT.* MAYBE *NEVER.*"
DANGER
TION ZONE
WELL, THAT WAS WEIRD.
NEVER HAD TO THROW ANYONE'S BAIL, BEFORE.
SORRY, ROOMIE. I DIDN'T KNOW WHO ELSE TO CALL.
I'M STARVING. YOU WOULDN'T *BELIEVE* WHAT THEY SERVE IN THERE.
OPEN 24HRS
FIN'S FAST FARE
SO, WHAT *HAPPENED?*
I WAS AT THE OCCUPY GOTHAM DEMO, DOWNTOWN. WE ALL GOT ARRESTED.
BUT THEY LET EVERYONE GO, RIGHT?
YEAH, EXCEPT FOR THE PEOPLE WHO CHOSE TO TALK LOUDLY ABOUT THE POLICE SERGEANT'S MOTHER, IT TURNS OUT.
I'LL PAY YOU BACK, I PROMISE.
TO BE HONEST, I GUESS I THOUGHT YOU'D JUST CALL YOUR DAD AND WORK SOMETHING OUT.
HEH.
Huh. She's really down.
Never seen her like this.
IF YOU KNEW THE COMMISSIONER, YOU'D KNOW HOW IMPOSSIBLE THAT WOULD BE.
COULD I JUST HAVE SOME COFFEE, AND I THINK SHE NEEDS A MENU?
SURE THING, HON.
STUPID *WAYNE* AND HIS STUPID *GENTRIFICATION.*
FORTY-EIGHT HOURS IN A HOLDING CELL...NOT AS FUN AS IT *SOUNDS,* GORDON.
NOT FOR ME, ANYWAY.

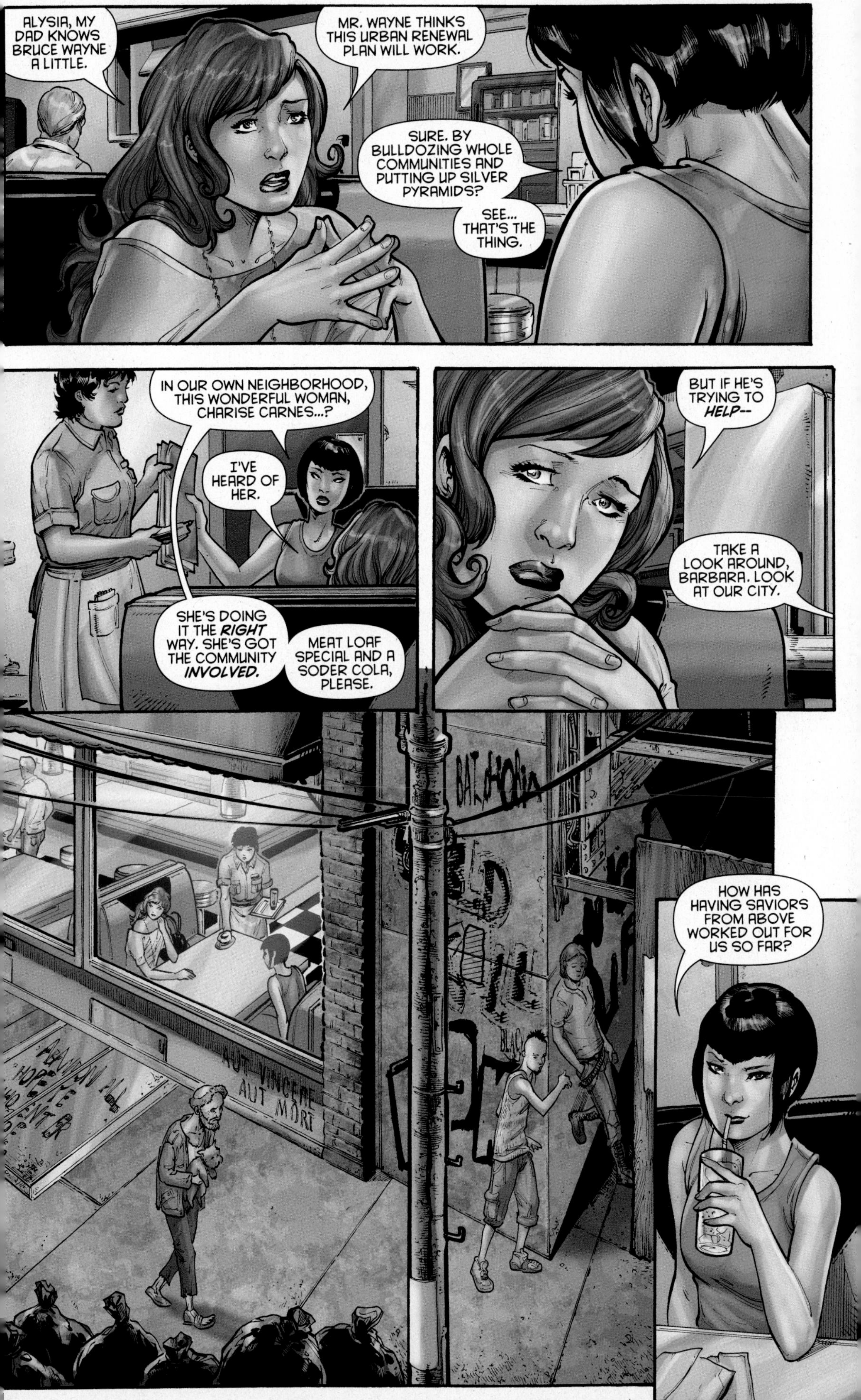
ALYSIA, MY DAD KNOWS BRUCE WAYNE A LITTLE.
MR. WAYNE THINKS THIS URBAN RENEWAL PLAN WILL WORK.
SURE. BY BULLDOZING WHOLE COMMUNITIES AND PUTTING UP SILVER PYRAMIDS?
SEE... THAT'S THE THING.
IN OUR OWN NEIGHBORHOOD, THIS WONDERFUL WOMAN, CHARISE CARNES...?
I'VE HEARD OF HER.
SHE'S DOING IT THE RIGHT WAY. SHE'S GOT THE COMMUNITY INVOLVED.
MEAT LOAF SPECIAL AND A SODER COLA, PLEASE.
BUT IF HE'S TRYING TO HELP--
TAKE A LOOK AROUND, BARBARA. LOOK AT OUR CITY.
AUT VINCERE AUT MORI
HOW HAS HAVING SAVIORS FROM ABOVE WORKED OUT FOR US SO FAR?

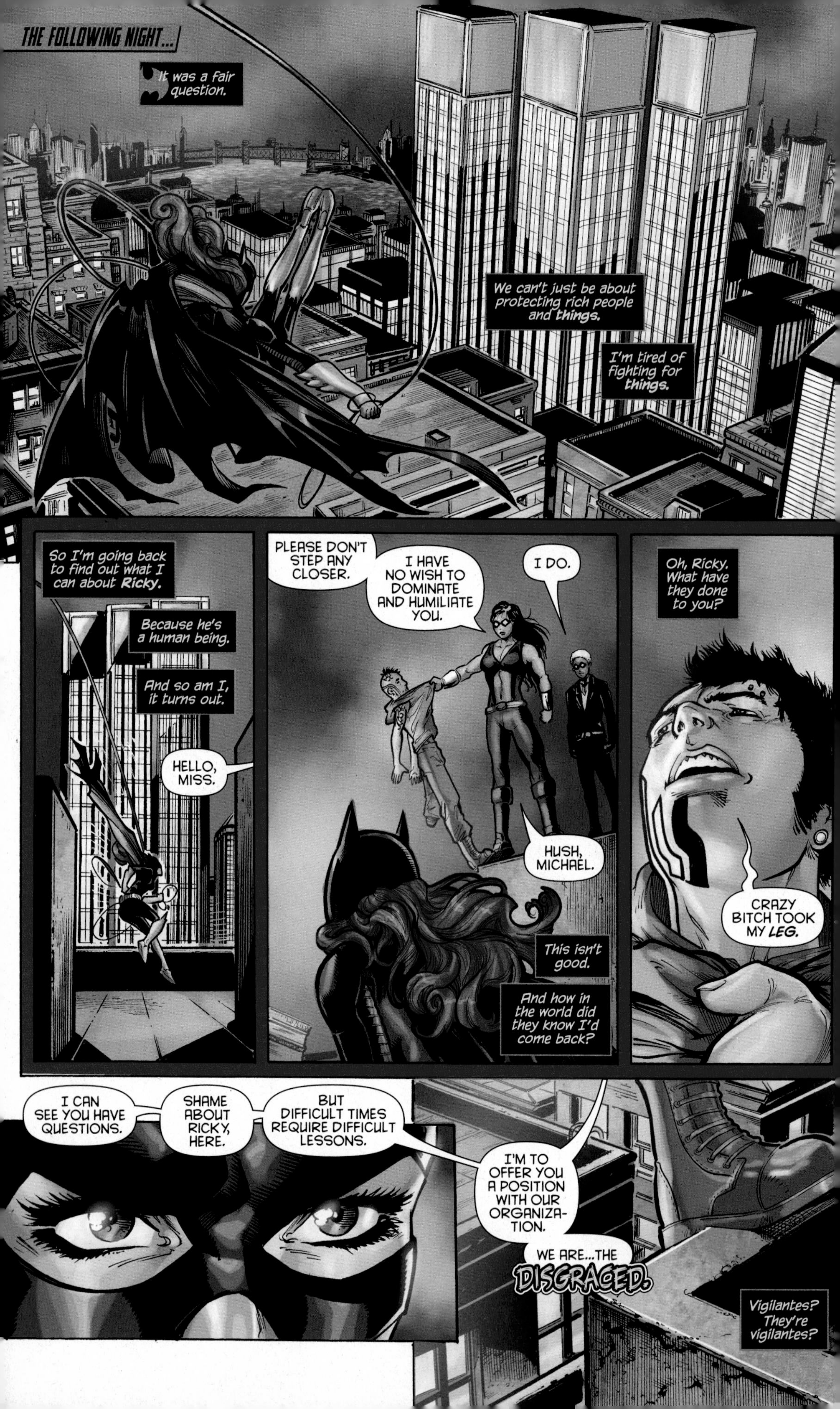

THE FOLLOWING NIGHT...
It was a fair question.
We can't just be about protecting rich people and *things.*
I'm tired of fighting for *things.*
So I'm going back to find out what I can about *Ricky.*
Because he's a human being.
And so am I, it turns out.
HELLO, MISS.
PLEASE DON'T STEP ANY CLOSER.
I HAVE NO WISH TO DOMINATE AND HUMILIATE YOU.
I DO.
HUSH, MICHAEL.
This isn't good.
And how in the world did they know I'd come back?
Oh, Ricky. What have they done to you?
CRAZY BITCH TOOK MY *LEG.*
I CAN SEE YOU HAVE QUESTIONS.
SHAME ABOUT RICKY, HERE.
BUT DIFFICULT TIMES REQUIRE DIFFICULT LESSONS.
I'M TO OFFER YOU A POSITION WITH OUR ORGANIZA-TION.
WE ARE...THE DISGRACED.
Vigilantes? They're vigilantes?

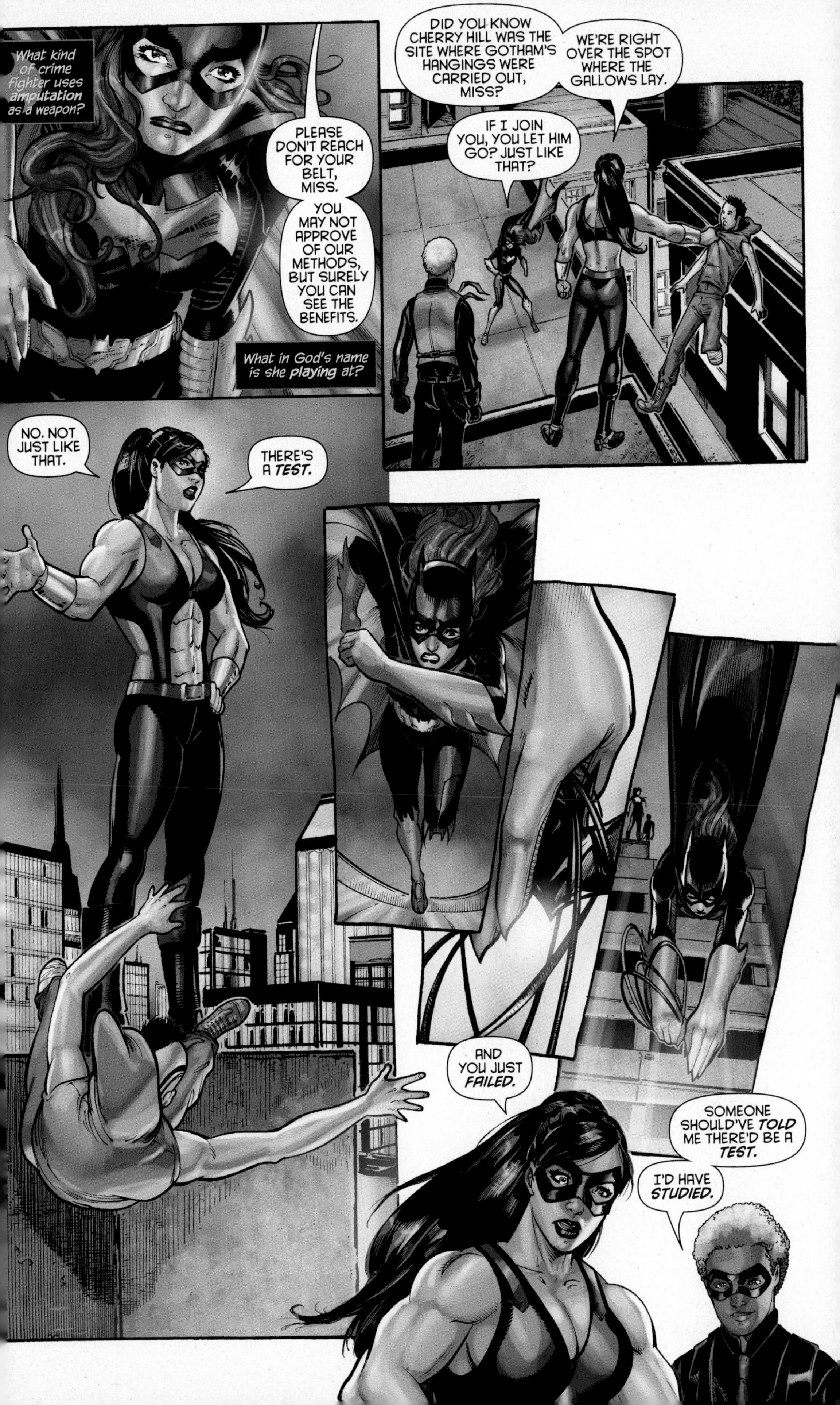
What kind of crime fighter uses amputation as a weapon?
PLEASE DON'T REACH FOR YOUR BELT, MISS.
YOU MAY NOT APPROVE OF OUR METHODS, BUT SURELY YOU CAN SEE THE BENEFITS.
What in God's name is she playing at?
DID YOU KNOW CHERRY HILL WAS THE SITE WHERE GOTHAM'S HANGINGS WERE CARRIED OUT, MISS?
WE'RE RIGHT OVER THE SPOT WHERE THE GALLOWS LAY.
IF I JOIN YOU, YOU LET HIM GO? JUST LIKE THAT?
NO. NOT JUST LIKE THAT.
THERE'S A TEST.
AND YOU JUST FAILED.
SOMEONE SHOULD'VE TOLD ME THERE'D BE A TEST.
I'D HAVE STUDIED.

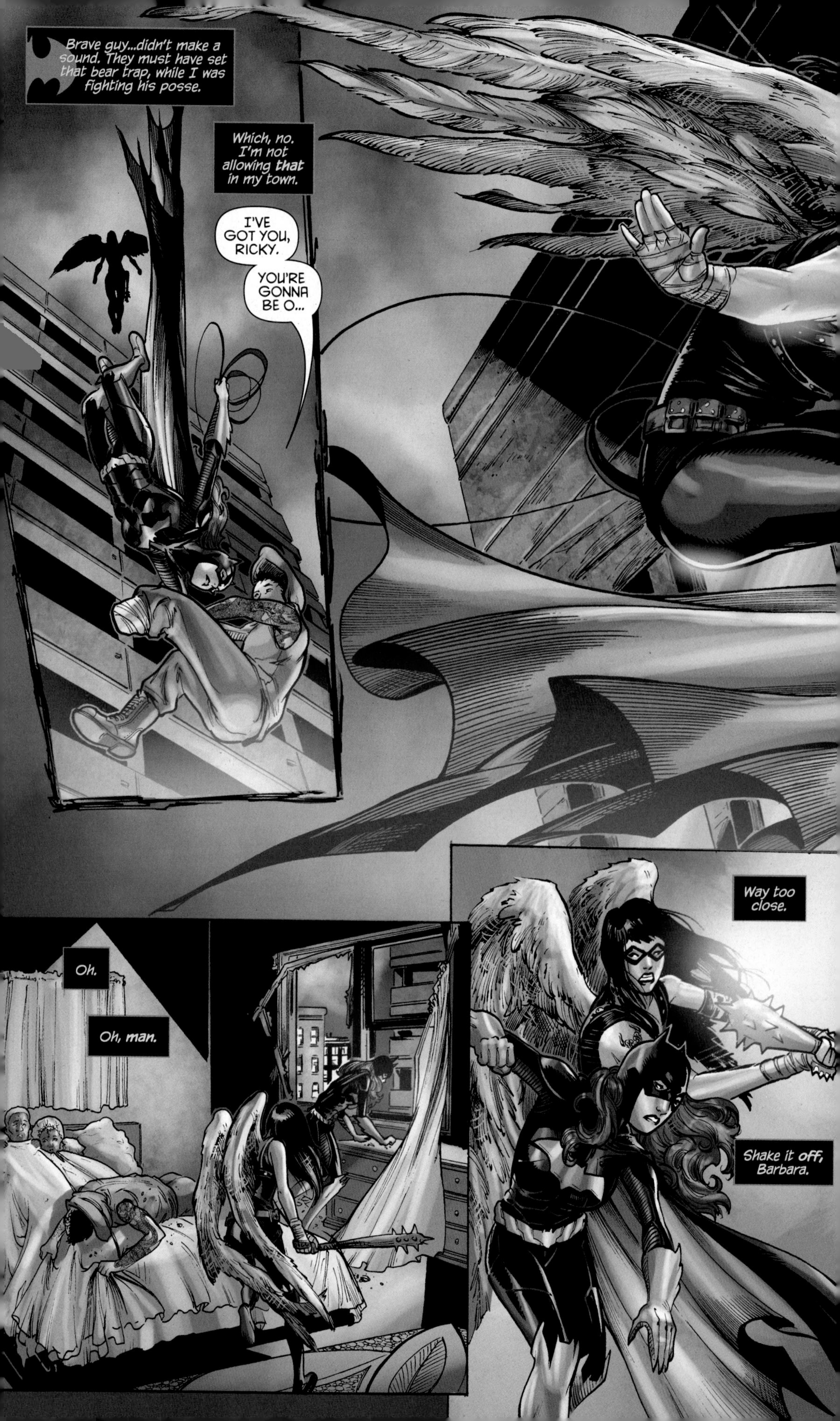
Brave guy...didn't make a sound. They must have set that bear trap, while I was fighting his posse.
Which, no. I'm not allowing **that** in my town.
I'VE GOT YOU, RICKY.
YOU'RE GONNA BE O...
Oh.
Oh, **man**.
Way too close.
Shake it **off**, Barbara.

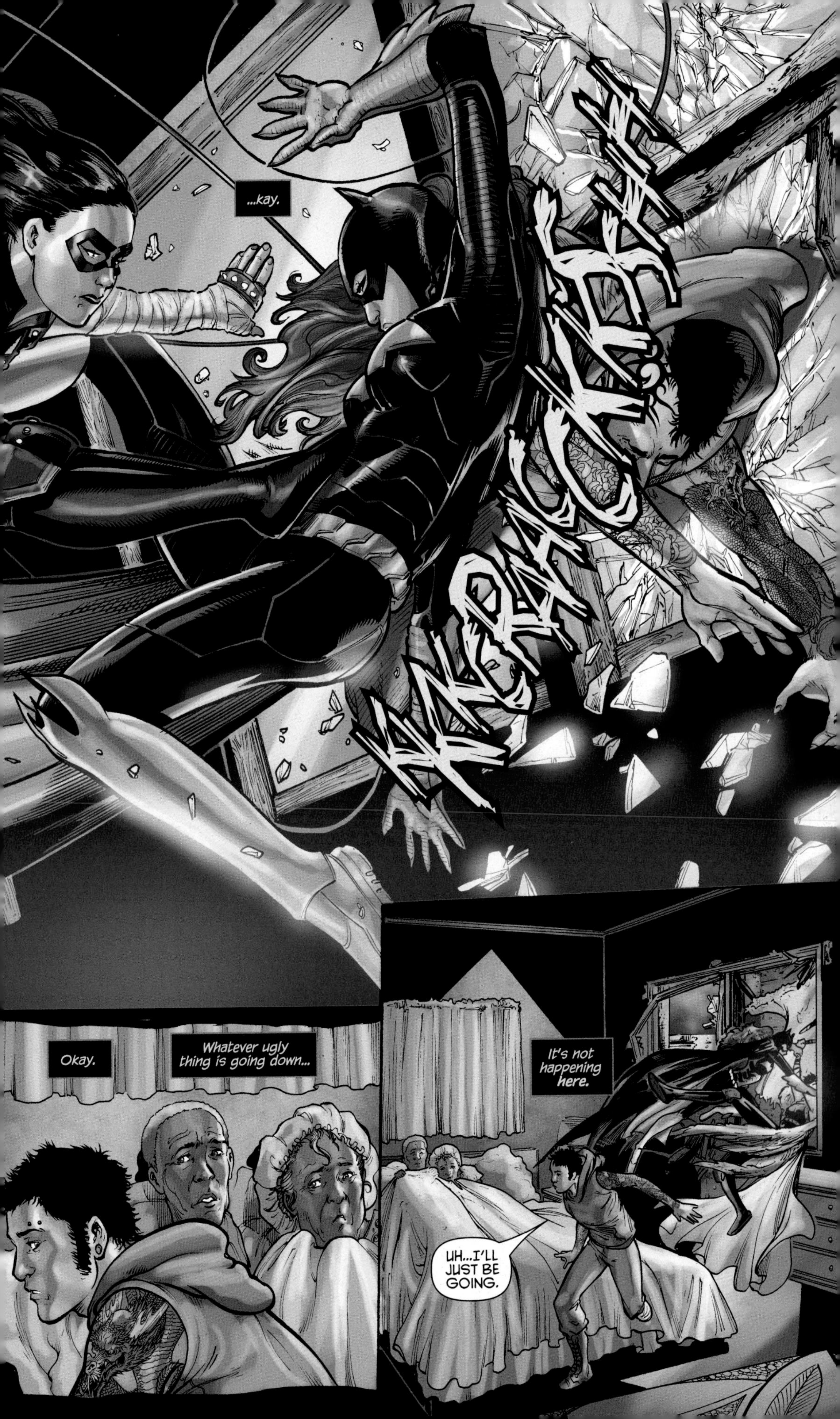
...kay.
KRAKASH
Okay.
Whatever ugly thing is going down...
It's not happening here.
UH...I'LL JUST BE GOING.

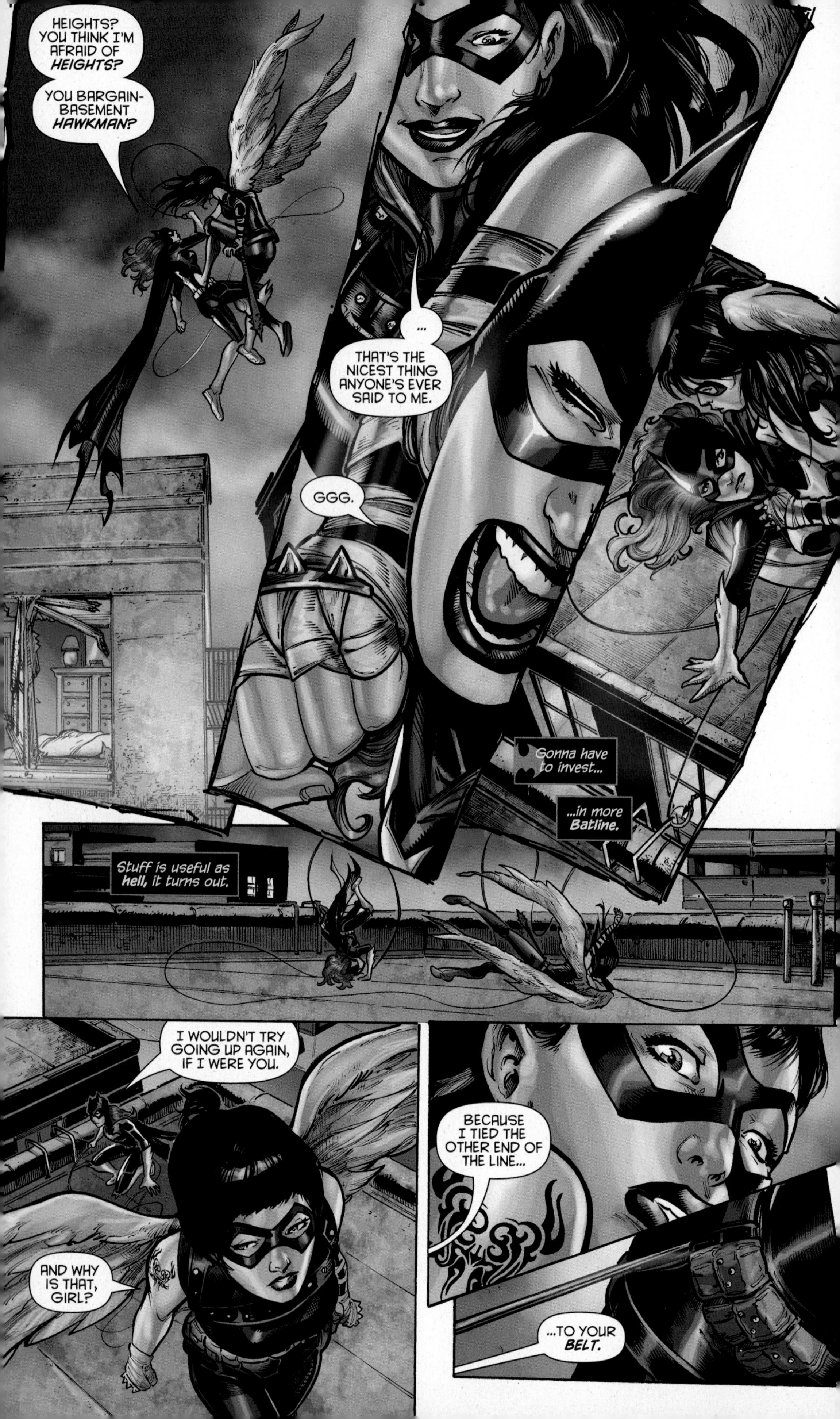
HEIGHTS? YOU THINK I'M AFRAID OF *HEIGHTS?*
YOU BARGAIN-BASEMENT *HAWKMAN?*
...
THAT'S THE NICEST THING ANYONE'S EVER SAID TO ME.
GGG.
Gonna have to invest...
...in more ***Batline.***
Stuff is useful as ***hell,*** *it turns out.*
I WOULDN'T TRY GOING UP AGAIN, IF I WERE YOU.
AND WHY IS THAT, GIRL?
BECAUSE I TIED THE OTHER END OF THE LINE...
...TO YOUR ***BELT.***

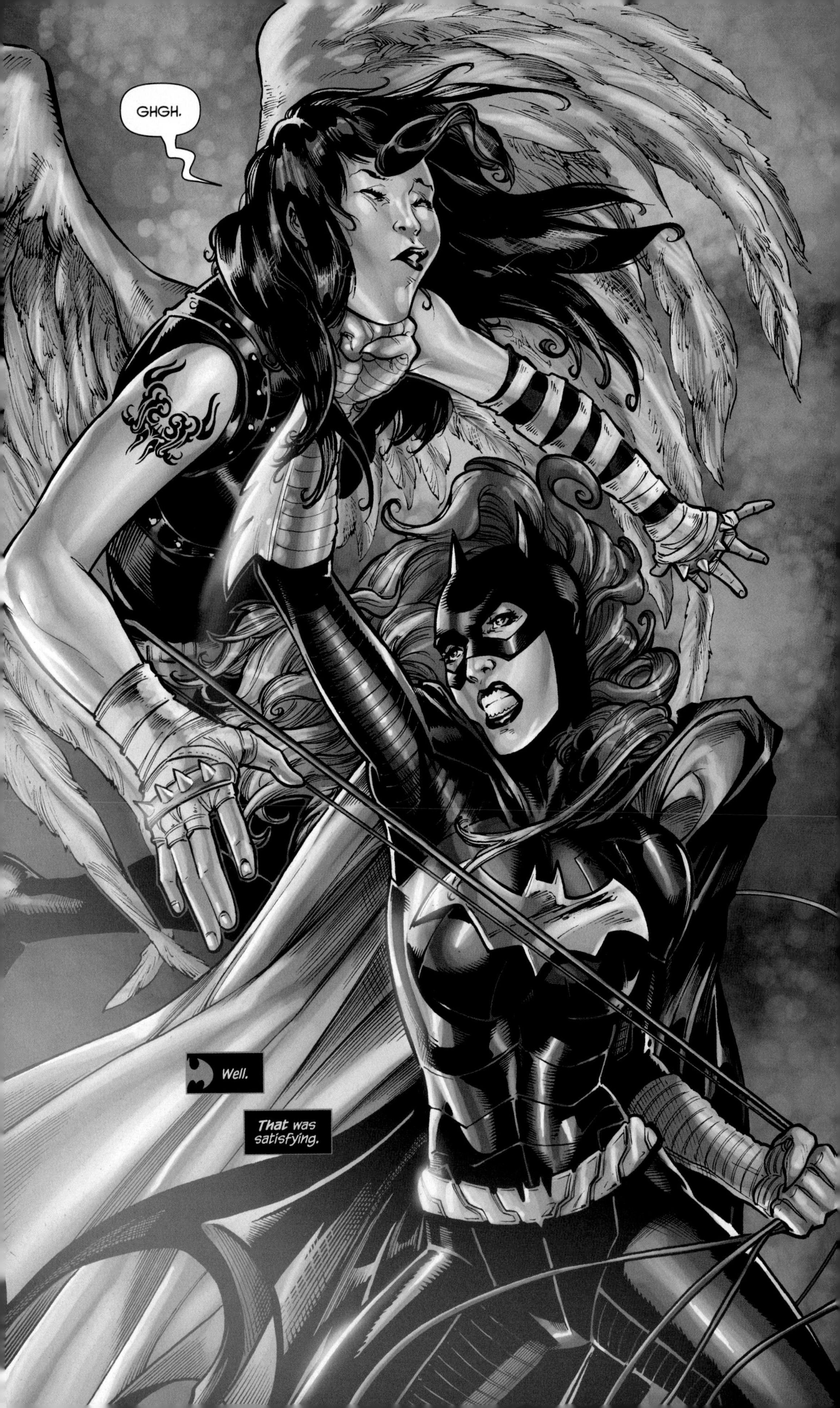
GHGH.
Well.
That was satisfying.

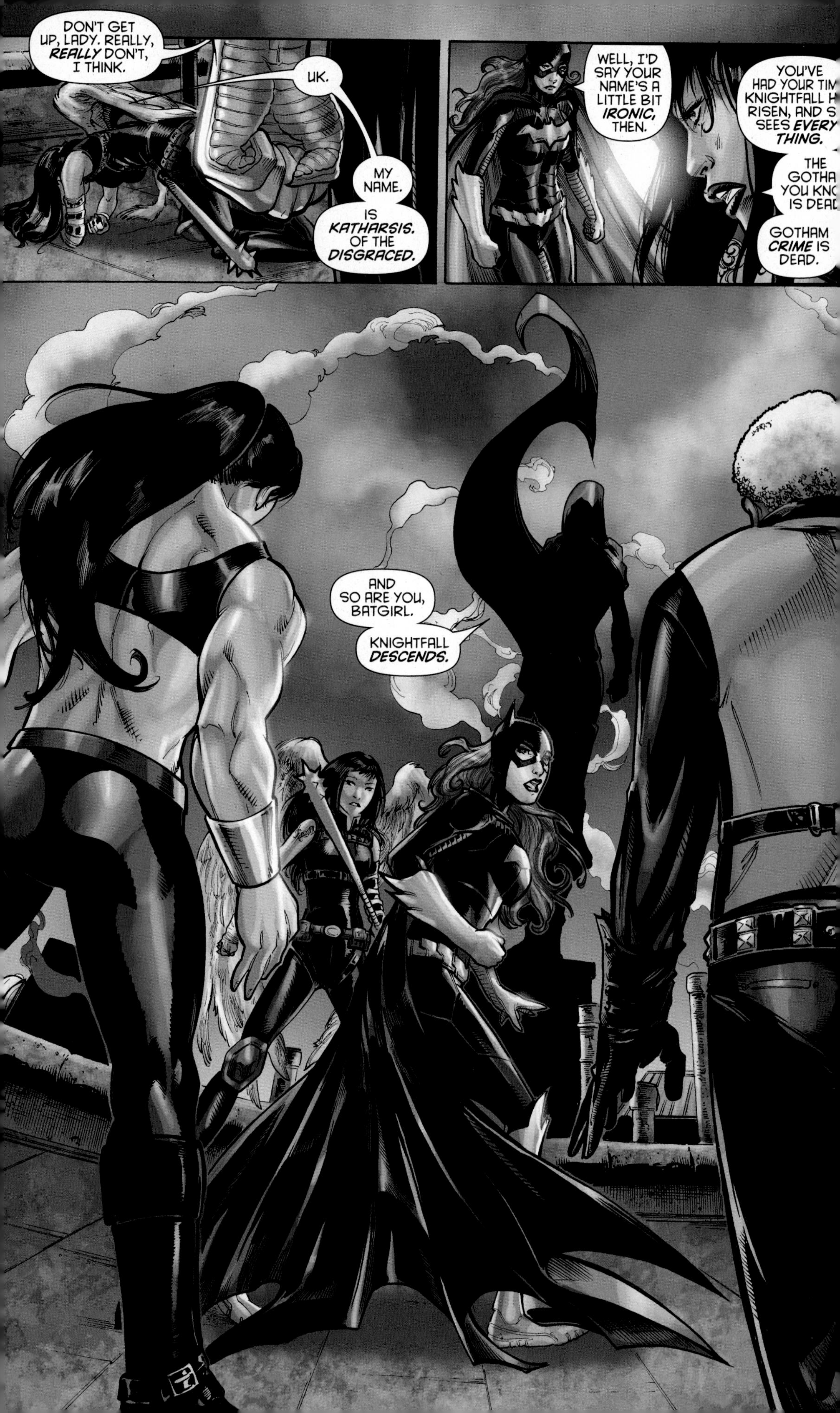
DON'T GET UP, LADY. REALLY, *REALLY* DON'T, I THINK.
UK.
MY NAME.
IS *KATHARSIS.* OF THE *DISGRACED.*
WELL, I'D SAY YOUR NAME'S A LITTLE BIT *IRONIC,* THEN.
YOU'VE HAD YOUR TIM KNIGHTFALL H RISEN, AND S SEES *EVERY THING.*
THE GOTHA YOU KNO IS DEAD
GOTHAM *CRIME* IS DEAD.
AND SO ARE YOU, BATGIRL.
KNIGHTFALL *DESCENDS.*

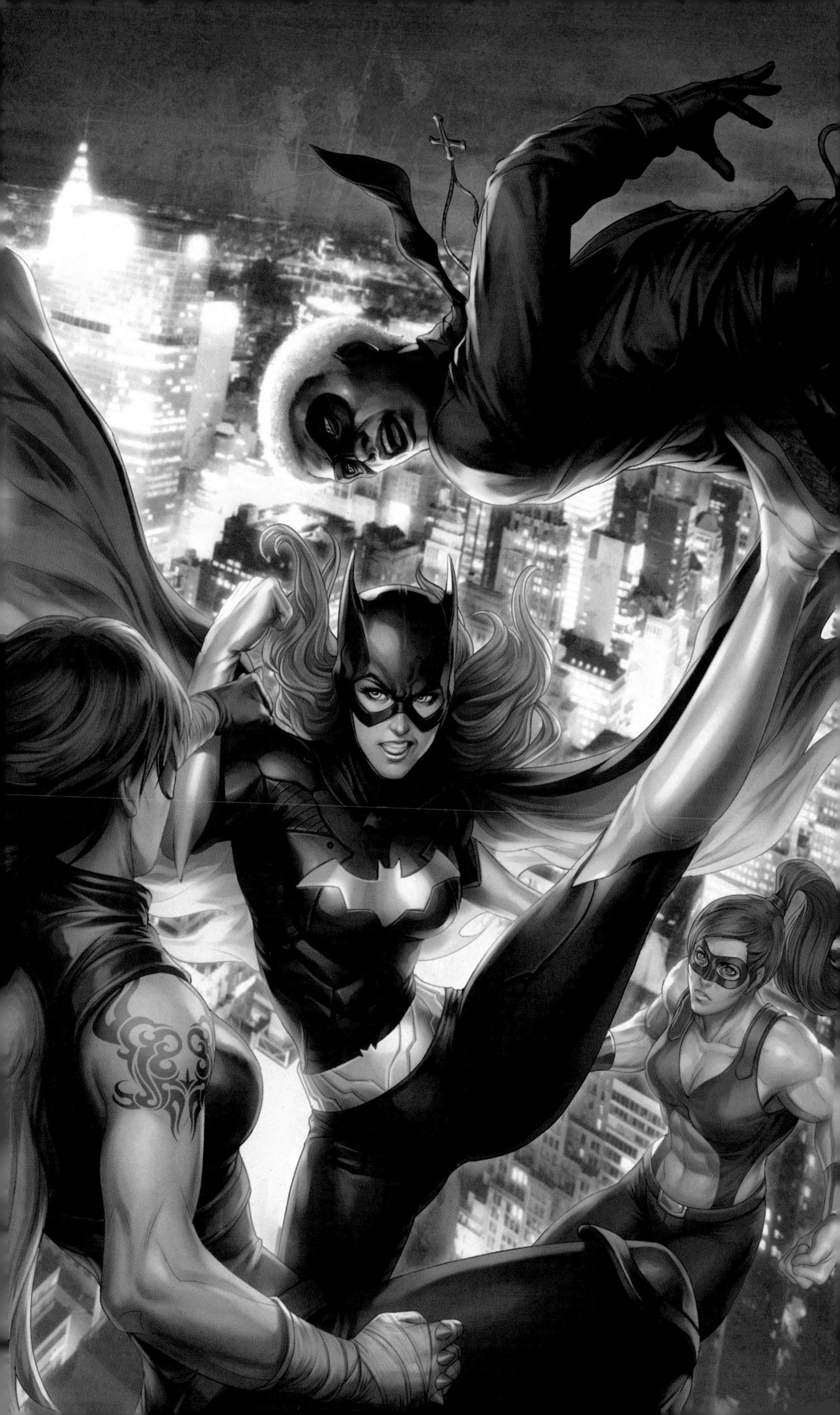

HEART OF COLD STEEL

GAIL SIMONE writer **ARDIAN SYAF** penciller **VICENTE CIFUENTES** inker cover by STANLEY "ARTGERM" LAU

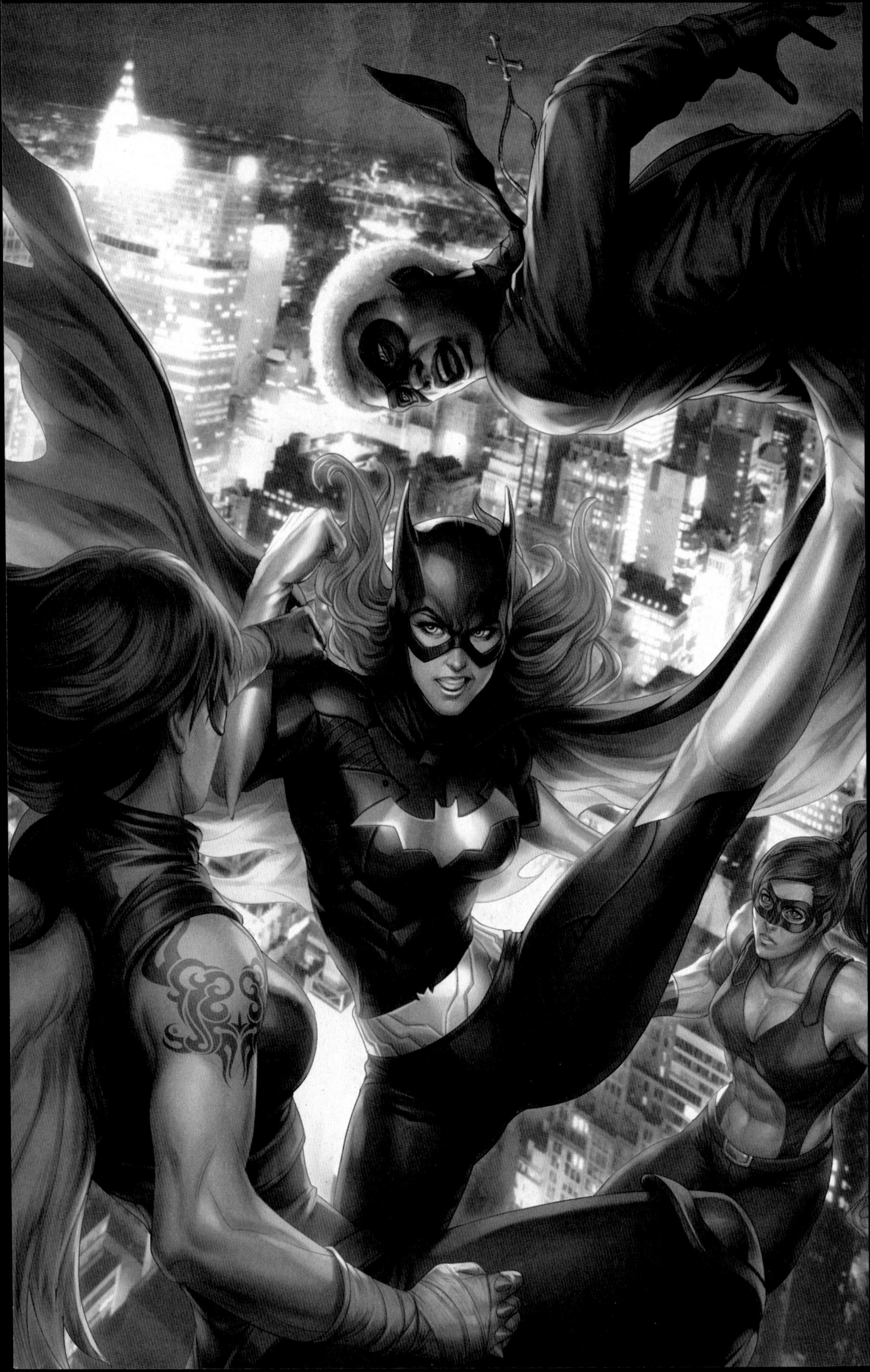

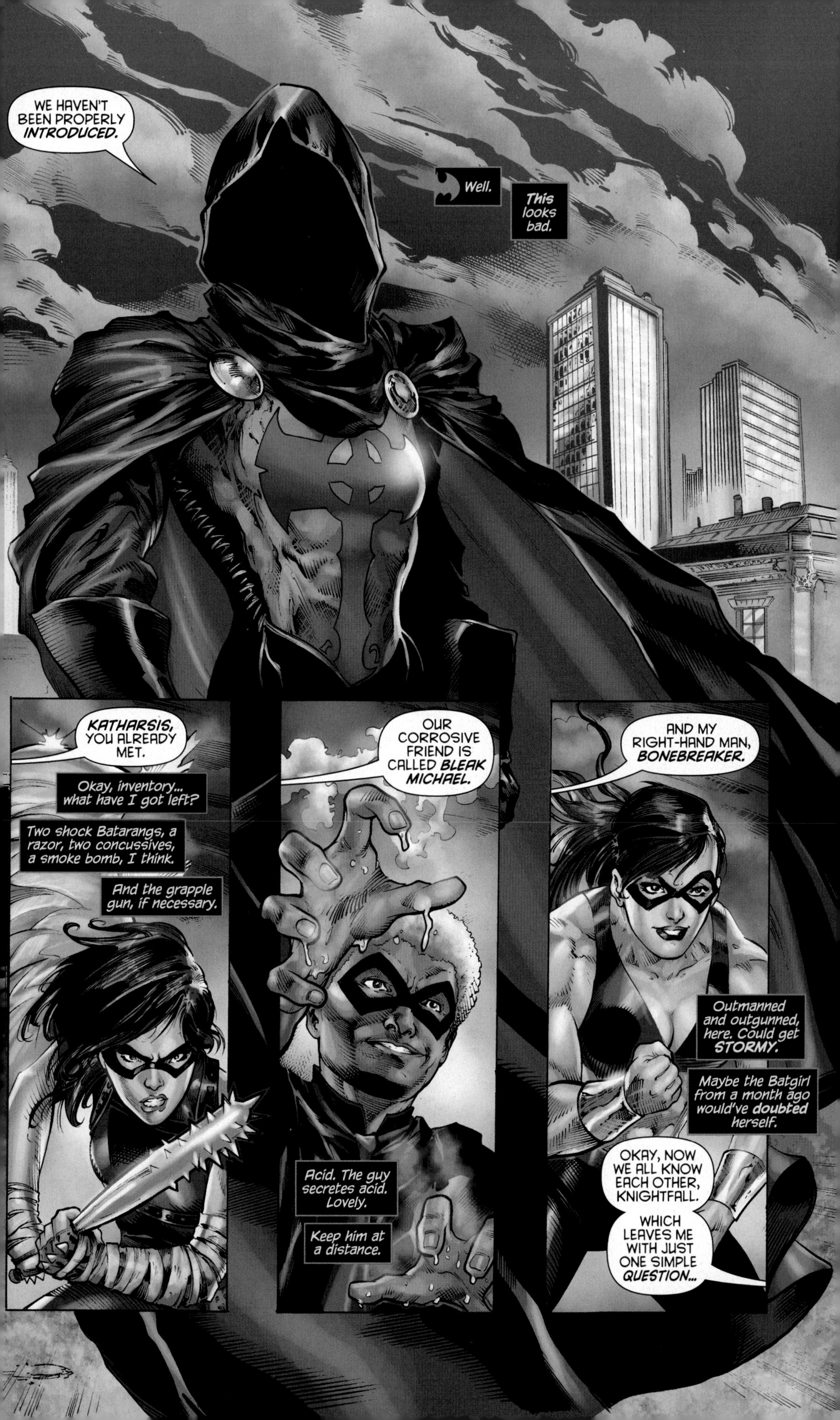
WE HAVEN'T BEEN PROPERLY INTRODUCED.
Well.
This looks bad.
KATHARSIS, YOU ALREADY MET.
Okay, inventory... what have I got left?
Two shock Batarangs, a razor, two concussives, a smoke bomb, I think.
And the grapple gun, if necessary.
OUR CORROSIVE FRIEND IS CALLED BLEAK MICHAEL.
Acid. The guy secretes acid. Lovely.
Keep him at a distance.
AND MY RIGHT-HAND MAN, BONEBREAKER.
Outmanned and outgunned, here. Could get STORMY.
Maybe the Batgirl from a month ago would've doubted herself.
OKAY, NOW WE ALL KNOW EACH OTHER, KNIGHTFALL.
WHICH LEAVES ME WITH JUST ONE SIMPLE QUESTION...

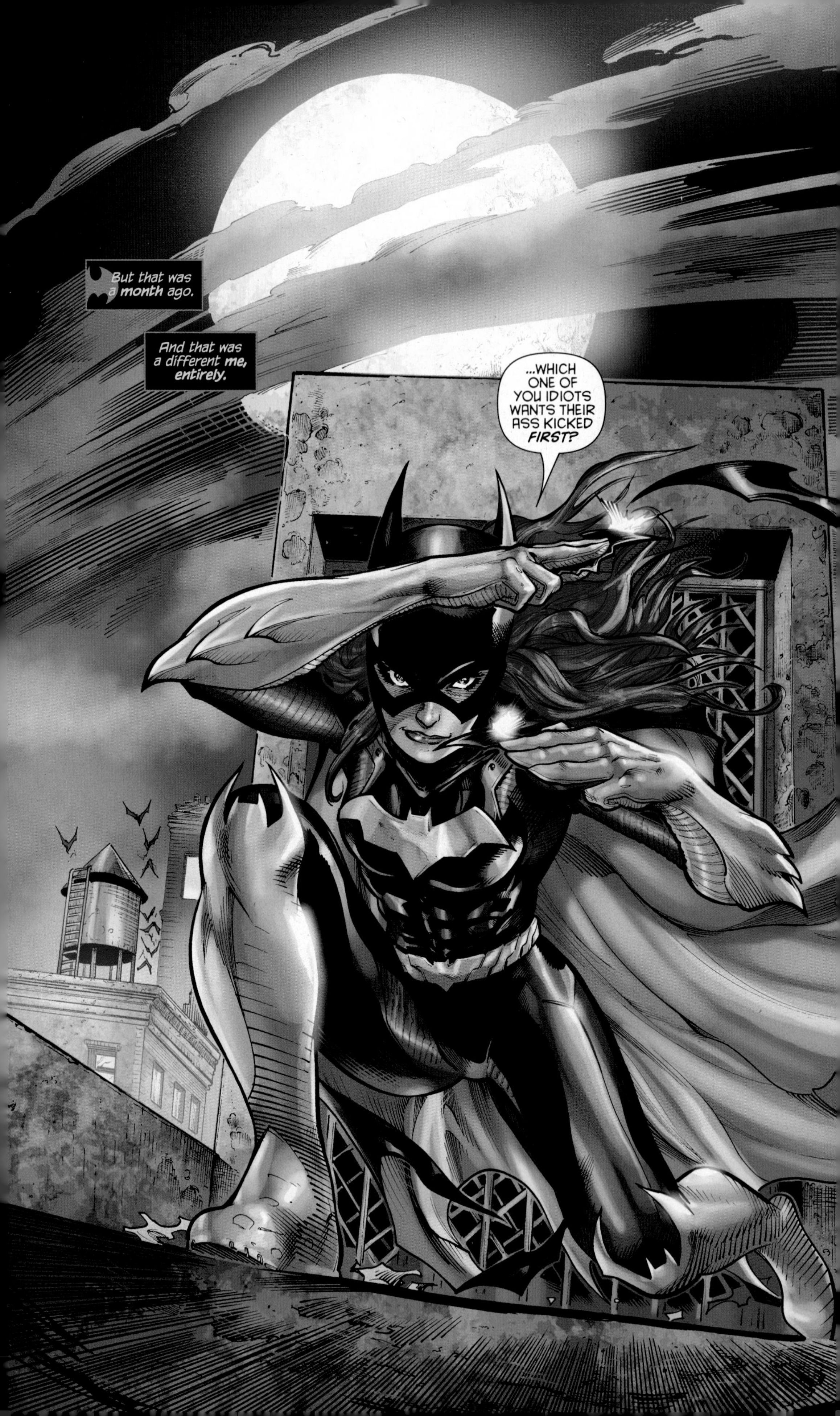

But that was a month ago.
And that was a different me, entirely.
...WHICH ONE OF YOU IDIOTS WANTS THEIR ASS KICKED FIRST?

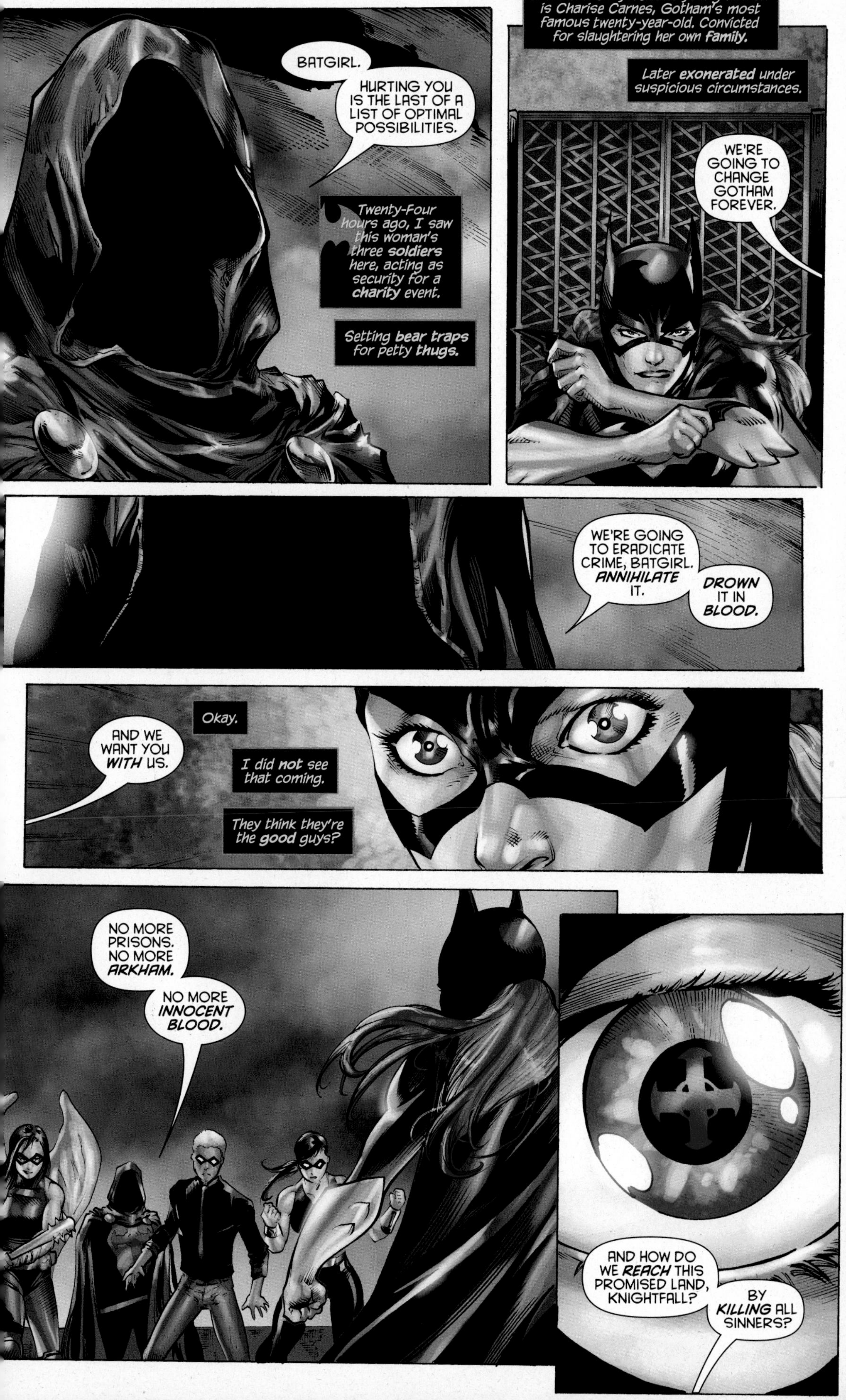
BATGIRL.
HURTING YOU IS THE LAST OF A LIST OF OPTIMAL POSSIBILITIES.
Twenty-Four hours ago, I saw this woman's three soldiers here, acting as security for a charity event.
Setting bear traps for petty thugs.
I think the mysterious young woman is Charise Carnes, Gotham's most famous twenty-year-old. Convicted for slaughtering her own family.
Later exonerated under suspicious circumstances.
WE'RE GOING TO CHANGE GOTHAM FOREVER.
WE'RE GOING TO ERADICATE CRIME, BATGIRL. ANNIHILATE IT.
DROWN IT IN BLOOD.
AND WE WANT YOU WITH US.
Okay.
I did not see that coming.
They think they're the good guys?
NO MORE PRISONS. NO MORE ARKHAM.
NO MORE INNOCENT BLOOD.
AND HOW DO WE REACH THIS PROMISED LAND, KNIGHTFALL?
BY KILLING ALL SINNERS?

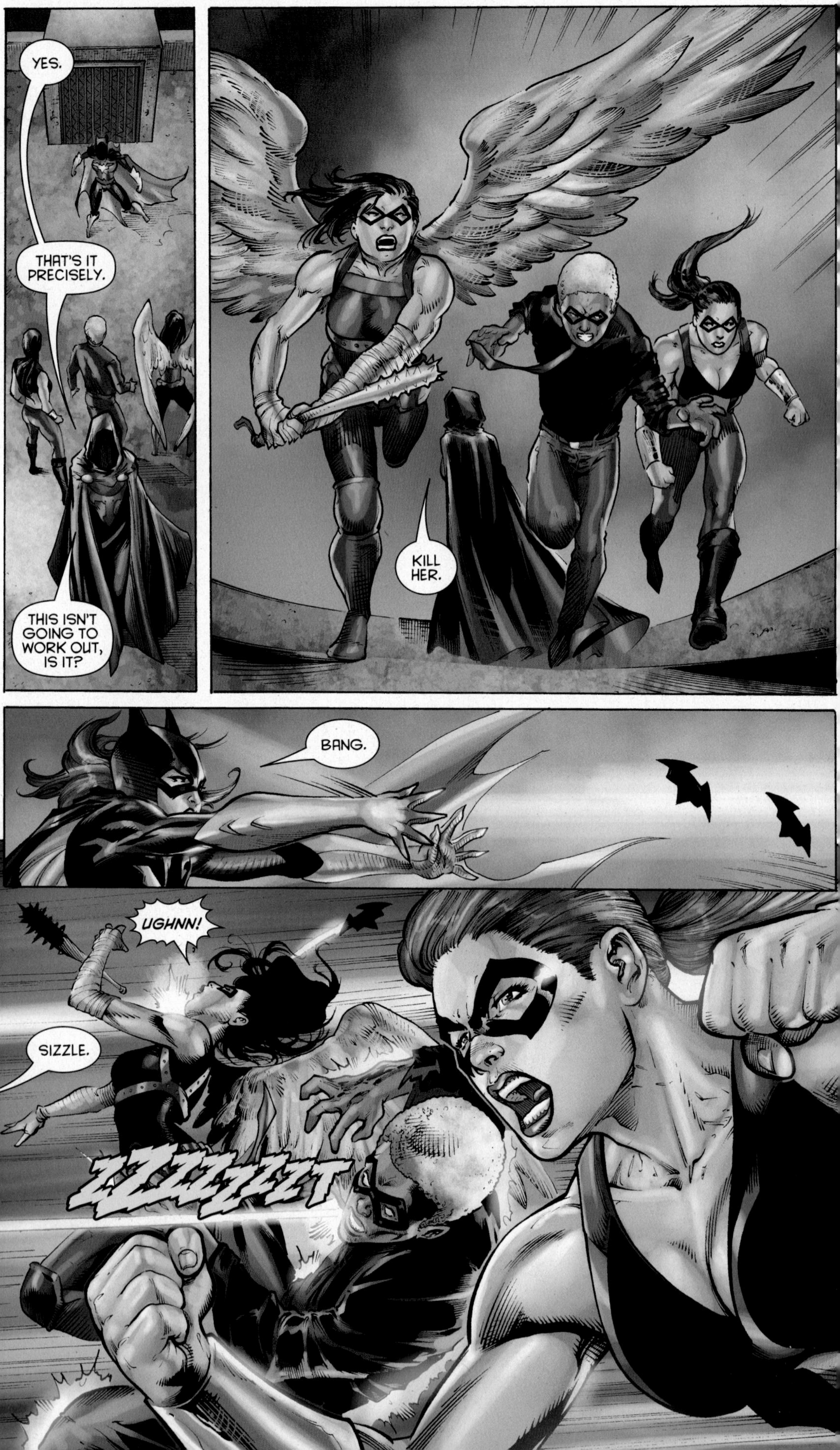
YES.
THAT'S IT PRECISELY.
THIS ISN'T GOING TO WORK OUT, IS IT?
KILL HER.
BANG.
UGHNN!
SIZZLE.
ZZZZZZZT

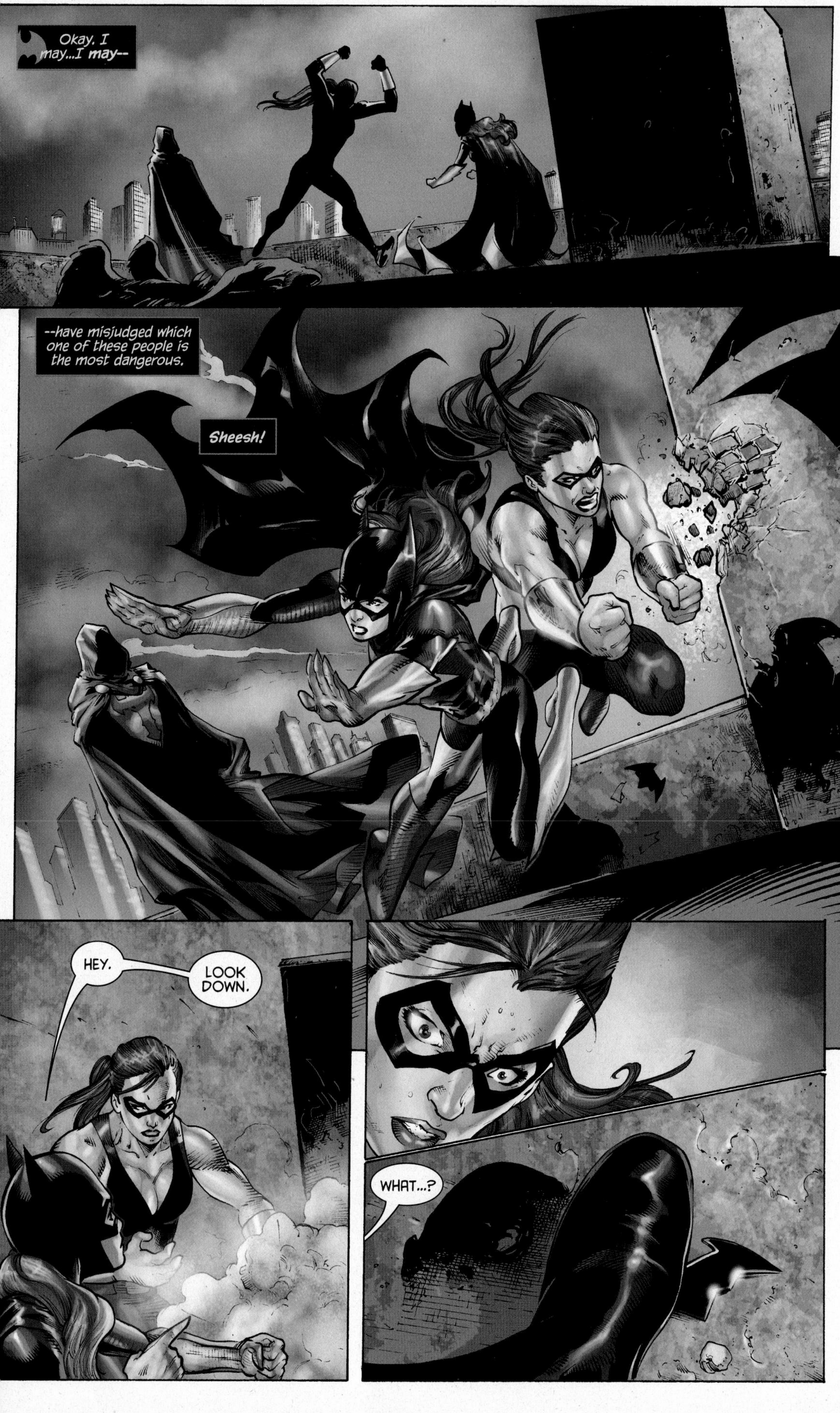
Okay. I may...I may--
--have misjudged which one of these people is the most dangerous.
Sheesh!
HEY.
LOOK DOWN.
WHAT...?

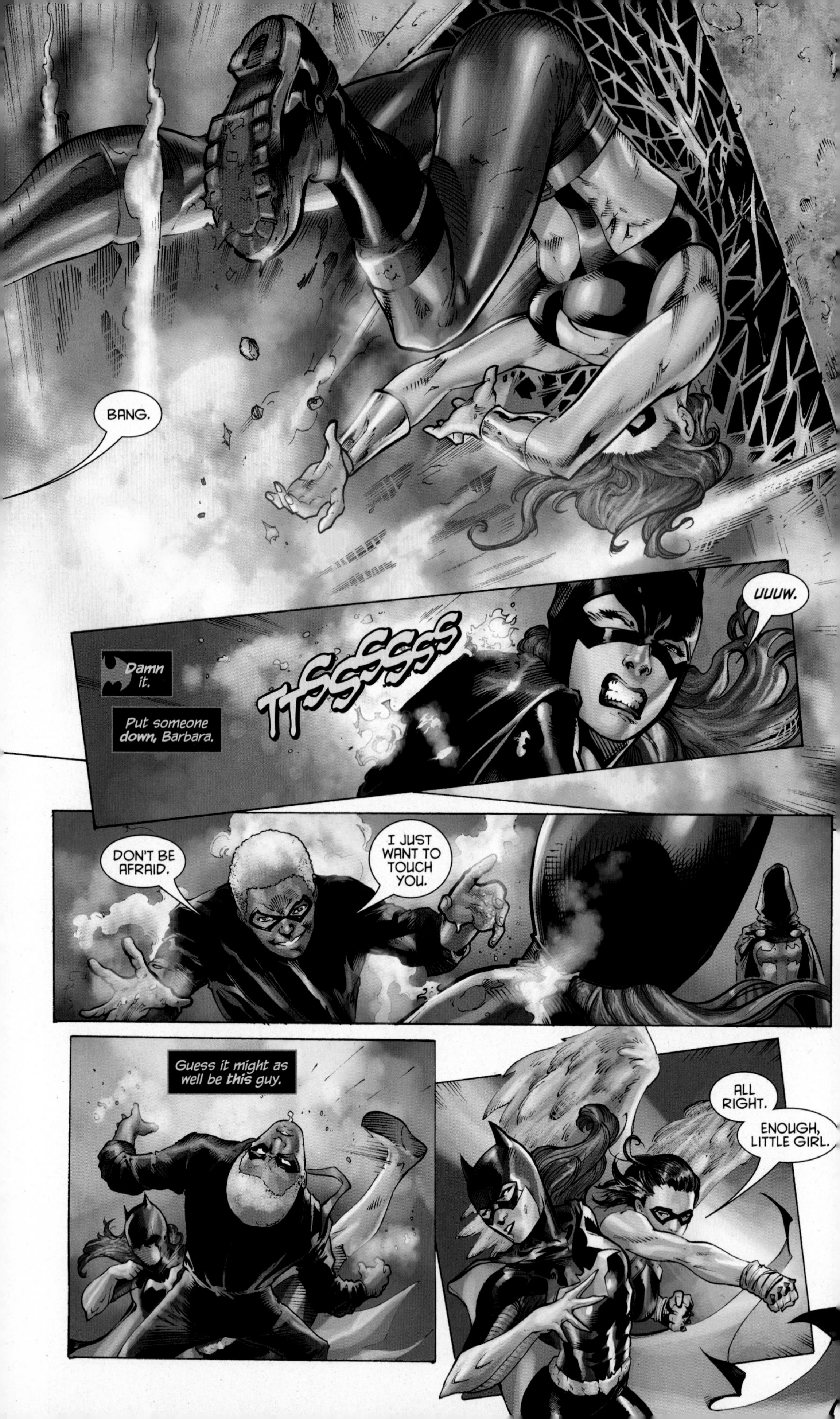
BANG.
Damn it.
Put someone down, Barbara.
TTSSSSSS
UUUW.
DON'T BE AFRAID.
I JUST WANT TO TOUCH YOU.
Guess it might as well be this guy.
ALL RIGHT.
ENOUGH, LITTLE GIRL.

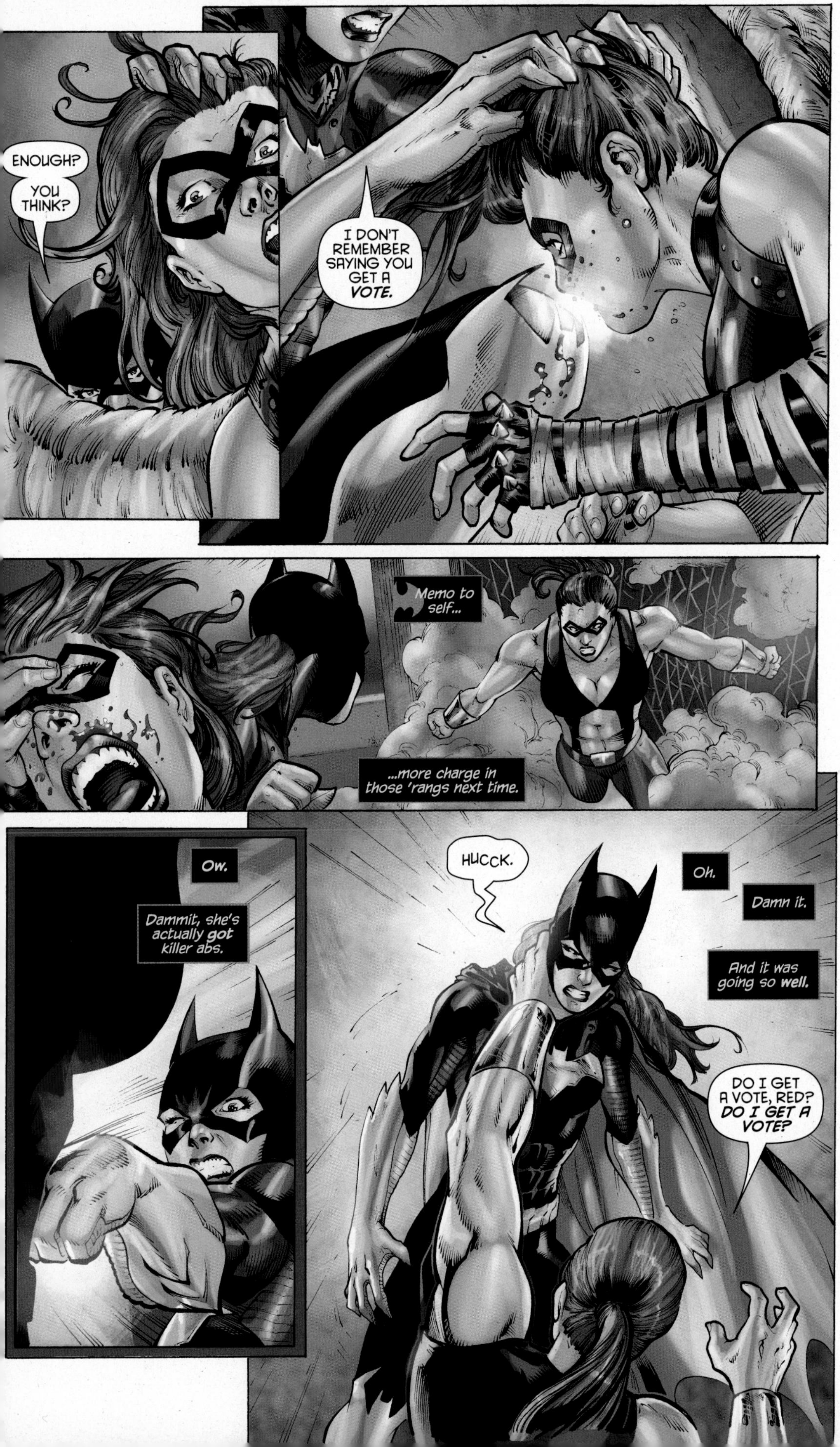
ENOUGH?
YOU THINK?
I DON'T REMEMBER SAYING YOU GET A VOTE.
Memo to self...
...more charge in those 'rangs next time.
Ow.
Dammit, she's actually got killer abs.
HUCCK.
Oh.
Damn it.
And it was going so well.
DO I GET A VOTE, RED? DO I GET A VOTE?

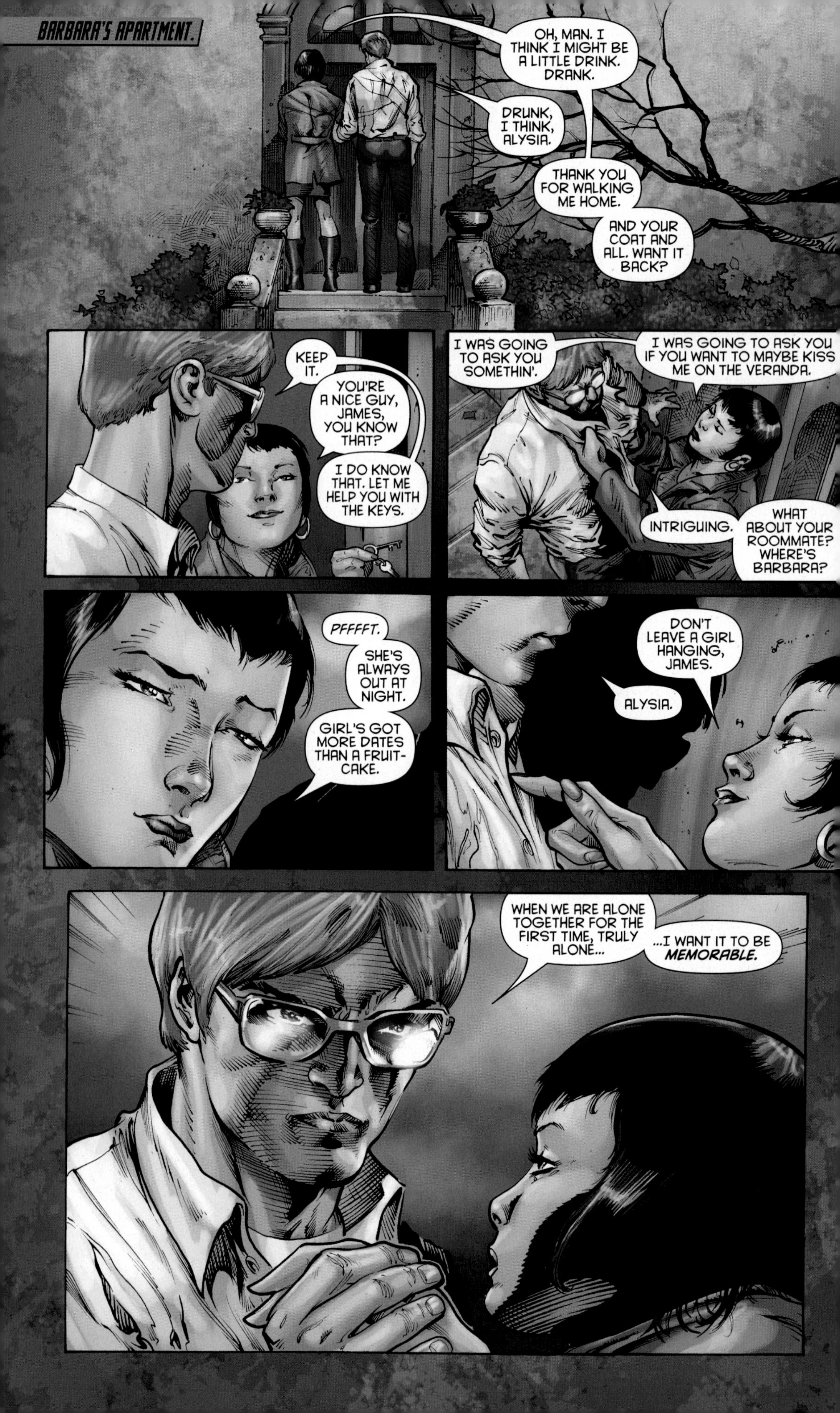
BARBARA'S APARTMENT.
OH, MAN. I THINK I MIGHT BE A LITTLE DRINK. DRANK.
DRUNK, I THINK, ALYSIA.
THANK YOU FOR WALKING ME HOME.
AND YOUR COAT AND ALL. WANT IT BACK?
KEEP IT.
YOU'RE A NICE GUY, JAMES, YOU KNOW THAT?
I DO KNOW THAT. LET ME HELP YOU WITH THE KEYS.
I WAS GOING TO ASK YOU SOMETHIN'.
I WAS GOING TO ASK YOU IF YOU WANT TO MAYBE KISS ME ON THE VERANDA.
INTRIGUING.
WHAT ABOUT YOUR ROOMMATE? WHERE'S BARBARA?
PFFFFT.
SHE'S ALWAYS OUT AT NIGHT.
GIRL'S GOT MORE DATES THAN A FRUIT-CAKE.
DON'T LEAVE A GIRL HANGING, JAMES.
ALYSIA.
WHEN WE ARE ALONE TOGETHER FOR THE FIRST TIME, TRULY ALONE...
...I WANT IT TO BE MEMORABLE.

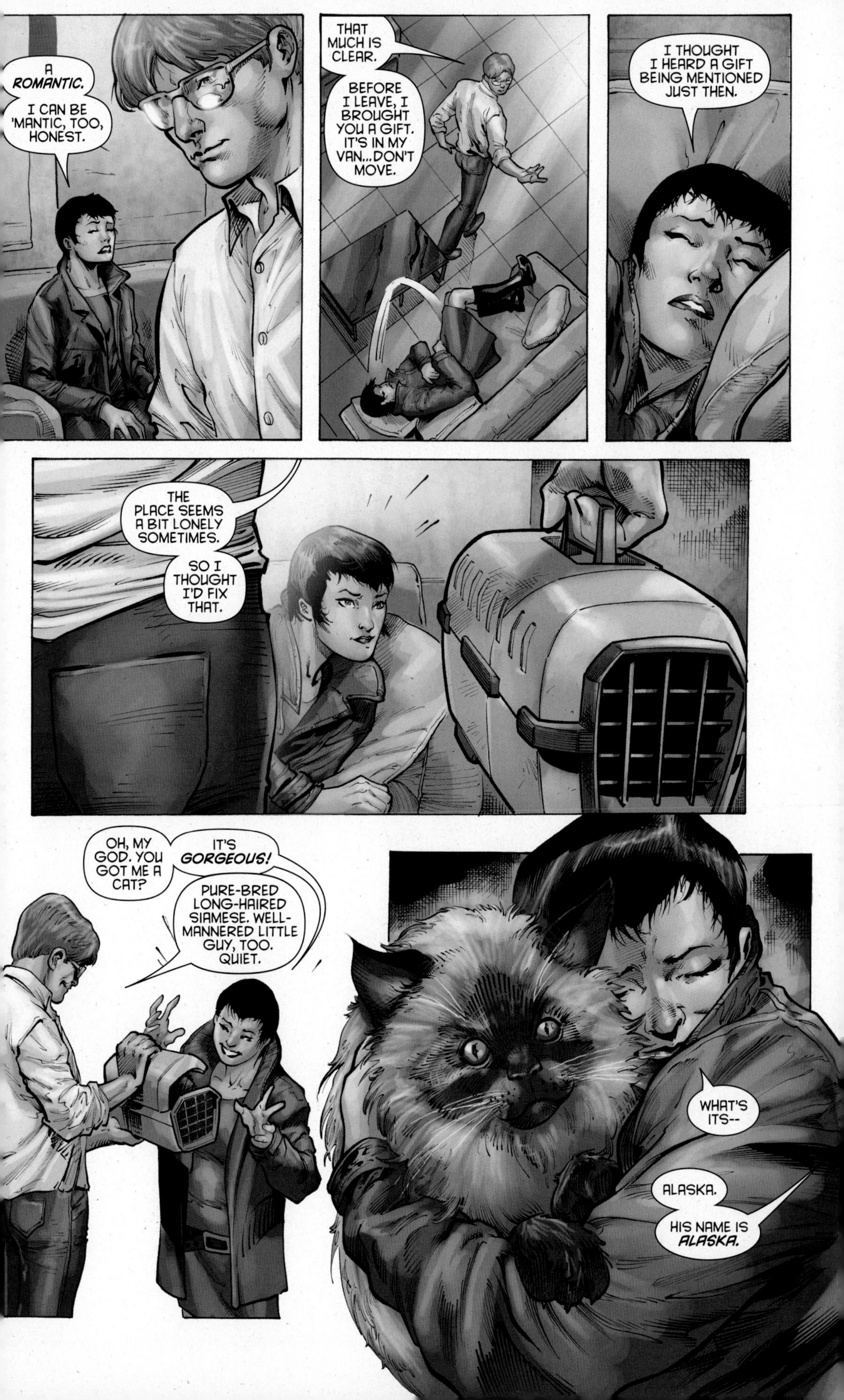
A ROMANTIC.
I CAN BE 'MANTIC, TOO, HONEST.
THAT MUCH IS CLEAR.
BEFORE I LEAVE, I BROUGHT YOU A GIFT. IT'S IN MY VAN...DON'T MOVE.
I THOUGHT I HEARD A GIFT BEING MENTIONED JUST THEN.
THE PLACE SEEMS A BIT LONELY SOMETIMES.
SO I THOUGHT I'D FIX THAT.
OH, MY GOD. YOU GOT ME A CAT?
IT'S GORGEOUS!
PURE-BRED LONG-HAIRED SIAMESE. WELL-MANNERED LITTLE GUY, TOO. QUIET.
WHAT'S ITS--
ALASKA.
HIS NAME IS ALASKA.

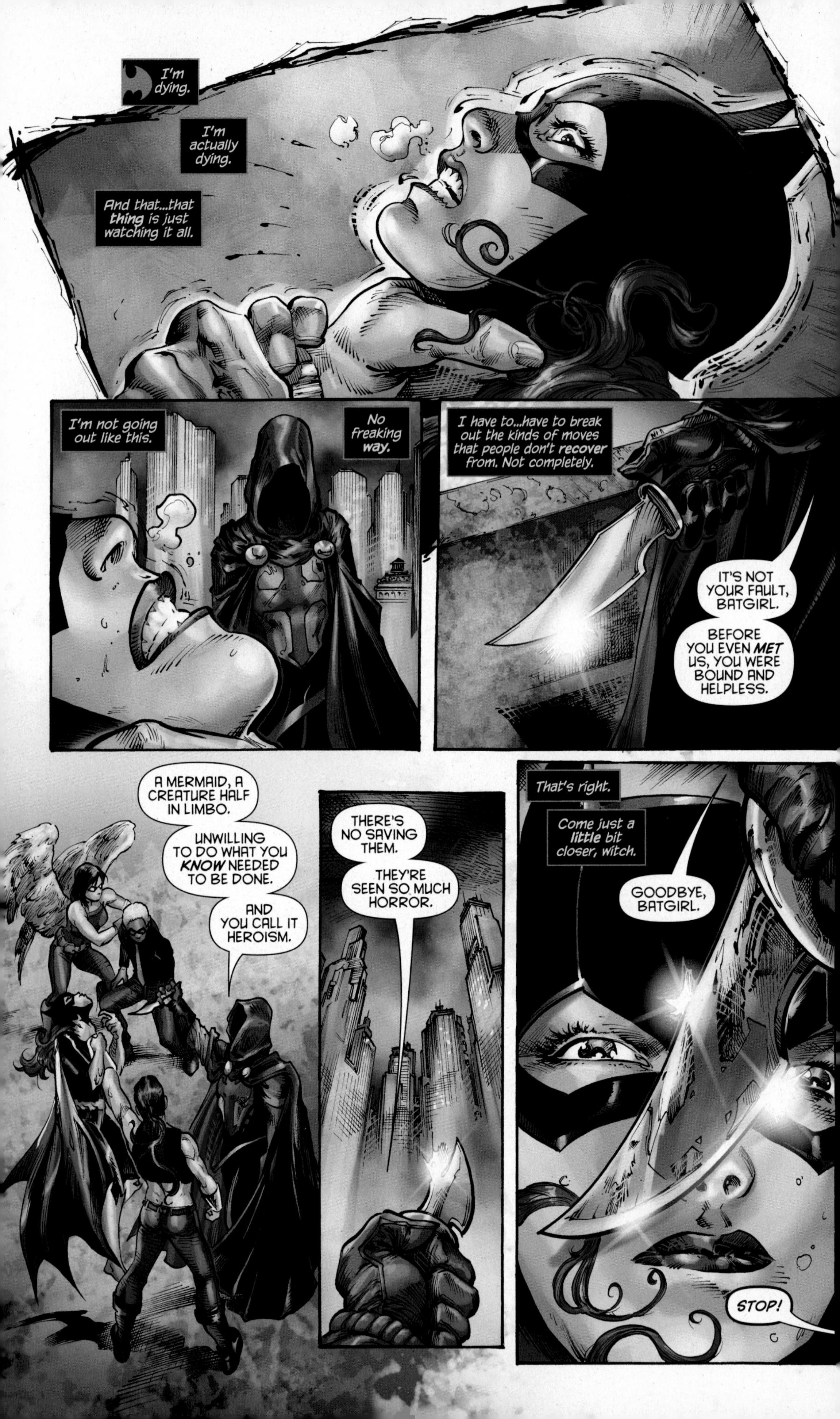
I'm dying.
I'm actually dying.
And that...that thing is just watching it all.
I'm not going out like this.
No freaking way.
I have to...have to break out the kinds of moves that people don't recover from. Not completely.
IT'S NOT YOUR FAULT, BATGIRL.
BEFORE YOU EVEN MET US, YOU WERE BOUND AND HELPLESS.
A MERMAID, A CREATURE HALF IN LIMBO.
UNWILLING TO DO WHAT YOU KNOW NEEDED TO BE DONE.
AND YOU CALL IT HEROISM.
THERE'S NO SAVING THEM.
THEY'RE SEEN SO MUCH HORROR.
That's right.
Come just a little bit closer, witch.
GOODBYE, BATGIRL.
STOP!

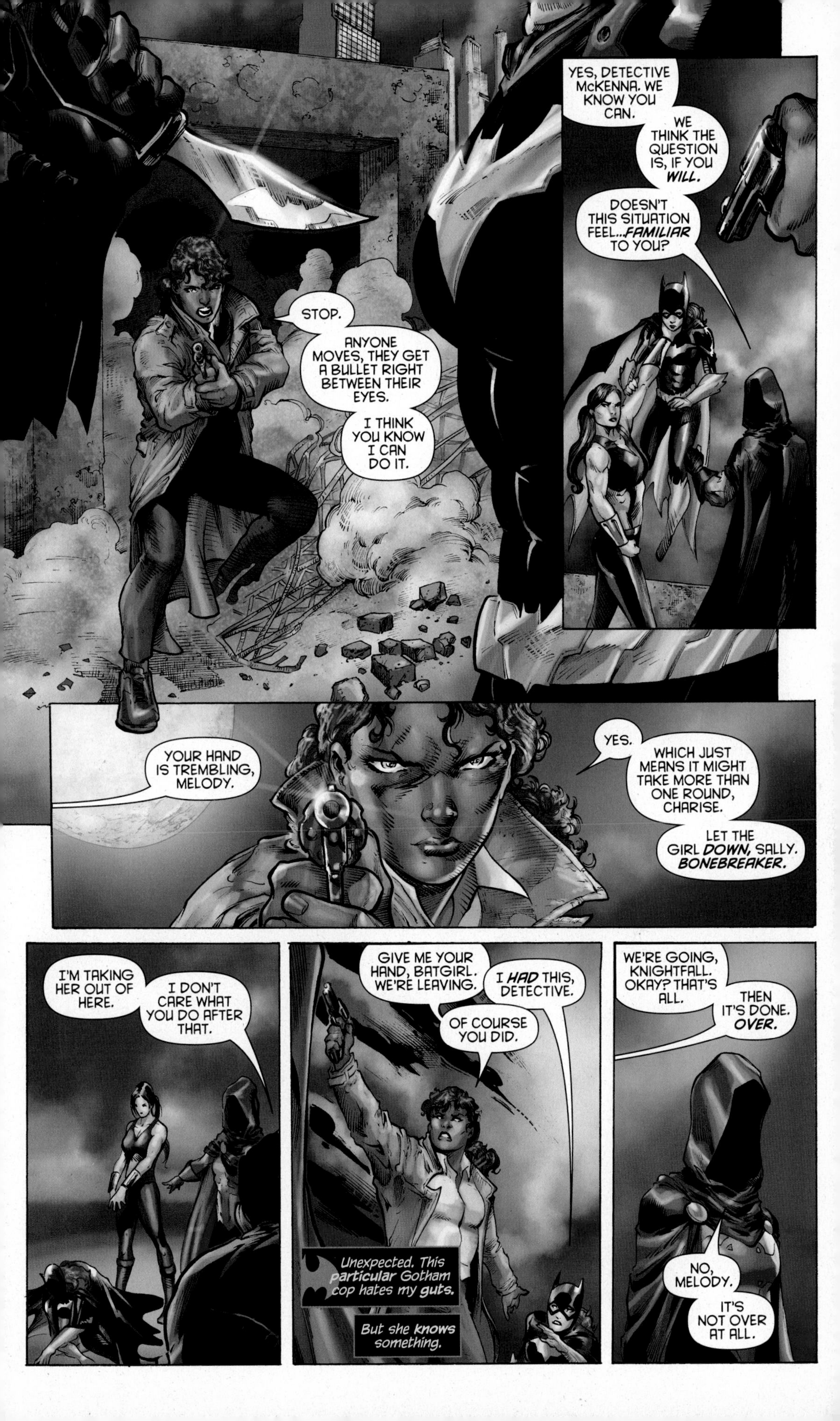
STOP.
ANYONE MOVES, THEY GET A BULLET RIGHT BETWEEN THEIR EYES.
I THINK YOU KNOW I CAN DO IT.
YES, DETECTIVE McKENNA. WE KNOW YOU CAN.
WE THINK THE QUESTION IS, IF YOU *WILL.*
DOESN'T THIS SITUATION FEEL...*FAMILIAR* TO YOU?
YOUR HAND IS TREMBLING, MELODY.
YES.
WHICH JUST MEANS IT MIGHT TAKE MORE THAN ONE ROUND, CHARISE.
LET THE GIRL *DOWN,* SALLY. *BONEBREAKER.*
I'M TAKING HER OUT OF HERE.
I DON'T CARE WHAT YOU DO AFTER THAT.
GIVE ME YOUR HAND, BATGIRL. WE'RE LEAVING.
I *HAD* THIS, DETECTIVE.
OF COURSE YOU DID.
Unexpected. This **particular** Gotham cop hates my **guts.**
But she **knows** something.
WE'RE GOING, KNIGHTFALL. OKAY? THAT'S ALL.
THEN IT'S DONE. *OVER.*
NO, MELODY.
IT'S NOT OVER AT ALL.

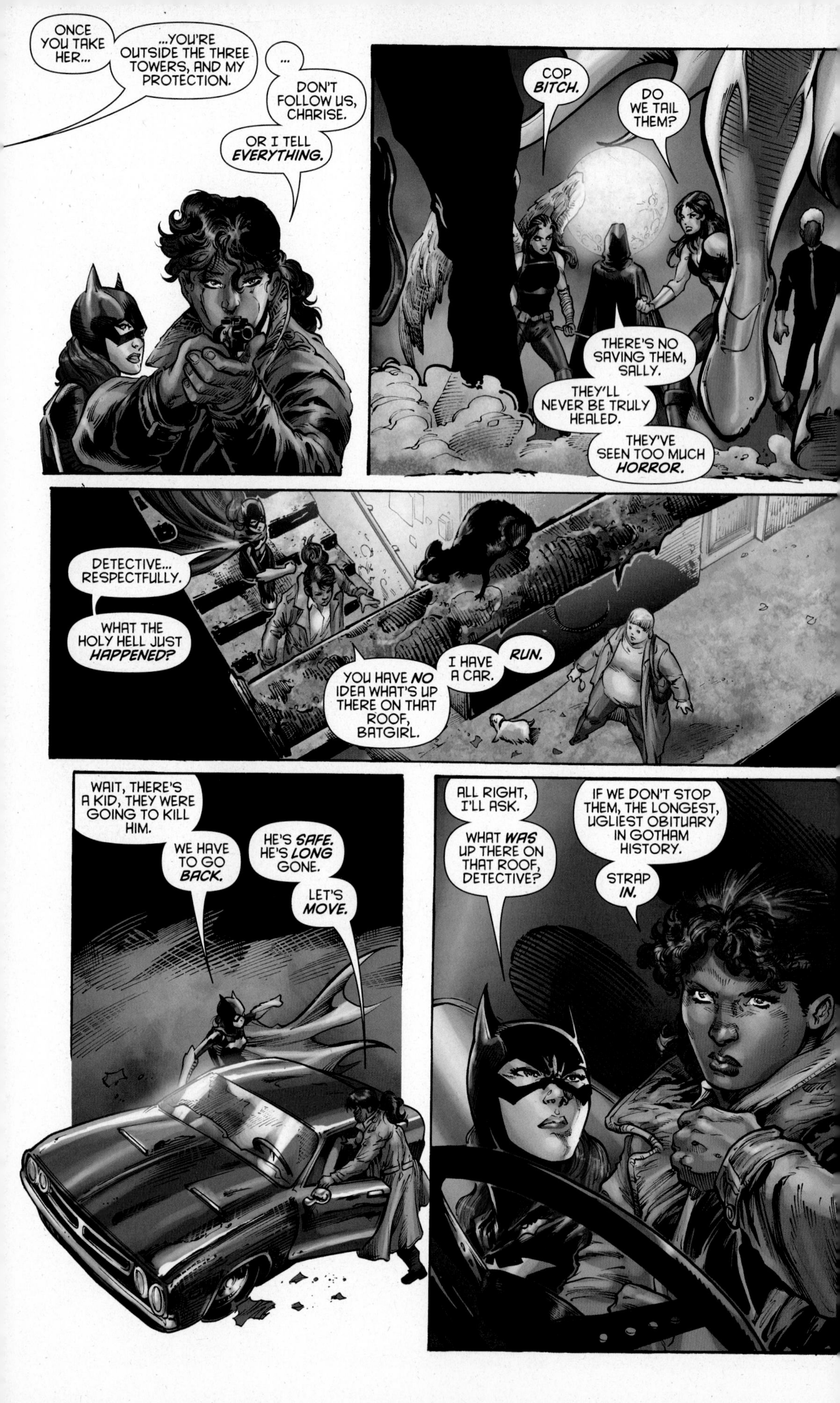
ONCE YOU TAKE HER...
...YOU'RE OUTSIDE THE THREE TOWERS, AND MY PROTECTION.
...
DON'T FOLLOW US, CHARISE.
OR I TELL EVERYTHING.
COP BITCH.
DO WE TAIL THEM?
THERE'S NO SAVING THEM, SALLY.
THEY'LL NEVER BE TRULY HEALED.
THEY'VE SEEN TOO MUCH HORROR.
DETECTIVE... RESPECTFULLY.
WHAT THE HOLY HELL JUST HAPPENED?
YOU HAVE NO IDEA WHAT'S UP THERE ON THAT ROOF, BATGIRL.
I HAVE A CAR.
RUN.
WAIT, THERE'S A KID, THEY WERE GOING TO KILL HIM.
WE HAVE TO GO BACK.
HE'S SAFE. HE'S LONG GONE.
LET'S MOVE.
ALL RIGHT, I'LL ASK.
WHAT WAS UP THERE ON THAT ROOF, DETECTIVE?
IF WE DON'T STOP THEM, THE LONGEST, UGLIEST OBITUARY IN GOTHAM HISTORY.
STRAP IN.

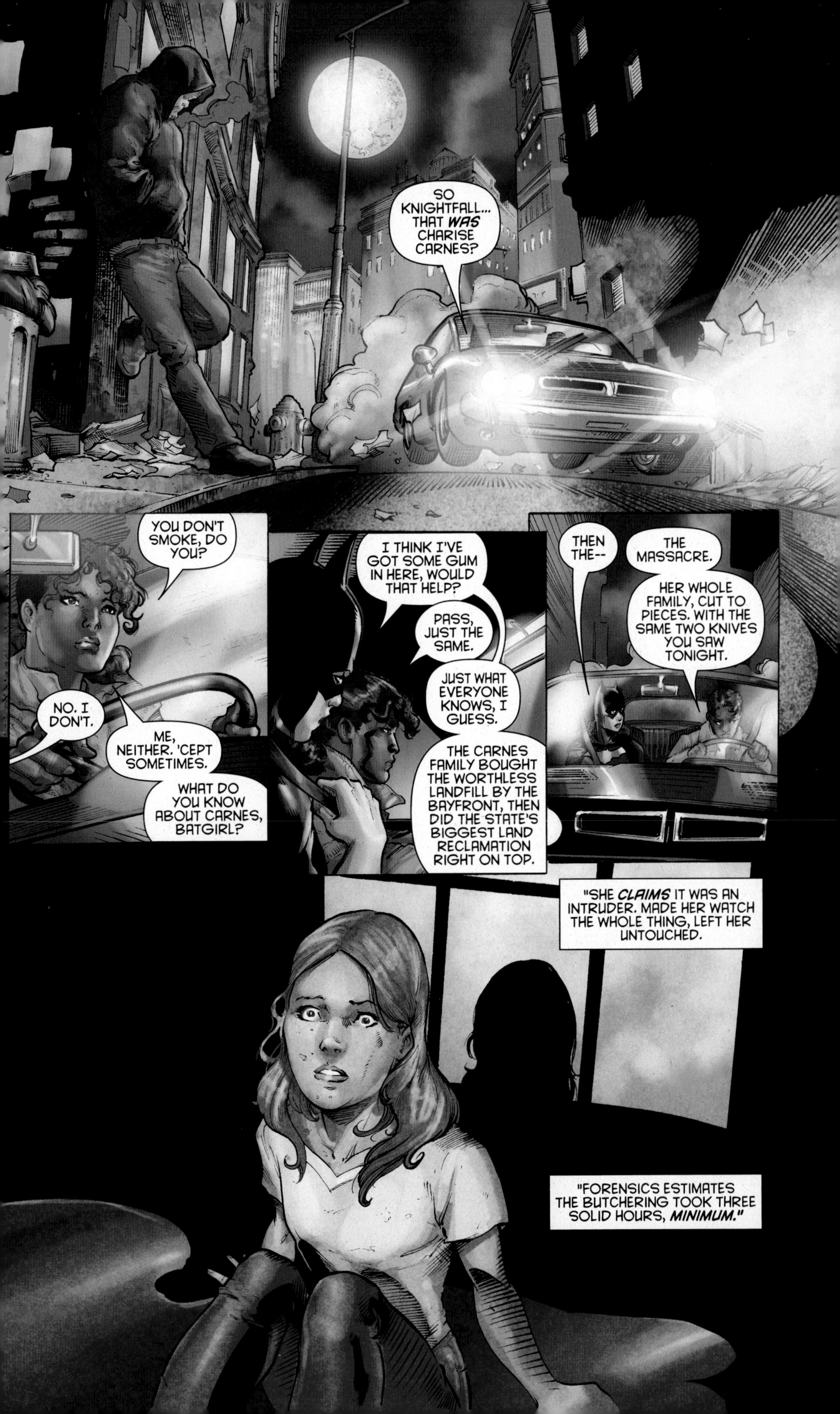
SO KNIGHTFALL... THAT *WAS* CHARISE CARNES?
YOU DON'T SMOKE, DO YOU?
NO. I DON'T.
ME, NEITHER. 'CEPT SOMETIMES.
WHAT DO YOU KNOW ABOUT CARNES, BATGIRL?
I THINK I'VE GOT SOME GUM IN HERE, WOULD THAT HELP?
PASS, JUST THE SAME.
JUST WHAT EVERYONE KNOWS, I GUESS.
THE CARNES FAMILY BOUGHT THE WORTHLESS LANDFILL BY THE BAYFRONT, THEN DID THE STATE'S BIGGEST LAND RECLAMATION RIGHT ON TOP.
THEN THE--
THE MASSACRE.
HER WHOLE FAMILY, CUT TO PIECES. WITH THE SAME TWO KNIVES YOU SAW TONIGHT.
"SHE *CLAIMS* IT WAS AN INTRUDER. MADE HER WATCH THE WHOLE THING, LEFT HER UNTOUCHED.
"FORENSICS ESTIMATES THE BUTCHERING TOOK THREE SOLID HOURS, *MINIMUM.*"

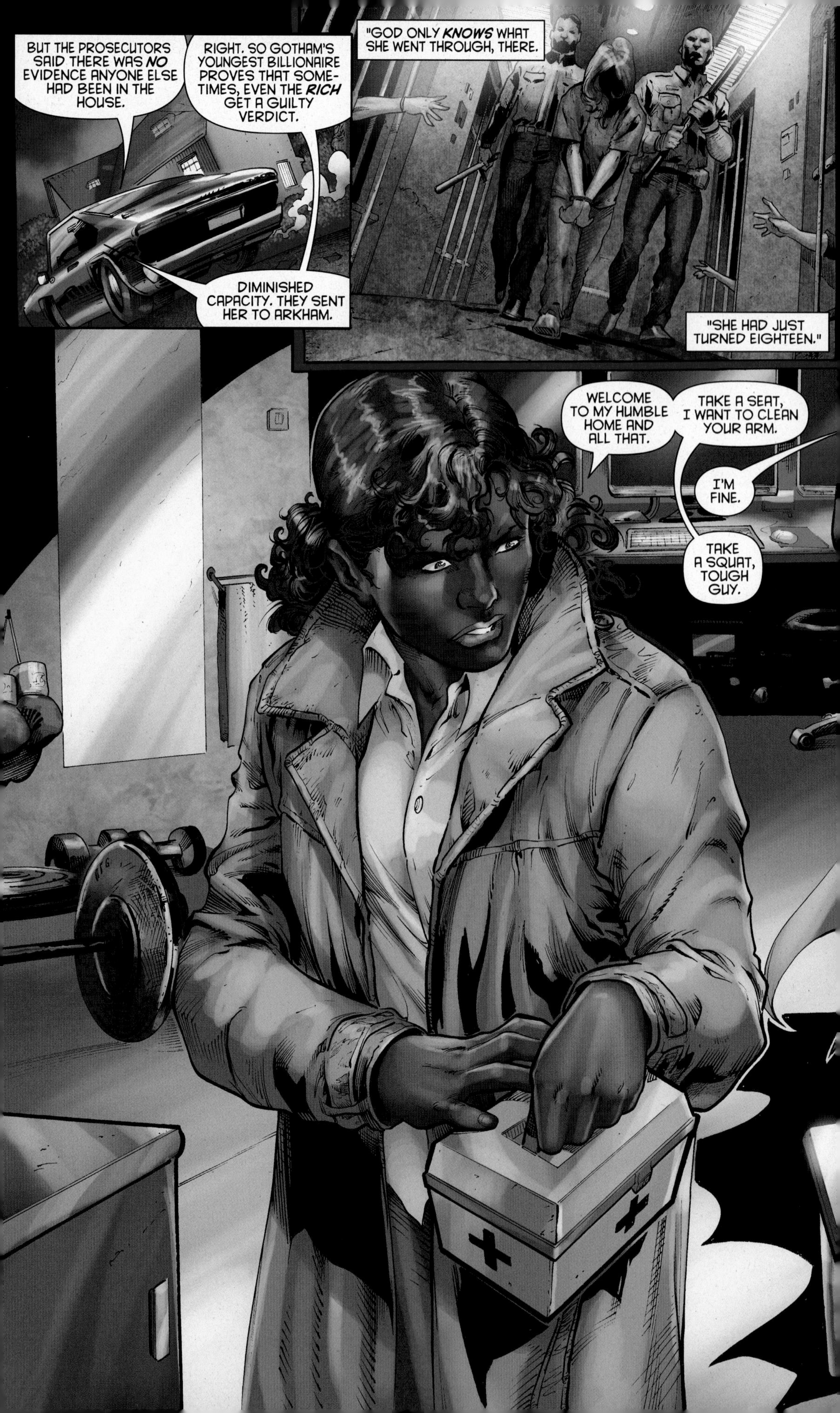

BUT THE PROSECUTORS SAID THERE WAS NO EVIDENCE ANYONE ELSE HAD BEEN IN THE HOUSE.
RIGHT. SO GOTHAM'S YOUNGEST BILLIONAIRE PROVES THAT SOMETIMES, EVEN THE RICH GET A GUILTY VERDICT.
DIMINISHED CAPACITY. THEY SENT HER TO ARKHAM.
"GOD ONLY KNOWS WHAT SHE WENT THROUGH, THERE.
"SHE HAD JUST TURNED EIGHTEEN."
WELCOME TO MY HUMBLE HOME AND ALL THAT.
TAKE A SEAT, I WANT TO CLEAN YOUR ARM.
I'M FINE.
TAKE A SQUAT, TOUGH GUY.

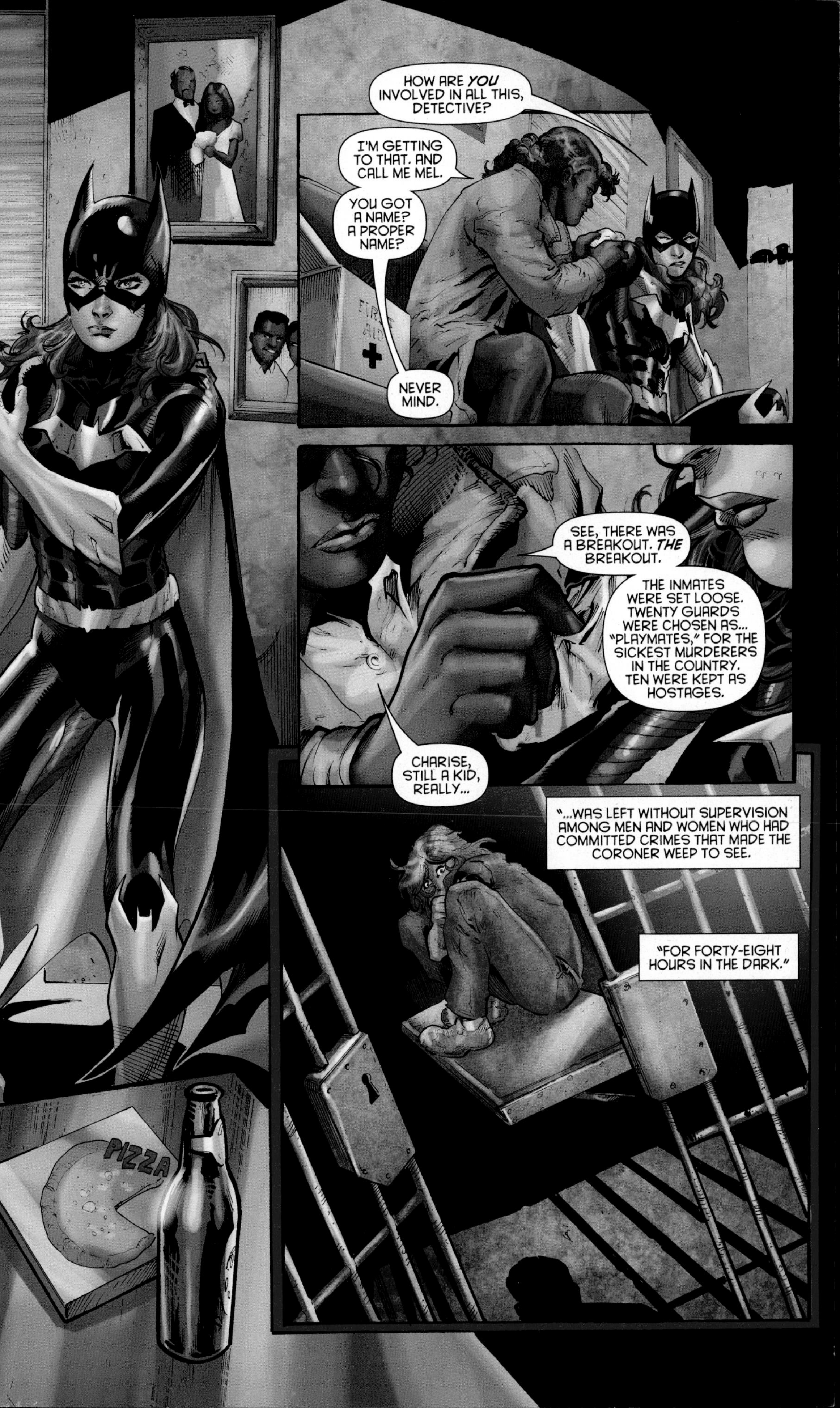
HOW ARE *YOU* INVOLVED IN ALL THIS, DETECTIVE?
I'M GETTING TO THAT. AND CALL ME MEL.
YOU GOT A NAME? A PROPER NAME?
NEVER MIND.
FIRST AID
SEE, THERE WAS A BREAKOUT. *THE* BREAKOUT.
THE INMATES WERE SET LOOSE. TWENTY GUARDS WERE CHOSEN AS... "PLAYMATES," FOR THE SICKEST MURDERERS IN THE COUNTRY. TEN WERE KEPT AS HOSTAGES.
CHARISE, STILL A KID, REALLY...
"...WAS LEFT WITHOUT SUPERVISION AMONG MEN AND WOMEN WHO HAD COMMITTED CRIMES THAT MADE THE CORONER WEEP TO SEE.
"FOR FORTY-EIGHT HOURS IN THE DARK."
PIZZA

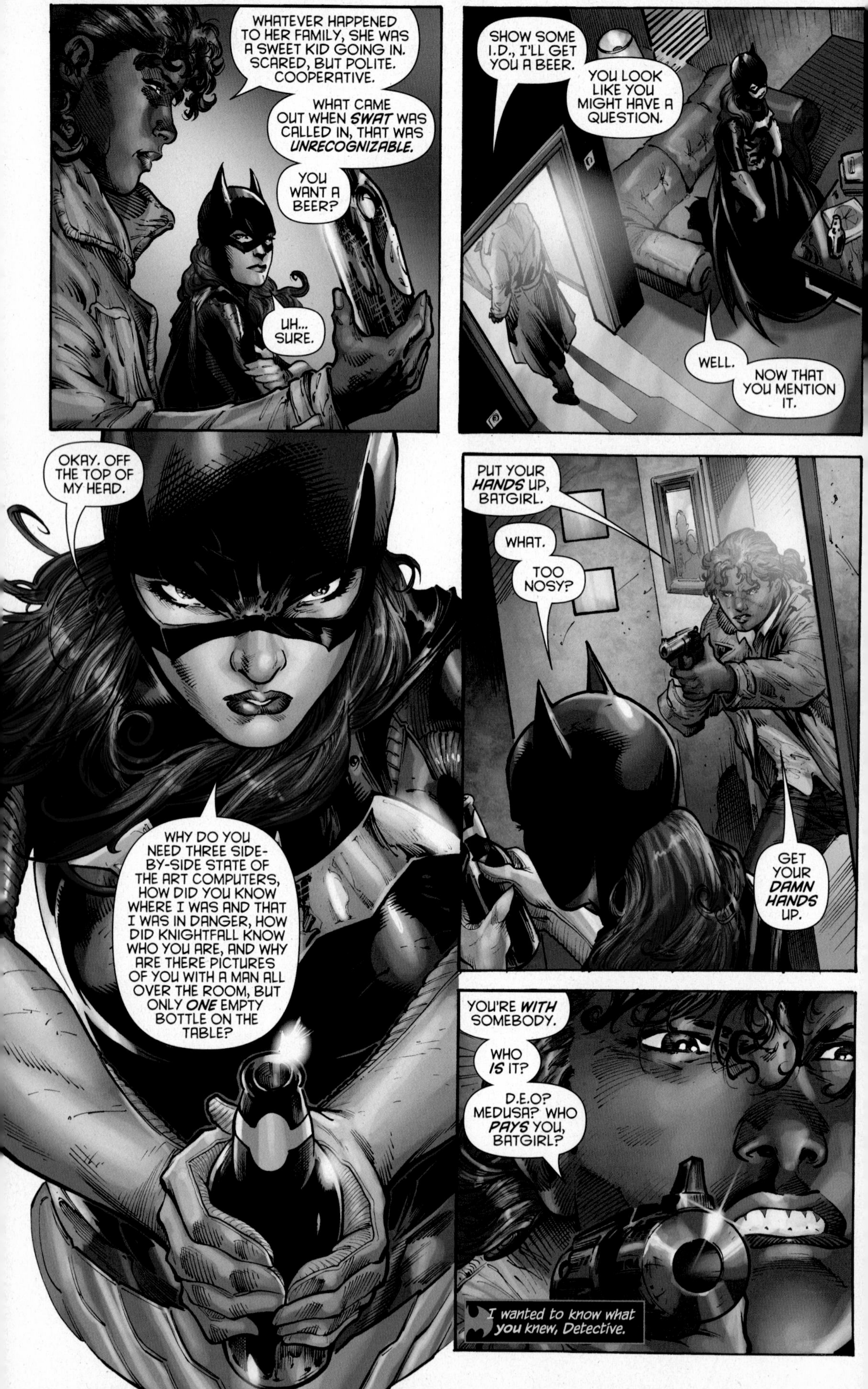
WHATEVER HAPPENED TO HER FAMILY, SHE WAS A SWEET KID GOING IN. SCARED, BUT POLITE. COOPERATIVE.
WHAT CAME OUT WHEN SWAT WAS CALLED IN, THAT WAS UNRECOGNIZABLE.
YOU WANT A BEER?
UH... SURE.
SHOW SOME I.D., I'LL GET YOU A BEER.
YOU LOOK LIKE YOU MIGHT HAVE A QUESTION.
WELL.
NOW THAT YOU MENTION IT.
OKAY. OFF THE TOP OF MY HEAD.
WHY DO YOU NEED THREE SIDE-BY-SIDE STATE OF THE ART COMPUTERS, HOW DID YOU KNOW WHERE I WAS AND THAT I WAS IN DANGER, HOW DID KNIGHTFALL KNOW WHO YOU ARE, AND WHY ARE THERE PICTURES OF YOU WITH A MAN ALL OVER THE ROOM, BUT ONLY ONE EMPTY BOTTLE ON THE TABLE?
PUT YOUR HANDS UP, BATGIRL.
WHAT.
TOO NOSY?
GET YOUR DAMN HANDS UP.
YOU'RE WITH SOMEBODY.
WHO IS IT?
D.E.O? MEDUSA? WHO PAYS YOU, BATGIRL?
I wanted to know what you knew, Detective.

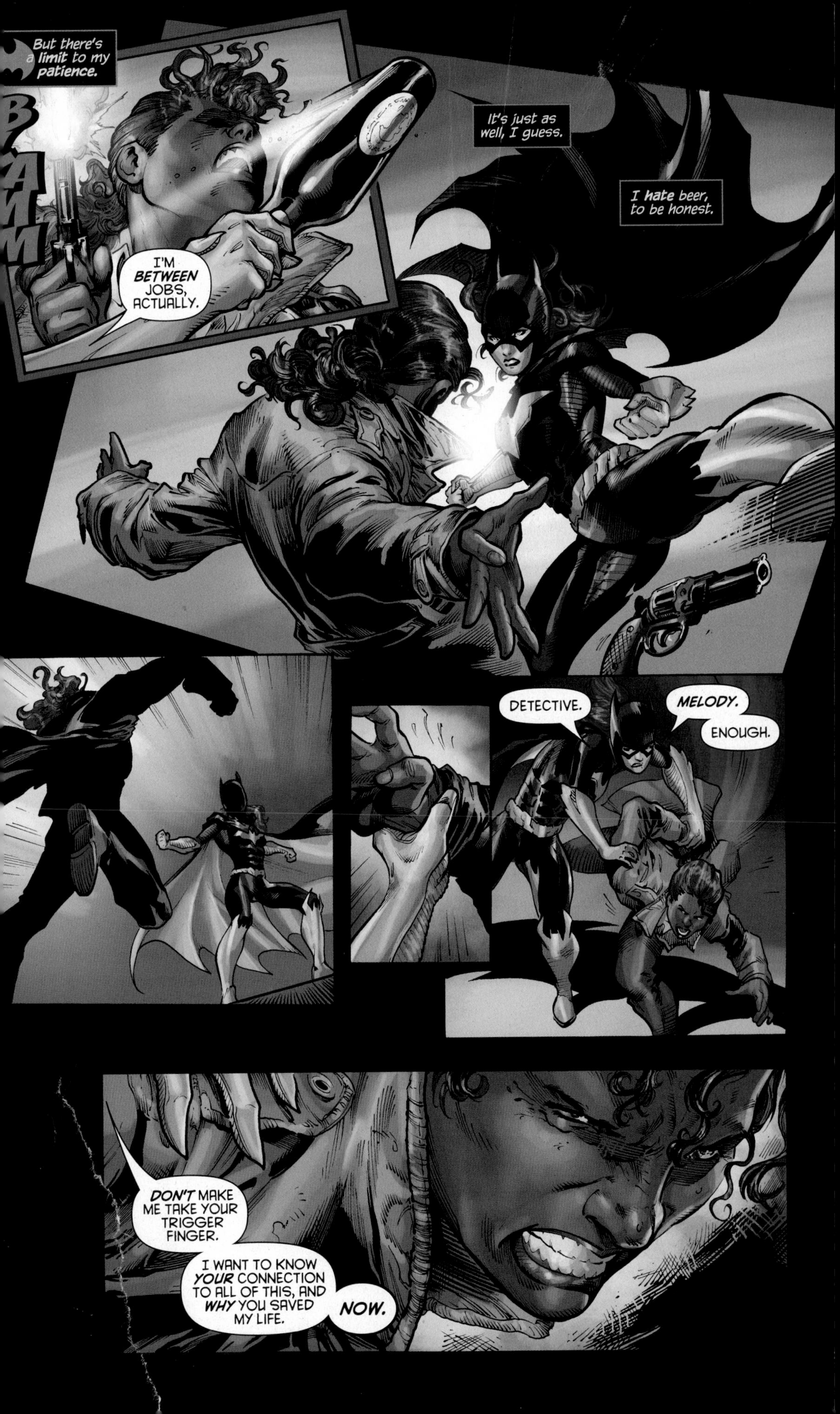
But there's a limit to my patience.
BLAM
I'M BETWEEN JOBS, ACTUALLY.
It's just as well, I guess.
I hate beer, to be honest.
DETECTIVE.
MELODY.
ENOUGH.
DON'T MAKE ME TAKE YOUR TRIGGER FINGER.
I WANT TO KNOW YOUR CONNECTION TO ALL OF THIS, AND WHY YOU SAVED MY LIFE.
NOW.

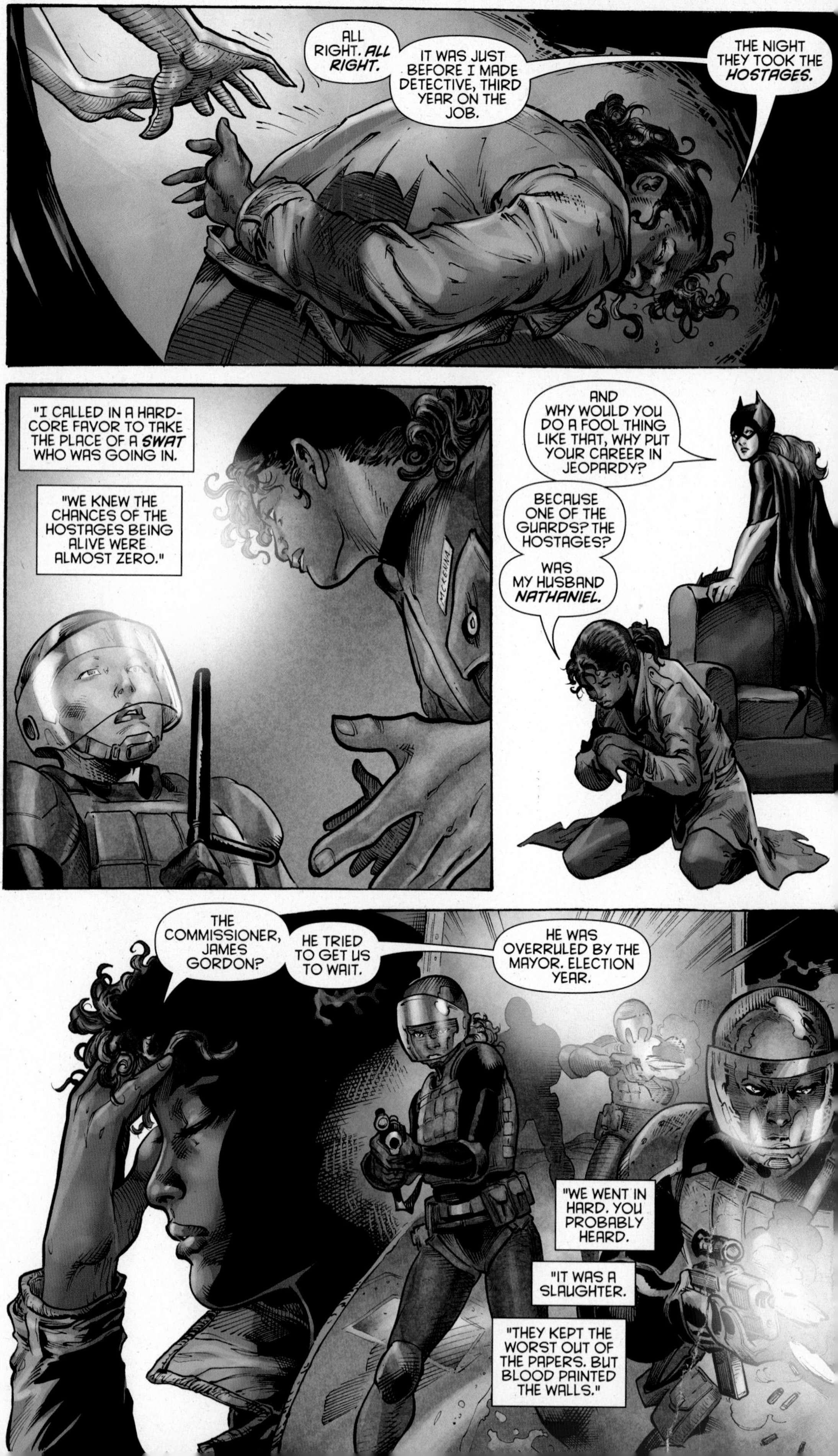

ALL RIGHT. ALL RIGHT.
IT WAS JUST BEFORE I MADE DETECTIVE, THIRD YEAR ON THE JOB.
THE NIGHT THEY TOOK THE HOSTAGES.
"I CALLED IN A HARD-CORE FAVOR TO TAKE THE PLACE OF A SWAT WHO WAS GOING IN.
"WE KNEW THE CHANCES OF THE HOSTAGES BEING ALIVE WERE ALMOST ZERO."
MCKENNA
AND WHY WOULD YOU DO A FOOL THING LIKE THAT, WHY PUT YOUR CAREER IN JEOPARDY?
BECAUSE ONE OF THE GUARDS? THE HOSTAGES?
WAS MY HUSBAND NATHANIEL.
THE COMMISSIONER, JAMES GORDON?
HE TRIED TO GET US TO WAIT.
HE WAS OVERRULED BY THE MAYOR. ELECTION YEAR.
"WE WENT IN HARD. YOU PROBABLY HEARD.
"IT WAS A SLAUGHTER.
"THEY KEPT THE WORST OUT OF THE PAPERS. BUT BLOOD PAINTED THE WALLS."

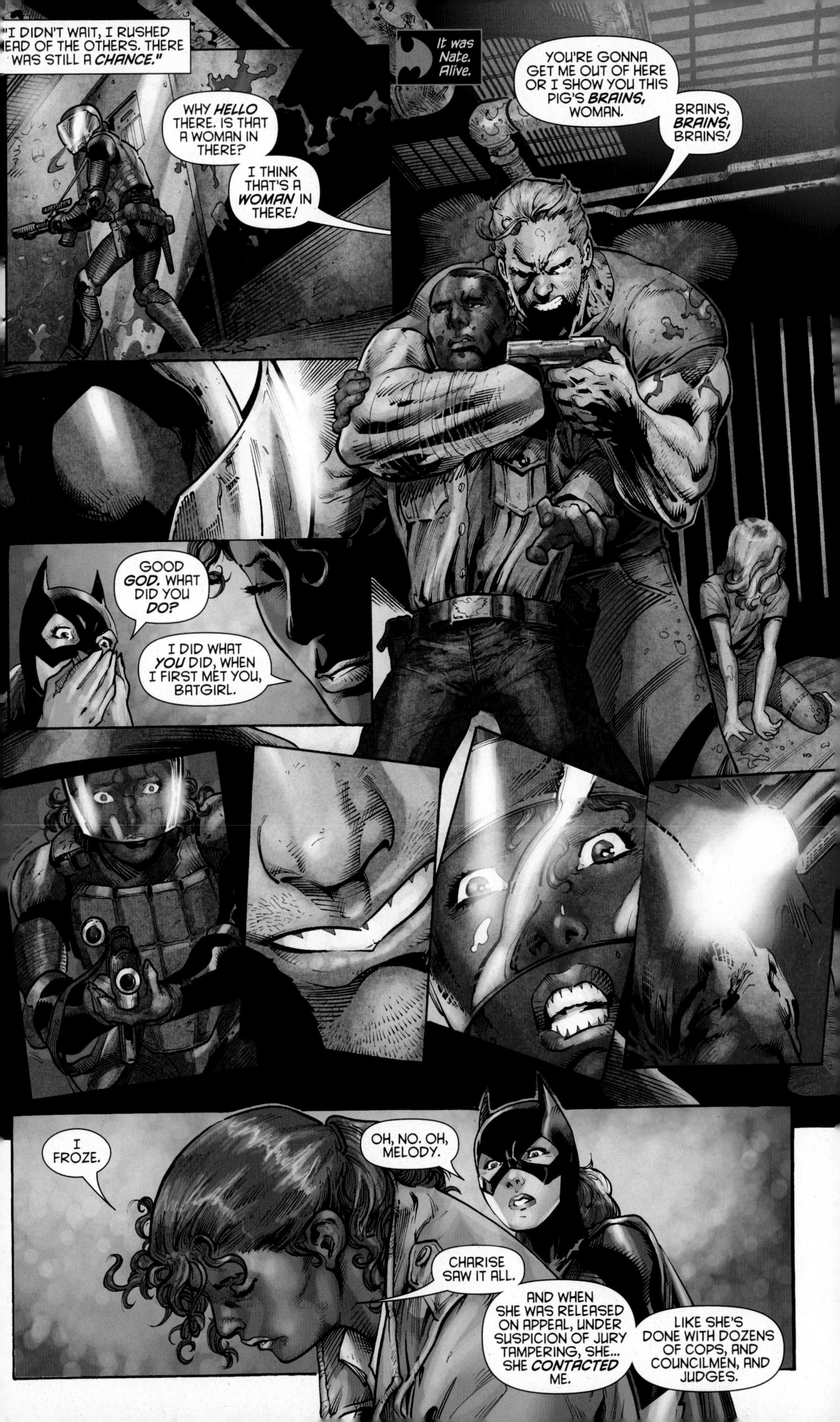
"I DIDN'T WAIT, I RUSHED
EAD OF THE OTHERS. THERE
WAS STILL A CHANCE."
WHY HELLO THERE. IS THAT A WOMAN IN THERE?
I THINK THAT'S A WOMAN IN THERE!
It was Nate. Alive.
YOU'RE GONNA GET ME OUT OF HERE OR I SHOW YOU THIS PIG'S BRAINS, WOMAN.
BRAINS, BRAINS, BRAINS!
GOOD GOD. WHAT DID YOU DO?
I DID WHAT YOU DID, WHEN I FIRST MET YOU, BATGIRL.
I FROZE.
OH, NO. OH, MELODY.
CHARISE SAW IT ALL.
AND WHEN SHE WAS RELEASED ON APPEAL, UNDER SUSPICION OF JURY TAMPERING, SHE... SHE CONTACTED ME.
LIKE SHE'S DONE WITH DOZENS OF COPS, AND COUNCILMEN, AND JUDGES.

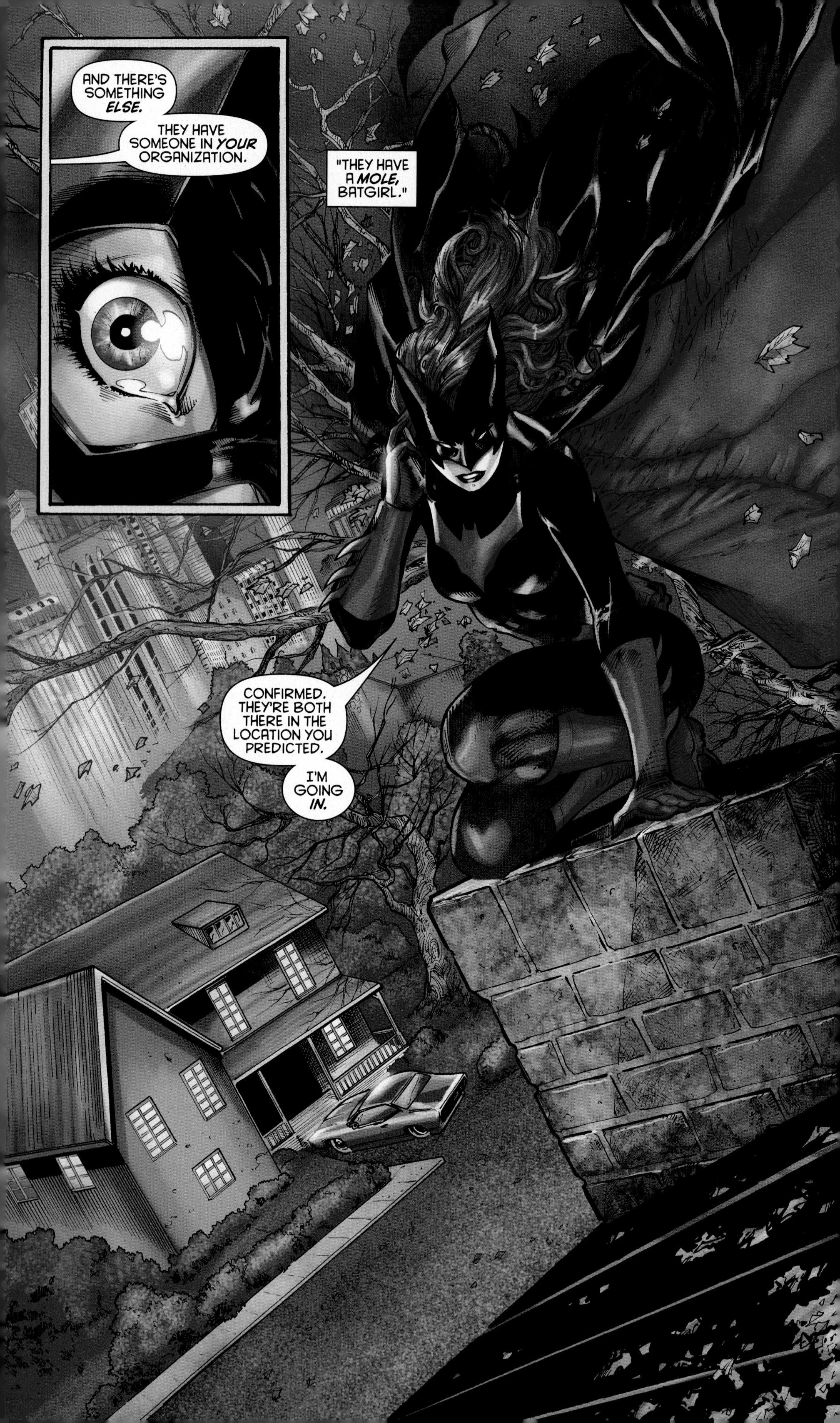
AND THERE'S SOMETHING *ELSE.*
THEY HAVE SOMEONE IN *YOUR* ORGANIZATION.
"THEY HAVE A *MOLE,* BATGIRL."
CONFIRMED. THEY'RE BOTH THERE IN THE LOCATION YOU PREDICTED.
I'M GOING *IN.*

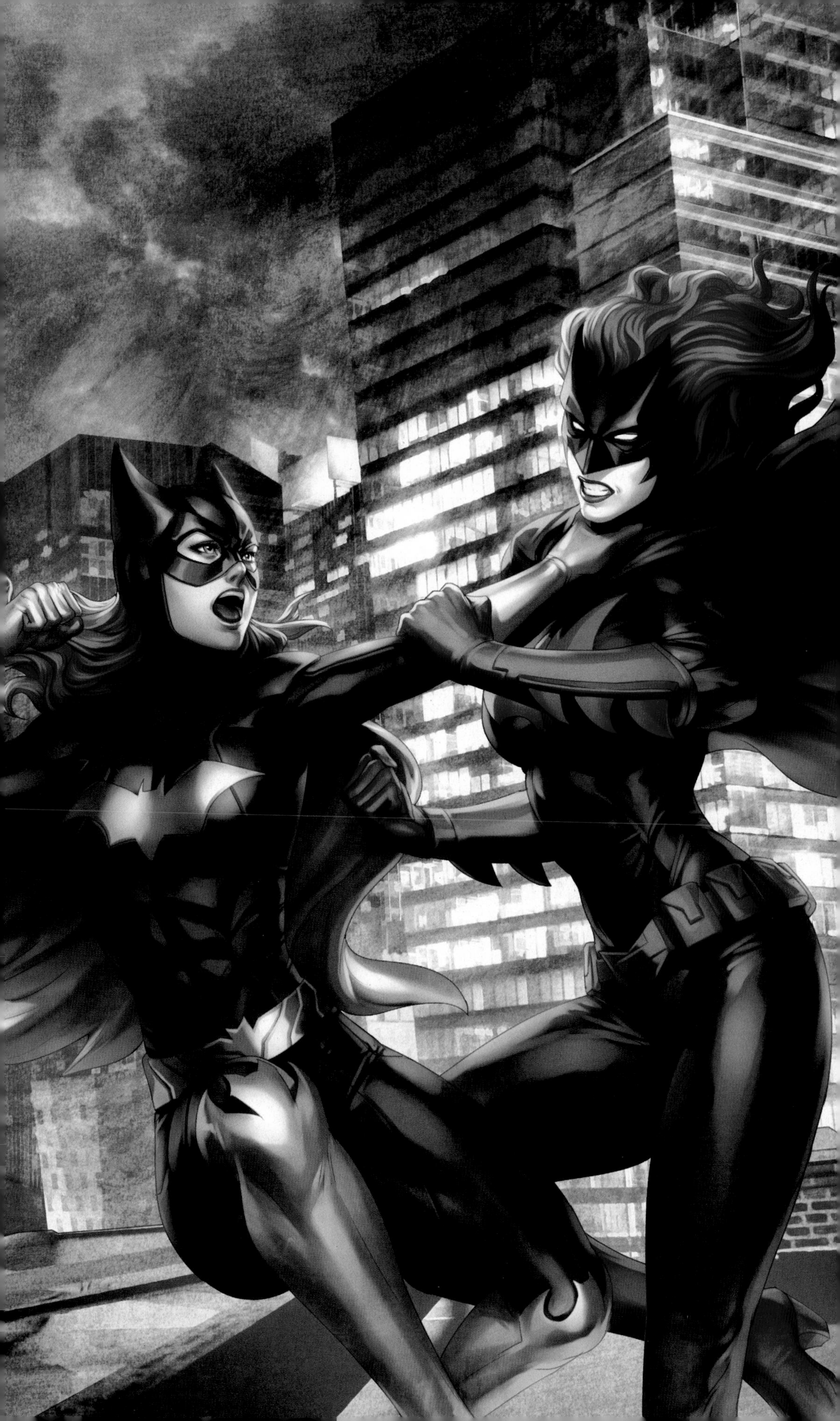

GAIL SIMONE writer ARDIAN SYAF penciller VICENTE CIFUENTES inker cover by STANLEY "ARTGERM" LAU

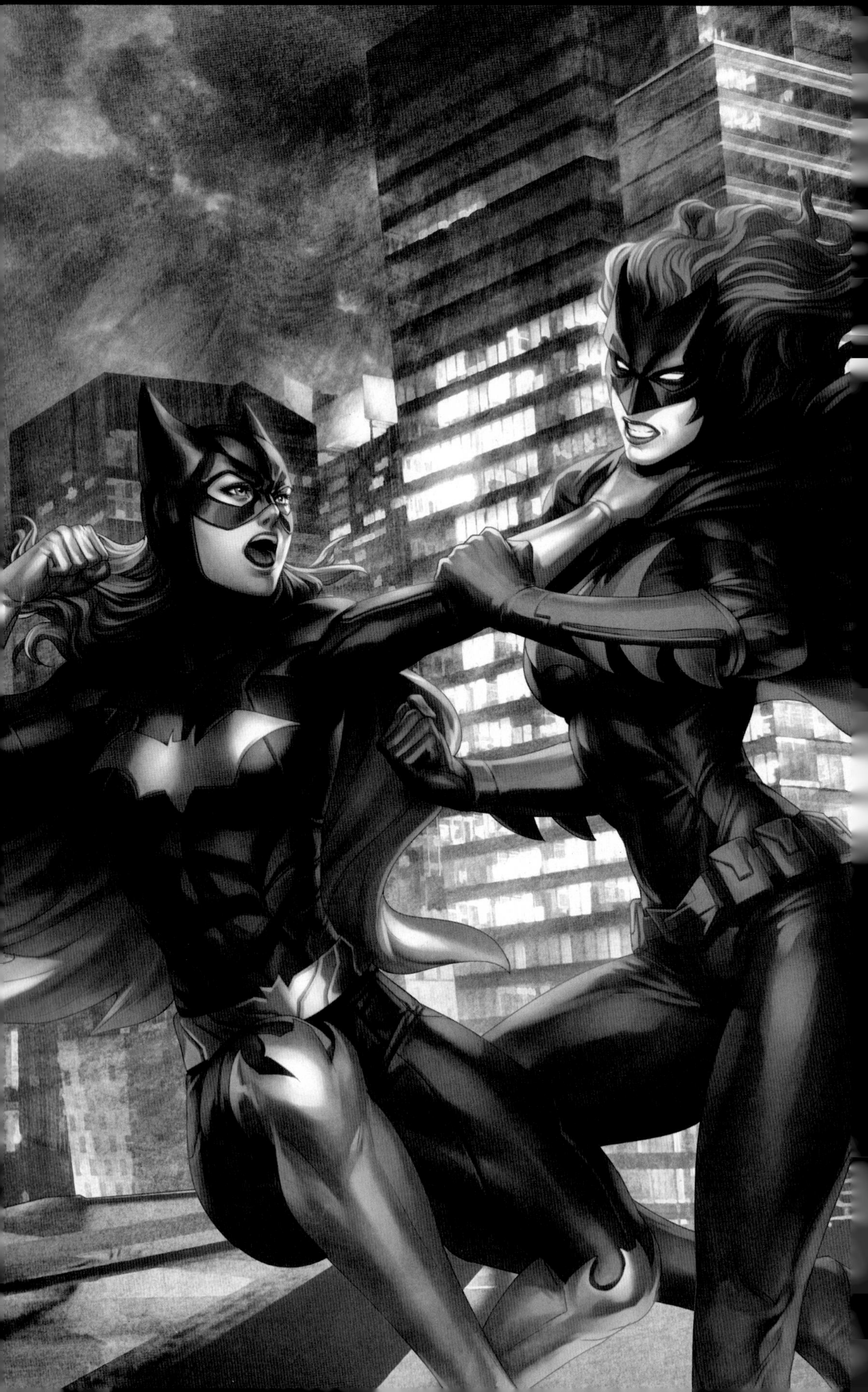

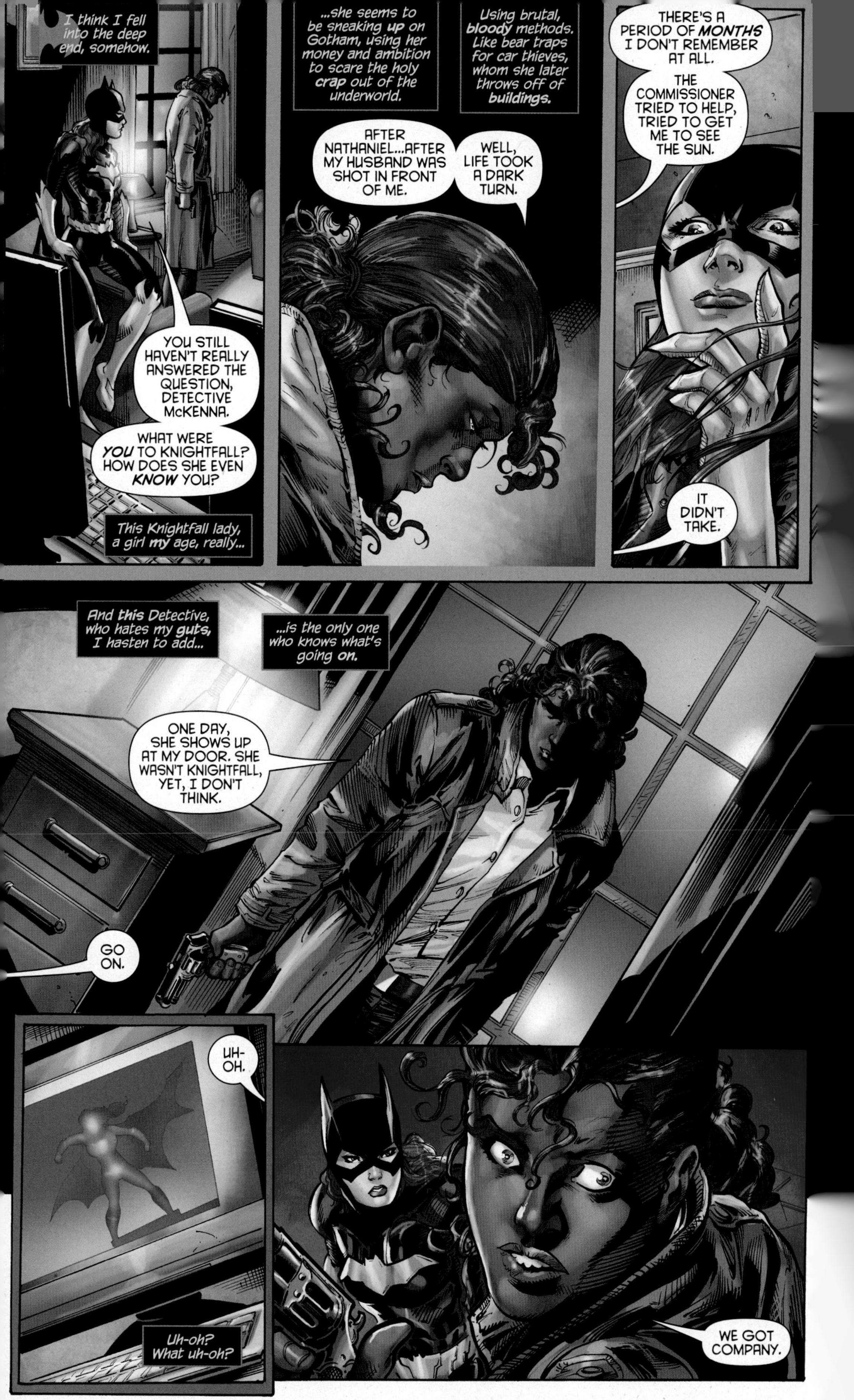

I think I fell into the deep end, somehow.
YOU STILL HAVEN'T REALLY ANSWERED THE QUESTION, DETECTIVE McKENNA.
WHAT WERE *YOU* TO KNIGHTFALL? HOW DOES SHE EVEN *KNOW* YOU?
This Knightfall lady, a girl *my* age, really...
...she seems to be sneaking *up* on Gotham, using her money and ambition to scare the holy *crap* out of the underworld.
Using brutal, *bloody* methods. Like bear traps for car thieves, whom she later throws off of *buildings.*
AFTER NATHANIEL...AFTER MY HUSBAND WAS SHOT IN FRONT OF ME.
WELL, LIFE TOOK A DARK TURN.
THERE'S A PERIOD OF *MONTHS* I DON'T REMEMBER AT ALL.
THE COMMISSIONER TRIED TO HELP, TRIED TO GET ME TO SEE THE SUN.
IT DIDN'T TAKE.
And *this* Detective, who hates my *guts,* I hasten to add...
...is the only one who knows what's going *on.*
ONE DAY, SHE SHOWS UP AT MY DOOR. SHE WASN'T KNIGHTFALL, YET, I DON'T THINK.
GO ON.
UH-OH.
Uh-oh? What uh-oh?
WE GOT COMPANY.

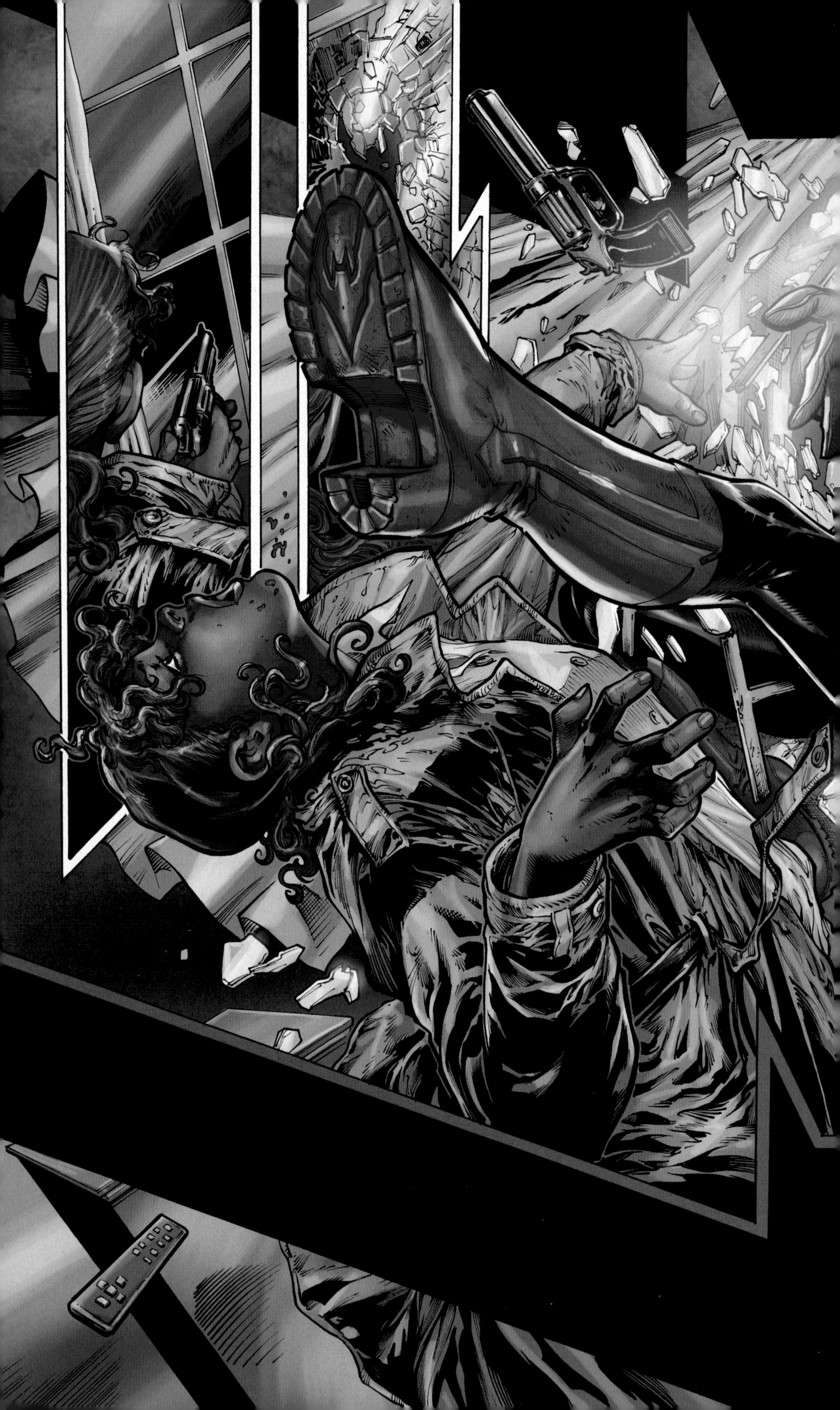

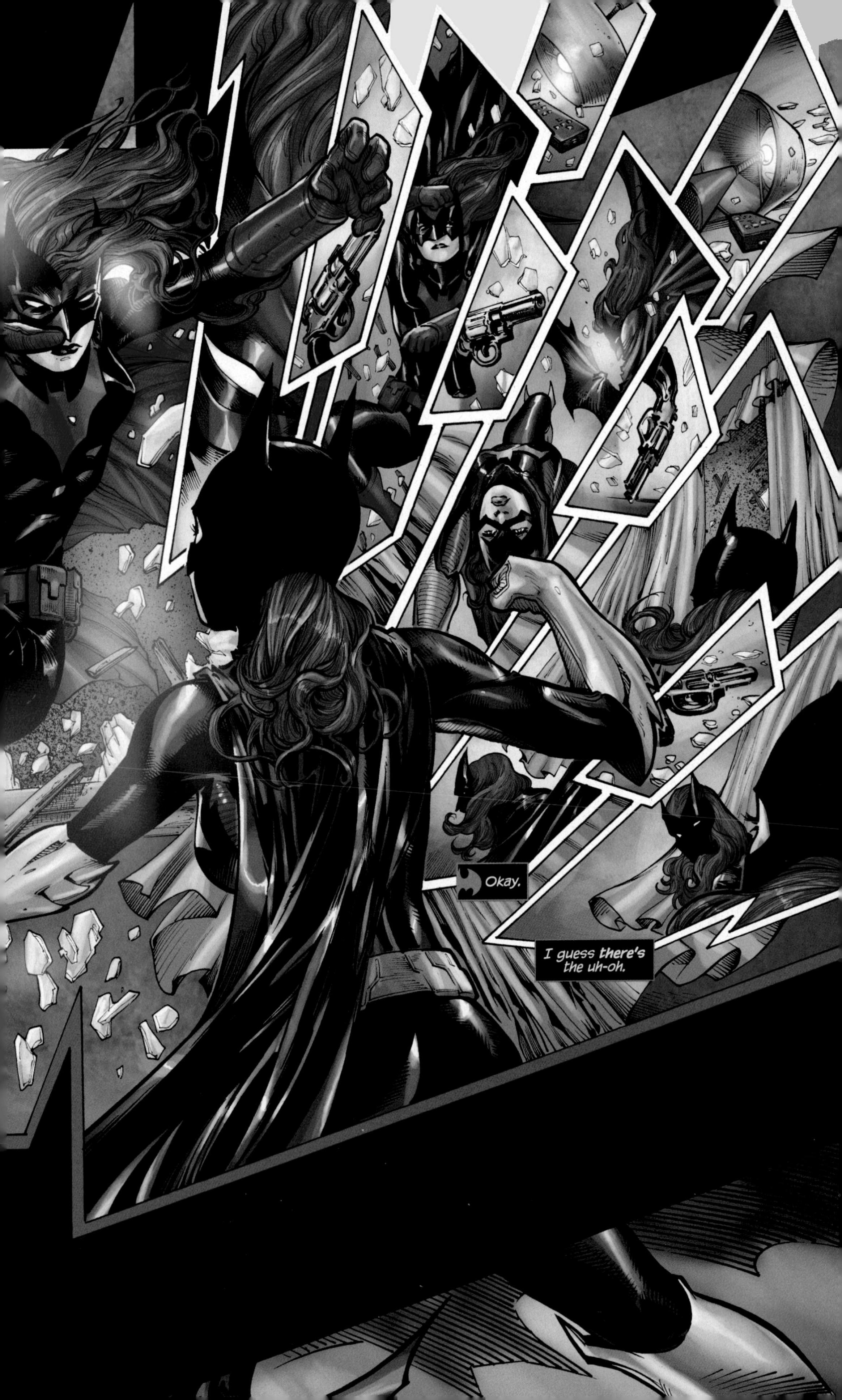
Okay.
I guess there's the uh-oh.

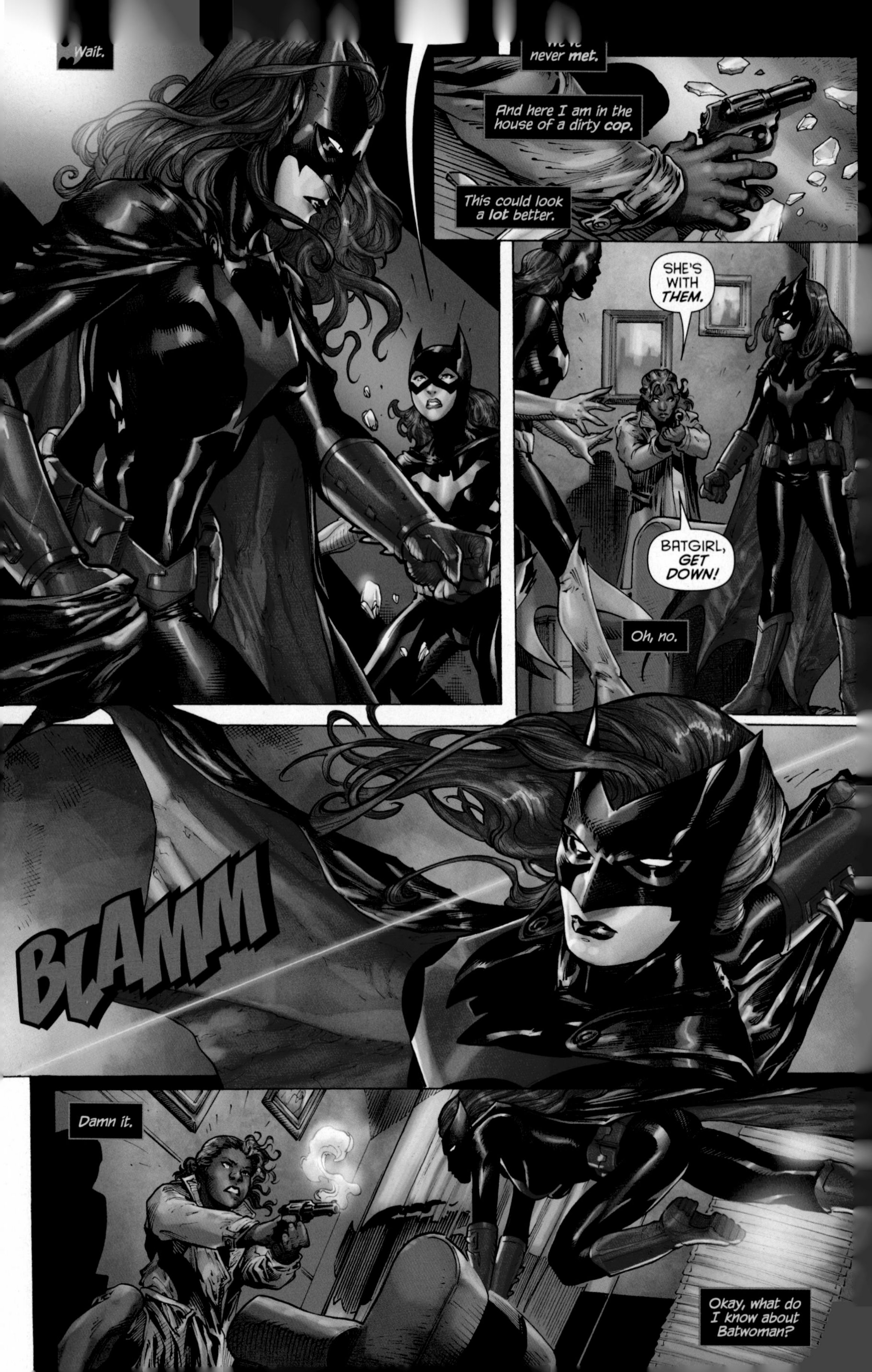
Wait.
never met.
And here I am in the house of a dirty cop.
This could look a lot better.
SHE'S WITH THEM.
BATGIRL, GET DOWN!
Oh, no.
BLAMM
Damn it.
Okay, what do I know about Batwoman?

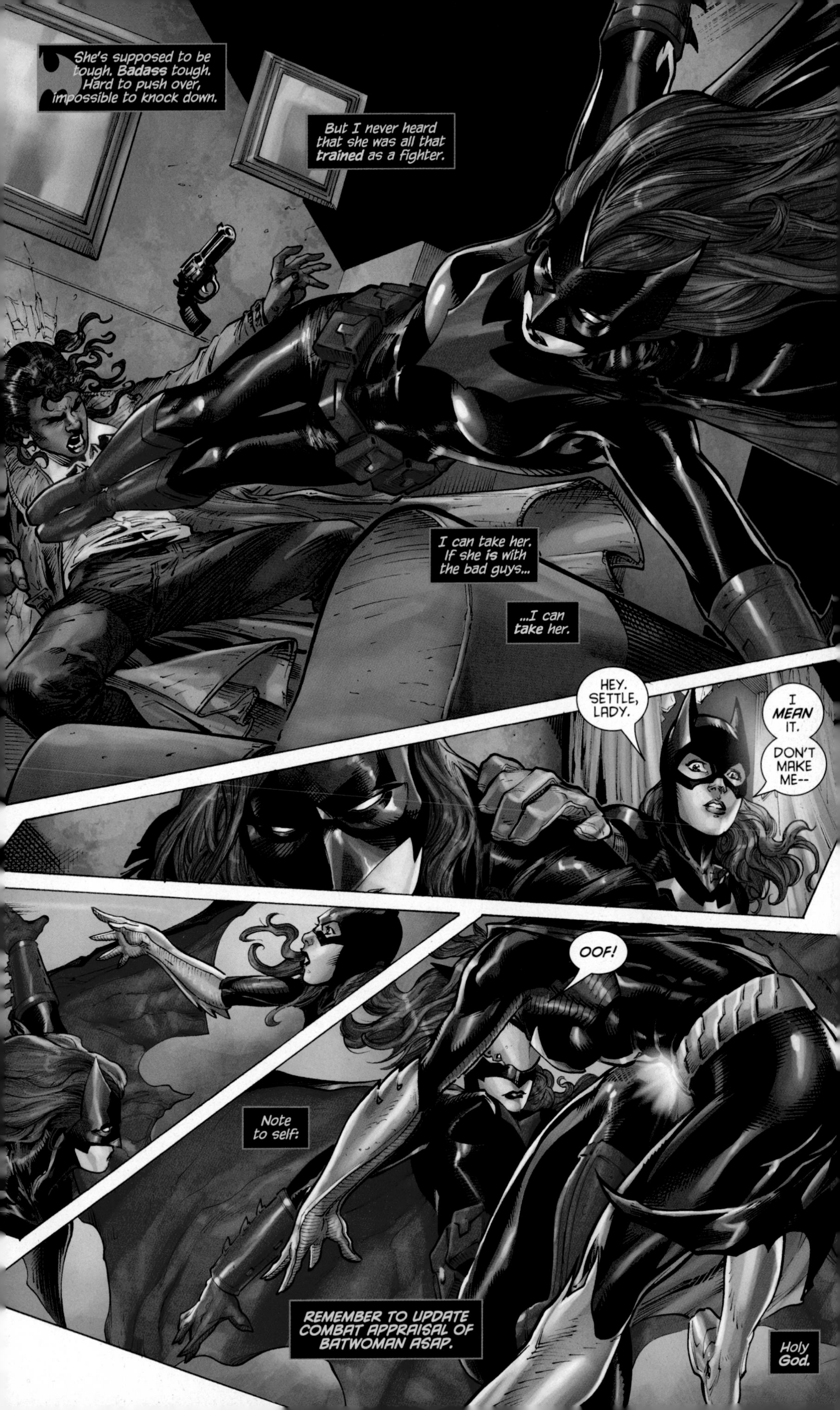

She's supposed to be tough. Badass tough. Hard to push over, impossible to knock down.
But I never heard that she was all that trained as a fighter.
I can take her. If she is with the bad guys...
...I can take her.
HEY. SETTLE, LADY.
I MEAN IT.
DON'T MAKE ME--
OOF!
Note to self:
REMEMBER TO UPDATE COMBAT APPRAISAL OF BATWOMAN ASAP.
Holy God.

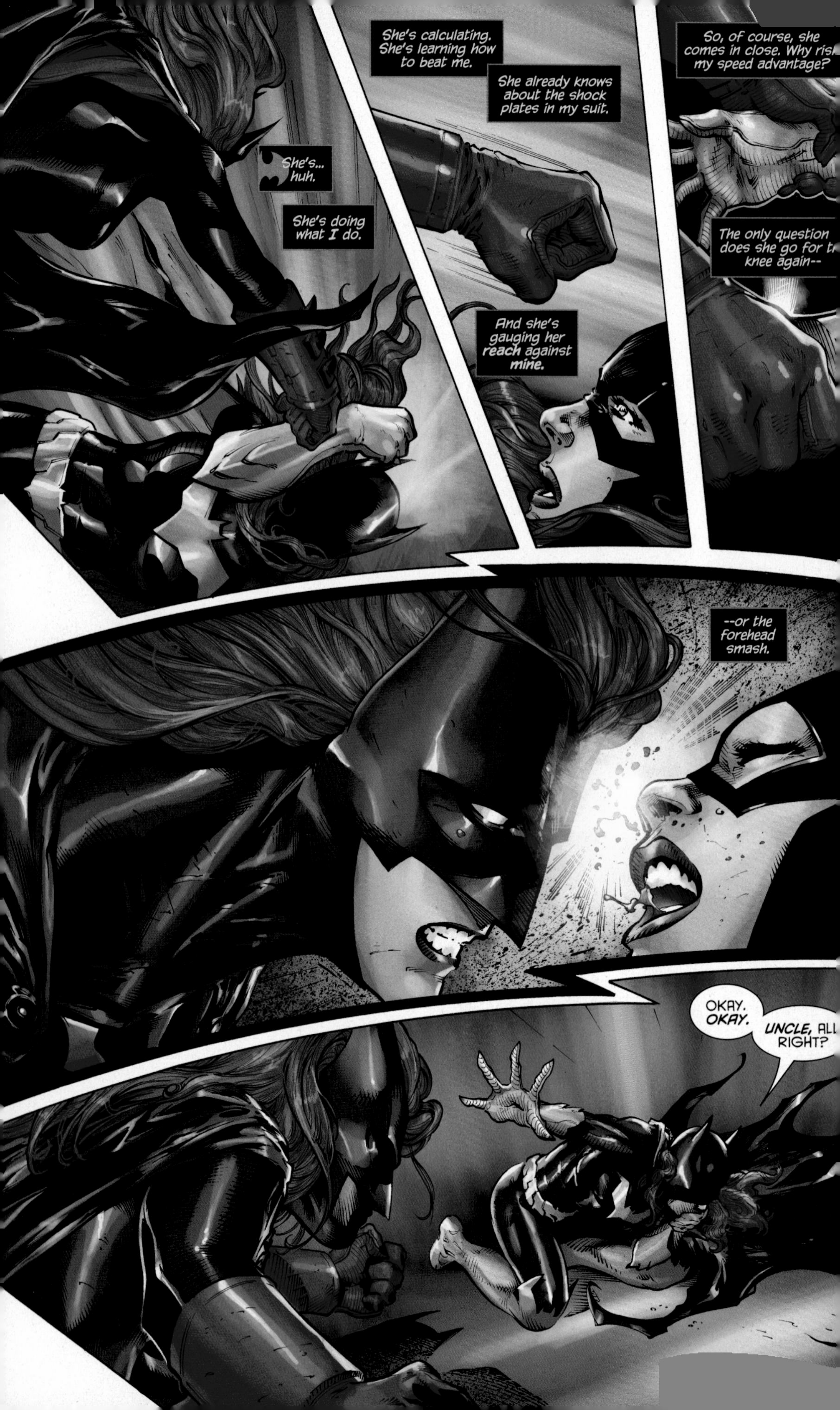
She's... huh.
She's doing what I do.
She's calculating. She's learning how to beat me.
She already knows about the shock plates in my suit.
And she's gauging her reach against mine.
So, of course, she comes in close. Why risk my speed advantage?
The only question does she go for the knee again--
--or the forehead smash.
OKAY. OKAY.
UNCLE, ALL RIGHT?

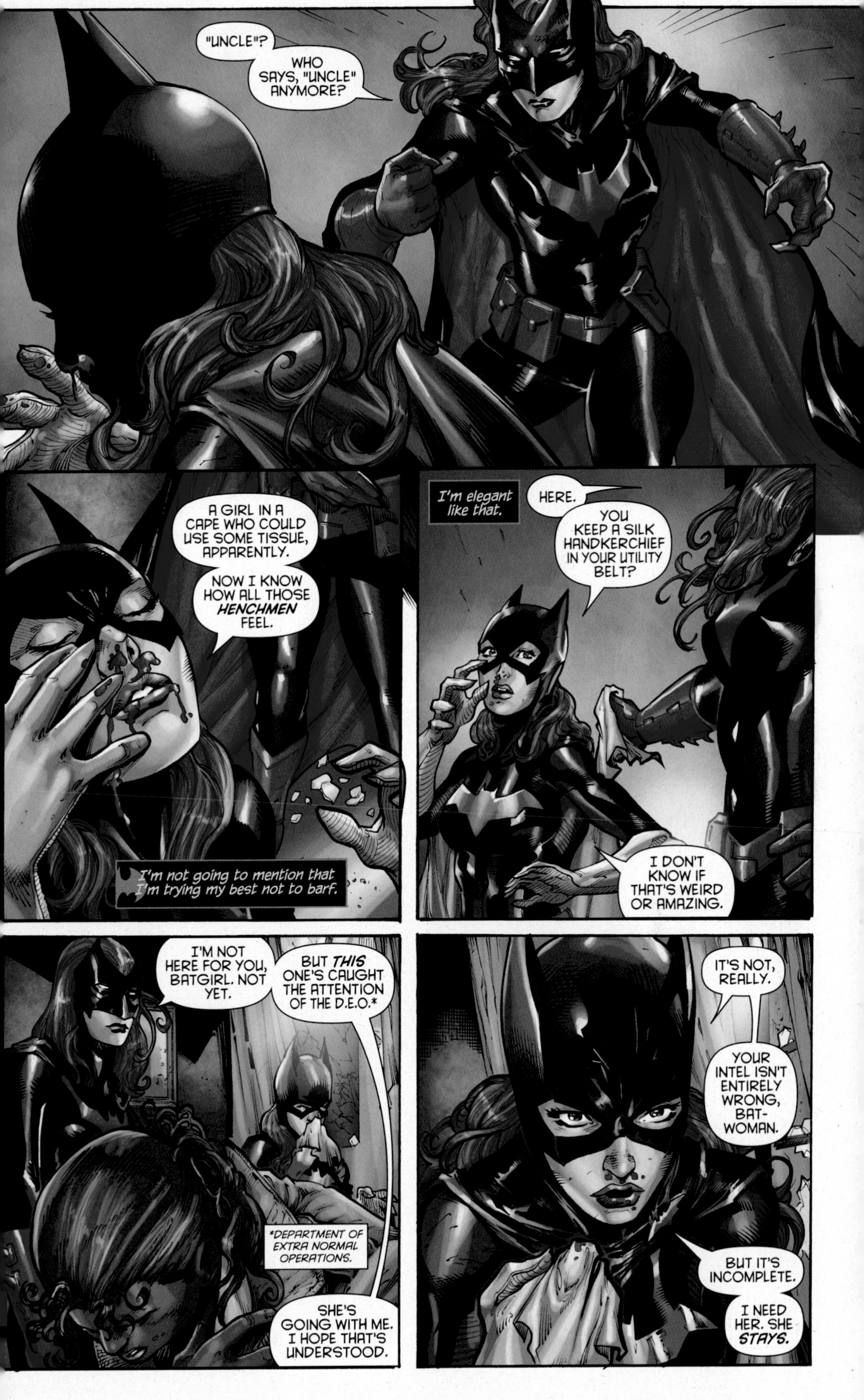
"UNCLE"?
WHO SAYS, "UNCLE" ANYMORE?
A GIRL IN A CAPE WHO COULD USE SOME TISSUE, APPARENTLY.
NOW I KNOW HOW ALL THOSE *HENCHMEN* FEEL.
I'm not going to mention that I'm trying my best not to barf.
I'm elegant like that.
HERE.
YOU KEEP A SILK HANDKERCHIEF IN YOUR UTILITY BELT?
I DON'T KNOW IF THAT'S WEIRD OR AMAZING.
I'M NOT HERE FOR YOU, BATGIRL. NOT YET.
BUT *THIS* ONE'S CAUGHT THE ATTENTION OF THE D.E.O.*
*DEPARTMENT OF EXTRA NORMAL OPERATIONS.
SHE'S GOING WITH ME. I HOPE THAT'S UNDERSTOOD.
IT'S NOT, REALLY.
YOUR INTEL ISN'T ENTIRELY WRONG, BAT-WOMAN.
BUT IT'S INCOMPLETE.
I NEED HER. SHE *STAYS.*

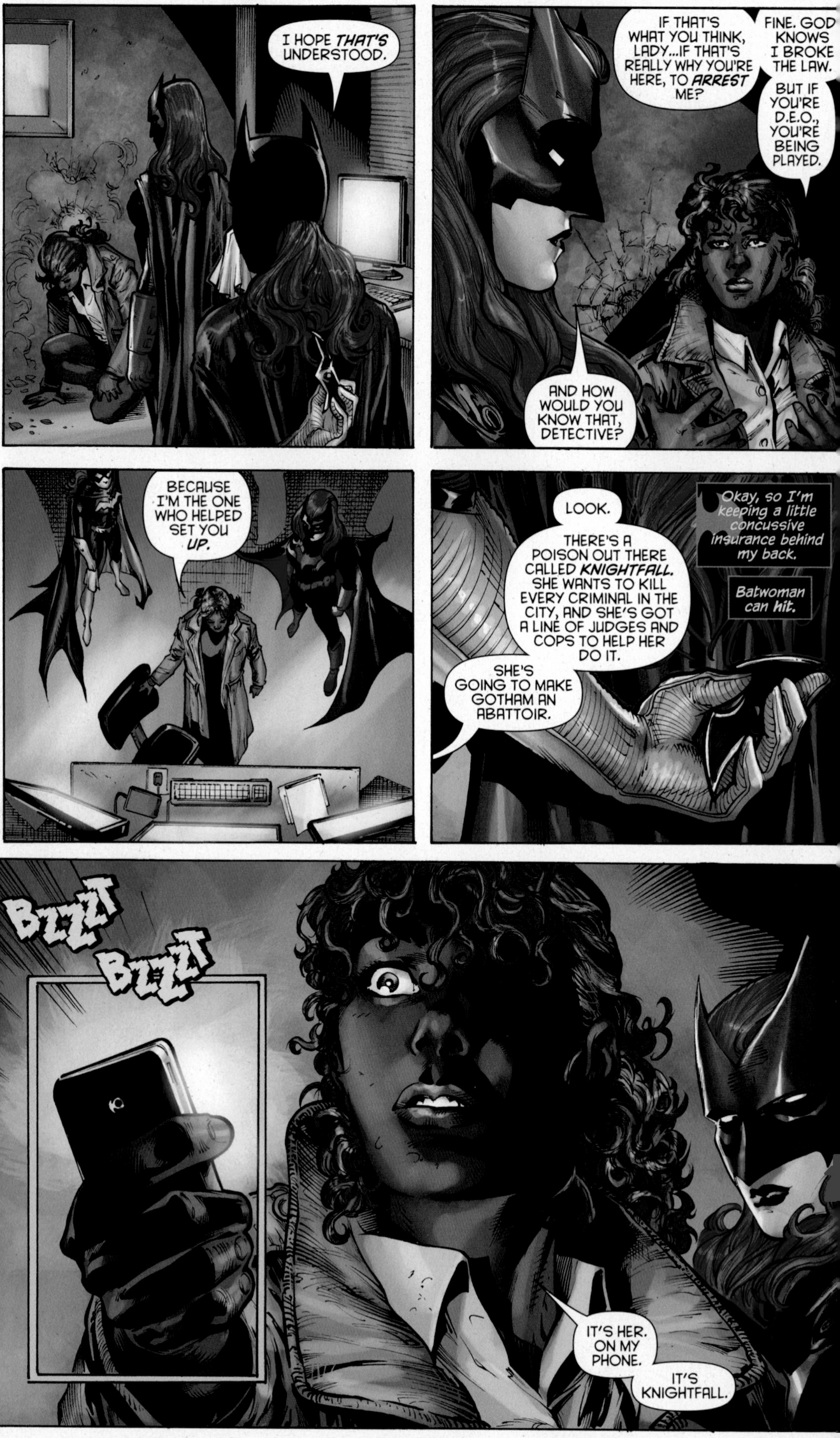
I HOPE THAT'S UNDERSTOOD.
IF THAT'S WHAT YOU THINK, LADY...IF THAT'S REALLY WHY YOU'RE HERE, TO ARREST ME?
FINE. GOD KNOWS I BROKE THE LAW.
BUT IF YOU'RE D.E.O., YOU'RE BEING PLAYED.
AND HOW WOULD YOU KNOW THAT, DETECTIVE?
BECAUSE I'M THE ONE WHO HELPED SET YOU UP.
LOOK.
THERE'S A POISON OUT THERE CALLED KNIGHTFALL. SHE WANTS TO KILL EVERY CRIMINAL IN THE CITY, AND SHE'S GOT A LINE OF JUDGES AND COPS TO HELP HER DO IT.
SHE'S GOING TO MAKE GOTHAM AN ABATTOIR.
Okay, so I'm keeping a little concussive insurance behind my back.
Batwoman can hit.
BZZZT
BZZZT
IT'S HER. ON MY PHONE.
IT'S KNIGHTFALL.

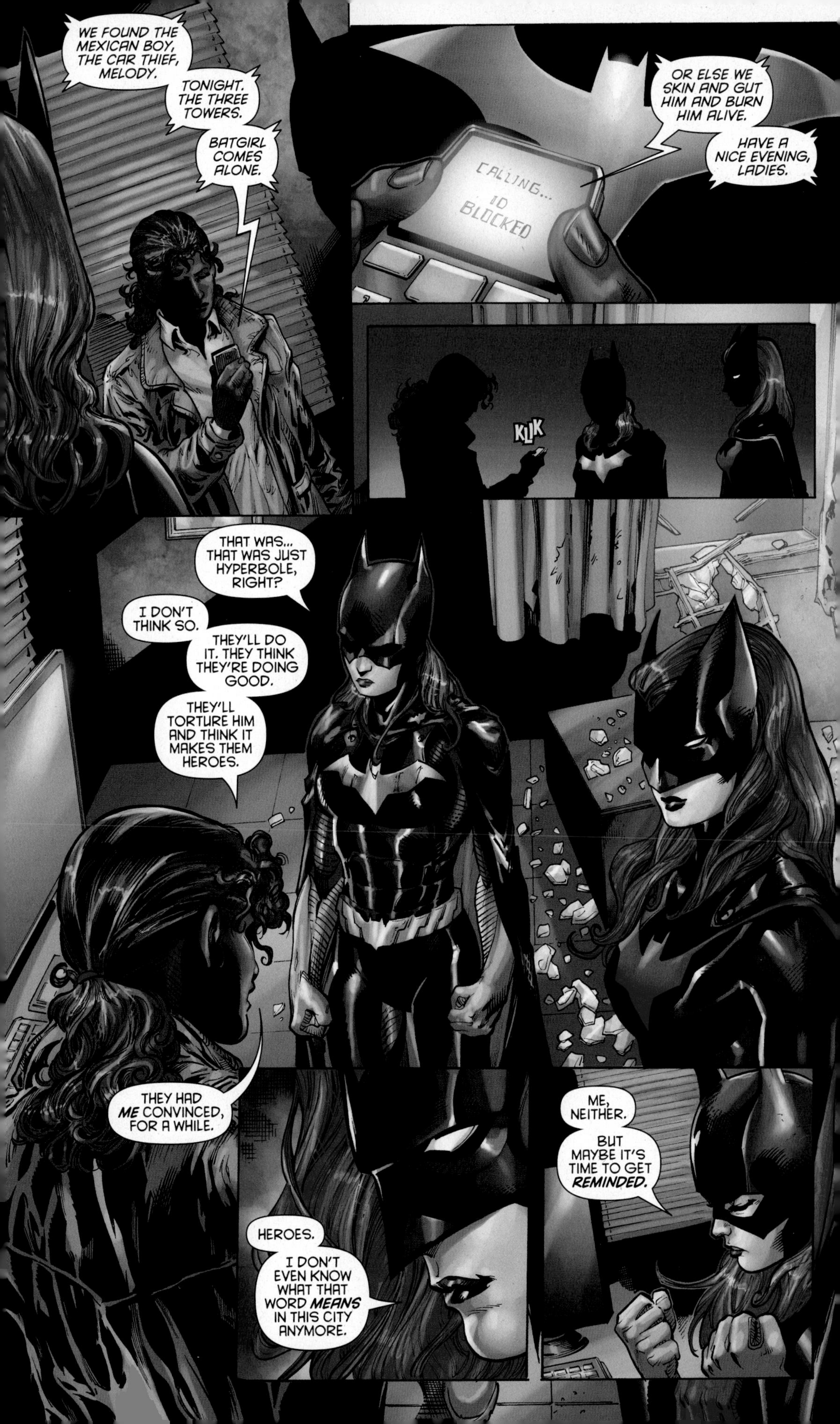
WE FOUND THE MEXICAN BOY, THE CAR THIEF, MELODY.
TONIGHT. THE THREE TOWERS.
BATGIRL COMES ALONE.
CALLING... ID BLOCKED
OR ELSE WE SKIN AND GUT HIM AND BURN HIM ALIVE.
HAVE A NICE EVENING, LADIES.
KLIK
THAT WAS... THAT WAS JUST HYPERBOLE, RIGHT?
I DON'T THINK SO.
THEY'LL DO IT. THEY THINK THEY'RE DOING GOOD.
THEY'LL TORTURE HIM AND THINK IT MAKES THEM HEROES.
THEY HAD **ME** CONVINCED, FOR A WHILE.
HEROES.
I DON'T EVEN KNOW WHAT THAT WORD **MEANS** IN THIS CITY ANYMORE.
ME, NEITHER.
BUT MAYBE IT'S TIME TO GET **REMINDED.**

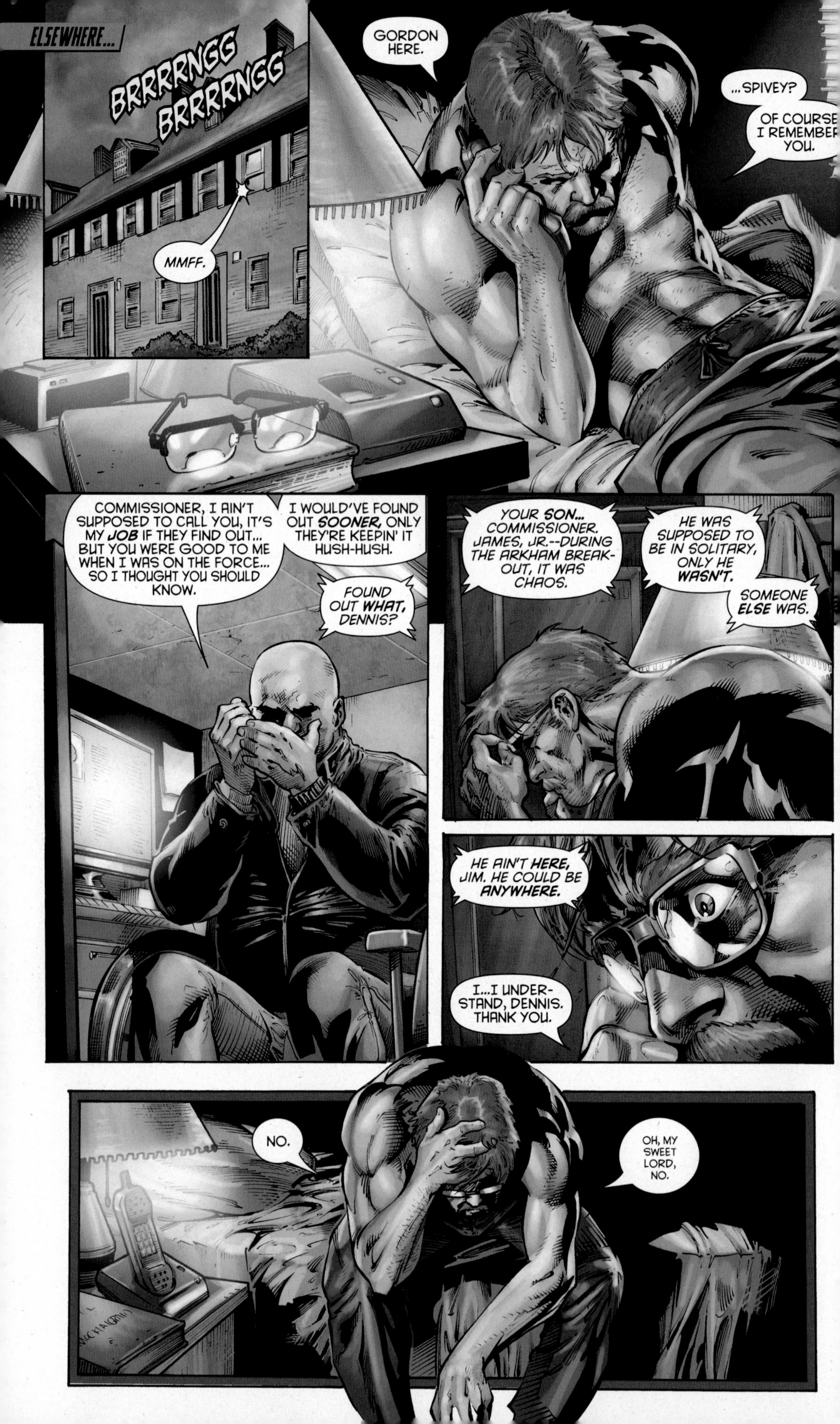
ELSEWHERE...
BRRRRNGG BRRRRNGG
MMFF.
GORDON HERE.
...SPIVEY?
OF COURSE I REMEMBER YOU.
COMMISSIONER, I AIN'T SUPPOSED TO CALL YOU, IT'S MY JOB IF THEY FIND OUT... BUT YOU WERE GOOD TO ME WHEN I WAS ON THE FORCE... SO I THOUGHT YOU SHOULD KNOW.
I WOULD'VE FOUND OUT SOONER, ONLY THEY'RE KEEPIN' IT HUSH-HUSH.
FOUND OUT WHAT, DENNIS?
YOUR SON... COMMISSIONER. JAMES, JR.--DURING THE ARKHAM BREAK-OUT, IT WAS CHAOS.
HE WAS SUPPOSED TO BE IN SOLITARY, ONLY HE WASN'T.
SOMEONE ELSE WAS.
HE AIN'T HERE, JIM. HE COULD BE ANYWHERE.
I...I UNDER-STAND, DENNIS. THANK YOU.
NO.
OH, MY SWEET LORD, NO.

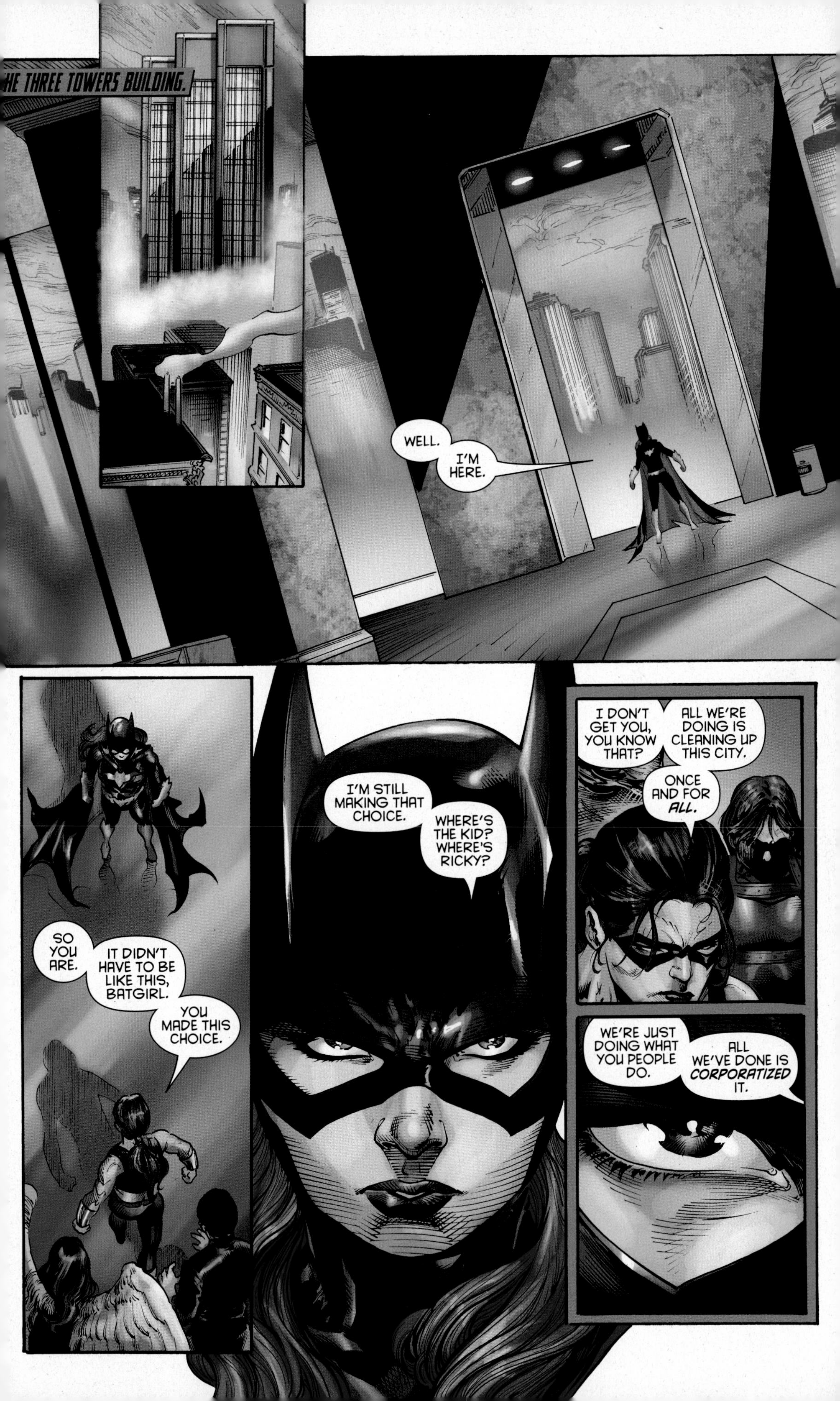

HE THREE TOWERS BUILDING.
WELL.
I'M HERE.
SO YOU ARE.
IT DIDN'T HAVE TO BE LIKE THIS, BATGIRL.
YOU MADE THIS CHOICE.
I'M STILL MAKING THAT CHOICE.
WHERE'S THE KID? WHERE'S RICKY?
I DON'T GET YOU, YOU KNOW THAT?
ALL WE'RE DOING IS CLEANING UP THIS CITY.
ONCE AND FOR ALL.
WE'RE JUST DOING WHAT YOU PEOPLE DO.
ALL WE'VE DONE IS CORPORATIZED IT.

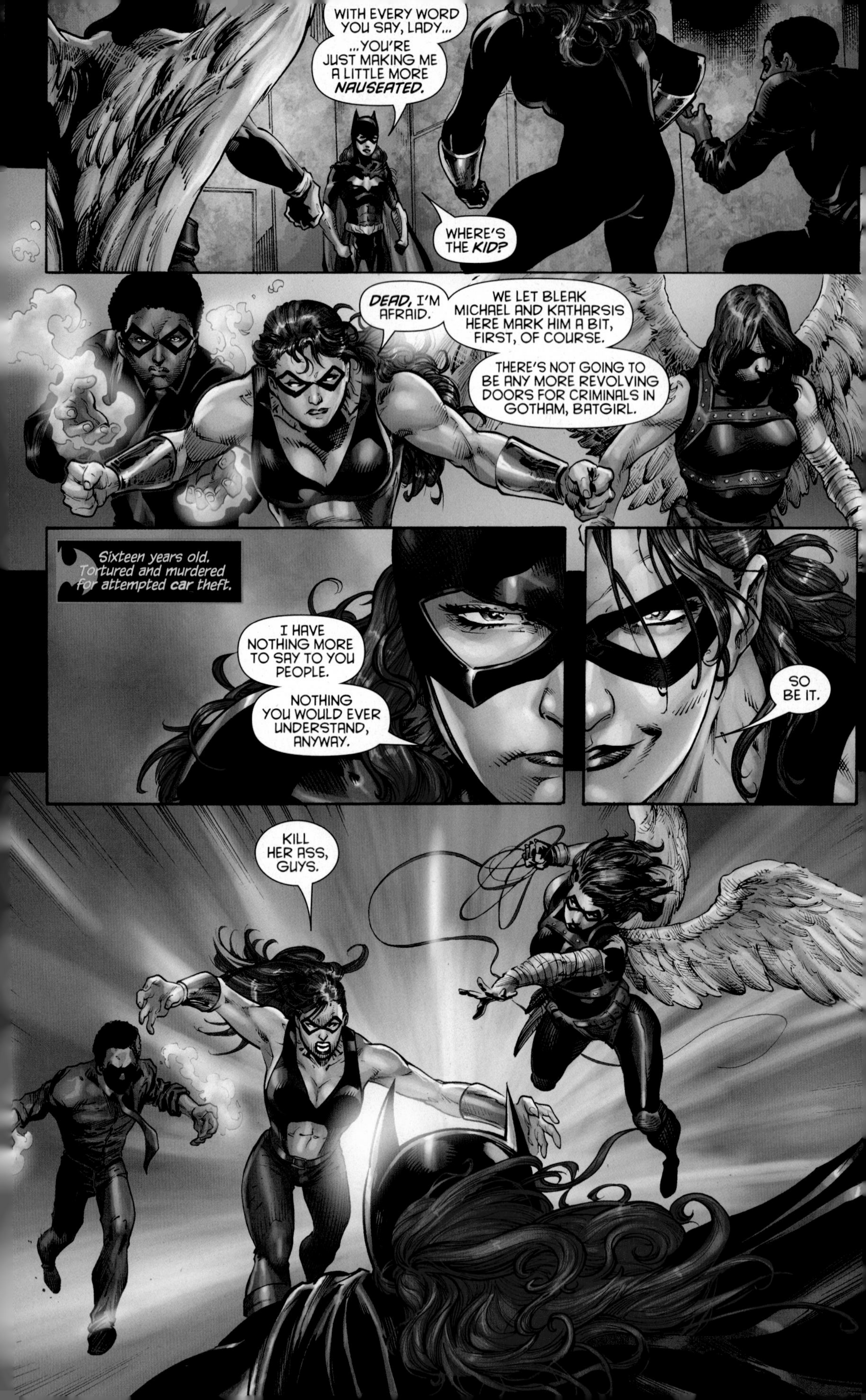
WITH EVERY WORD YOU SAY, LADY...
...YOU'RE JUST MAKING ME A LITTLE MORE *NAUSEATED.*
WHERE'S THE *KID?*
DEAD, I'M AFRAID.
WE LET BLEAK MICHAEL AND KATHARSIS HERE MARK HIM A BIT, FIRST, OF COURSE.
THERE'S NOT GOING TO BE ANY MORE REVOLVING DOORS FOR CRIMINALS IN GOTHAM, BATGIRL.
Sixteen years old. Tortured and murdered for attempted **car** theft.
I HAVE NOTHING MORE TO SAY TO YOU PEOPLE.
NOTHING YOU WOULD EVER UNDERSTAND, ANYWAY.
SO BE IT.
KILL HER ASS, GUYS.

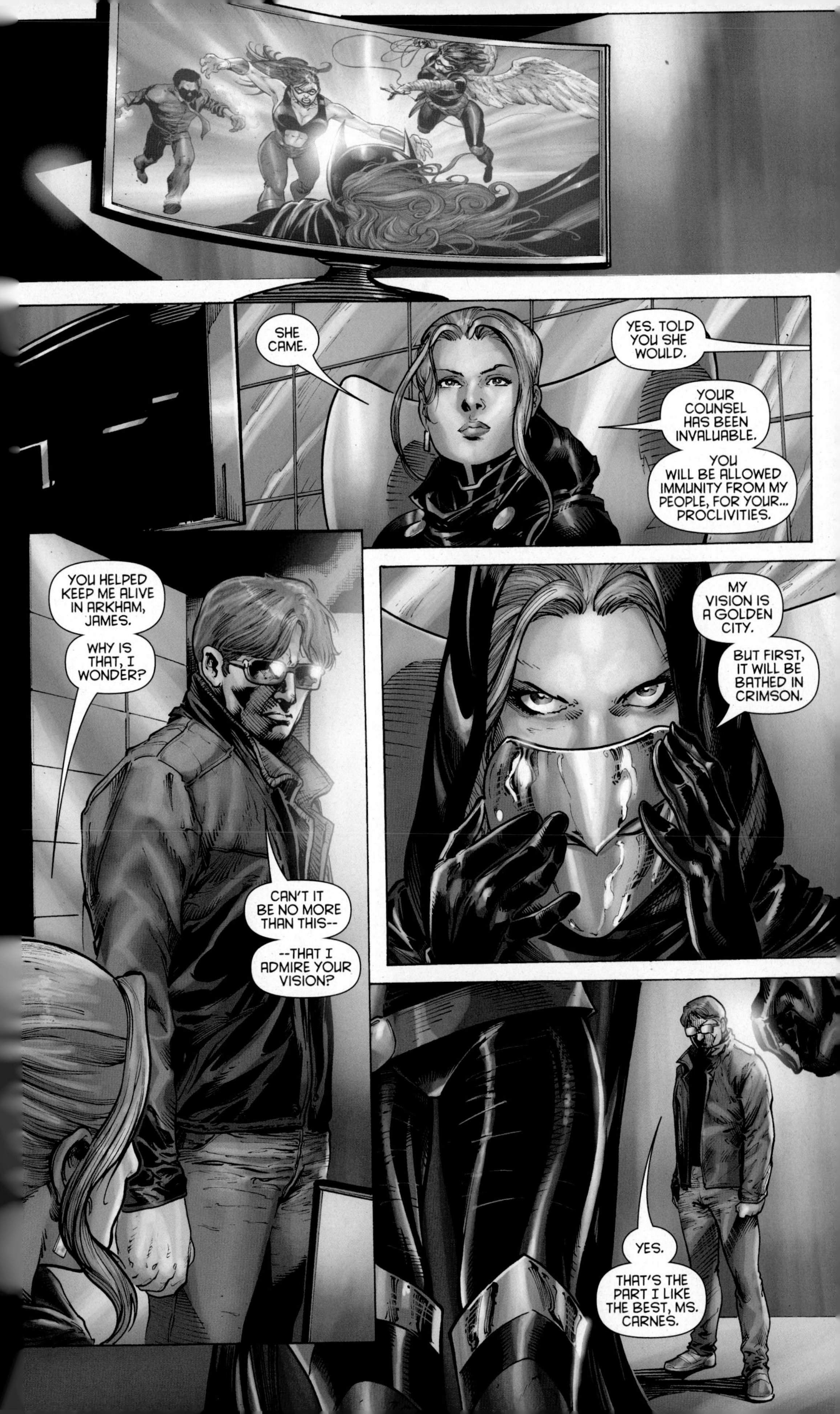
SHE CAME.
YES. TOLD YOU SHE WOULD.
YOUR COUNSEL HAS BEEN INVALUABLE.
YOU WILL BE ALLOWED IMMUNITY FROM MY PEOPLE, FOR YOUR... PROCLIVITIES.
YOU HELPED KEEP ME ALIVE IN ARKHAM, JAMES.
WHY IS THAT, I WONDER?
CAN'T IT BE NO MORE THAN THIS--
--THAT I ADMIRE YOUR VISION?
MY VISION IS A GOLDEN CITY.
BUT FIRST, IT WILL BE BATHED IN CRIMSON.
YES.
THAT'S THE PART I LIKE THE BEST, MS. CARNES.

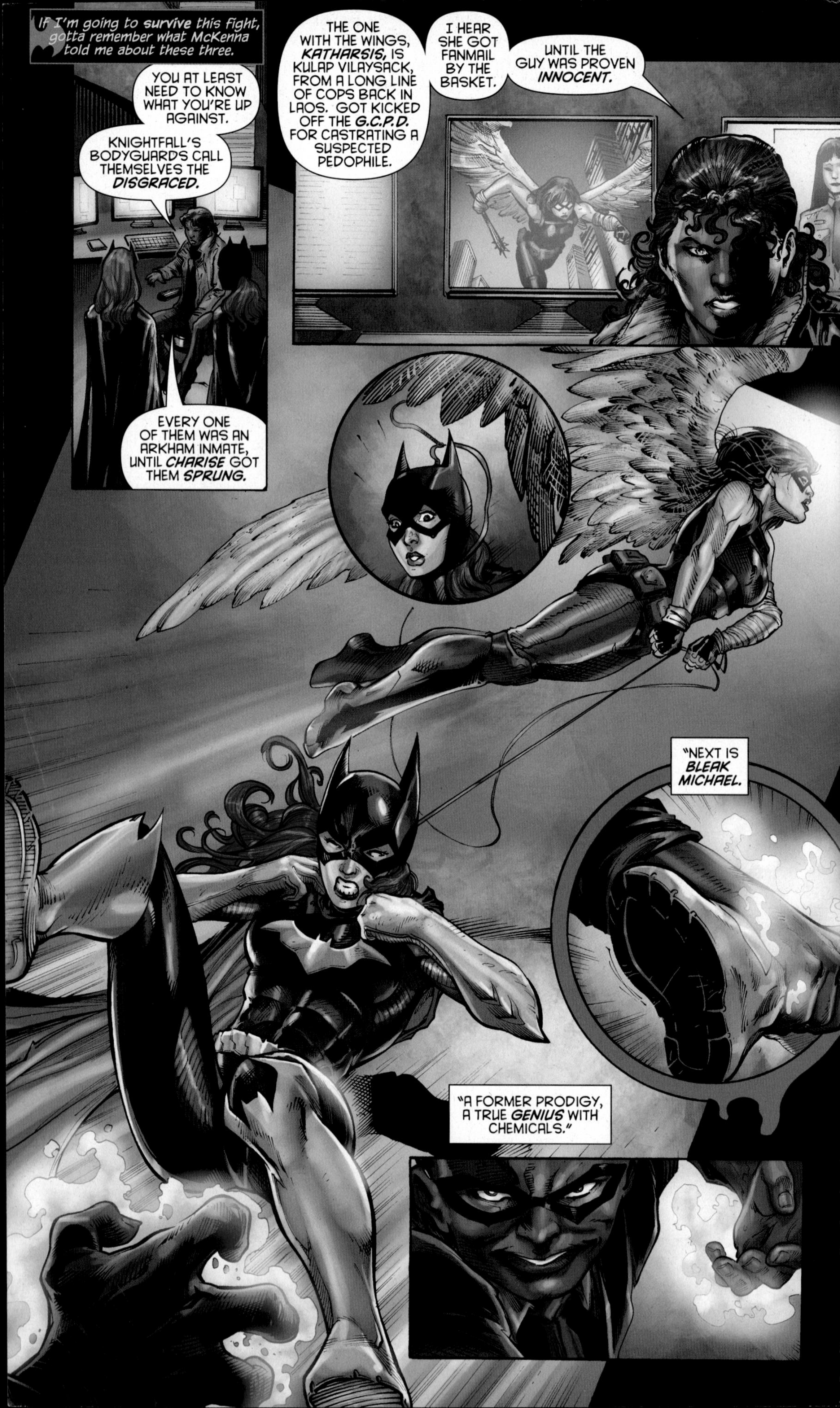
If I'm going to survive this fight, gotta remember what McKenna told me about these three.
YOU AT LEAST NEED TO KNOW WHAT YOU'RE UP AGAINST.
KNIGHTFALL'S BODYGUARDS CALL THEMSELVES THE DISGRACED.
EVERY ONE OF THEM WAS AN ARKHAM INMATE, UNTIL CHARISE GOT THEM SPRUNG.
THE ONE WITH THE WINGS, KATHARSIS, IS KULAP VILAYSACK, FROM A LONG LINE OF COPS BACK IN LAOS. GOT KICKED OFF THE G.C.P.D. FOR CASTRATING A SUSPECTED PEDOPHILE.
I HEAR SHE GOT FANMAIL BY THE BASKET.
UNTIL THE GUY WAS PROVEN INNOCENT.
"NEXT IS BLEAK MICHAEL.
"A FORMER PRODIGY, A TRUE GENIUS WITH CHEMICALS."

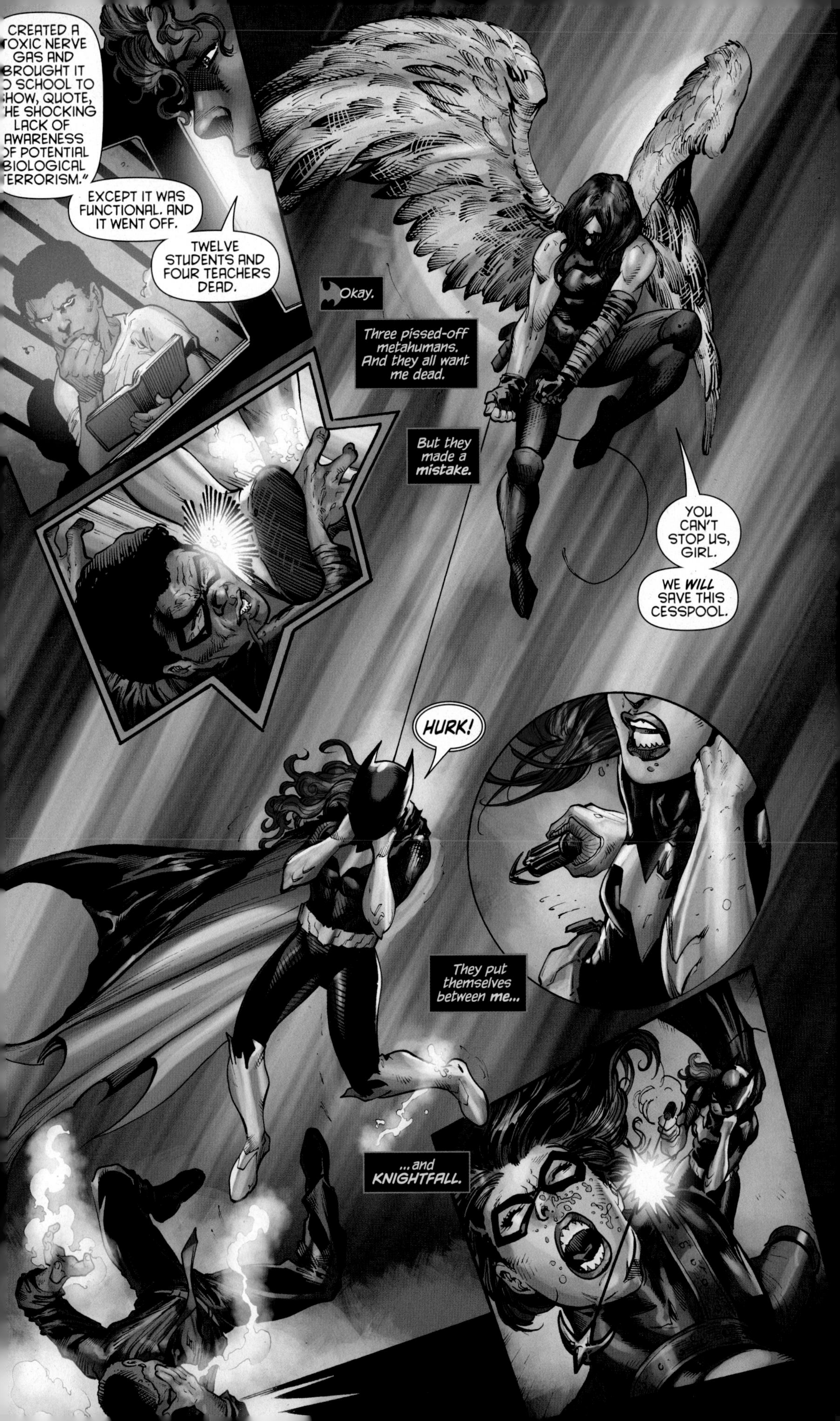

CREATED A TOXIC NERVE GAS AND BROUGHT IT TO SCHOOL TO SHOW, QUOTE, "THE SHOCKING LACK OF AWARENESS OF POTENTIAL BIOLOGICAL TERRORISM."
EXCEPT IT WAS FUNCTIONAL. AND IT WENT OFF.
TWELVE STUDENTS AND FOUR TEACHERS DEAD.
Okay.
Three pissed-off metahumans. And they all want me dead.
But they made a mistake.
YOU CAN'T STOP US, GIRL.
WE WILL SAVE THIS CESSPOOL.
HURK!
They put themselves between me...
...and KNIGHTFALL.

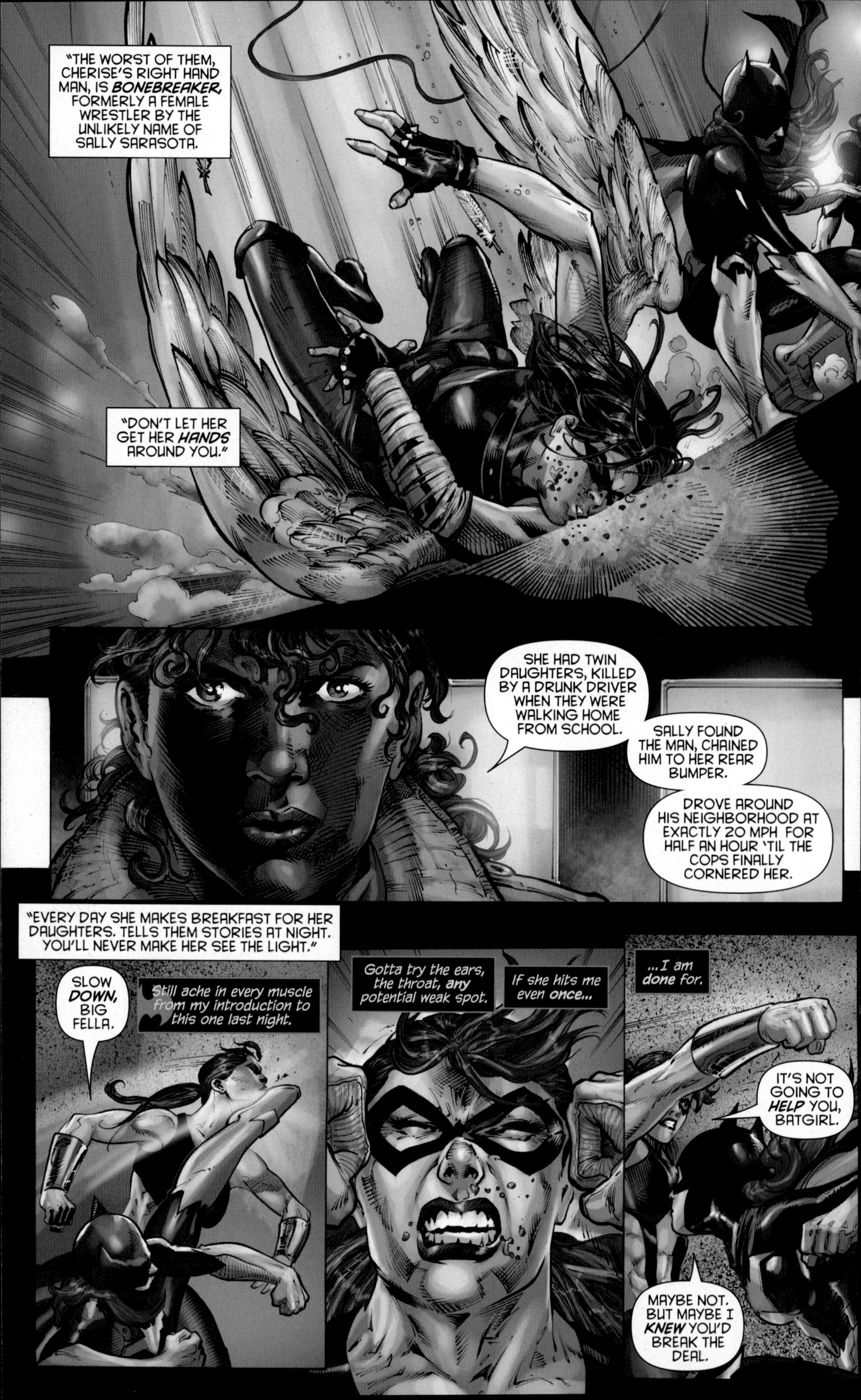
"THE WORST OF THEM, CHERISE'S RIGHT HAND MAN, IS BONEBREAKER, FORMERLY A FEMALE WRESTLER BY THE UNLIKELY NAME OF SALLY SARASOTA.
"DON'T LET HER GET HER HANDS AROUND YOU."
SHE HAD TWIN DAUGHTERS, KILLED BY A DRUNK DRIVER WHEN THEY WERE WALKING HOME FROM SCHOOL.
SALLY FOUND THE MAN, CHAINED HIM TO HER REAR BUMPER.
DROVE AROUND HIS NEIGHBORHOOD AT EXACTLY 20 MPH FOR HALF AN HOUR 'TIL THE COPS FINALLY CORNERED HER.
"EVERY DAY SHE MAKES BREAKFAST FOR HER DAUGHTERS. TELLS THEM STORIES AT NIGHT. YOU'LL NEVER MAKE HER SEE THE LIGHT."
SLOW DOWN, BIG FELLA.
Still ache in every muscle from my introduction to this one last night.
Gotta try the ears, the throat, any potential weak spot.
If she hits me even once...
...I am done for.
IT'S NOT GOING TO HELP YOU, BATGIRL.
MAYBE NOT. BUT MAYBE I KNEW YOU'D BREAK THE DEAL.

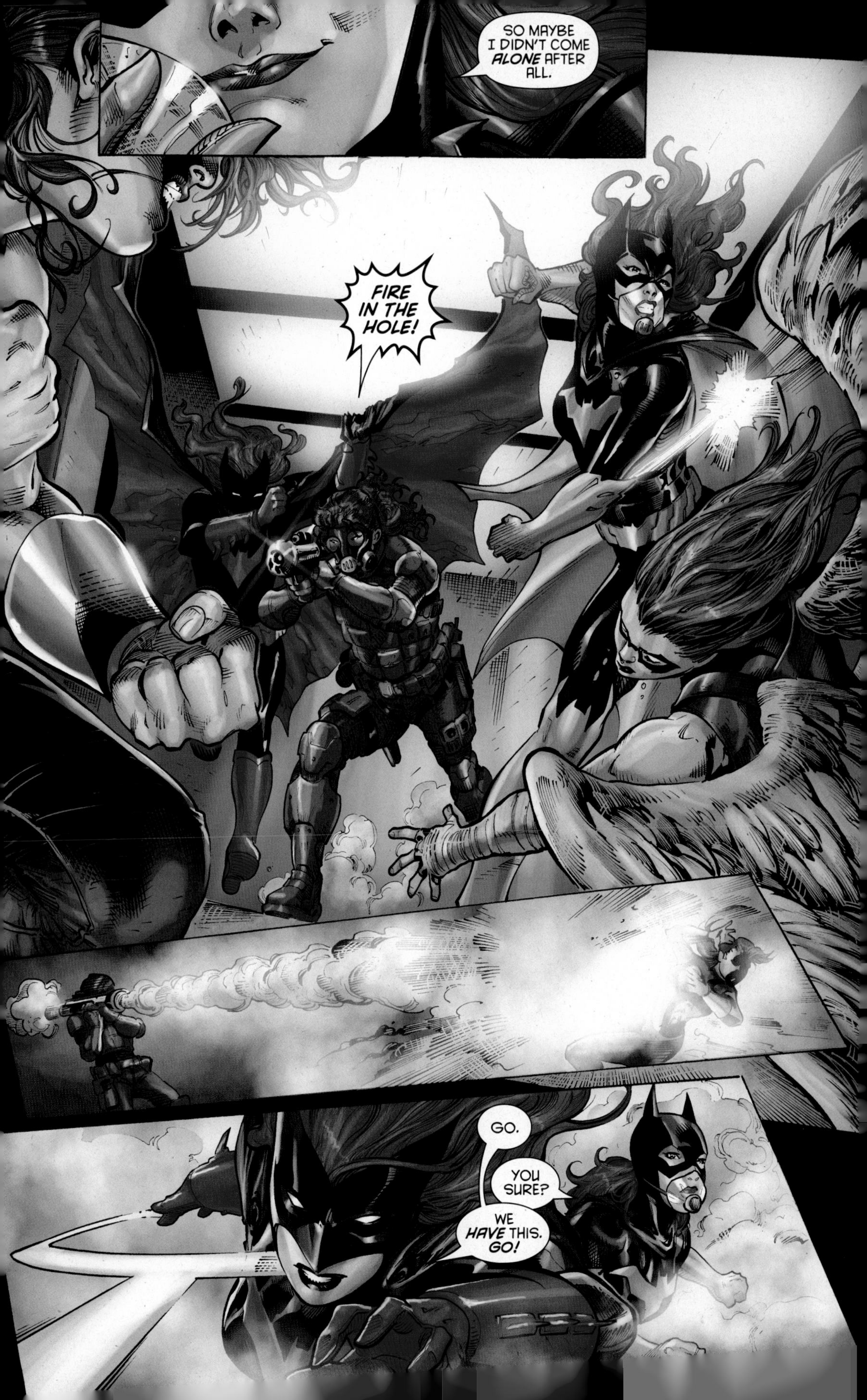
SO MAYBE I DIDN'T COME *ALONE* AFTER ALL.
FIRE IN THE HOLE!
GO.
YOU SURE?
WE *HAVE* THIS. *GO!*

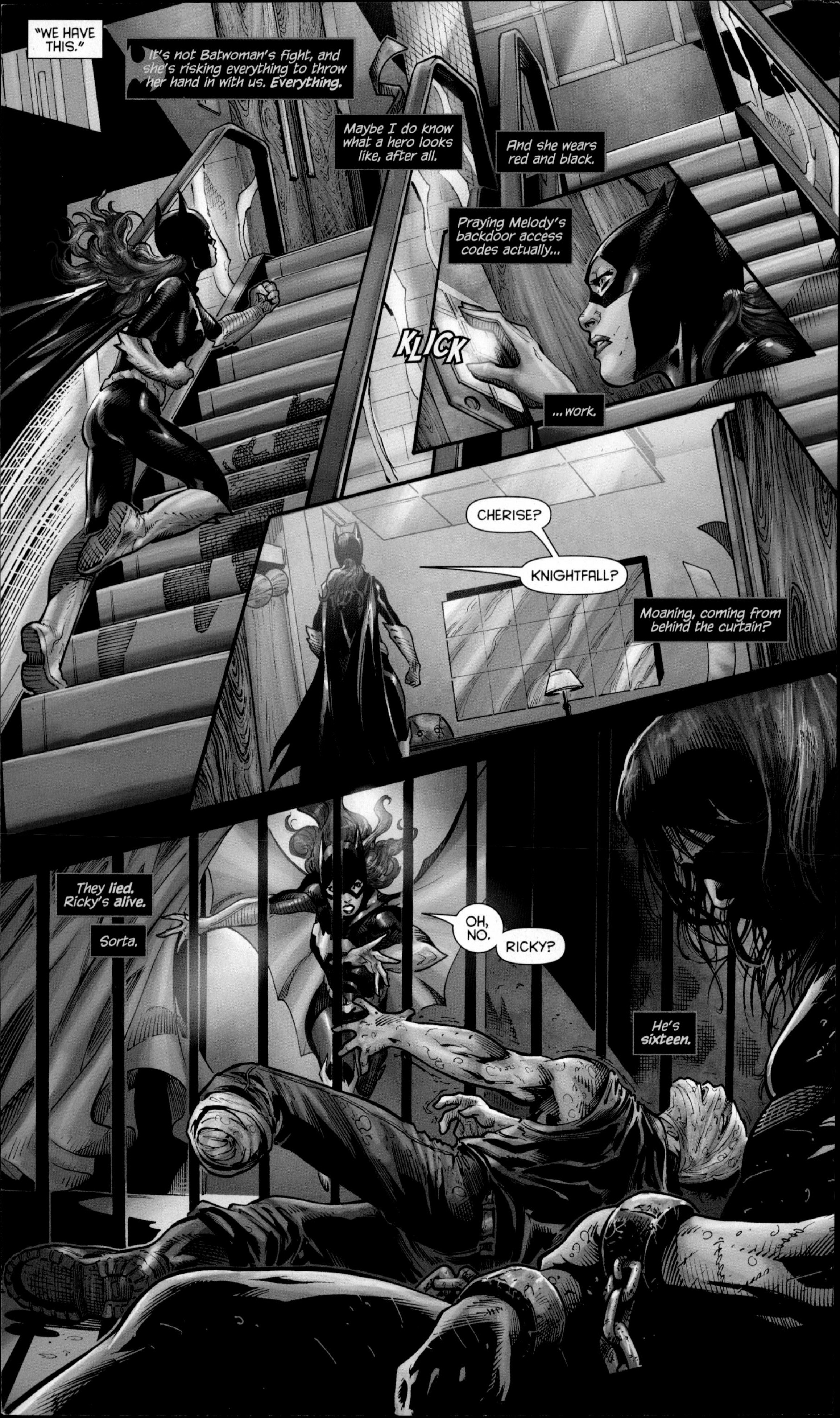

"WE HAVE THIS."
It's not Batwoman's fight, and she's risking everything to throw her hand in with us. Everything.
Maybe I do know what a hero looks like, after all.
And she wears red and black.
Praying Melody's backdoor access codes actually...
KLICK
...work.
CHERISE?
KNIGHTFALL?
Moaning, coming from behind the curtain?
They lied. Ricky's alive.
Sorta.
OH, NO.
RICKY?
He's sixteen.

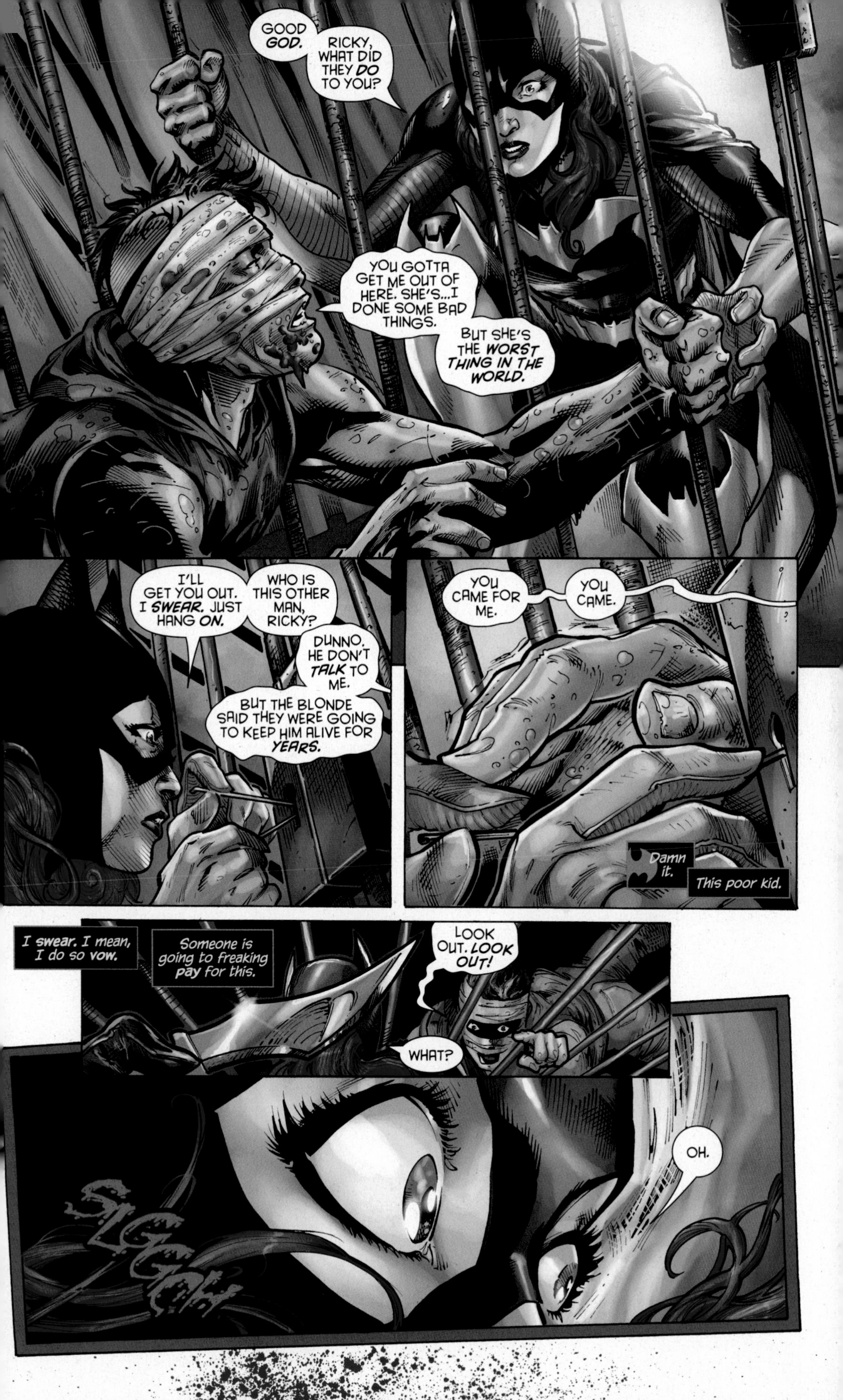
GOOD GOD.
RICKY, WHAT DID THEY DO TO YOU?
YOU GOTTA GET ME OUT OF HERE. SHE'S...I DONE SOME BAD THINGS.
BUT SHE'S THE WORST THING IN THE WORLD.
I'LL GET YOU OUT. I SWEAR. JUST HANG ON.
WHO IS THIS OTHER MAN, RICKY?
DUNNO. HE DON'T TALK TO ME.
BUT THE BLONDE SAID THEY WERE GOING TO KEEP HIM ALIVE FOR YEARS.
YOU CAME.
YOU CAME FOR ME.
Damn it.
This poor kid.
I swear. I mean, I do so vow.
Someone is going to freaking pay for this.
LOOK OUT. LOOK OUT!
WHAT?
OH.
SLGGH

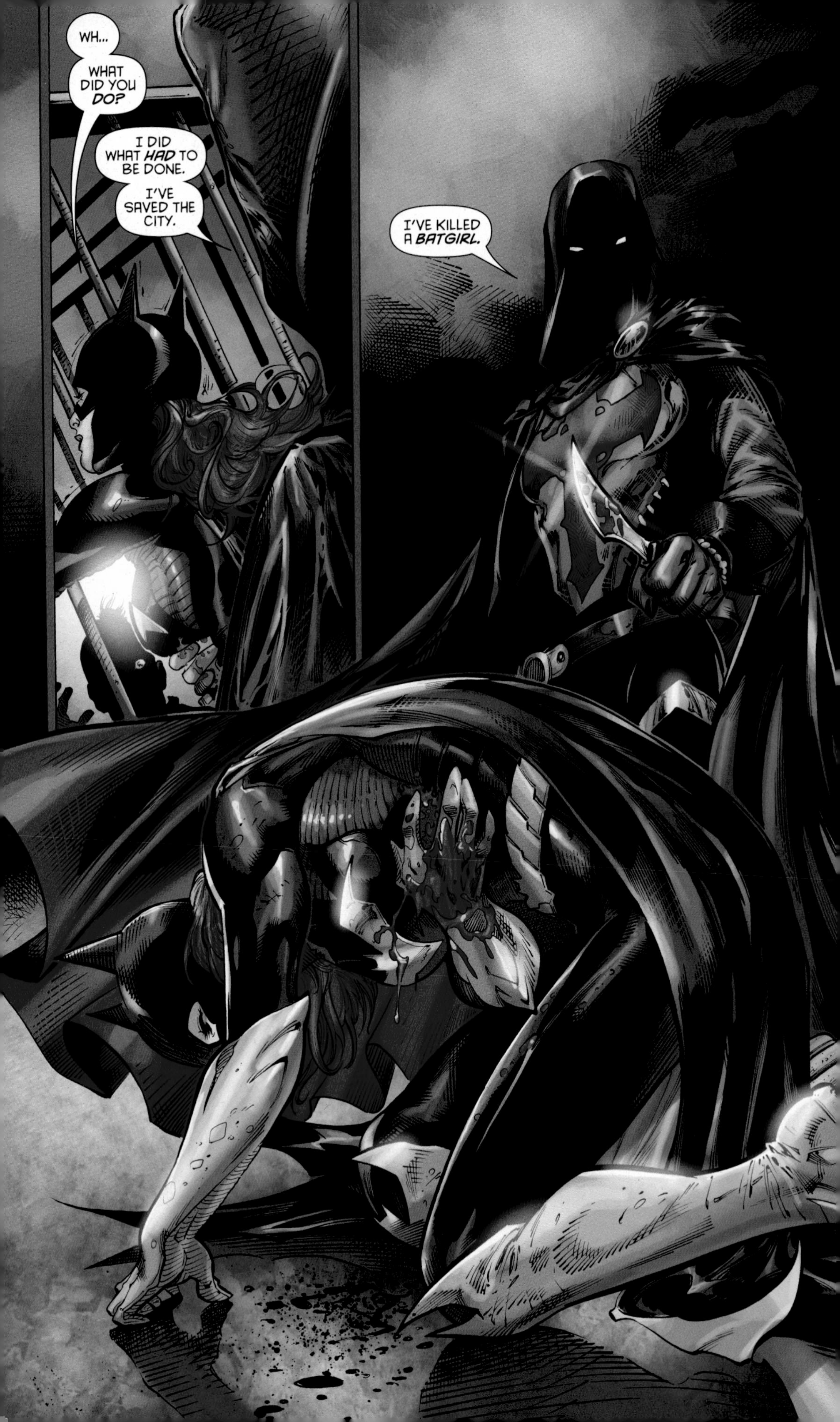
WH...
WHAT DID YOU *DO?*
I DID WHAT *HAD* TO BE DONE.
I'VE SAVED THE CITY.
I'VE KILLED A *BATGIRL.*

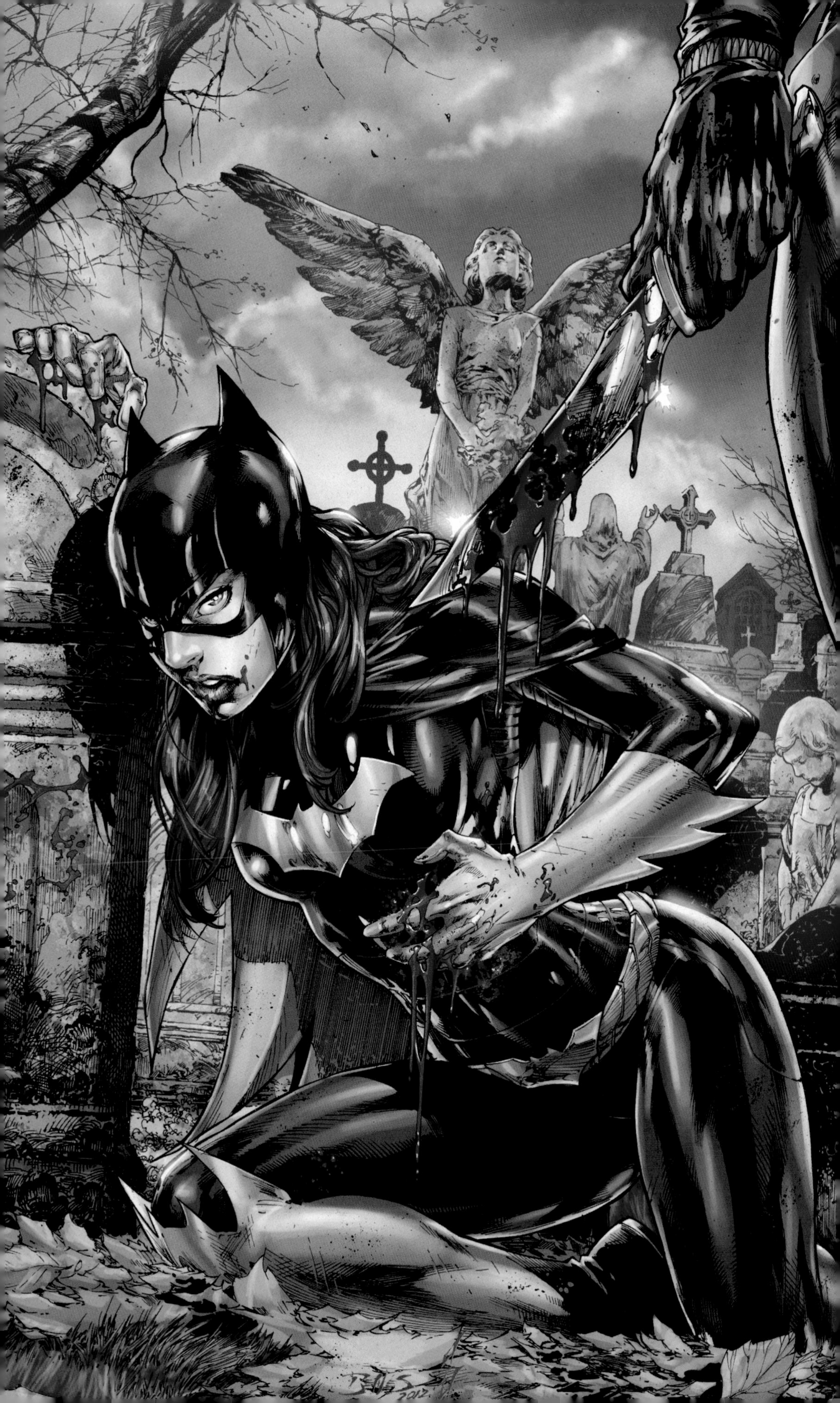

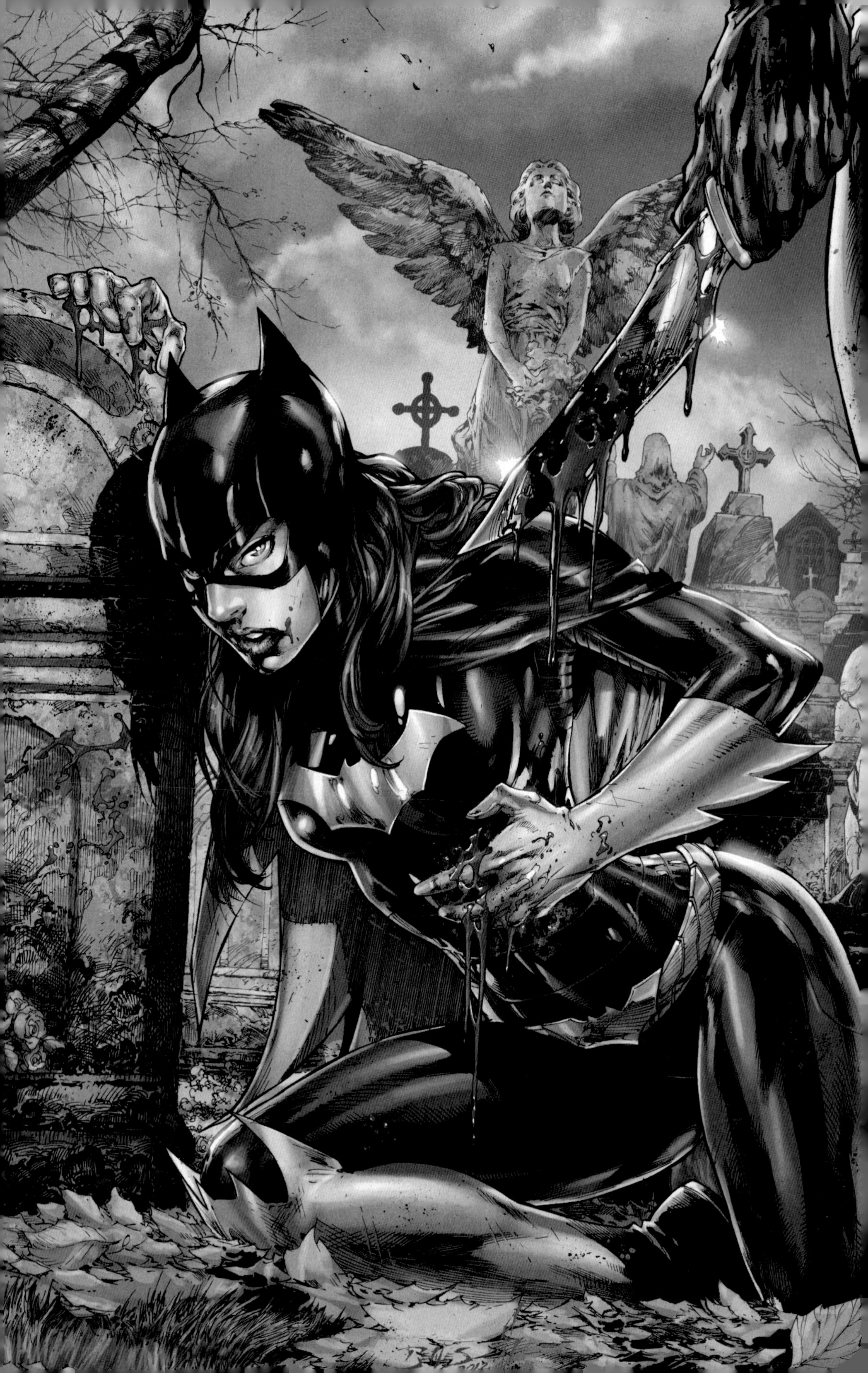

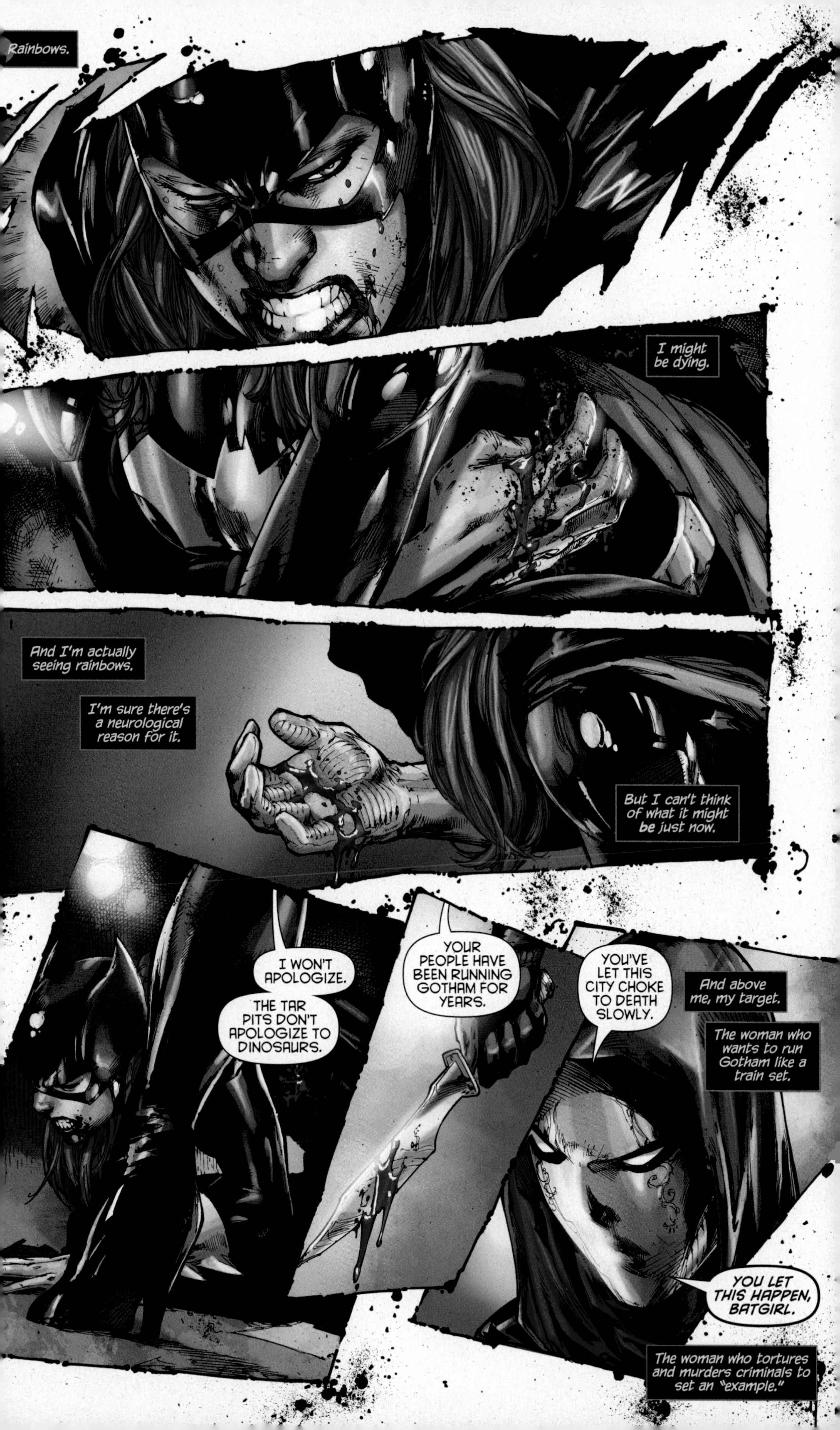

Rainbows.
I might be dying.
And I'm actually seeing rainbows.
I'm sure there's a neurological reason for it.
But I can't think of what it might be just now.
I WON'T APOLOGIZE.
THE TAR PITS DON'T APOLOGIZE TO DINOSAURS.
YOUR PEOPLE HAVE BEEN RUNNING GOTHAM FOR YEARS.
YOU'VE LET THIS CITY CHOKE TO DEATH SLOWLY.
And above me, my target.
The woman who wants to run Gotham like a train set.
YOU LET THIS HAPPEN, BATGIRL.
The woman who tortures and murders criminals to set an "example."

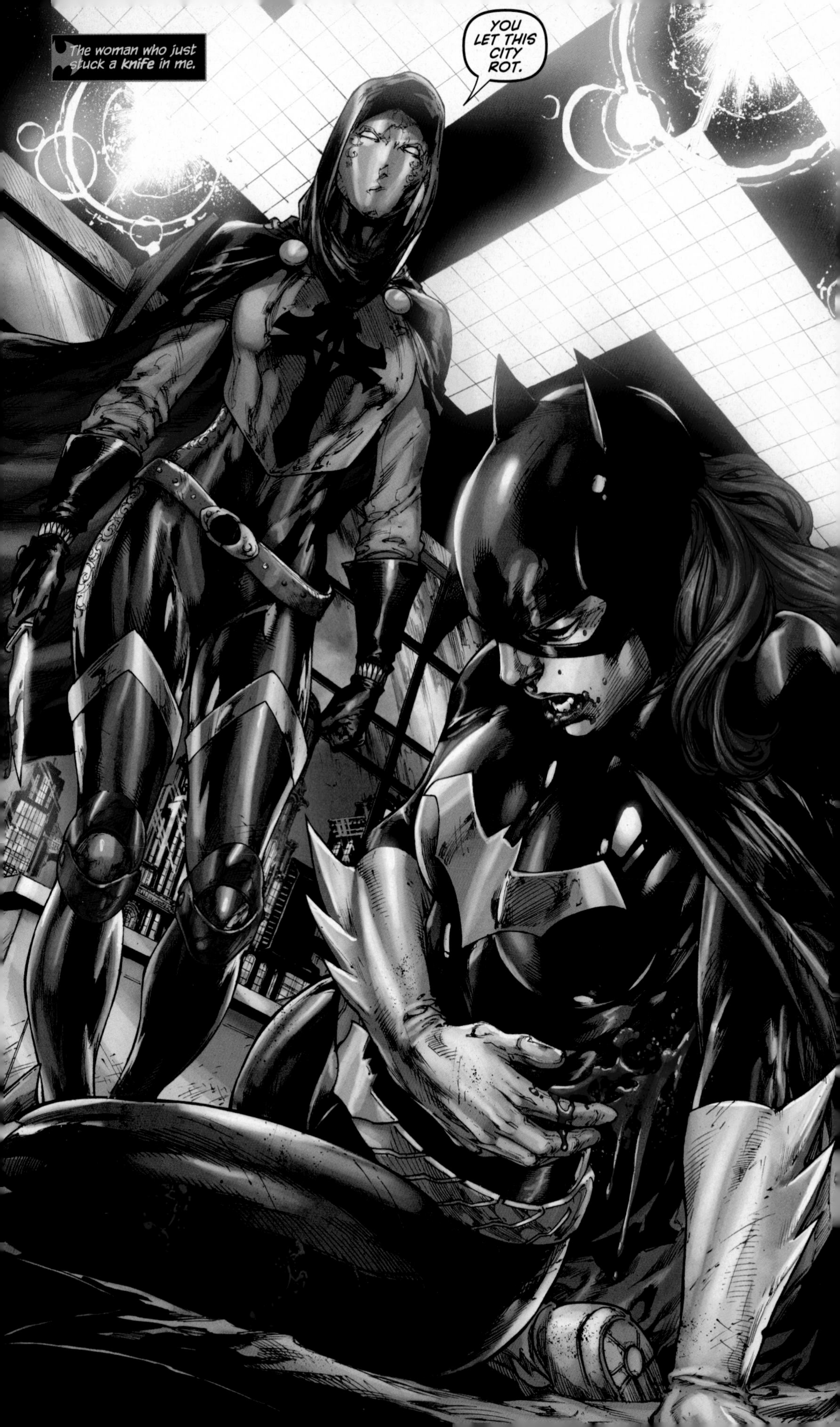
The woman who just stuck a knife in me.
YOU LET THIS CITY ROT.

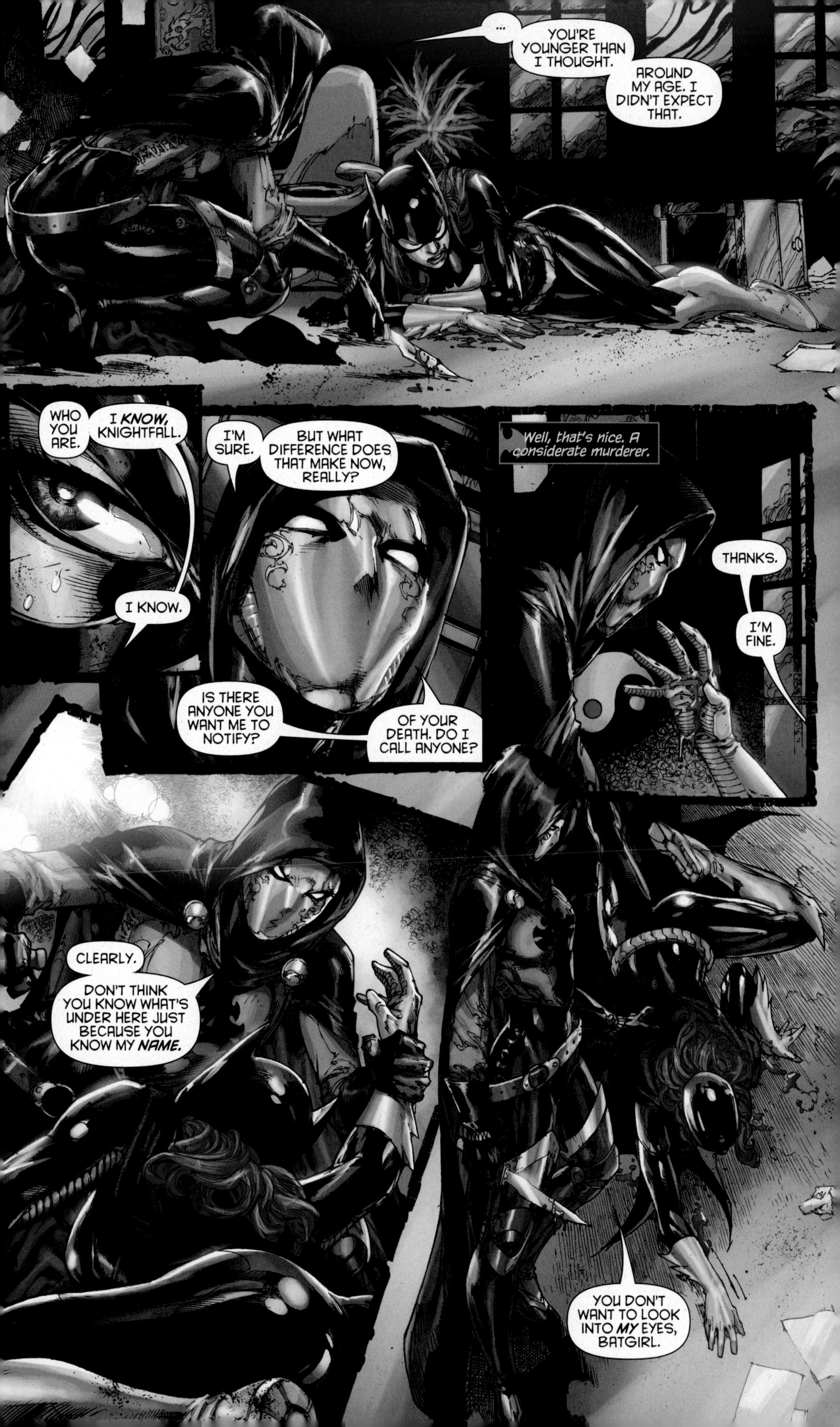
...
YOU'RE YOUNGER THAN I THOUGHT.
AROUND MY AGE. I DIDN'T EXPECT THAT.
WHO YOU ARE.
I *KNOW,* KNIGHTFALL.
I KNOW.
I'M SURE.
BUT WHAT DIFFERENCE DOES THAT MAKE NOW, REALLY?
IS THERE ANYONE YOU WANT ME TO NOTIFY?
OF YOUR DEATH. DO I CALL ANYONE?
Well, that's nice. A considerate murderer.
THANKS.
I'M FINE.
CLEARLY.
DON'T THINK YOU KNOW WHAT'S UNDER HERE JUST BECAUSE YOU KNOW MY ***NAME.***
YOU DON'T WANT TO LOOK INTO ***MY*** EYES, BATGIRL.

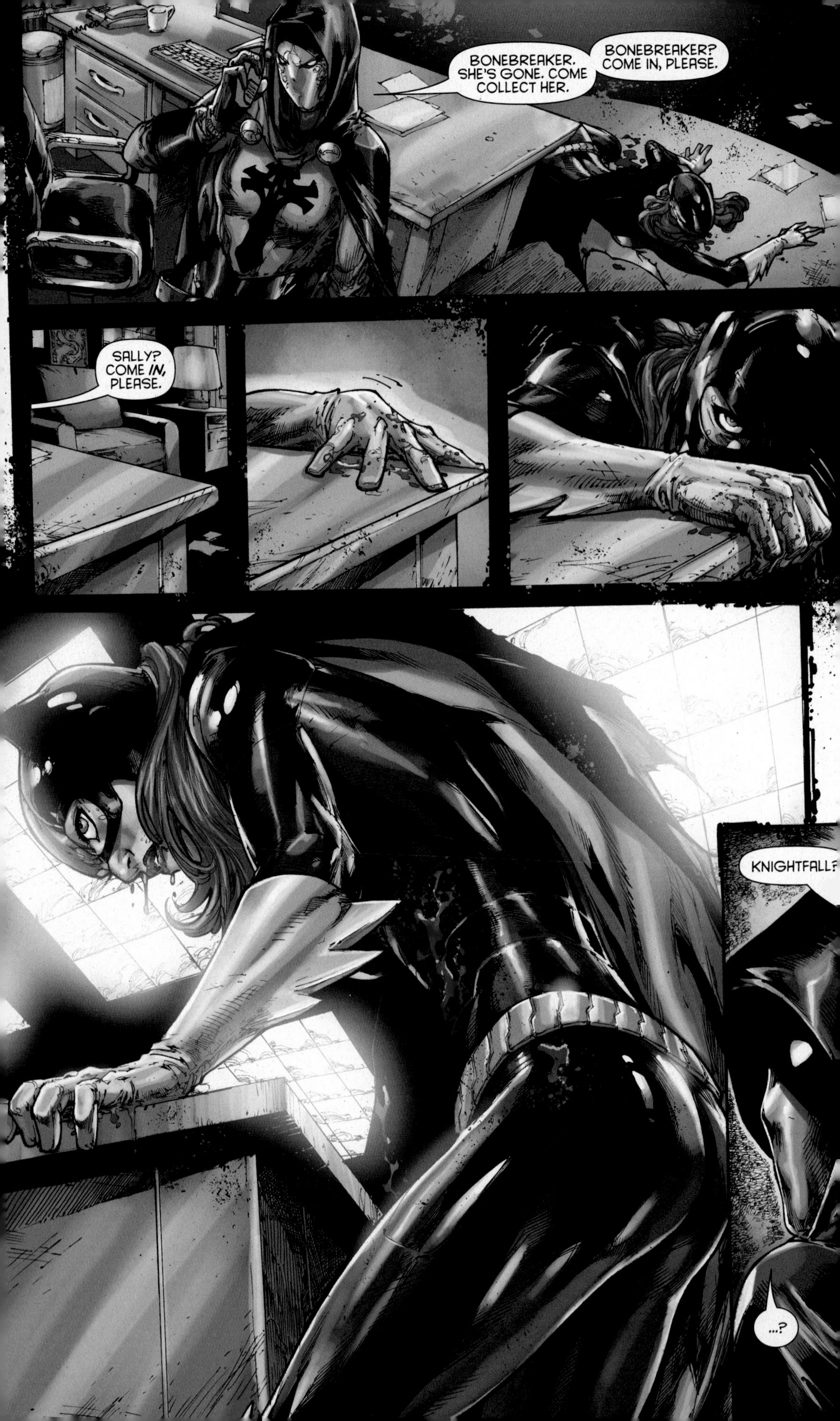
BONEBREAKER? COME IN, PLEASE.
BONEBREAKER. SHE'S GONE. COME COLLECT HER.
SALLY? COME IN, PLEASE.
KNIGHTFALL?
...?

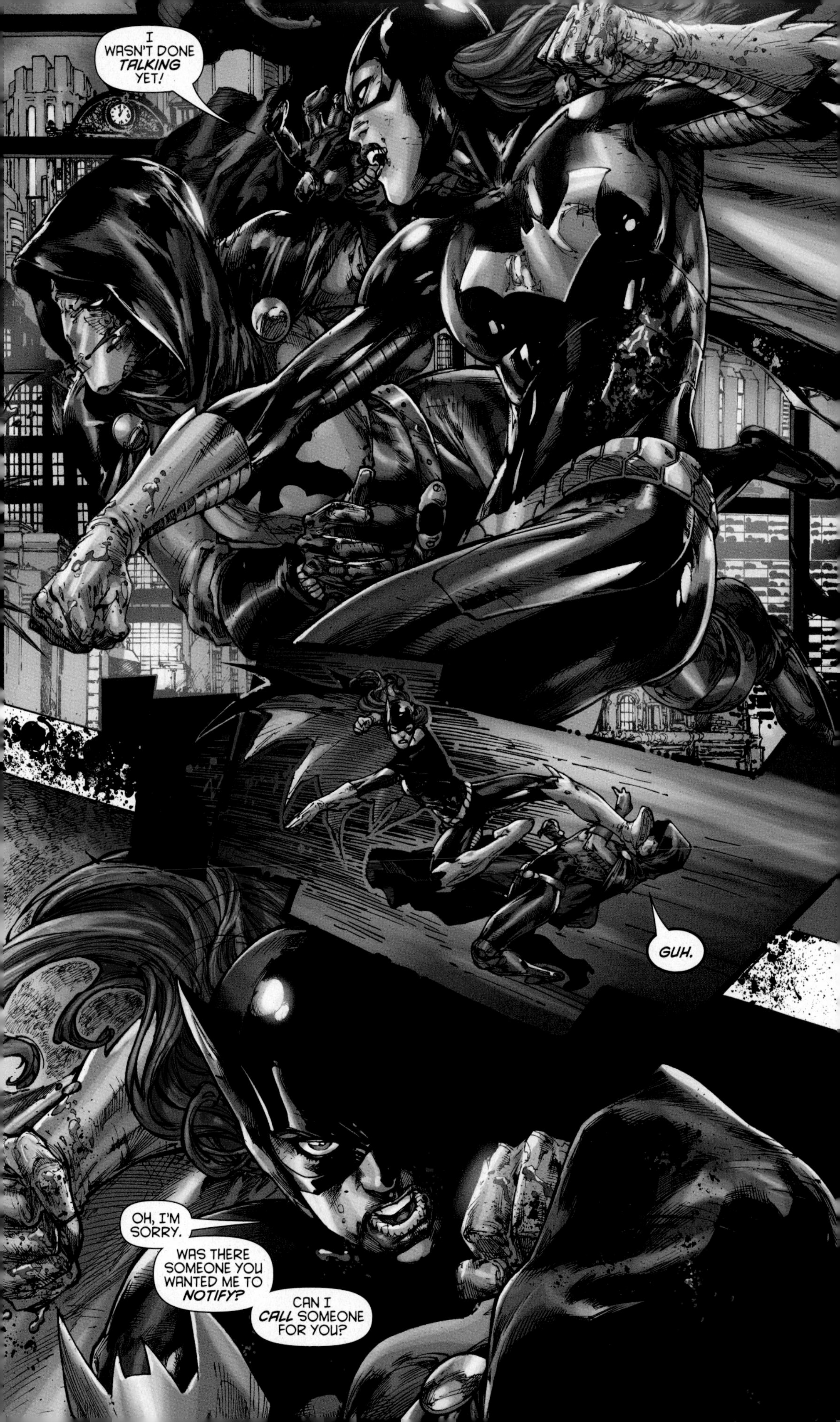
I WASN'T DONE *TALKING* YET!
GUH.
OH, I'M SORRY.
WAS THERE SOMEONE YOU WANTED ME TO *NOTIFY?*
CAN I *CALL* SOMEONE FOR YOU?

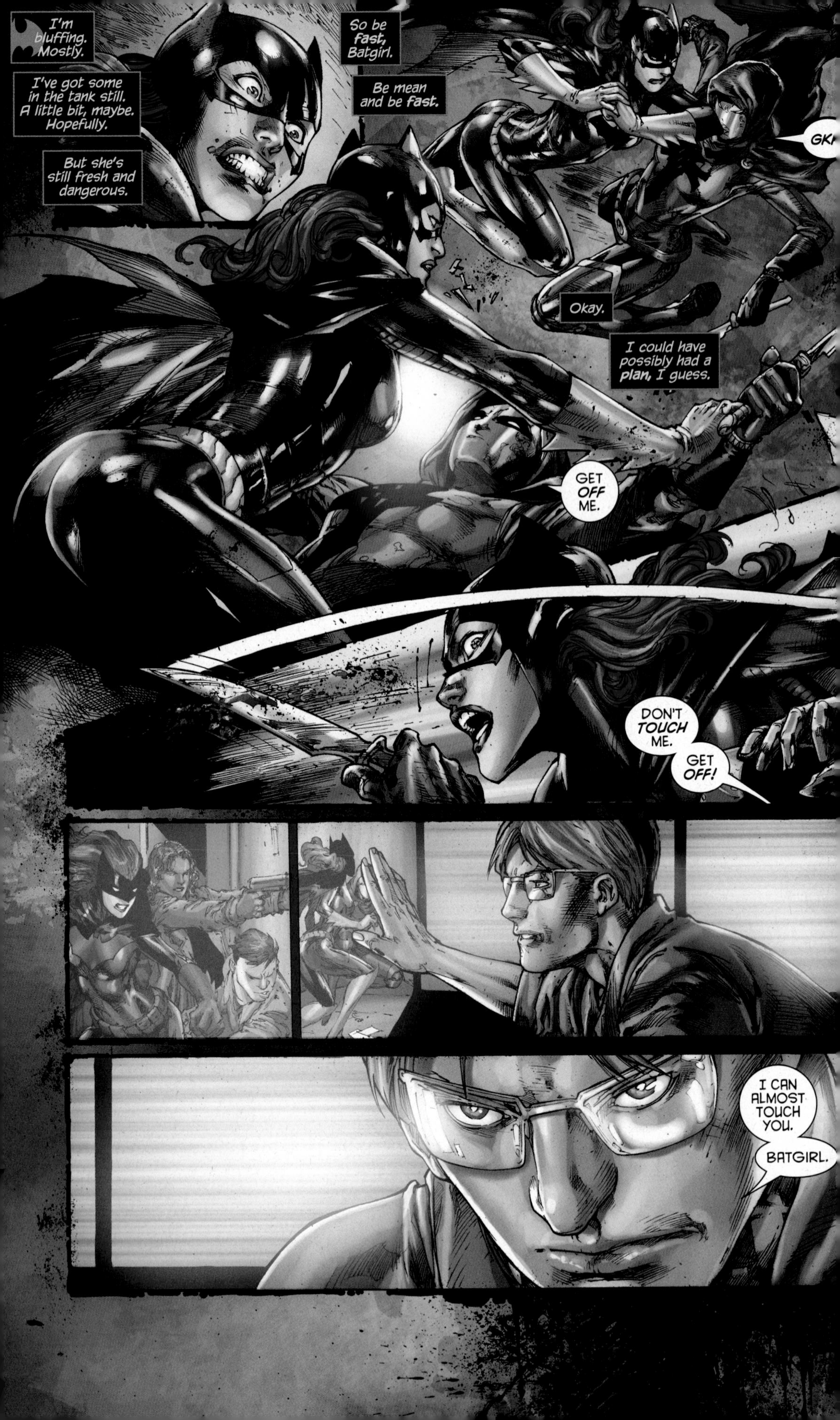
I'm bluffing. Mostly.
I've got some in the tank still. A little bit, maybe. Hopefully.
But she's still fresh and dangerous.
So be fast, Batgirl.
Be mean and be fast.
GK!
Okay.
I could have possibly had a plan, I guess.
GET OFF ME.
DON'T TOUCH ME.
GET OFF!
I CAN ALMOST TOUCH YOU.
BATGIRL.

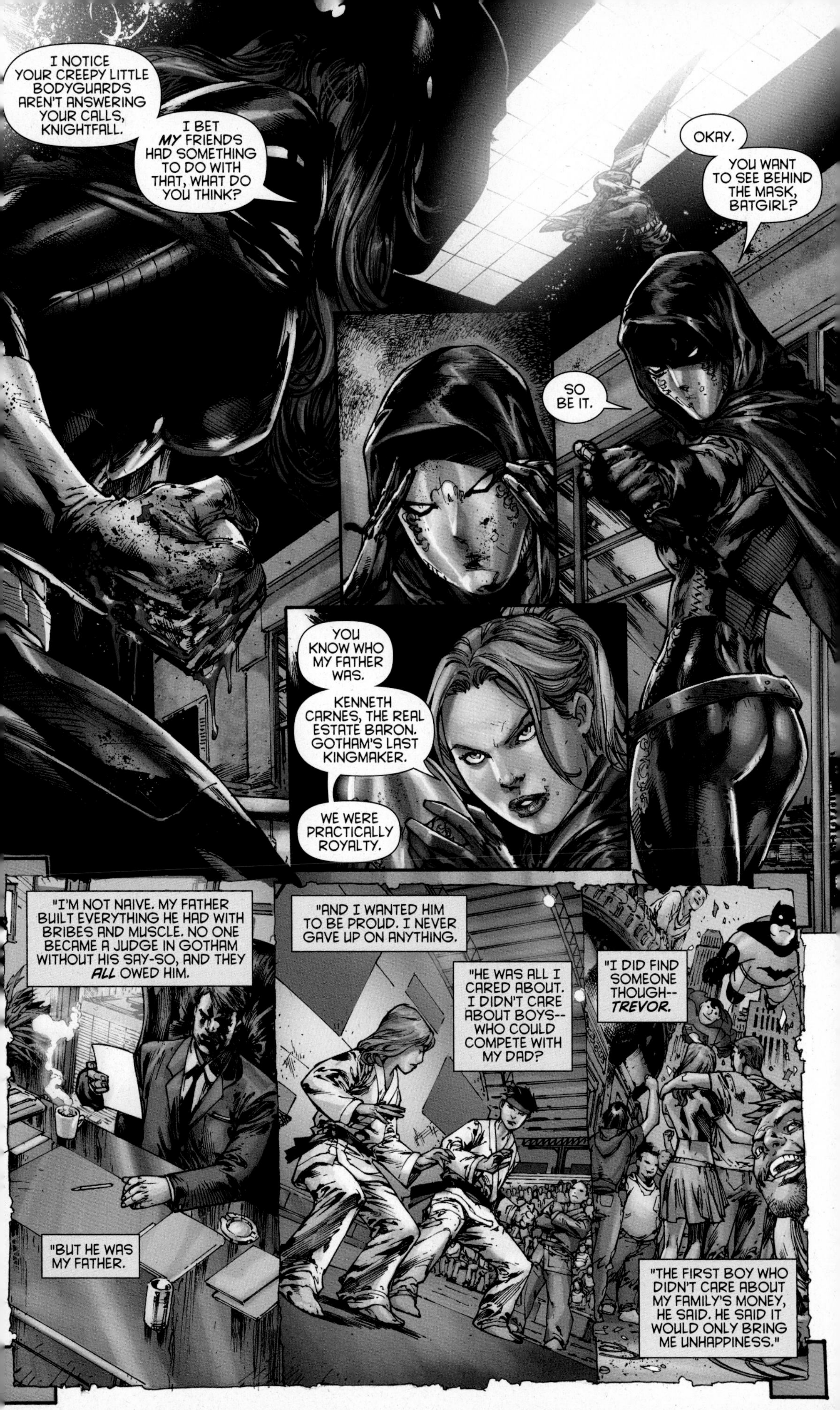
I NOTICE YOUR CREEPY LITTLE BODYGUARDS AREN'T ANSWERING YOUR CALLS, KNIGHTFALL.
I BET *MY* FRIENDS HAD SOMETHING TO DO WITH THAT, WHAT DO YOU THINK?
OKAY.
YOU WANT TO SEE BEHIND THE MASK, BATGIRL?
SO BE IT.
YOU KNOW WHO MY FATHER WAS.
KENNETH CARNES, THE REAL ESTATE BARON. GOTHAM'S LAST KINGMAKER.
WE WERE PRACTICALLY ROYALTY.
"I'M NOT NAIVE. MY FATHER BUILT EVERYTHING HE HAD WITH BRIBES AND MUSCLE. NO ONE BECAME A JUDGE IN GOTHAM WITHOUT HIS SAY-SO, AND THEY *ALL* OWED HIM.
"BUT HE WAS MY FATHER.
"AND I WANTED HIM TO BE PROUD. I NEVER GAVE UP ON ANYTHING.
"HE WAS ALL I CARED ABOUT. I DIDN'T CARE ABOUT BOYS-- WHO COULD COMPETE WITH MY DAD?
"I DID FIND SOMEONE THOUGH-- *TREVOR.*
"THE FIRST BOY WHO DIDN'T CARE ABOUT MY FAMILY'S MONEY, HE SAID. HE SAID IT WOULD ONLY BRING ME UNHAPPINESS."

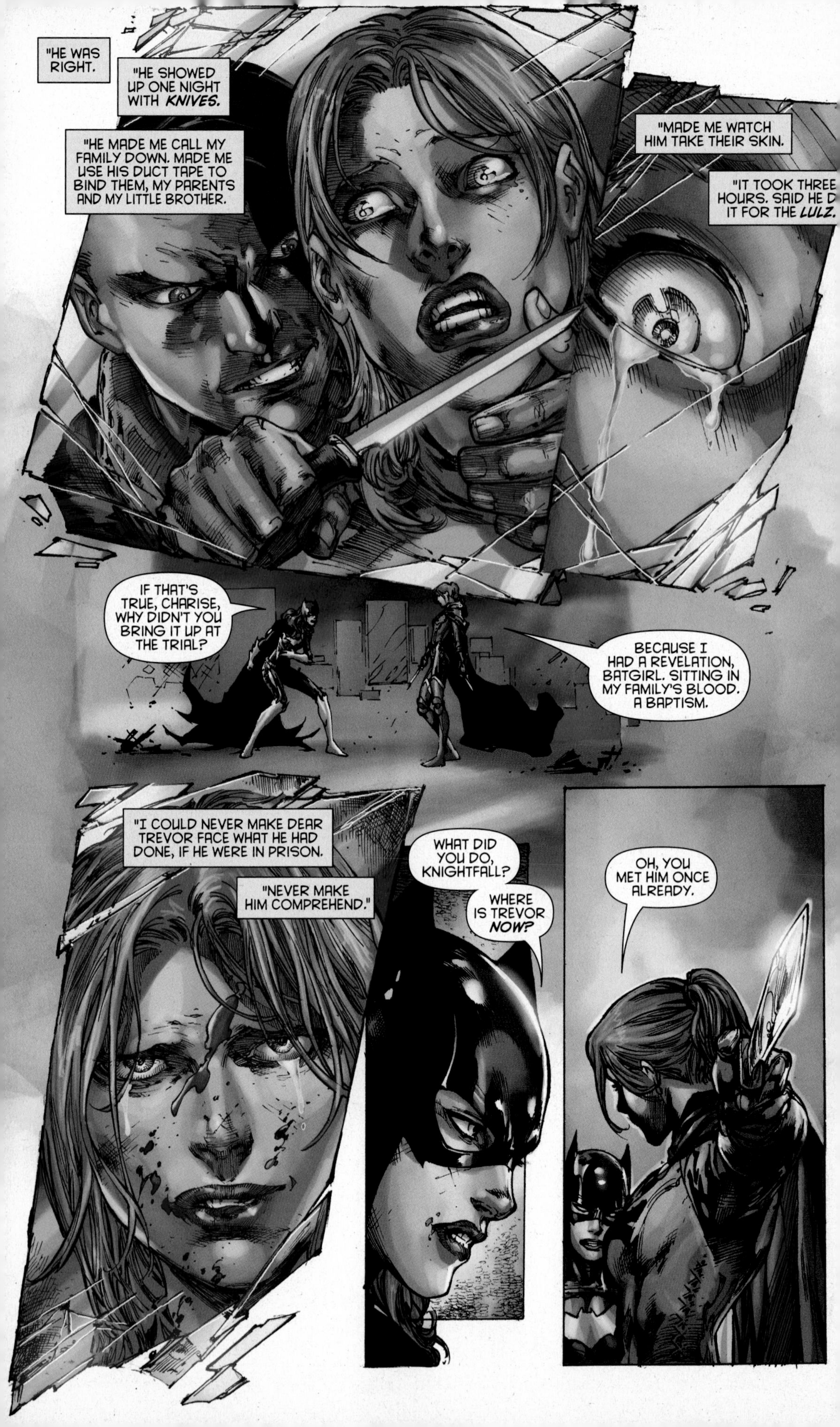

"HE WAS RIGHT.
"HE SHOWED UP ONE NIGHT WITH KNIVES.
"HE MADE ME CALL MY FAMILY DOWN. MADE ME USE HIS DUCT TAPE TO BIND THEM, MY PARENTS AND MY LITTLE BROTHER.
"MADE ME WATCH HIM TAKE THEIR SKIN.
"IT TOOK THREE HOURS. SAID HE D IT FOR THE LULZ.
IF THAT'S TRUE, CHARISE, WHY DIDN'T YOU BRING IT UP AT THE TRIAL?
BECAUSE I HAD A REVELATION, BATGIRL. SITTING IN MY FAMILY'S BLOOD. A BAPTISM.
"I COULD NEVER MAKE DEAR TREVOR FACE WHAT HE HAD DONE, IF HE WERE IN PRISON.
"NEVER MAKE HIM COMPREHEND."
WHAT DID YOU DO, KNIGHTFALL?
WHERE IS TREVOR NOW?
OH, YOU MET HIM ONCE ALREADY.

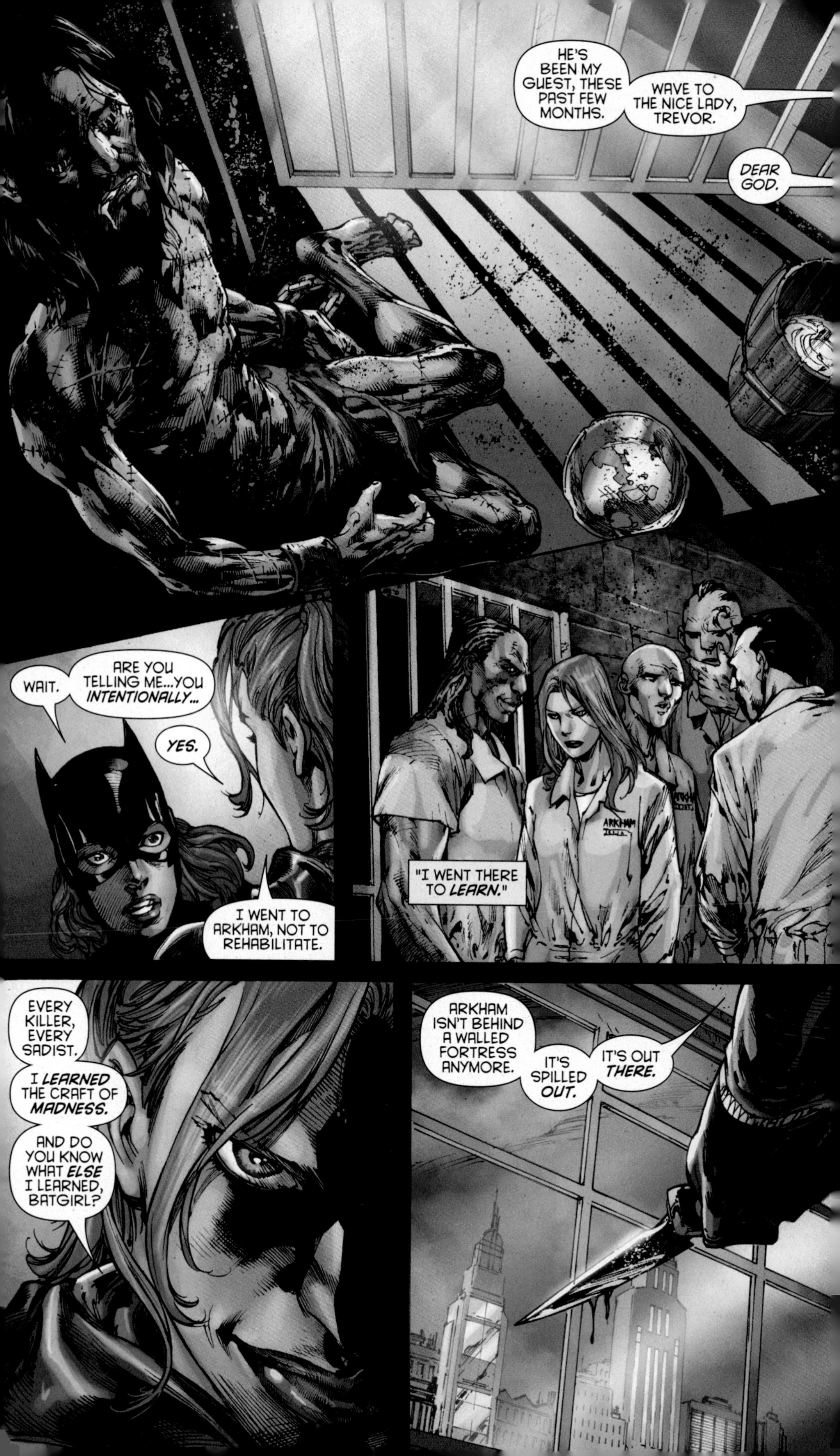
HE'S BEEN MY GUEST, THESE PAST FEW MONTHS.
WAVE TO THE NICE LADY, TREVOR.
DEAR GOD.
WAIT.
ARE YOU TELLING ME...YOU INTENTIONALLY...
YES.
I WENT TO ARKHAM, NOT TO REHABILITATE.
"I WENT THERE TO LEARN."
ARKHAM
EVERY KILLER, EVERY SADIST.
I LEARNED THE CRAFT OF MADNESS.
AND DO YOU KNOW WHAT ELSE I LEARNED, BATGIRL?
ARKHAM ISN'T BEHIND A WALLED FORTRESS ANYMORE.
IT'S SPILLED OUT.
IT'S OUT THERE.

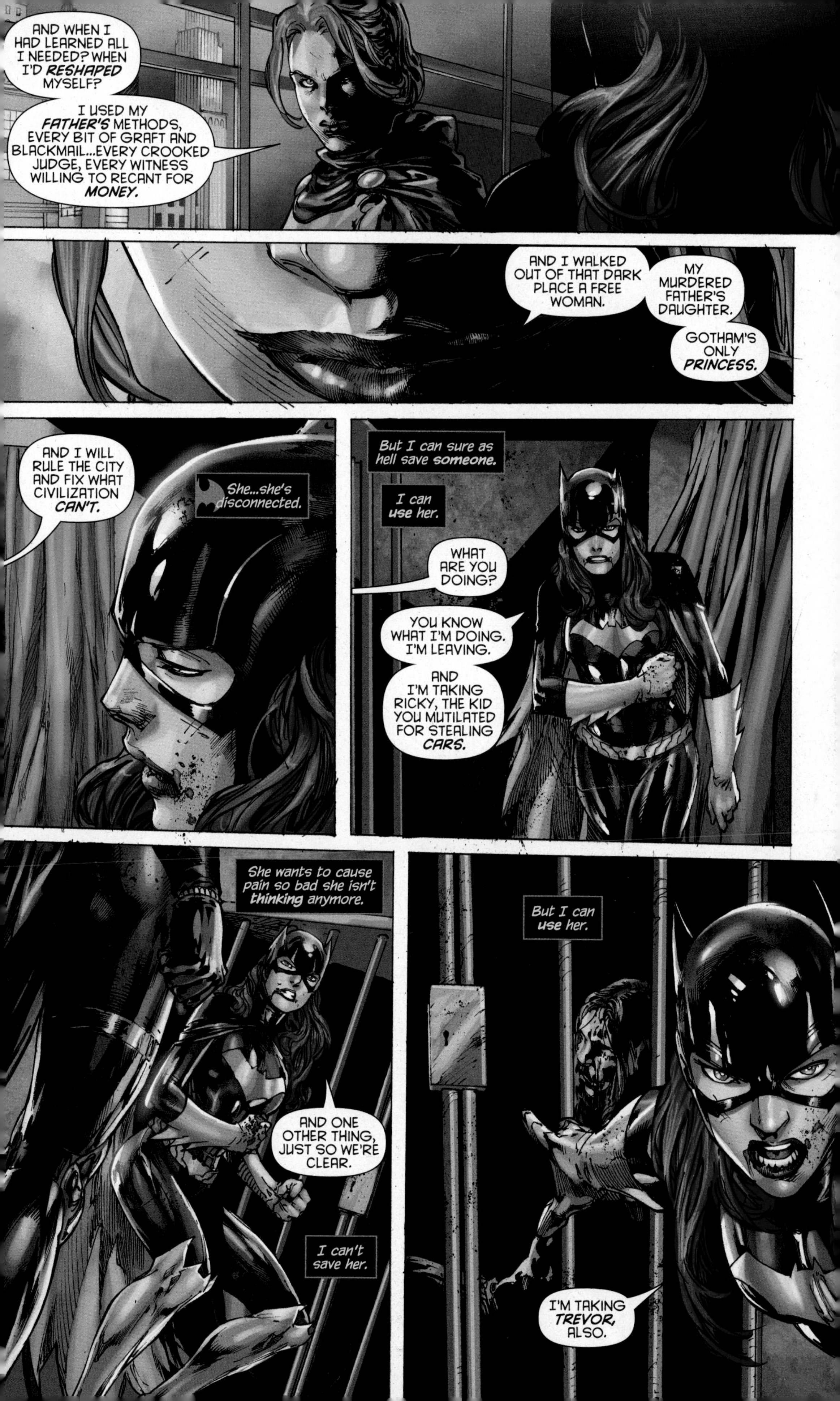
AND WHEN I HAD LEARNED ALL I NEEDED? WHEN I'D RESHAPED MYSELF?
I USED MY FATHER'S METHODS, EVERY BIT OF GRAFT AND BLACKMAIL...EVERY CROOKED JUDGE, EVERY WITNESS WILLING TO RECANT FOR MONEY.
AND I WALKED OUT OF THAT DARK PLACE A FREE WOMAN.
MY MURDERED FATHER'S DAUGHTER.
GOTHAM'S ONLY PRINCESS.
AND I WILL RULE THE CITY AND FIX WHAT CIVILIZATION CAN'T.
She...she's disconnected.
But I can sure as hell save someone.
I can use her.
WHAT ARE YOU DOING?
YOU KNOW WHAT I'M DOING. I'M LEAVING.
AND I'M TAKING RICKY, THE KID YOU MUTILATED FOR STEALING CARS.
She wants to cause pain so bad she isn't thinking anymore.
AND ONE OTHER THING, JUST SO WE'RE CLEAR.
I can't save her.
But I can use her.
I'M TAKING TREVOR, ALSO.

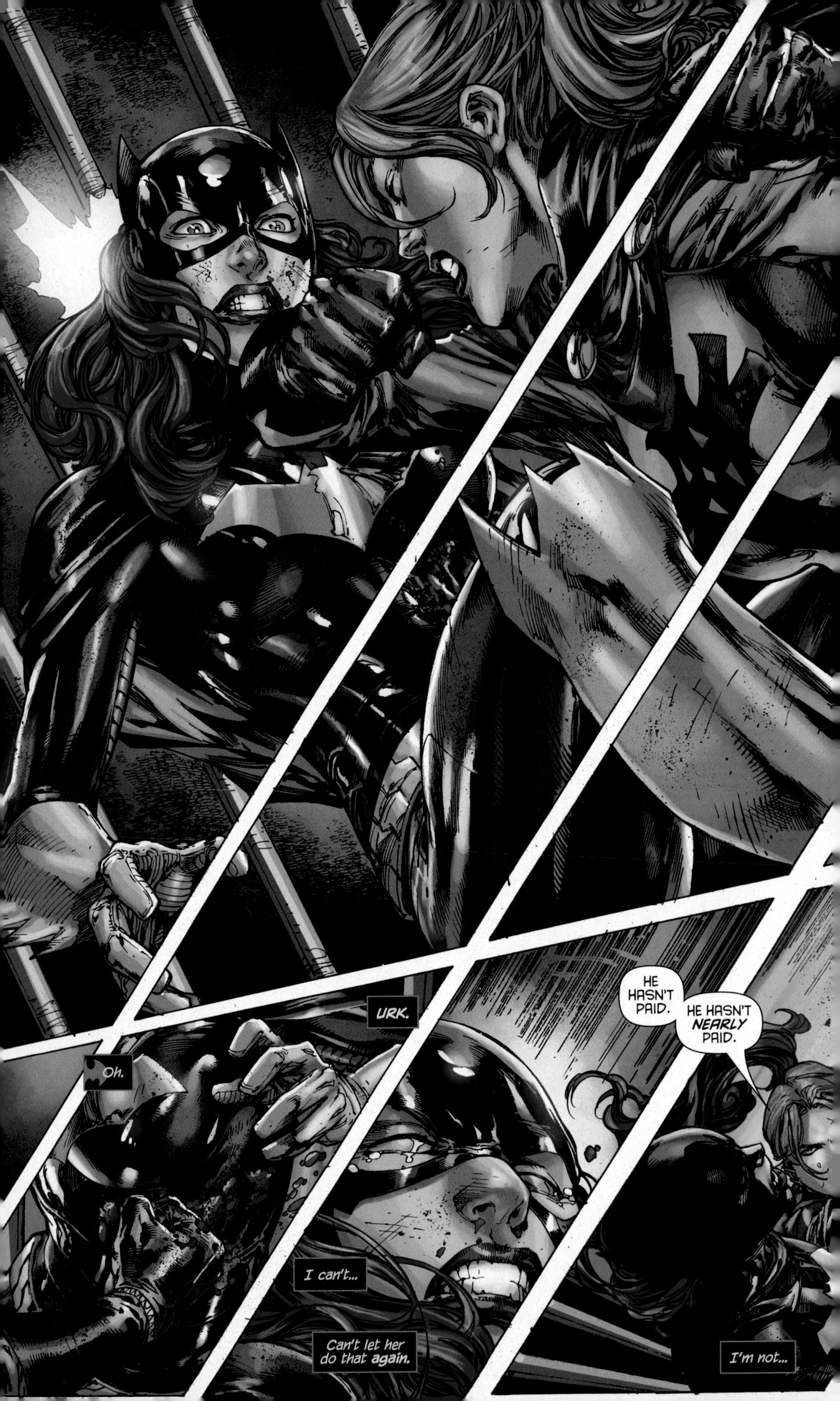
URK.
Oh.
I can't...
Can't let her do that again.
HE HASN'T PAID.
HE HASN'T NEARLY PAID.
I'm not...

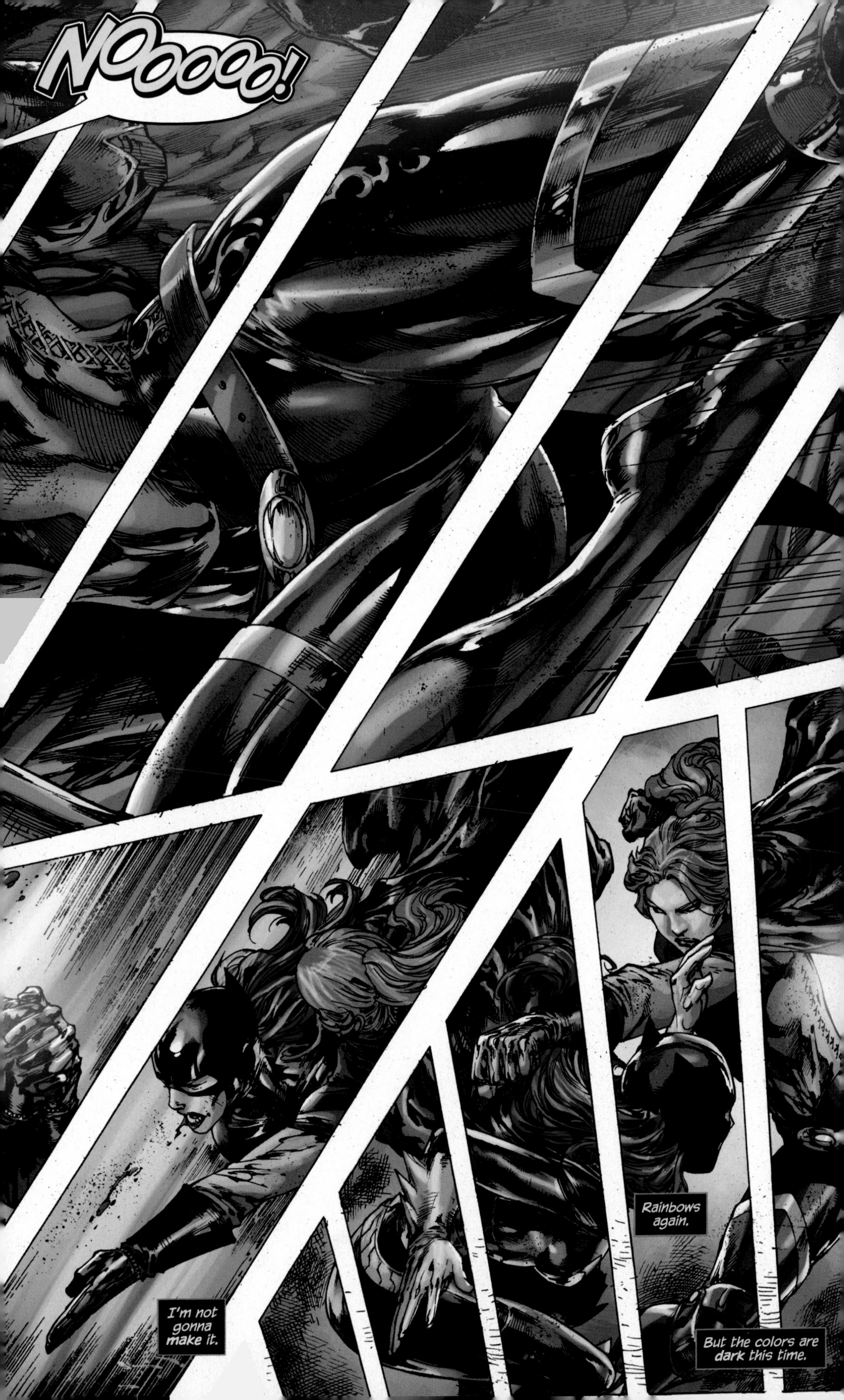
NOOOOOO!
I'm not gonna make it.
Rainbows again.
But the colors are dark this time.

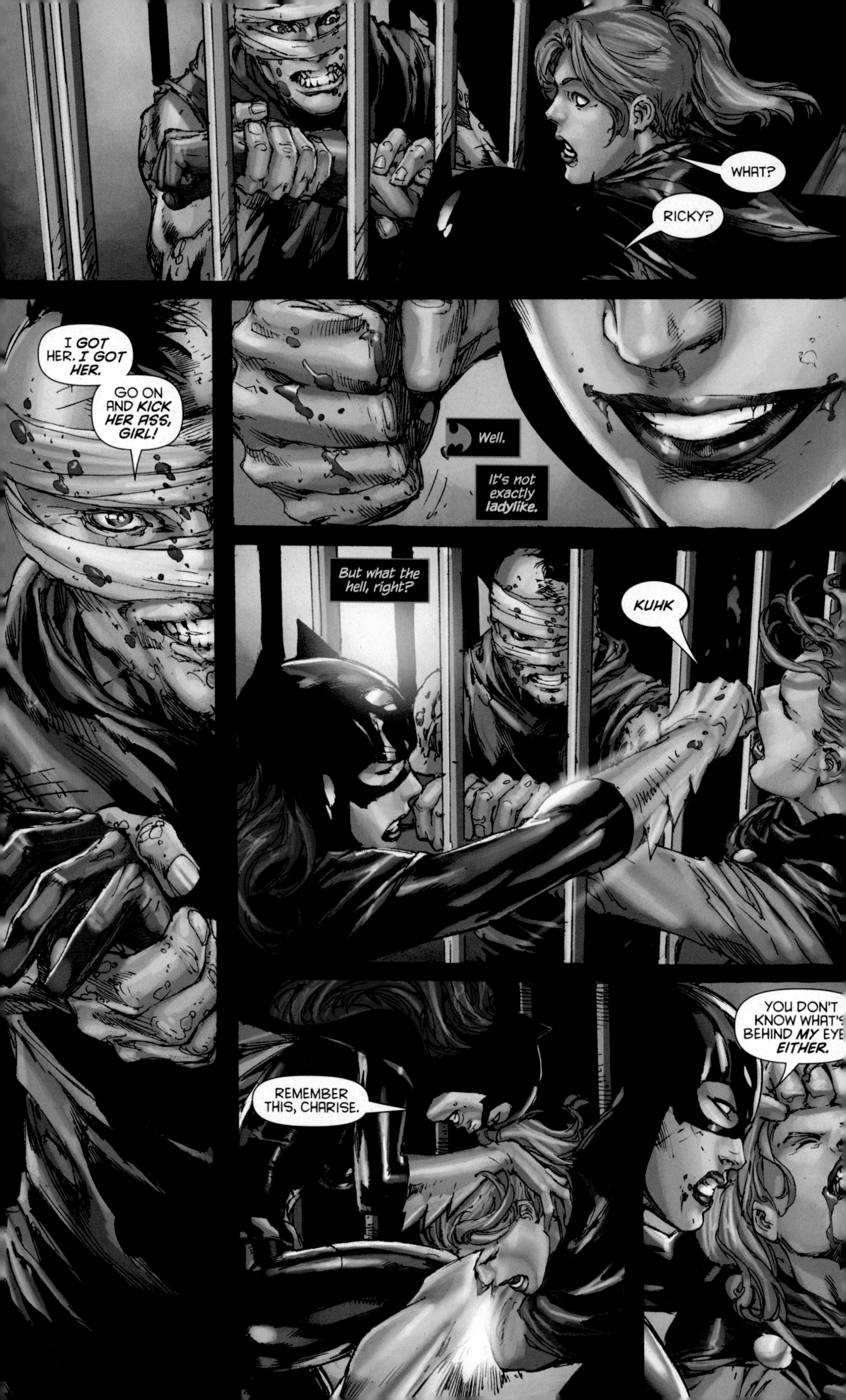
WHAT?
RICKY?
I GOT HER. I GOT HER.
GO ON AND KICK HER ASS, GIRL!
Well.
It's not exactly ladylike.
But what the hell, right?
KUHK
REMEMBER THIS, CHARISE.
YOU DON'T KNOW WHAT'S BEHIND MY EYE EITHER.

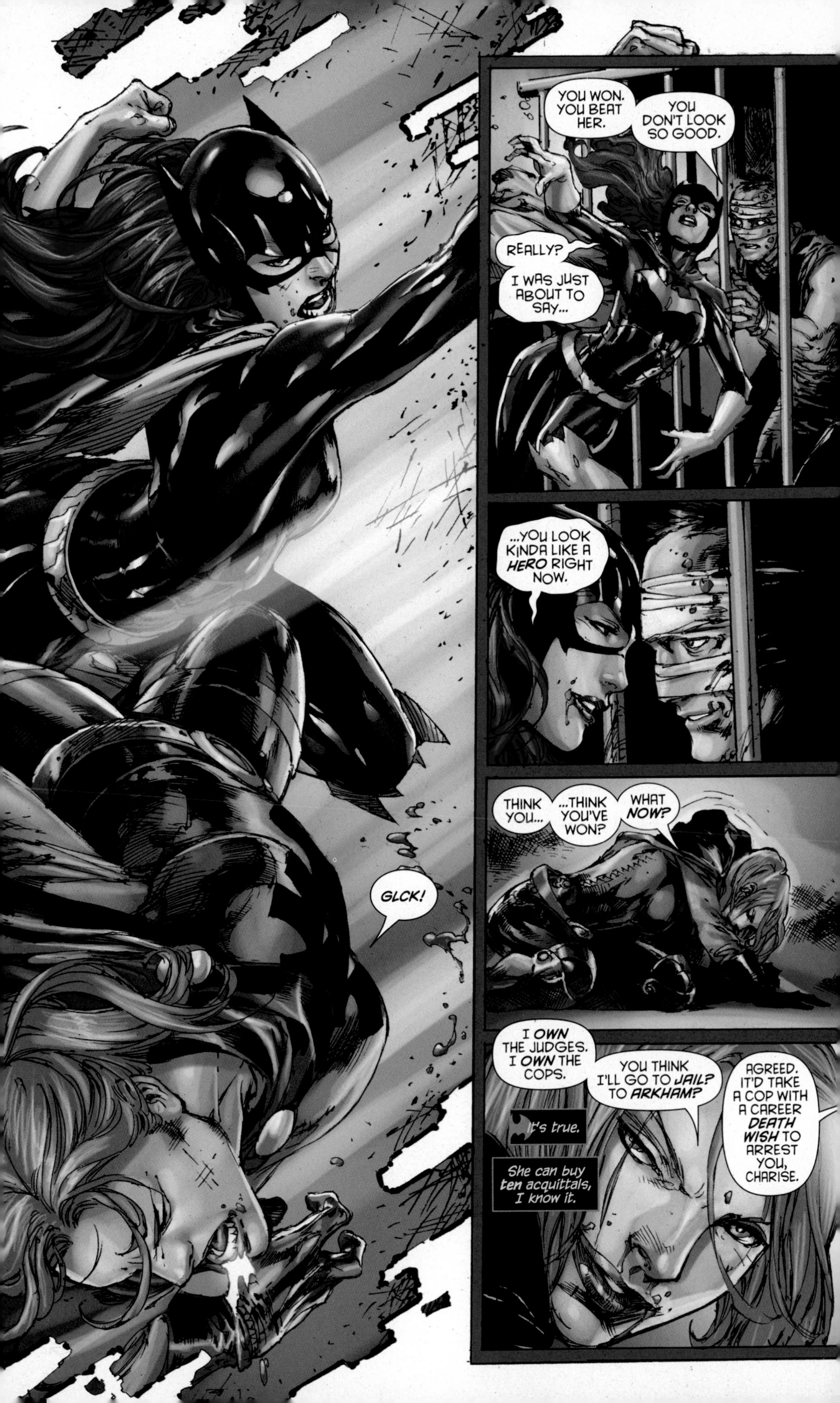
GLCK!
YOU WON. YOU BEAT HER.
YOU DON'T LOOK SO GOOD.
REALLY?
I WAS JUST ABOUT TO SAY...
...YOU LOOK KINDA LIKE A *HERO* RIGHT NOW.
THINK YOU...
...THINK YOU'VE WON?
WHAT *NOW?*
I *OWN* THE JUDGES. I *OWN* THE COPS.
YOU THINK I'LL GO TO *JAIL?* TO *ARKHAM?*
It's true.
She can buy **ten** acquittals, I know it.
AGREED. IT'D TAKE A COP WITH A CAREER *DEATH WISH* TO ARREST YOU, CHARISE.

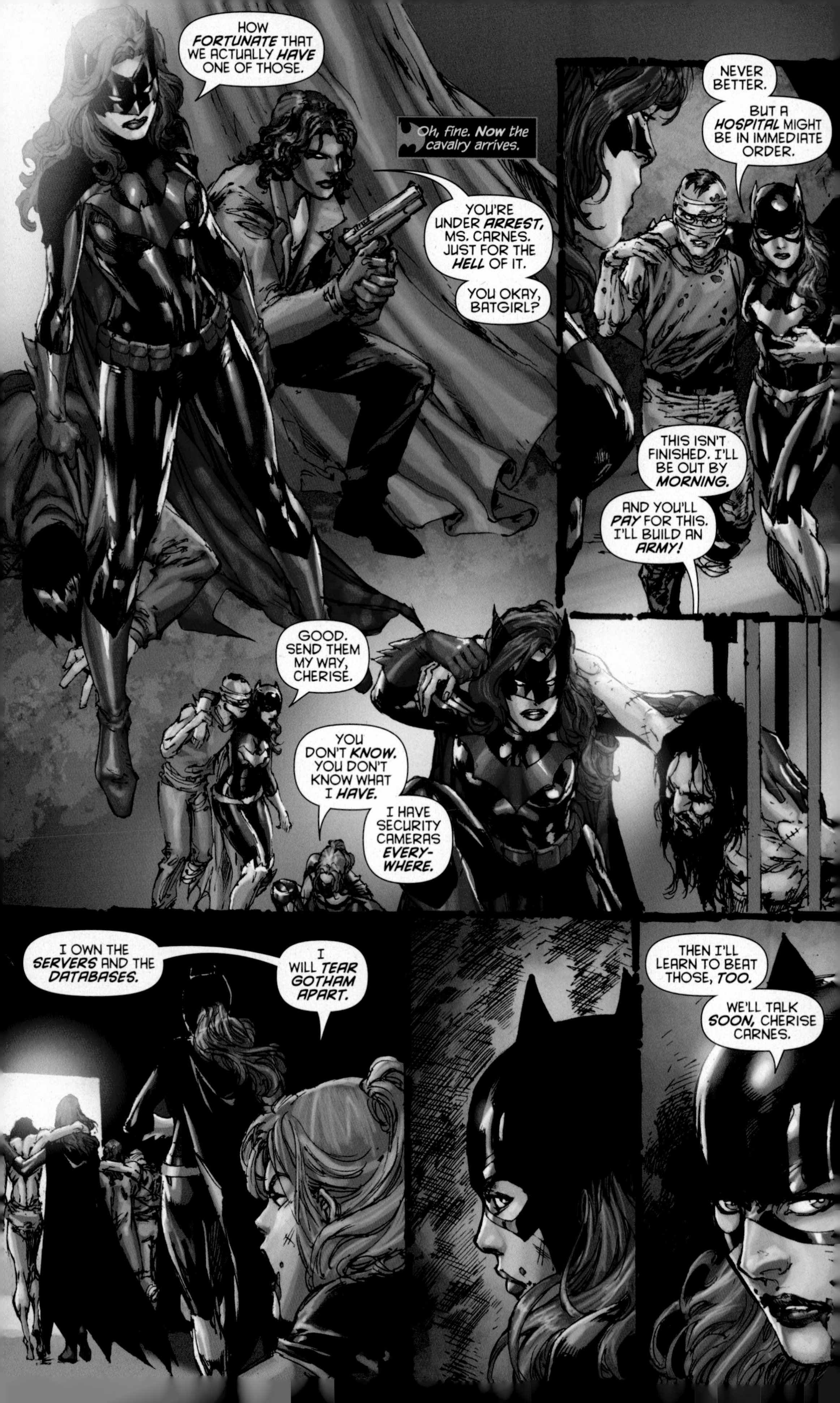
HOW FORTUNATE THAT WE ACTUALLY HAVE ONE OF THOSE.
Oh, fine. Now the cavalry arrives.
YOU'RE UNDER ARREST, MS. CARNES. JUST FOR THE HELL OF IT.
YOU OKAY, BATGIRL?
NEVER BETTER.
BUT A HOSPITAL MIGHT BE IN IMMEDIATE ORDER.
THIS ISN'T FINISHED. I'LL BE OUT BY MORNING.
AND YOU'LL PAY FOR THIS. I'LL BUILD AN ARMY!
GOOD. SEND THEM MY WAY, CHERISE.
YOU DON'T KNOW. YOU DON'T KNOW WHAT I HAVE.
I HAVE SECURITY CAMERAS EVERY-WHERE.
I OWN THE SERVERS AND THE DATABASES.
I WILL TEAR GOTHAM APART.
THEN I'LL LEARN TO BEAT THOSE, TOO.
WE'LL TALK SOON, CHERISE CARNES.

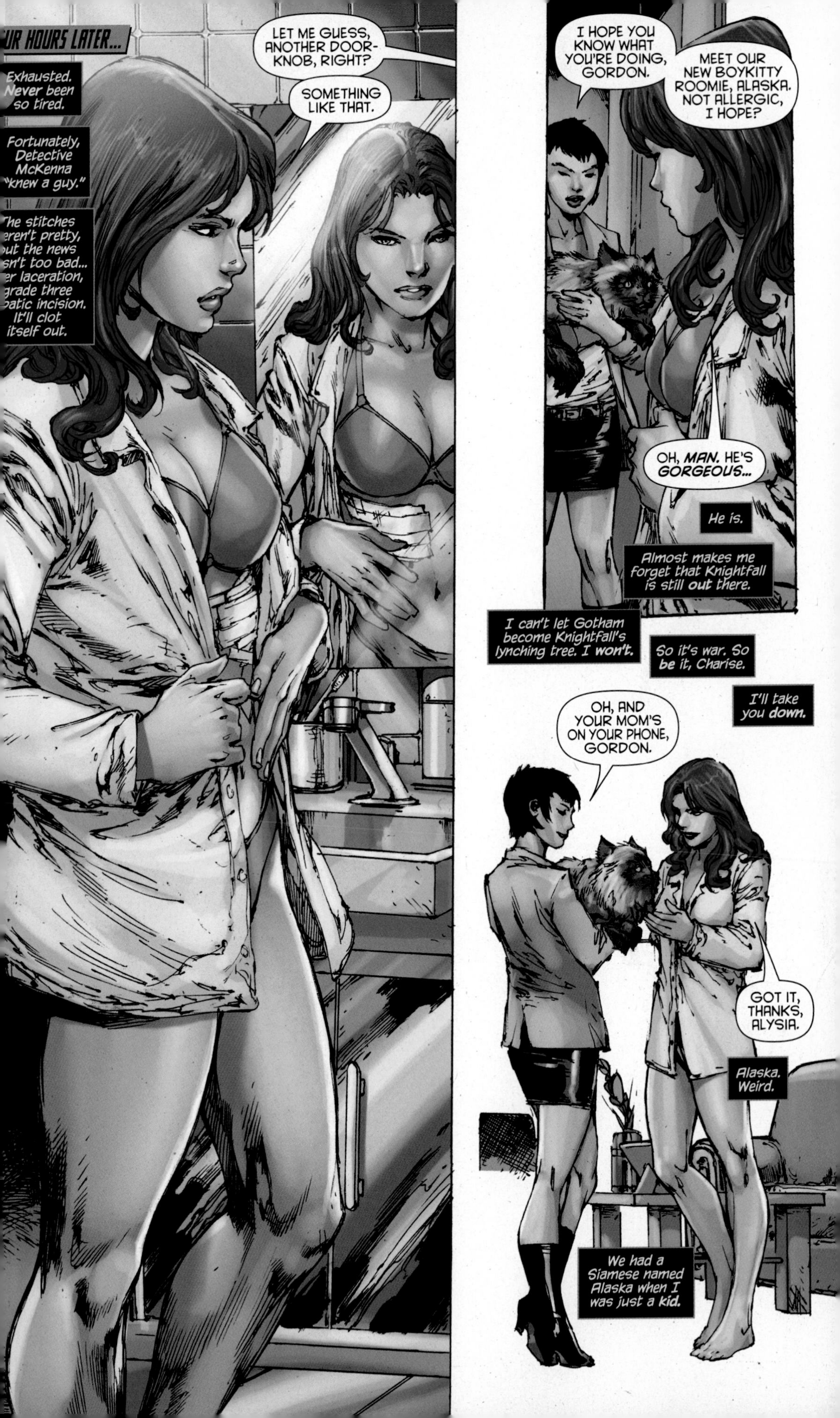

UR HOURS LATER...
Exhausted. Never been so tired.
LET ME GUESS, ANOTHER DOOR-KNOB, RIGHT?
SOMETHING LIKE THAT.
Fortunately, Detective McKenna "knew a guy."
he stitches eren't pretty, ut the news sn't too bad... er laceration, grade three patic incision. It'll clot itself out.
I HOPE YOU KNOW WHAT YOU'RE DOING, GORDON.
MEET OUR NEW BOYKITTY ROOMIE, ALASKA. NOT ALLERGIC, I HOPE?
OH, MAN. HE'S GORGEOUS...
He is.
Almost makes me forget that Knightfall is still out there.
I can't let Gotham become Knightfall's lynching tree. I won't.
So it's war. So be it, Charise.
I'll take you down.
OH, AND YOUR MOM'S ON YOUR PHONE, GORDON.
GOT IT, THANKS, ALYSIA.
Alaska. Weird.
We had a Siamese named Alaska when I was just a kid.

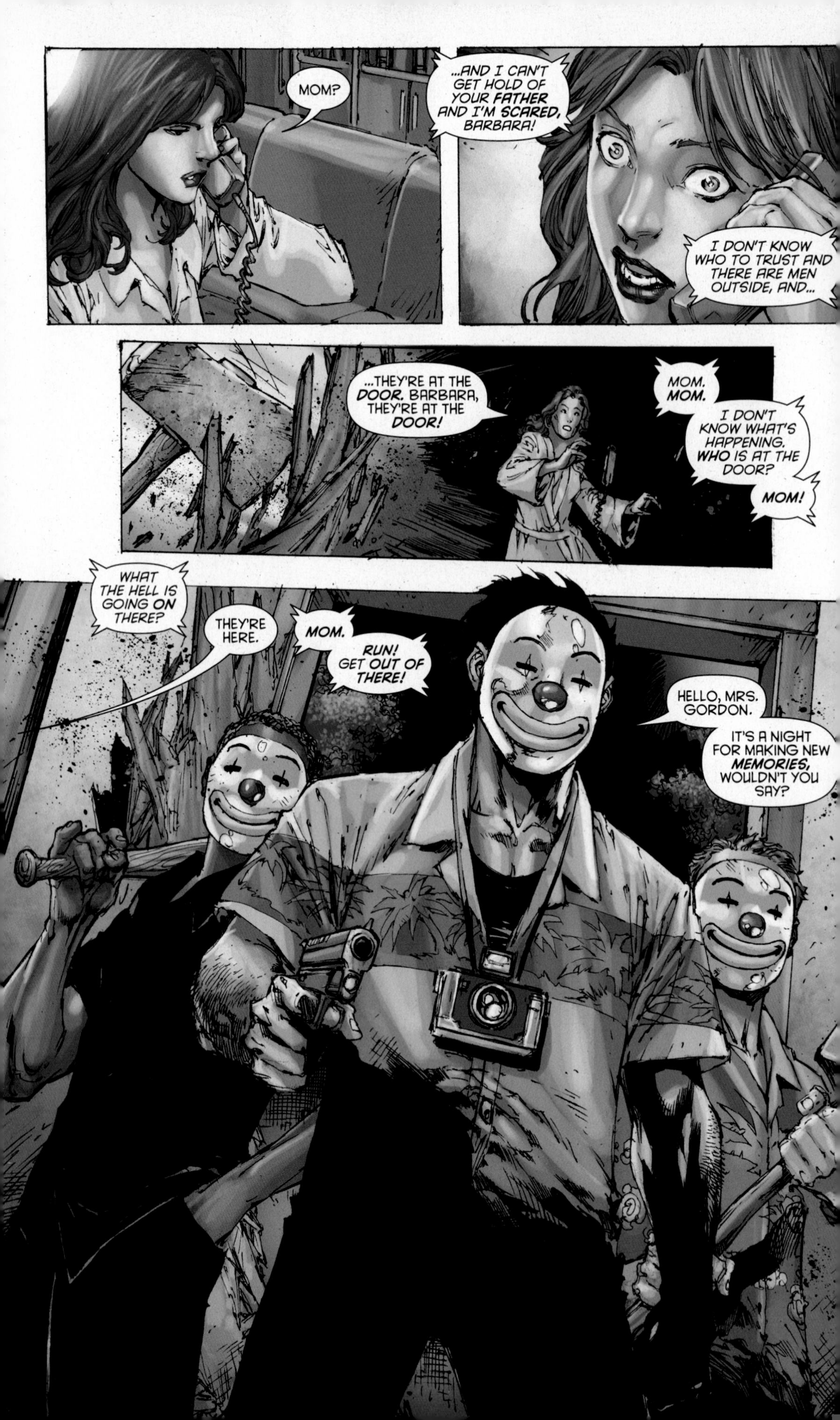

MOM?
...AND I CAN'T GET HOLD OF YOUR FATHER AND I'M SCARED, BARBARA!
I DON'T KNOW WHO TO TRUST AND THERE ARE MEN OUTSIDE, AND...
...THEY'RE AT THE DOOR. BARBARA, THEY'RE AT THE DOOR!
MOM. MOM.
I DON'T KNOW WHAT'S HAPPENING. WHO IS AT THE DOOR?
MOM!
WHAT THE HELL IS GOING ON THERE?
THEY'RE HERE.
MOM.
RUN! GET OUT OF THERE!
HELLO, MRS. GORDON.
IT'S A NIGHT FOR MAKING NEW MEMORIES, WOULDN'T YOU SAY?

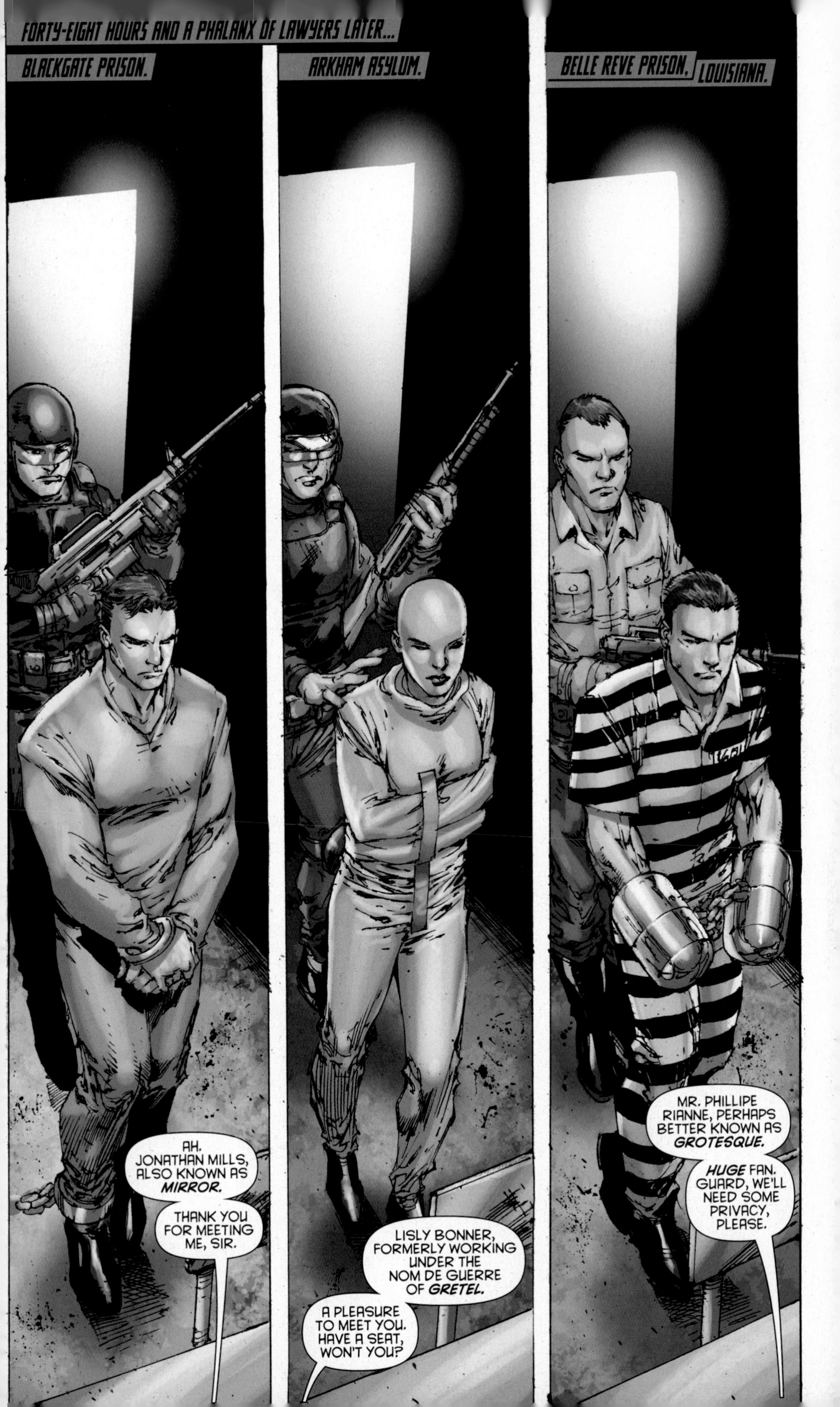
FORTY-EIGHT HOURS AND A PHALANX OF LAWYERS LATER...
BLACKGATE PRISON.
AH. JONATHAN MILLS, ALSO KNOWN AS MIRROR.
THANK YOU FOR MEETING ME, SIR.
ARKHAM ASYLUM.
LISLY BONNER, FORMERLY WORKING UNDER THE NOM DE GUERRE OF GRETEL.
A PLEASURE TO MEET YOU. HAVE A SEAT, WON'T YOU?
BELLE REVE PRISON, LOUISIANA.
MR. PHILLIPE RIANNE, PERHAPS BETTER KNOWN AS GROTESQUE.
HUGE FAN. GUARD, WE'LL NEED SOME PRIVACY, PLEASE.

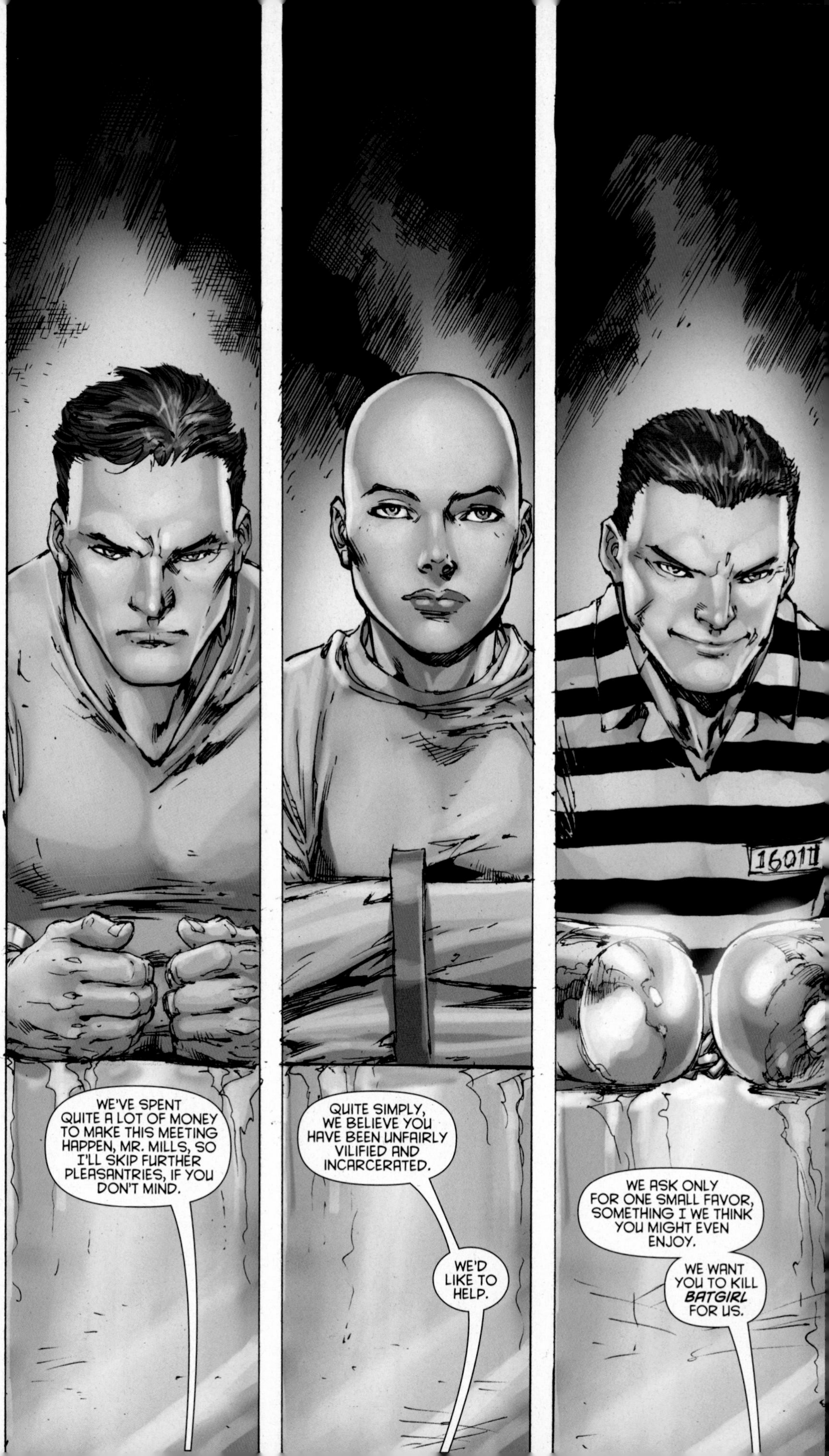

WE'VE SPENT QUITE A LOT OF MONEY TO MAKE THIS MEETING HAPPEN, MR. MILLS, SO I'LL SKIP FURTHER PLEASANTRIES, IF YOU DON'T MIND.
QUITE SIMPLY, WE BELIEVE YOU HAVE BEEN UNFAIRLY VILIFIED AND INCARCERATED.
WE'D LIKE TO HELP.
16011
WE ASK ONLY FOR ONE SMALL FAVOR, SOMETHING I WE THINK YOU MIGHT EVEN ENJOY.
WE WANT YOU TO KILL *BATGIRL* FOR US.

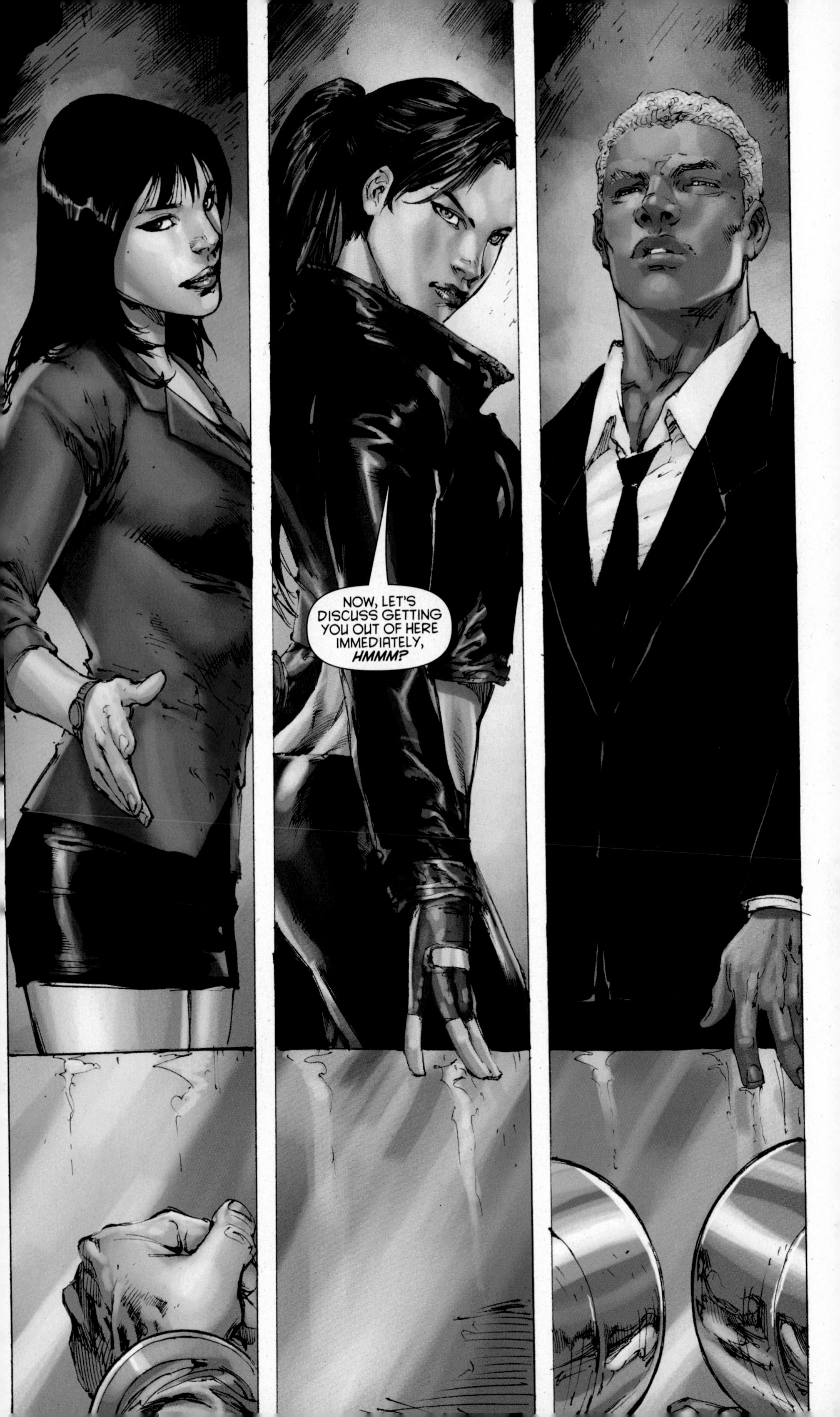
NOW, LET'S DISCUSS GETTING YOU OUT OF HERE IMMEDIATELY, *HMMM?*

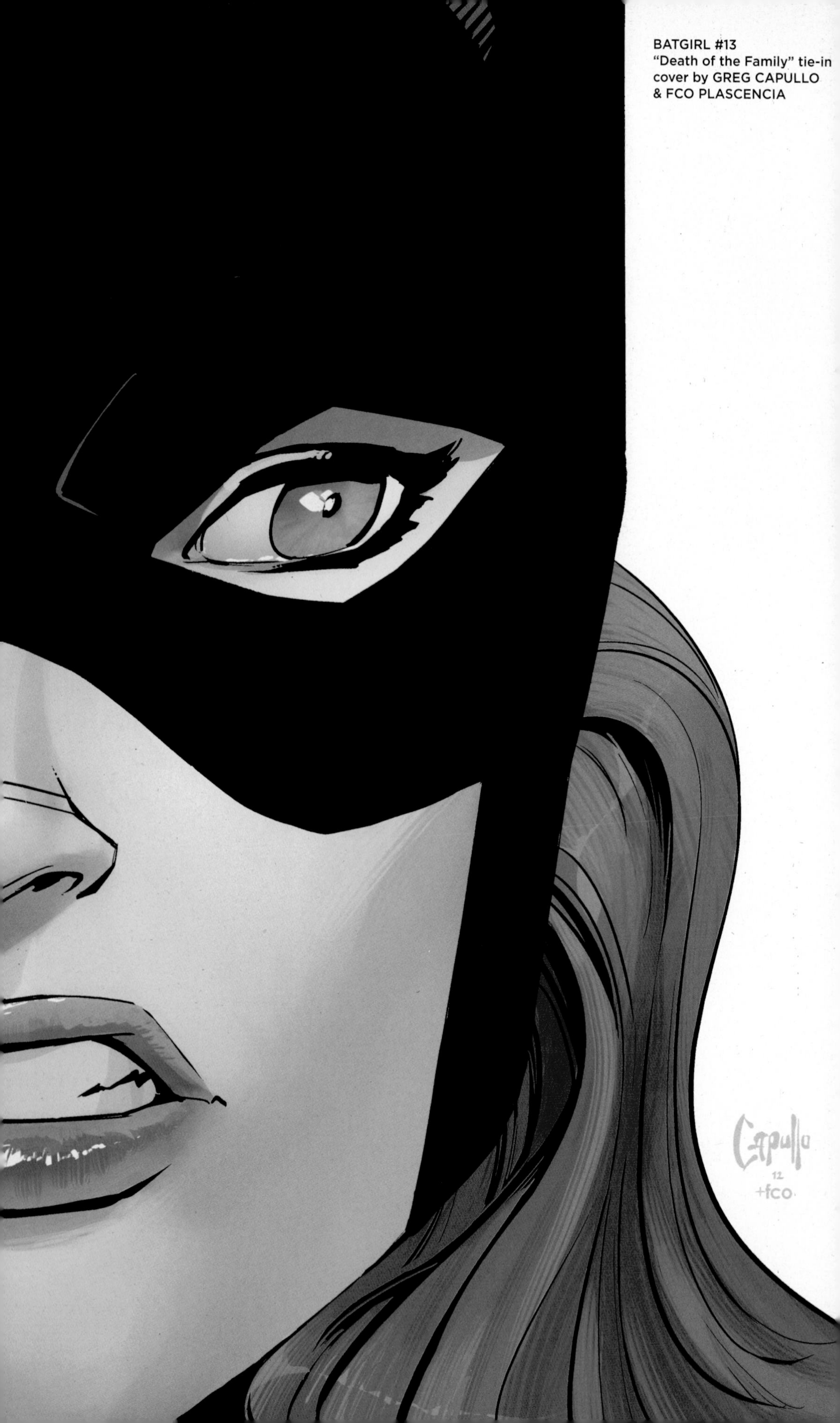
Capullo
12
+fco

BATGIRL #13
"Death of the Family" tie-in
cover by GREG CAPULLO
& FCO PLASCENCIA

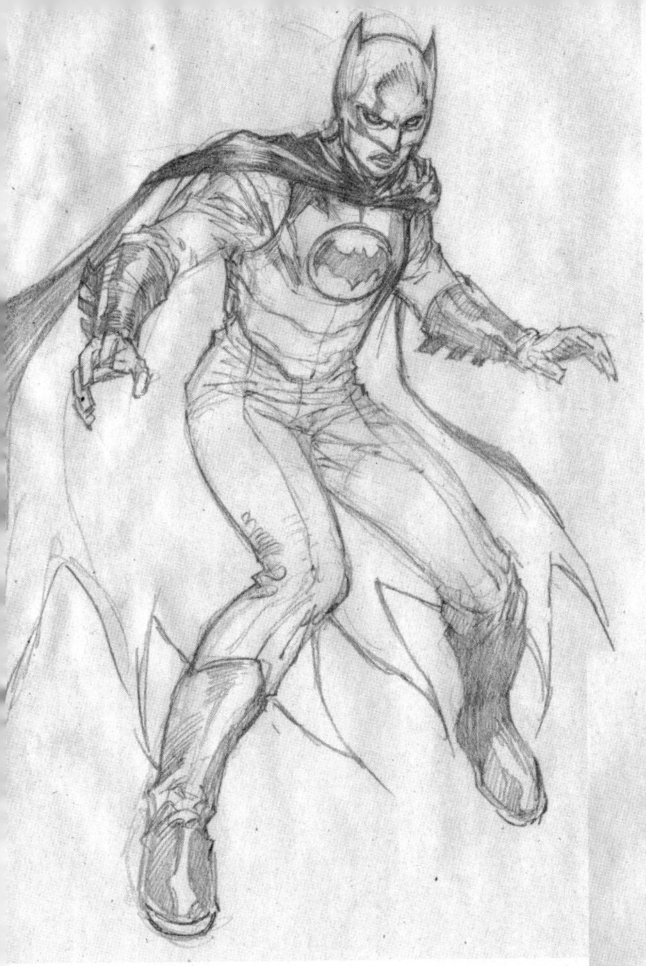

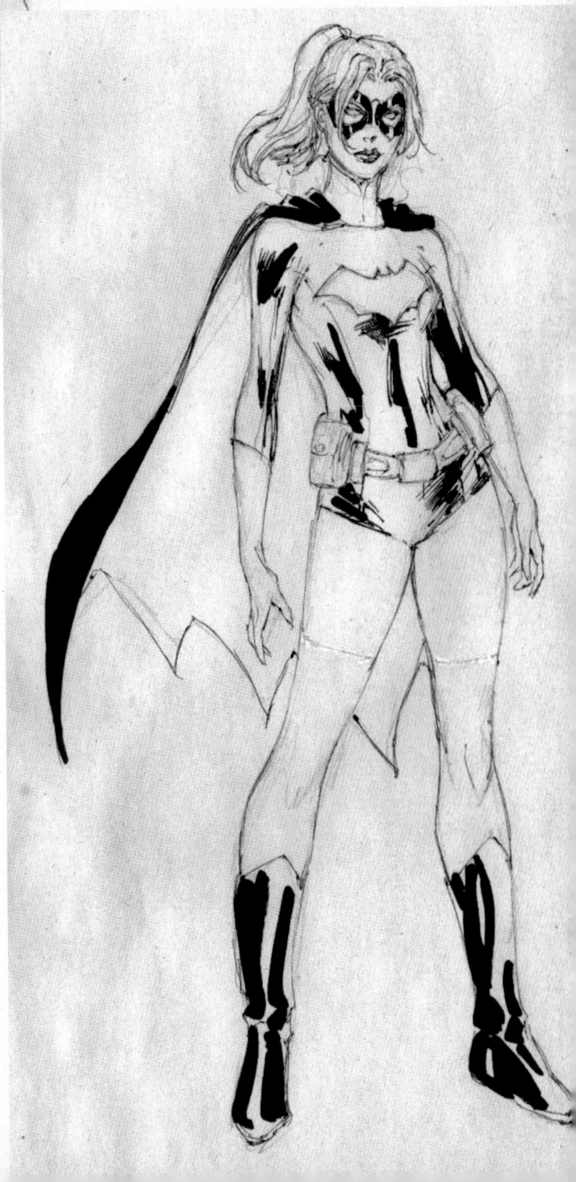

Young Batgirl costume designs by Ed Benes

Layout of BATGIRL #9 page 13 by Ardian Syaf

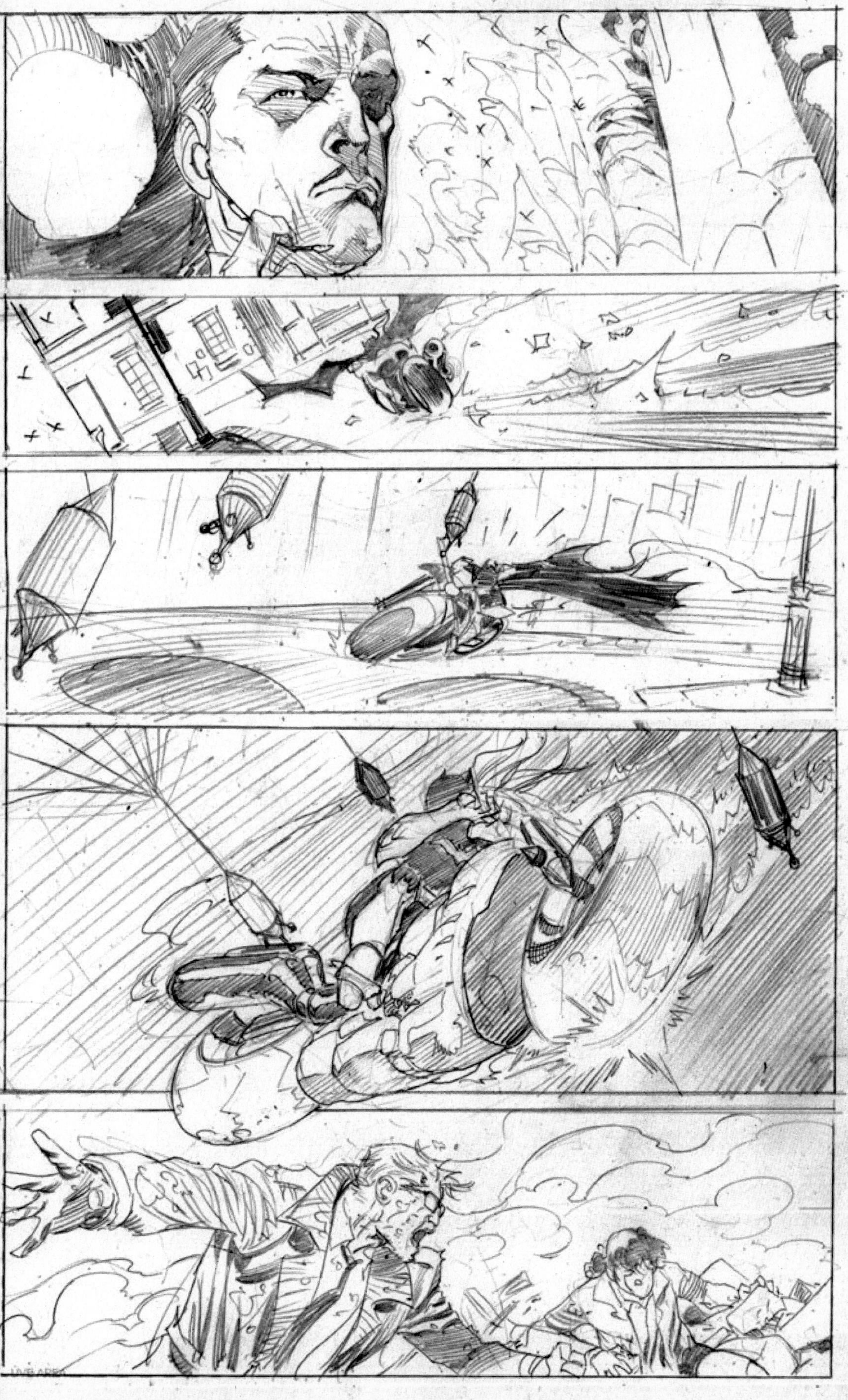

Cover sketches by Ardian Syaf

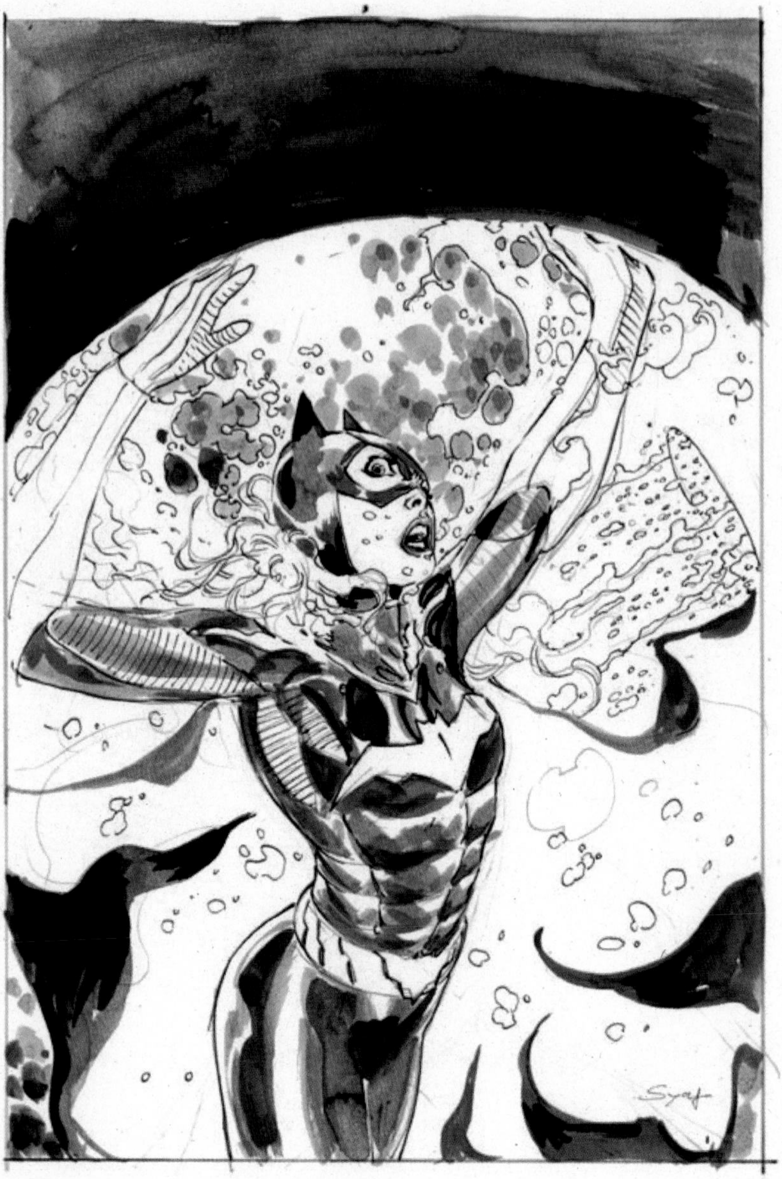
Syaf

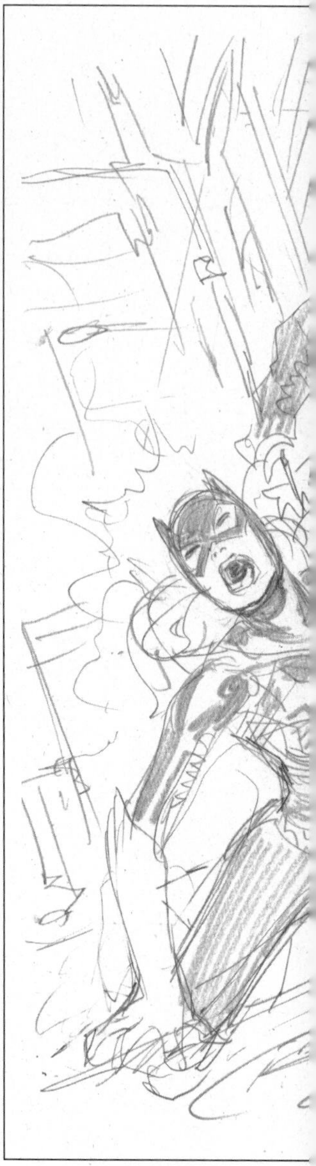

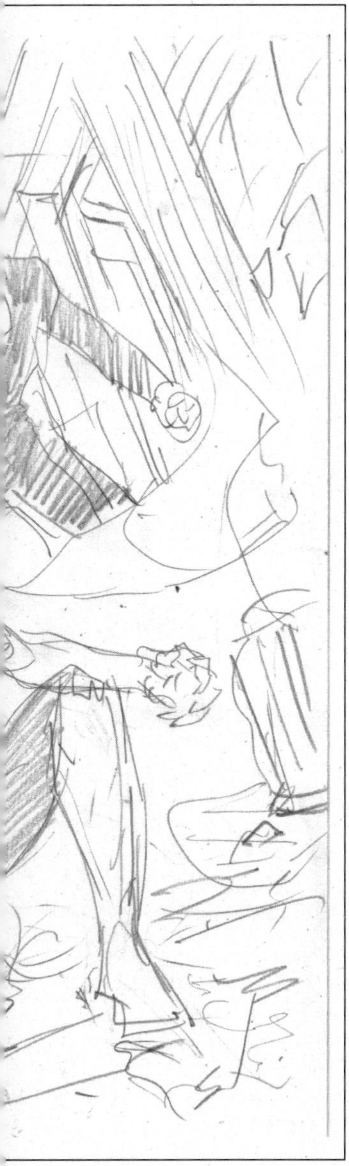

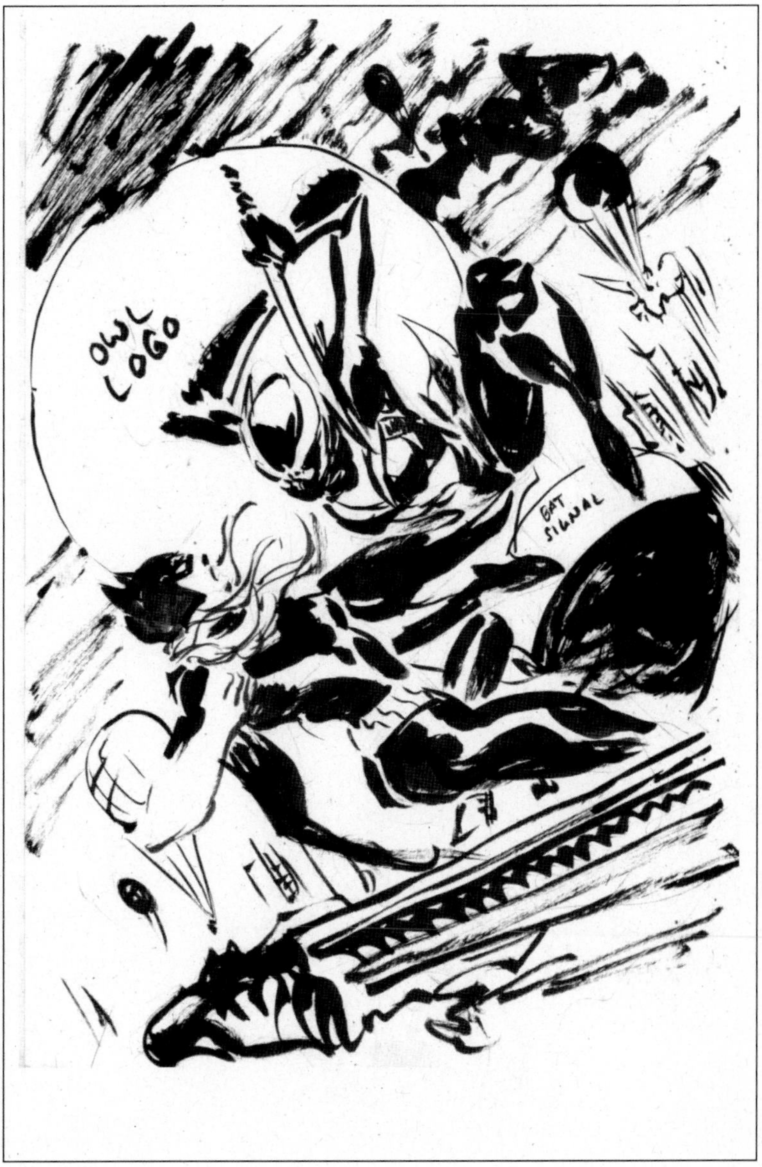
OWL LOGO
BAT SIGNAL

Cover roughs by Ed Benes

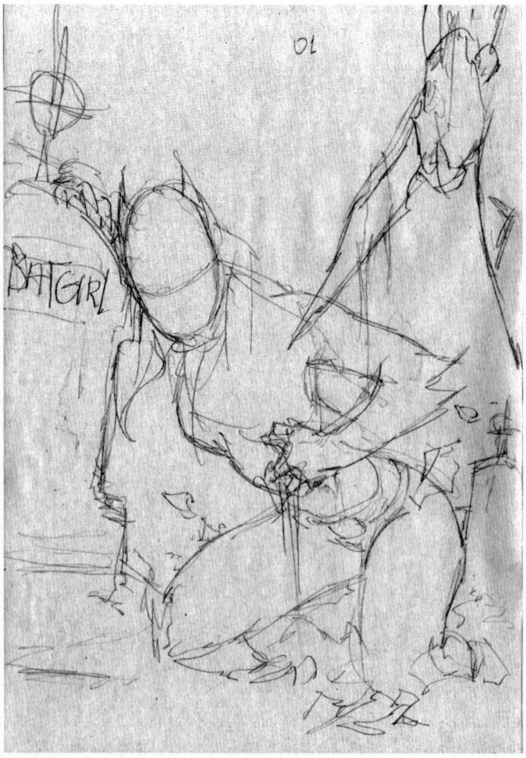
01
BATGIRL

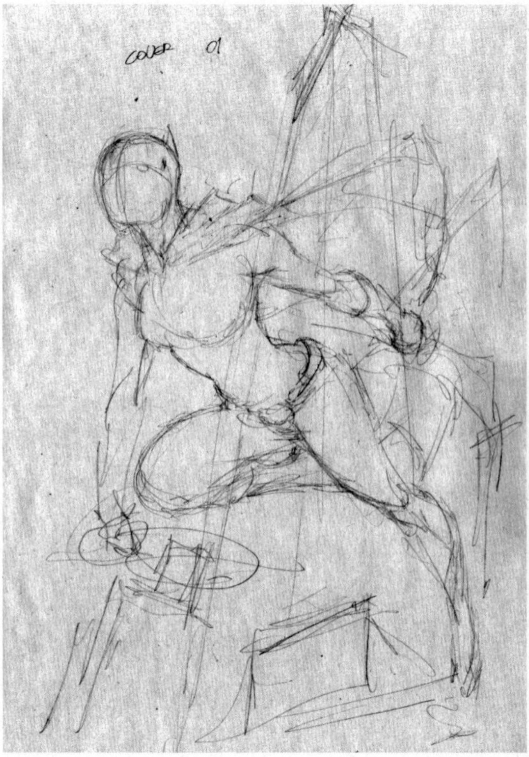
COVER 01

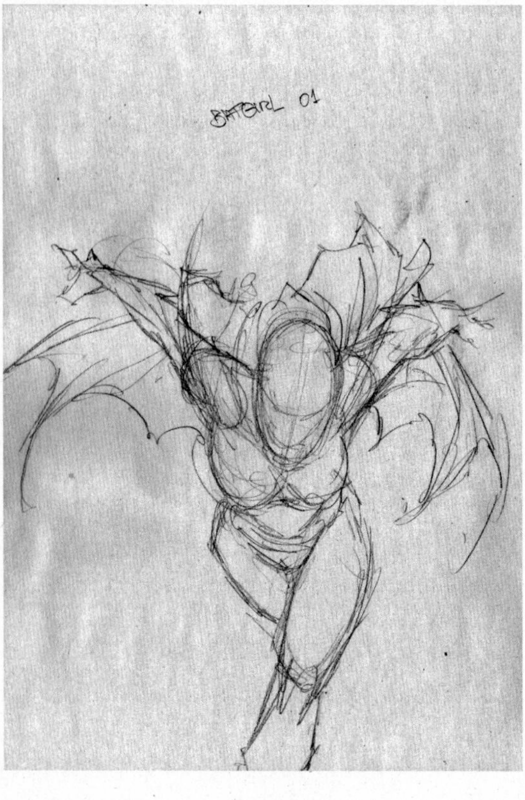
BATGIRL 01

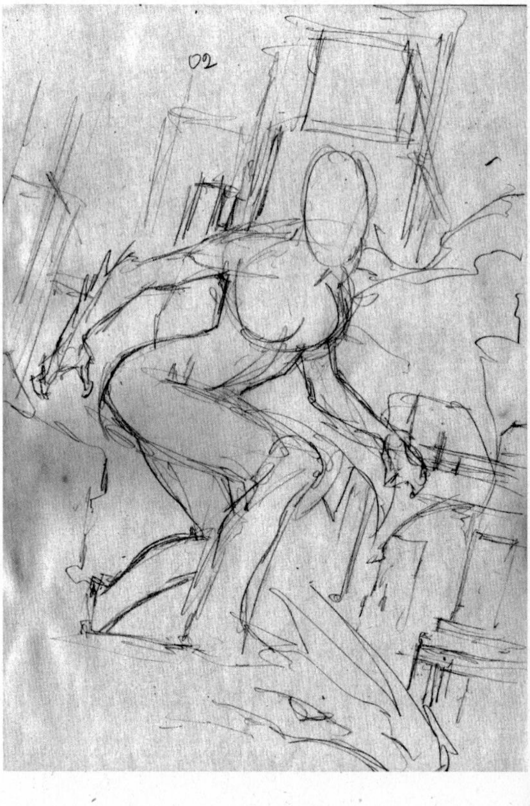
02

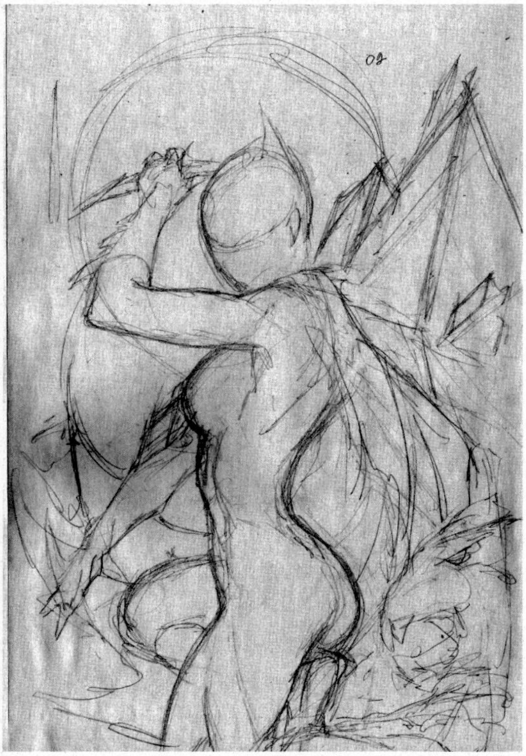
02

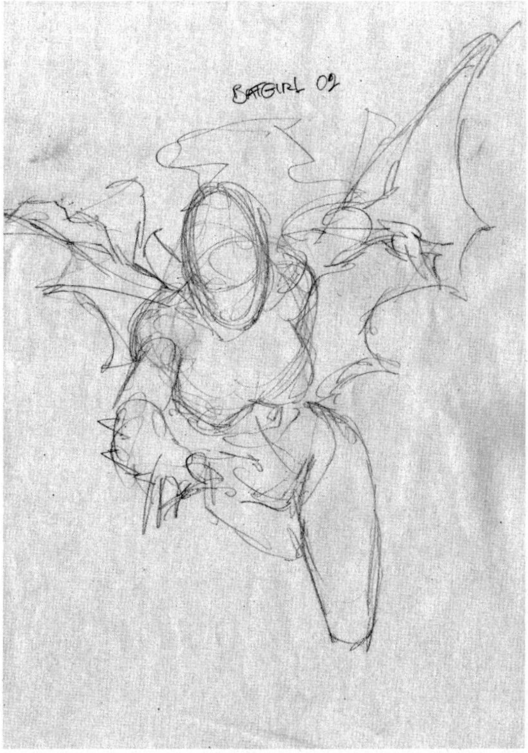
BATGIRL 02

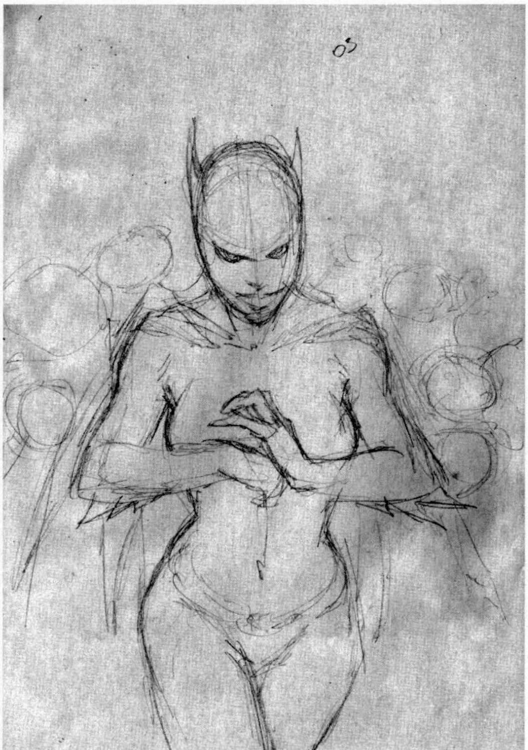
05

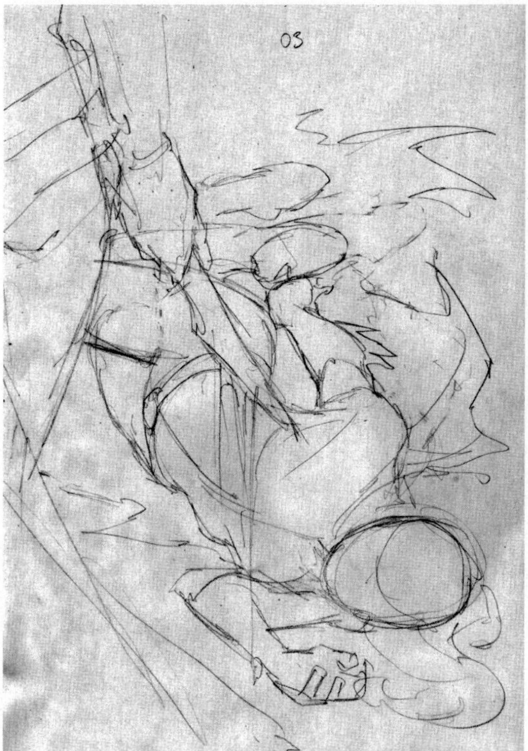
03

Pencilled art for BATGIRL #13 second printing cover by Ed Benes

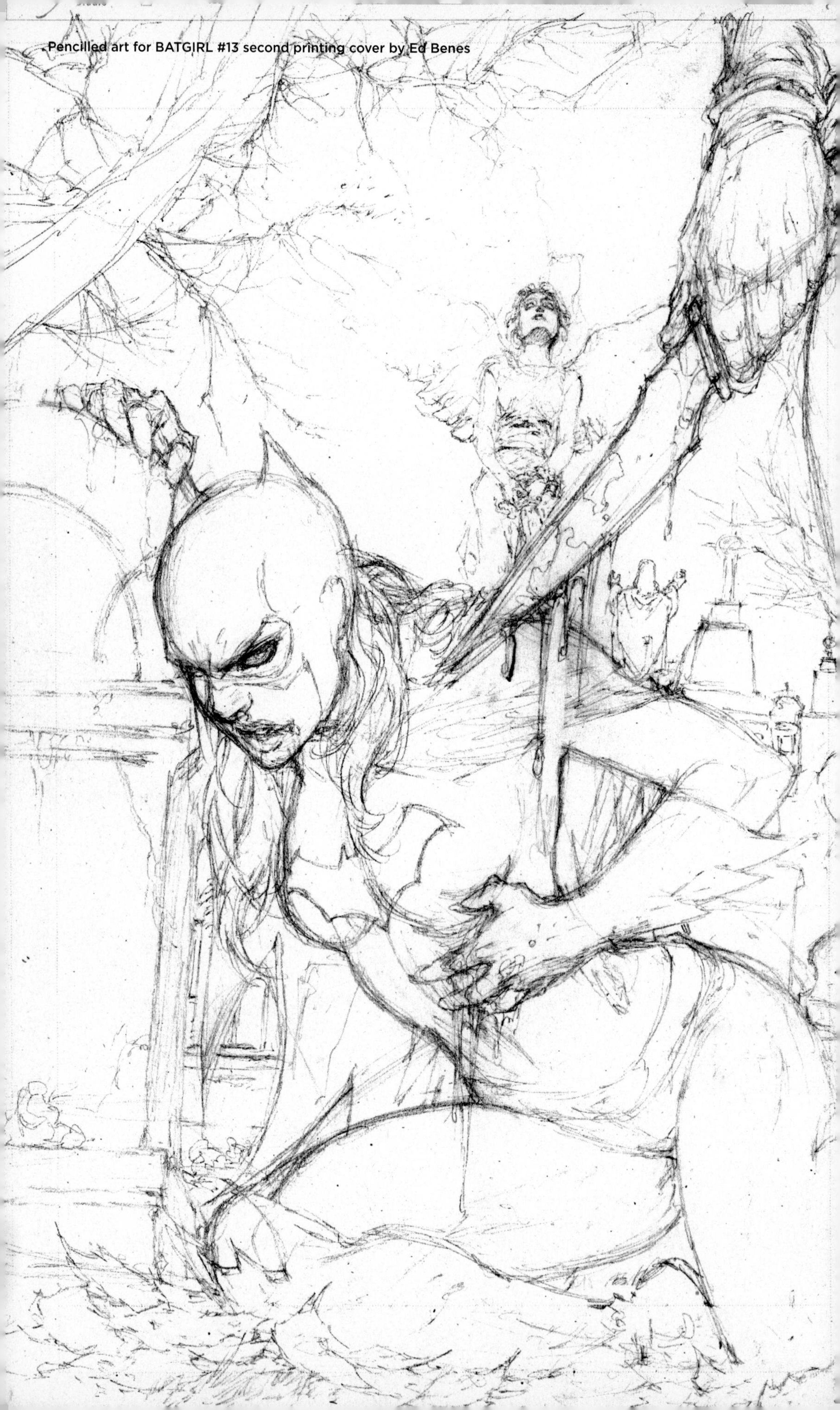

START AT THE BEGINNING!

BATMAN VOLUME 1: THE COURT OF OWLS

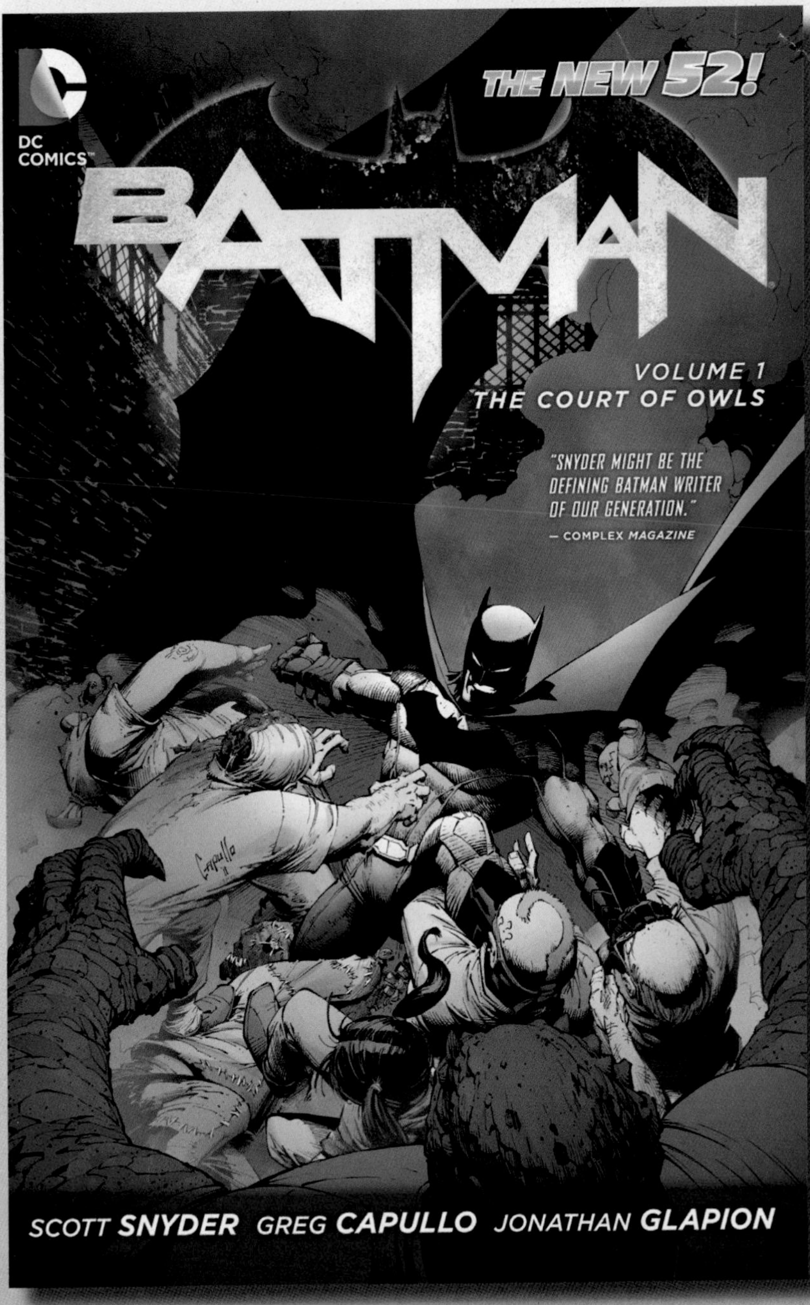

BATMAN VOL. 2: THE CITY OF OWLS

with SCOTT SNYDER and GREG CAPULLO

BATMAN VOL. 3: DEATH OF THE FAMILY

with SCOTT SNYDER and GREG CAPULLO

BATMAN: NIGHT OF THE OWLS

with SCOTT SNYDER and GREG CAPULLO

DC COMICS

THE NEW 52!

BATMAN

VOLUME 1
THE COURT OF OWLS

"SNYDER MIGHT BE THE DEFINING BATMAN WRITER OF OUR GENERATION."
— COMPLEX MAGAZINE

SCOTT **SNYDER** GREG **CAPULLO** JONATHAN **GLAPION**

"Simone and artist Ardian Syaf not only do justice to Babs' legacy, but build in a new complexity that is the starting point for a future full of new storytelling possibilities. A hell of a ride."—IGN

START AT THE BEGINNING!

BATGIRL
VOLUME 1: THE DARKEST REFLECTION

BATGIRL VOL. 2: KNIGHTFALL DESCENDS

BATGIRL VOL. 3: DEATH OF THE FAMILY

BATWOMAN VOL. 1: HYDROLOGY

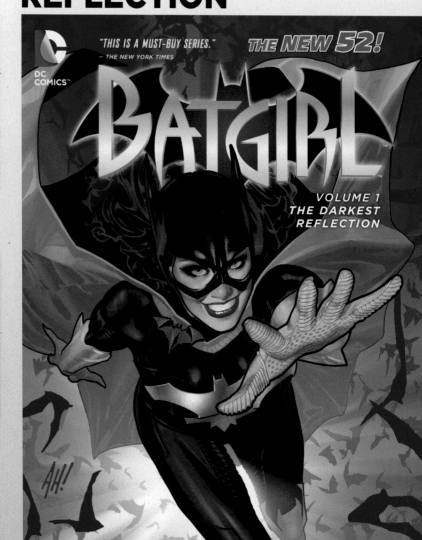

"THIS IS A MUST-BUY SERIES." — THE NEW YORK TIMES

THE NEW 52!

DC COMICS™

BATGIRL

VOLUME 1 THE DARKEST REFLECTION

GAIL SIMONE   ARDIAN SYAF   VICENTE CIFUENTES